BANDITS, MISFITS, AND SUPERHEROES

BANDITS, MISFITS, AND SUPERHEROES

Whiteness and Its Borderlands in American Comics and Graphic Novels

JOSEF BENSON AND **DOUG SINGSEN**

University Press of Mississippi / Jackson

The University Press of Mississippi is the scholarly publishing agency of the Mississippi Institutions of Higher Learning: Alcorn State University, Delta State University, Jackson State University, Mississippi State University, Mississippi University for Women, Mississippi Valley State University, University of Mississippi, and University of Southern Mississippi.

www.upress.state.ms.us

The University Press of Mississippi is a member of the Association of University Presses.

Any discriminatory or derogatory language or hate speech regarding race, ethnicity, religion, sex, gender, class, national origin, age, or disability that have been retained or appear in elided form is in no way an endorsement of the use of such language outside a scholarly context.

Copyright © 2022 by University Press of Mississippi
All rights reserved

First printing 2022
∞

Library of Congress Cataloging-in-Publication Data

Names: Benson, Josef, 1974– author. | Singsen, Doug, author.
Title: Bandits, misfits, and superheroes : whiteness and its borderlands in American comics and graphic novels / Josef Benson, Doug Singsen.
Description: Jackson : University Press of Mississippi, 2022. | Includes bibliographical references and index.
Identifiers: LCCN 2021048484 (print) | LCCN 2021048485 (ebook) | ISBN 978-1-4968-3833-9 (hardback) | ISBN 978-1-4968-3834-6 (paperback) | ISBN 978-1-4968-3836-0 (epub) | ISBN 978-1-4968-3835-3 (epub) | ISBN 978-1-4968-3838-4 (pdf) | ISBN 978-1-4968-3837-7 (pdf)
Subjects: LCSH: Comic books, strips, etc.—United States—History and criticism. | Comic books, strips, etc.—Social aspects—United States. | Racism—United States—Comic books, strips, etc. | Racism and the arts—United States. | Whites—Race identity—United States—Comic books, strips, etc. | Outlaws—Comic books, strips, etc. | Superheroes—Comic books, strips, etc.
Classification: LCC PN6725 .B3765 2022 (print) | LCC PN6725 (ebook) | DDC 741.5/3529—dc23/eng/20211128
LC record available at https://lccn.loc.gov/2021048484
LC ebook record available at https://lccn.loc.gov/2021048485

British Library Cataloging-in-Publication Data available

DEDICATIONS

We dedicate this book to our sons, Lazarus and Benji.

CONTENTS

INTRODUCTION 3

CHAPTER ONE: Race and Racism in the Birth of the Superhero 16

CHAPTER TWO: The Southern Outlaw and the White Indian in Western Comics. 43

CHAPTER THREE: Colonialism and Primitivism in US Comics 67

CHAPTER FOUR: Civil Rights and the Limits of Liberalism 90

CHAPTER FIVE: Robert Crumb's Cathartic Racism. 127

CHAPTER SIX: Jewish Exceptionalism and Assimilation in the 1970s and 1980s 152

CHAPTER SEVEN: Racial Borderlands in Alternative Comics. 174

CHAPTER EIGHT: The Deconstruction of the White Superhero in *Watchmen*. 197

CHAPTER NINE: Frank Miller's Hypermasculine Whiteness and the Defense
of Western Culture 221

CHAPTER TEN: Reskinning Narratives: Taking Off the Mask 246

CONCLUSION 266

NOTES 272

BIBLIOGRAPHY 274

INDEX. 284

ACKNOWLEDGMENTS

We would like to thank Vijay Shah for his interest and faith in this project. We would also like to thank the folks at Popular Culture Association and American Culture Association (PCA-ACA), especially Nicole Freim and the comics group, for providing a forum in which we could share early chapters.

BANDITS, MISFITS, AND SUPERHEROES

INTRODUCTION

Whiteness pervades American culture, but many people, especially whites, are unaware or only fleetingly aware of its presence all around them. The simultaneous pervasiveness and invisibility of whiteness are often compared to the way that water surrounds a fish (e.g., Tochluk, 11). Fish live their entire lives surrounded by water, never encountering any other environment. Their entire being has evolved to exist in water, so they are not even aware of its presence or its influence on their lives. Similarly, whiteness influences all areas of American life and culture yet remains imperceptible to many Americans. Indeed, a large part of its power stems from its imperceptibility. Joe Feagin has argued that most white people carry with them and apply a set of racial assumptions, often without even being aware that they are doing so, a bundle of assumptions that he terms the white racial frame. These assumptions provide a justification for the advantages that whites enjoy in American society and for the mistreatment, oppression, and exploitation experienced by people of color. Whiteness has always connoted a sense of power and subjugation, a note of contradistinctive exceptionality, a raison d'être for exploitation, enslavement, and murder. Political whiteness functions as a construct of normativity whereby those in power tacitly and sometimes unwittingly define themselves as a raceless, monolithic group inherently worthy of privilege and power, while others exist as inherently inferior. Because most people do not perceive the white frame, they are not even aware that they are employing it and consequently are unable to recognize or counteract its effects. When it is pointed out, they often react dismissively or angrily, accusing the messenger of manufacturing charges of racism for political reasons. Robin DiAngelo describes these emotional and often hostile responses by whites toward anyone who broaches the white racial frame as "white fragility" (54). DiAngelo points out that white fragility stems from whites existing within an insulated, racially stress-free environment where they "have not had to build the cognitive or affective skills or develop the stamina that would allow for constructive engagement across racial divides" (57).

Whiteness has a powerful impact on how both whites and people of color define their identities. In *Playing in the Dark: Whiteness and the Literary Imagination*, one of the seminal texts of whiteness studies, Toni Morrison writes that the construction of blackness "is the vehicle by which the American self knows itself not as enslaved, but free; not repulsive, but desirable; not helpless, but licensed and powerful; not history-less, but historical; not damned, but innocent; not blind accident of evolution, but a progressive fulfillment of destiny" (52). Whiteness does not exist without nonwhiteness and vice versa; they define each other. While the discipline of ethnic studies initially focused on recovering the lost or buried histories of people of color, it has become clear that to fully unpack and understand the construction of race, it is necessary to name and analyze whiteness as well as blackness and brownness. Thus Morrison has called for scholars "to avert the critical gaze from the racial object to the racial subject; from the described and imagined to the describers and imaginers; from the serving to the served" (90). We share Morrison's goal of analyzing "the impact of notions of racial hierarchy, racial exclusion, and racial vulnerability and availability on nonblacks" while also recognizing with her that whiteness and nonwhiteness are always dialectically intertwined (11). In interrogating and mapping the construction of whiteness, therefore, we are also always interrogating and mapping the construction of other racial identities as well.

In addition to defining itself against other racial identities, whiteness is also internally divided. White identity is normally constructed as a single, monolithic identity, but this pretense of unity masks a reality of internal division and hierarchy. Most notably, in the late nineteenth century and the early twentieth, recent immigrants to America from southern and eastern Europe were not considered fully white. Depending on the situation, they could be granted provisional or partial inclusion within the charmed circle of whiteness, but more commonly they were categorized as nonwhite and denied the benefits that came with this status. Yet at the same time, they always received preferential treatment compared to other groups that were even farther down the racial hierarchy, including African Americans, Mexicans and other Hispanic groups, and Asians. The new immigrants from southern and eastern Europe were, in the whiteness scholar David Roediger's description, "'inbetween' hard racism and full inclusion—neither securely white nor nonwhite" (*Working toward Whiteness*, 12). This group included Jewish immigrants, who played a disproportionately important role in comics history. Jewish writers and artists were responsible for the creation of Superman, Batman, Captain America, Iron Man, Spider-Man, the Hulk, the X-Men, and many more of the most iconic characters in American comics.

All these characters reveal the imprint of the Jewish experience, although usually in ways that are disguised or camouflaged. In particular, the Jewish experience of being both an insider and an outsider—an experience that directly reflects the Jewish experience of being considered provisionally but not fully white—is a constant theme of superhero comics. The internal fragmentation of whiteness also appears in a myriad of other ways that we explore throughout the book.

American comics have for most of their existence reflected the white supremacist culture out of which they arose. Superheroes and comic books in general are products of whiteness that both signal and hide its presence, blending into the cultural landscape as myths that serve to buttress and sustain white supremacy. Even when comics creators and publishers sought to advance an antiracist agenda, very often a lack of awareness of their own whiteness and the ideological baggage that goes along with it undermined their efforts. The inability or refusal to recognize the existence of the white racial frame through which they viewed the world resulted in the unintentional imposition of racist stereotypes and other white supremacist ideas. In addition to the conscious or unconscious application of this white racial frame, comics creators often bring other stereotypes and biases to their work, such as misogyny and homophobia that complicate and undermine their attempts to project an antiracist message.

Even the industry's sacred cows, such as Jerry Siegel and Joe Shuster, Jack Jackson, William Gaines, Stan Lee, Robert Crumb, Will Eisner, and Frank Miller, have not been able to distance themselves from the problematic racism embedded in their narratives, regardless of their intentions or explanations. Very early and unintentionally, we found ourselves focusing on industry giants like William Gaines from EC Comics, Stan Lee from Marvel, and Will Eisner, in part because of their tremendous influence and impact on the comics industry, but also because there was so little critical assessment of their work in relation to race. One might view our book in part as a sober assessment of some of the giants of the industry and their role in perpetuating racism throughout the history of comics.

While American comic books and graphic novels are rooted in a culture of white supremacy, their relationship to whiteness is complex and contradictory. On the one hand, comics have frequently upheld the hegemony of white identity within American culture. They are best known for giving birth to the superhero that has functioned for most of comics history as an ideal version of the heterosexual white male and archetypal symbol of white America derived from the outlaw bandit first instantiated as an opponent of emancipation and multiculturalism. Nonwhite characters appear rarely in comics and almost never as leading characters, making comic books and graphic novels perhaps the least racially diverse medium in American popular culture. This racial exclusivity applies to both mainstream comics and their underground and alternative counterparts that questioned many aspects of hegemonic white identity but did not display any more racial inclusivity than the mainstream culture they rejected.

While people of color were relegated to the margins or the dark side of comic books for many years, beginning with the Man of Steel, white superheroes were presented as possessing a single consciousness free of fragmentation. In the words of Morrison, "Images of blackness can be evil *and* protective, rebellious *and* forgiving, fearful *and* desirable—all of the self-contradictory features of the self. Whiteness, alone, is mute, meaningless, unfathomable, pointless, frozen, veiled, curtained, dreaded, senseless, implacable" (59). Despite the dual personae of most superheroes that hint at a fragmented consciousness, these fetishized cultural identities symbolize paragons of heteronormative and hypermasculine monolithic whiteness while masking a splintered consciousness or sexual borderland. Superheroes' dual identities may point to a fragmented consciousness, but they are never presented that way. They are normalized and simply come with the territory that, despite the dual identities, still purports to represent monolithic whiteness. One might then understand whiteness as the denial of internal fragmentation. The myth of monolithic and heteronormative whiteness is required to maintain a static racial and sexual power structure wherein whiteness appears whole and integrated in comparison to nonwhiteness or sexual nonnormativity, which appears fragmented and inferior. Additionally, the myth also masks the origin of whiteness as economically expedient and comprising an evolving number of ethnicities over hundreds of years. Monolithic whiteness includes heteronormativity. For example, in Nazi Germany, homosexuals were categorized as a "third sex" and deemed an "official minority" that threatened the "racial purity" of the state (Plant, 30, 33–34, 100).

On the other hand, comics' position in relation to hegemonic white identity has been complicated for much of their history by existing on the margins of the white social order, targeted by elected officials, librarians, and other community leaders as an inferior form of literature detrimental to the development of the children and adolescents who were comics' primary consumers. Yet, with a few notable exceptions, mainstream comics typically responded to this denigration not by questioning the society that rejected them but by attempting to prove their usefulness to it as upholders of hegemonic whiteness through the creation of heroic, all-American, white characters. Superheroes serve as powerful cultural and ideological symbols employed to affirm and defend an unjust law and an unjust culture. They are figments of ideological state apparatuses, powerful myths that influence people their whole lives.

Since ideologies of whiteness and white supremacy appear across all types of comics, this book is not limited to just one genre, such as superheroes. Instead we examine many genres, including westerns, horror comics, crime comics, funny animal comics, underground comix, autobiography, literary fiction, and historical fiction. Because of the breadth of material we cover, we cannot examine any one topic in exhaustive depth, and we are very aware that this history inevitably contains many absences and gaps. We cannot hope to cover all issues that are relevant to whiteness. What we have attempted to do is assess a few of the industry giants, highlight some of the most important episodes in American comic books' constructions of whiteness, and show how they relate to one another and form a larger pattern. By including such a wide range of material, we are able to chart how whiteness has been constructed over the whole history of American comic books. This also allows us to examine how interconnected all these genres are, often in unexpected and surprising ways.

One example of this appears in the use of tropes derived from blackface minstrelsy in superhero comics of the 1930s and 1940s. The most notable of these blackface characters was Will Eisner's awfully racist portrayal of Ebony White, the first sidekick of the Spirit, a superhero detective. This use of blackface minstrelsy reappeared in the late 1960s in the work of Robert Crumb, who worked in the underground comix style rather than the mainstream superhero genre. The underground or postunderground cartoonists Art Spiegelman and Harvey Pekar took up relations between Blacks and Jews as a more general concern. Finally, the alternative cartoonist Chris Ware provided a direct response to Ebony White with his own character Chalky Black, a white boy (and later man) who is as extreme an example of one stereotype of whiteness as Ebony White was of blackness. Mainstream/superhero and underground/alternative comics are usually seen as occupying mutually exclusive cultural spaces, so the parallels and overlaps between them are important because of how they debunk and complicate this assumption. They also demonstrate once again how whiteness pervades American culture, spanning subcultures that might initially appear to have nothing in common.

The goal of this book is to analyze, understand, and critique constructions of whiteness, that is, the racial and ethnic identities of white people. Until about a half century ago, race was understood as a biological reality and was defined in the United States through the one-drop rule, which stipulated that anyone with even "one drop" of Black ancestry was Black and therefore subject to racist discrimination, violence, and inferior social status. The one-drop rule was also used to justify the sexual control of white women and the persecution of Black men, who were supposedly unable to control their violent lust for white women. This biological myth of racialized blood became so potent a metaphor for race that not only did people firmly believe it, as many still do, but white women became a sort of symbol of negative potential for their alleged singular power to taint the purity of whiteness through miscegenation and the possible procreation of "mongrelized" babies. This notion hearkens back to slavery and the law that the racial status of the child follows that of the mother. If the mother was Black, then the child was Black regardless of the race of the father. This facilitated the common practice of white slave masters raping their Black slaves without worrying about how to incorporate the resulting children into the estate. By this twisted logic, only white women could have white babies. Therefore, controlling the sexuality of white women became paramount in maintaining the purity of the white race. Likewise, Black men were seen as potential threats to white purity and were branded as sexually rapacious not only to justify their murder post-Reconstruction but also to put the fear of God into white women by indoctrinating them into thinking that Black men were beastly, violent rapists to be avoided at all costs. These beliefs were eventually challenged and relegated to the margins of mainstream political and cultural discourse, but they never disappeared, and they continue to underlie race relations in the United States today.

By contrast, we understand whiteness to be a social construct, like blackness and all racial and ethnic identities. As Noel Ignatiev and John Garvey have written, "Race is not a biological but a social fact, constructed through history. The white race consists of those people who partake of the privileges of the white skin in this society" (279). The differences in visual appearance, or phenotype, between different racial or ethnic groups are real, but no scientific basis exists for separating people by phenotype into racial or ethnic categories. First, phenotypical attributes such as skin, hair, and eye color or the shape of various facial features vary heavily within racial and ethnic groups as well as between them. Thus no biological basis exists for drawing the line between different racial or ethnic groups in one place rather than in another. While phenotypical differences are real, they cannot be used to construct scientifically valid racial or ethnic identities. Second, there is no correlation between differences in phenotype and the relative intelligence, morality, strength, agility, or level of civilizational advancement of different racial or ethnic groups. The idea that such differences do exist was central to the racist science of eugenics in the late nineteenth and early twentieth century and to other forms of biological racism.

Although racial categories have no biological basis, they have nevertheless been socially constructed to buttress systems of oppression. Racism against Africans, for instance, was promulgated in the late 1600s and early 1700s in the United States to prevent poor white farmers from fraternizing and making common cause with Black slaves. It was nurtured and maintained to justify the institution of slavery, which was essential to the American economy of the colonial and antebellum eras and made white plantation owners, merchants, and bankers a great deal of money. Since the end of slavery, the institutions that guarantee white supremacy have gone through a series of transformations, including the development of the convict-leasing system in the late nineteenth century, Jim Crow segregation in the early twentieth century, and most recently the war on drugs, the prison-industrial complex, and the school-to-prison pipeline (Alexander, 20–58).

Race is thus a social construct that serves to maintain white supremacy and advance the perceived interests of whites, in particular upper-class, powerful whites, who receive far greater benefits from the system of white supremacy than do working-class or poor whites. In fact, working-class and poor whites are harmed in many ways by the maintenance of white supremacy, since racism is often used as an excuse to pit white and minority workers against one another and to eliminate government programs that help working-class and poor people of all races.

Individual whites absorb racist ideas from the institutions of American culture and from the behavior of people around them, but the system of white supremacy as a whole is the collective product of the American cultural landscape, not of any one individual. We are therefore not as concerned in this book with the question of whether individual comic book writers, artists, editors, or publishers are racist. This is not because they were not racist; in many and arguably most cases, they were. We are not as concerned with the question of individual culpability or guilt because it is of limited use in helping us understand how white supremacy functions. What we are more interested in are the codes, tropes, and structures through which white supremacy expresses and reproduces itself in the medium of comic books. The individuals who created these comics did not have to be consciously aware of what they were doing. They absorbed the ideology of whiteness and white supremacy throughout their lives and, like the fish swimming in the water, were unaware or not fully aware of its existence and influence on them. Thus many individuals who produced highly racist characters and stories did not consider themselves racist. They were unaware of how whiteness pervades American society and structured their reality, creating what Joe Feagin has called the white racial frame, through which they viewed the world without being aware of it.

We also reject the notion that analyzing the structures of whiteness and white supremacy in earlier eras is ahistorical and presentist or that the expression and perpetuation of white supremacy were inevitable in earlier times. The label of "political correctness," which is so often used to dismiss any and all critiques of social injustice today, did not exist in the 1930s, but that does not mean there was not an active antiracist movement then. The medium of comic books was pioneered in the United States in the 1930s, a time when America could look back on a century of concerted, organized antiracist struggles. The abolitionist movement of the pre-Civil War era gave rise to leaders such as Sojourner Truth and Frederick Douglass, who continued to trumpet the cause of Black freedom and racial equality for decades after the war ended. The National Association for the Advancement of Colored People was founded in 1909, the Universal Negro Improvement Association and African Communities League was founded in 1914, and the Congress of Racial Equality was founded in 1942. All these people and groups worked tirelessly and publicly to promote the rights of Black Americans, and it would have been difficult for any American to be totally unaware of their existence or activities. One of the most famous struggles for racial justice of the pre–civil rights era occurred in the early 1930s in the highly publicized and controversial trial of the Scottsboro Boys, a group of nine Black teenagers who were falsely accused of raping two white women on a train in 1931. The case dragged on for five years through multiple retrials and placed the issue of racial justice unavoidably and undeniably on the agenda of American society in this period.

There is thus nothing presentist about criticizing the racism of comic books from the 1930s. To claim that "everyone was racist" in those days as an excuse for the widespread prevalence of racist cultural material is simply to ignore the facts and erase the true history of the fight for racial justice in the United States, which has been going on continuously for centuries. Three key moments in the fight for racial justice that preceded the creation of comic books were the abolitionist movement of the nineteenth century, the Reconstruction period after the Civil War, and the Harlem Renaissance of the 1920s. The claim that racism has always been an inevitable and uncontested aspect of American society is, in fact, a prime example of the invisibility of whiteness and white privilege that Shelly Tochluk points out. The false assumption that white supremacy went unquestioned before the civil rights movement of the 1960s serves to provide an excuse for exempting whites of previous eras from criticism for their racist acts and expressions. This in turn perpetuates the invisibility of white supremacy by disallowing criticism of cultural products that promote and defend it.

We see one example of such an argument in a 2010 article written by Duy Tano, editor in chief of the *Comics Cube*. The article, titled "Addressing Ebony White—Was Will Eisner Racist?," serves as an example of many of the approaches to whiteness that we are arguing against here, including the focus on individual culpability, the use of historical context as an excuse for racism, and the declaration that critiquing racism from earlier eras is ahistorical. However, we do not wish to point the finger too strongly at Tano, since he later recanted these views. In a 2015 reply to his own 2010 article, Tano wrote to one of his critics, "[You're] right. I've actually changed my view on this in the five years since I wrote it." Tano's article also reminds us that the ideology of white supremacy is absorbed and propagated not only by white people but by everyone within American culture, including people of color such as Tano, who identifies himself as Filipino in one of his comments in the article. The evolution in Tano's views demonstrates that the white racial frame is not inevitable or impermeable. With work and through exposure to analyses of how the white racial frame operates, we can learn to see and understand the mechanisms of white supremacy and ultimately replace them.

Michael Schumacher takes a different tack in excusing Eisner's racism in his biography of Eisner. Schumacher uses the inaccurate argument that no precedent for the concept of racial equality existed at the time of Ebony White's creation, writing that "the *Brown v. Board of Education* Supreme Court decision was a decade away and the civil rights movement two decades in the future," but he then goes on to argue that Ebony White was not actually a negative stereotype, or at least that his negative features were outweighed by his positive ones. Schumacher acknowledges that "whenever confronted with the Ebony issue in interviews—and there were many such occasions—Eisner would insist, first and foremost, that he felt no regrets for creating Ebony," and then sets about justifying this view (179). Schumacher cites Eisner's explanation that "Ebony had been brought into *The Spirit* as a means of infusing humor into the stories," much like other racist characters from Shakespeare's Shylock to the minstrel character of Rochester. According to Eisner and Schumacher, "No malice had been intended," and "stereotypes, in and of themselves, were not necessarily harmful" (179). Schumacher then goes on to mount a defense of Ebony, writing that "his actions were always positive, even heroic," ignoring the fact that this purported heroism was being attributed to a character who was being mercilessly mocked and belittled on practically every page on which he appeared (179).

Our purpose in this book is not necessarily to measure the career of Will Eisner or any other comics creator and determine what their overall impact has been or how racism in their work should be assessed. Our purpose here is to identify how whiteness has been defined, transformed, and occasionally undermined, over the course of American comic books' eighty years in existence. Before one can make any sweeping conclusions about the impact or value of Eisner's legacy, or the legacy of any comic book writer, artist, editor, or publisher, it is first necessary to make a bracing, honest accounting of their work, one that includes their failures as well as their successes. This book attempts to do so with respect to race and whiteness, but this is only one of many reevaluations that are necessary, with gender and sexuality being two of the other main categories that comics scholarship needs to consider.

We have structured the book into chapters dealing with major themes, works, and individual creators that have had a major impact on the construction of whiteness in American comic books and graphic novels. We organized these chapters in roughly chronological order, although there is necessarily a good deal of overlapping and backtracking in the chronological sequence of the chapters. We have no illusions that we have exhausted the subject and are fully aware that many more examples of the social construction of whiteness in comics remain to be examined.

Chapter 1 traces the genealogy of superheroes to the philosophy of Friedrich Nietzsche, early twentieth-century pulp heroes, the eugenics movement, science fiction fandom, and the Ku Klux Klan, among other sources. We also delineate the racist discourse of the Yellow Peril, the supposed threat of invasion from East Asia, and the complicated early contributions of Jewish comic book creators who subtly encoded their ethnic and religious heritage in their work while directing their ire at minorities farther down the racial hierarchy.

Chapter 2 argues that violence and the myth of racial blood purity represent the two most visible characteristics of the American western genre, which are represented in American comics by the figure of the gunfighter and the white Indian. The origins of the outlaw bandit and gunslinger in American culture and myth center on his repudiation of government-enforced emancipation. The white Indian, more often than not and despite his exposure to nonwhiteness, demonstrates his loyalties to the white power structure by using his knowledge of the other against him.

Chapter 3 shows how colonial occupation and military interventions in foreign countries have influenced several genres of American comic books. The first and most important comics genre to put forward colonialist and primitivist ideology was the jungle queen genre, in which a nearly superhuman white woman rules helpless Black Africans, but the same tropes also appear in superhero and Disney comics. In the late 1960s and early 1970s, however, the rising antiwar movement forced superhero comics to confront their history of colonialism and imperialism.

Chapter 4 argues that beginning in the mid-1950s, as the civil rights movement advanced, publishers such as EC Comics and later Marvel Comics began to impugn racism and discrimination in their comics. However, their efforts, along with those of the civil rights activist and anticomics crusader Fredric Wertham, were undermined by their own unexamined assumptions and biases about race, biases that demonstrated their possessive investment in white supremacy, especially in relation to gender and sexuality. As the civil rights movement adopted the ideas of Black nationalism, Marvel's superheroes responded by embracing the civil rights agenda but steadfastly condemning radical Black politics, which the company saw as a threat to white supremacy.

Chapter 5 points out that in the 1960s, Robert Crumb, the most prominent figure of the underground comix movement, became infamous and controversial for creating overtly racist comic book characters like Angelfood McSpade. Crumb's unapologetic attitude regarding these characters stems from his belief that he was simply offering an accurate portrayal of the white unconscious. However, he seemingly failed to understand the effects of these racist caricatures as well as his own role in advancing white supremacy.

Chapter 6 outlines a divide between a Jewish cartoonist from comics' first generation, Will Eisner, and a group of second-generation Jewish cartoonists over the identity of Jews as defined in relation to whites and other ethnic groups. Eisner adopts a narrative that posits Jews as the ideal white Americans. Coming from a diverse set of backgrounds, Art Spiegelman, Aline Kominsky-Crumb, and Harvey Pekar reject Eisner's narrative, acknowledging the messy reality of Jewishness in relation to white assimilation and nonwhites.

Chapter 7 asserts that in the 1980s and 1990s, a new generation of cartoonists began combining the iconoclasm of underground comix with longer narratives driven by literary ambitions. Known as alternative comics, these works advanced the artistic boundaries of comic books but had a mixed record regarding race. Alternative comics achieved some major breakthroughs in recognizing whiteness as a social construct and its impact on people of other races. Gilbert and Jaime Hernandez's *Love and Rockets* and Chris Ware's *Jimmy Corrigan* grappled seriously with the effects of whiteness, but other alternative comics perpetuated racist narratives, as in Jessica Abel's *La Perdida*.

Chapter 8 contends that Alan Moore, in his seminal graphic novel *Watchmen*, reinvigorated the superhero genre by employing postmodern techniques that have denaturalized the classic superhero and exposed the ideological underpinnings of the superhero genre. In favoring naturalistic, fragmented, and pluralistic worlds as backdrops for his characters, Moore exposed the classic superhero as a fraudulent social construction of heteronormative whiteness. Alan Moore's skeptical approach to the superhero weakened the classic superhero but strengthened the superhero genre and influenced later comics such as Marvel's *Civil War*.

Chapter 9 focuses on Frank Miller, a major figure in contemporary American comics. The one constant in Miller's universe is the presence of hypermasculine, hyperviolent white heroes who defend Western civilization against its various enemies, both internal and external. Paradoxically, in Miller's view, the only way to salvage the supposedly rational and freedom-loving civilization of the West is for it to become more violent and irrational than those threatening it. Miller's work can be linked to many currents in right-wing thought over the past three decades, including neoconservatism, libertarianism, and the alt-right, but the person whose ideology he is closest to is Donald Trump.

Chapter 10 recounts how, over the past several decades, the American comic publishers Marvel and DC have presented Black versions of traditional superheroes, such as Green Lantern, Iron Man, Superman, and Captain America. We argue that in most cases, the white superheroes give up their power unwillingly and quickly try to take it back. These reskinning narratives demonstrate both the investment that the fictional white superheroes have in their powers and the investment in whiteness of the narratives' authors, who in the 1980s and 1990s ultimately refused to supplant their white superheroes in any meaningful way. Marvel's limited series *Truth: Red, White & Black* (2002) represents a dramatic and important departure from this earlier pattern of reskinning by positing a parallel history to Captain America embodied in the Black Captain America Isaiah Bradley, who is presented as a highly capable superhero. As a result, Captain America is recontextualized as the beneficiary of white privilege within the dominant white racist cultural landscape. Even more recently, *Ms. Marvel: No Normal* (2014), featuring Kamala Khan, a Pakistani American born in Jersey City, displays the potential political power in reskinning narratives that operate beyond the pale of the original white superheroes.

Maybe it goes without saying, but we would like to note that in addition to being academics, we are also fans of comics. As academics who analyze cultural artifacts, we often find ourselves interrogating and scrutinizing what we love, often with disappointing results. Perhaps we do this *because* we love the artifacts so much and see their progressive potential. Nevertheless, we hope that in the following pages we are able to convince readers that comics have been carriers of white supremacy for nearly a century, and we agree with G.I. Joe that knowing is half the battle.

Chapter One

RACE AND RACISM IN THE BIRTH OF THE SUPERHERO

Superheroes were born out of a combustible mixture of cultural crosscurrents, many of which were deeply rooted in white supremacist ideologies. Nietzsche's theory of the Übermensch, eugenics, the Ku Klux Klan, pulp science fiction, the Yellow Peril scare, and the pressure on Jewish immigrants from eastern Europe to assimilate all helped lay the groundwork for the creation of the superhero, the linchpin of the American comic book industry. This cultural milieu clearly influenced superhero comics, but the exact nature of these influences on individual creators and characters is often difficult to retrace precisely. The racism of early superhero comics, on the other hand, is as overt and undeniable as it is repugnant. American culture was (and is) pervaded by a white supremacy that superheroes both reflected and perpetuated. They embodied everything that their creators saw as good and upright in the American character, which, in their eyes, could only manifest in whiteness. When nonwhite characters did appear in early superhero comics, they were at best dull-witted sidekicks and at worst barbaric villains who served to highlight the fundamental goodness of the white superheroes. As Fredric Wertham put it in *Seduction of the Innocent* (1954):

> Children have told us about how different peoples are represented to them in the lore of crime comics.... On the one hand is the tall, blond, regular-featured man sometimes disguised as a superman (or superman disguised as a man).... On the other hand are the inferior people: natives, primitives, savages, "ape men," Negroes, Jews, Indians, Italians, Slavs, Chinese and Japanese, immigrants of every description, people with irregular features, swarthy skins, physical deformities, Oriental features. (101)

Although the comic community has roundly dismissed Wertham because of his hyperbolic (and sexist and homophobic) opposition to comics, his description of the racial makeup of early comics in this passage is entirely correct.

To understand how whiteness influenced the first superheroes, it is essential to recognize that the definition of whiteness used at the time differed from the one we use today. From roughly 1880 to 1940, immigrants from southern and eastern Europe arrived in the United States in large numbers. These new European immigrants were not considered white, or not fully white, by the country's white Anglo-Saxon Protestant (WASP) establishment. David Roediger has described these immigrants as being neither fully white nor definitely nonwhite. Central and eastern Europeans were variously categorized as Slavic, semi-Oriental, Asiatic, Caucasian, and white, while southern Europeans could be categorized as Latin, Mediterranean, mixed, Caucasian, white, or dark white. More insulting terms included "guinea," "greaser," "dago," and "hunky" (35–47). Anglo-Saxons represented the paradigm of whiteness, followed by other northern Europeans, whom promoters of eugenics often referred to as Nordics in an attempt to provide a scientific justification for racism. Below the new immigrants from southern and eastern Europe were all those groups definitively regarded as nonwhite, including Blacks, Hispanics, Native Americans, and Asians. Asians in particular appeared constantly in early comic books as dehumanized, evil villains. During World War II, such dehumanizing representations of Asians were applied to the Japanese in comic books and elsewhere, but this built on earlier discourses that identified the Chinese and other Asian cultures as threats to Western culture. Superheroes served as a symbolic bulwark against the dangers that white Americans perceived in different ethnic and racial groups, from central and eastern Europeans to Chinese and Japanese.

In addition to obligatory whiteness, superheroes were also necessarily male. Women functioned in superhero narratives as damsels in distress and love interests with little narrative weight. The two great exceptions were Lois Lane and Wonder Woman, both of whom played major roles in their respective series, the former as a powerful supporting character and the latter as the main character in her own series. Both were depicted as formidable figures. Lois Lane functions as a symbol of how powerful women can overshadow and dominate weak men and of the male need to turn the tables on such women. Wonder Woman was a remarkable symbol of female independence, but she was granted this freedom only within the structures of white supremacy, which her comics epitomized, featuring some of the most virulently racist caricatures in early American comic books.

Ironically, this inchoate mishmash of white supremacist thought was in large part created by artists and writers who were barred from the charmed circle of whiteness by the racial ideology of the day. Most of the artists, writers, and editors who created the first superheroes were the children of recent Jewish immigrants, who, like other new European immigrants, were widely perceived as not white or not fully white. Jewish writers and artists included almost no direct allusions to their identity as Jews in their work (a significant fact in itself), but their ethnic background informed their comics on a subtextual level, especially in their early opposition to the Nazis. This did not mean that they opposed racism in the United States. On the contrary, Jewish cartoonists frequently depicted racial groups that were below them in America's racial hierarchy in viciously racist terms. Their racism against groups below them emphasized their relative closeness to whiteness and facilitated their assimilation into whiteness. In Roediger's words, "New immigrants proved 'apt students' of white supremacy," learning to stigmatize those below them to elevate their own status (119). Captain America, created by Joe Simon and Jack Kirby, both of whom were Jewish, is a prototypical example. As J. Richard Stevens has written, "African American characters in Captain [America] comics are consistent with the terrible racial stereotypes" typical of the 1940s and were depicted as brute savages or minstrel-show stereotypes who were, above all, stupid (51–52). Stevens writes, "Perhaps the worst example of African American stereotypes can be found in the character of Whitewash Jones," who is depicted as an incompetent coward whose main abilities are playing the harmonica and eating watermelons (52).

THE WHITE SUPERMAN FROM NIETZSCHE TO *ACTION COMICS*

Jerry Siegel and Joe Shuster created the first comic book superhero, Superman, but their idea of a human being with extraordinary powers or abilities was far from unique. The construction of whiteness applied to superheroes did not emerge full born in superhero comics. It was rooted in the philosophical, eugenicist, and science fiction supermen that preceded and influenced its development. While the general idea of a superman can be traced back to the mythological heroes of antiquity, the modern version of the superman developed in the final decades of the nineteenth century and the first decades of the twentieth. Multiple discourses postulated some kind of superman and contributed to the birth of the superhero, overlapping heavily and in confusing ways. Practically every ideology during this highly turbulent period had some version of a superman to offer, from fascism to socialism, science fiction to spiritualism, modernism to conservatism, and so on (G. Jones, *Men of Tomorrow*, 70). Since many of these discourses were diametrically opposed to each other, versions of the superman that drew on more than one of them are at best philosophically muddled, if not utterly incoherent.

The comic book superhero was one of the most polyvalent versions of the superman, incorporating a huge swath of these sources while removing or downplaying as much of their ideological content as possible. However, this ideological baggage did not entirely disappear. Instead it slipped below the surface, operating out of range of conscious perception.

One of the key sources for the superhero was Nietzsche's concept of the Übermensch, which has been translated as both "overman" and "superman." Nietzsche introduced the concept in *Thus Spoke Zarathustra*, which was published in four parts from 1883 to 1892, as a being who transcended traditional notions of morality and created a new way of living free from the shackles of the past. Nietzsche's views on race are complicated and contradictory. On the one hand, he saw Judaism as the source of what he called slave morality, which he used to describe any philosophy that advocated self-denial or equality among human beings. According to Nietzsche, the slave morality of Judaism spread throughout Western culture by way of Christianity (*Beyond Good and Evil / On the Genealogy of Morality*, 226–349). One of Nietzsche's main goals in postulating the Übermensch was to replace this slave morality with the quest to achieve the greatest possible vitality, self-development, and self-actualization of the individual. Greece and the Italian Renaissance, both formative periods in the history of Western civilization, were his main precedents for this state of being. Some interpreted Nietzsche's critique of Judaism as a call for white supremacy, but this oversimplifies Nietzsche's views considerably. Nietzsche implicated Christianity as well as Judaism in slave morality and was a fervent critic of German nationalism. He was hardly a wholehearted champion of Western culture or white ethnonationalism (148–58). German nationalists, however, adopted elements of his philosophy, culminating in the Nazis' co-optation of Nietzsche as a philosophical precursor. A hodgepodge of writers outside Germany also claimed him as an influence, including George Bernard Shaw, H. G. Wells, and H. L. Mencken (Bloom, 1–6; Ratner-Rosenhagen, 53–57; J. Batchelor, 5). These writers in turn influenced a generation of adventure writers in the pulps and elsewhere, who in turn influenced the first superheroes.

Eugenics was another strain of thought that fed into the creation of the superhero, overlapping heavily with Nietzschean ideas in the early twentieth century. George Bernard Shaw's use of the term "superman" in his 1903 book *Man and Superman* owed more to Shaw's support for eugenics than to Nietzsche's use of the term (Gavaler, *Superhero Comics*, 50–51). Eugenicists sought to create an ideal body governed by reason, discipline, and physical perfection, traits that they identified as uniquely belonging to the Nordic race. The eugenicists' ideal body was tall, blond, and white, in contrast to the short, swarthy, dark bodies of the Alpines and Mediterraneans (Nies, 20). According to Madison Grant's highly influential *The Passing of a Great Race* (1916), this ideal body was "statuesque," "very tall, fair skinned, with blond or brown hair and light colored airs," and possessed a "Roman, Norman, or aquiline nose" and "splendid fighting and moral qualities" (31). By contrast, Mediterraneans were "stunted," "dwarfed," "more or less swarthy," and of "primitive short stock," while "Alpines" from southern or central Europe were good workers but had no capacity for leadership (28). Eugenicists feared that Nordics would be replaced in America by Alpines, Mediterraneans, Asians, and Africans. Grant wrote in *The Passing of a Great Race* that "there is a great danger of a . . . replacement of a higher by a lower type here in America unless the native American uses his superior intelligence to protect himself and his children from competition with intrusive peoples drained from the lowest races of eastern Europe" (28). Eugenicists associated crime and slums with the new immigrants and believed that criminal proclivities were inherited. Such views were mainstream positions and repeatedly promoted in magazines like the *Saturday Evening Post* and *Collier's* (28, 35–36).

In the aftermath of World War I, eugenicists used the image of the powerful, disciplined, impenetrable white male body as a symbol for the reconstitution of society (13). According to Betsy Nies, "The desire to locate a towering white male who could rescue the country from a new immigrant presence permeated the popular consciousness" (39). Madison Grant called this kind of heroic white figure a "blond barbarian" (23). Captain America's origin story is firmly grounded in the eugenics movement, as he was created using a serum administered to him by a scientist working for the military, who declares:

> The serum coursing through his blood is rapidly building his body and brain tissues, until his stature and intelligence increase to an amazing degree! . . . There's power surging through those growing muscles. . . . Millions of cells forming at incredible speed! Behold! The crowning achievement of all my years of hard work! The first of a corps of super-agents whose mental and physical ability will make them a terror to spies and saboteurs! We shall call you Captain America, son! Because, like you—America shall gain the strength and the will to safeguard our shores! (Simon et al., 19)

The goal of the eugenics movement was precisely to create a superman through science. However, eugenicists did not restrict themselves to advocating selective breeding and sterilization of those considered socially undesirable. They also argued for controls on immigration from undesirable countries to prevent them from polluting the white American gene pool (Kline, 1–4; Nies, 27–36).

The American Legion, founded in 1919 in the interest of restoring white American society to a state of monolithic whiteness, shared eugenicists' antipathy for immigrants. The legionnaire embodied the American Legion, contrasting with the dark, disorganized immigrants and their radical politics represented in the revolutionary anarchist union of the Industrial Workers of the World (24). Superheroes such as Captain America later fulfilled a similar function in the aftermath of the Great Depression and the approach of another world war. Captain America is in many ways a superheroic version of the legionnaire, performing many of the same social and political functions.

The Ku Klux Klan offered another unsavory model for the superhero. As Chris Gavaler has argued, superheroes resembled Klansmen in that both were vigilantes who bypassed the police and courts to correct injustices that the regular authorities were incapable of addressing. The KKK was presented heroically in Thomas Dixon Jr.'s *The Clansman: An Historical Romance of the Ku Klux Klan* (1905) and in *The Birth of a Nation* (1915), D. W. Griffith's landmark film adaptation of Dixon's book (Gavaler, *Superhero Comics*, 78). After *The Birth of a Nation*, the KKK grew in size and expanded the range of issues around which it agitated. Chris Gavaler writes, "The second Klan embodied a cross-section of American middle-class racial and ethnic anxiety, focused primarily against a perception of urban crime, corruption and expanding immigrant populations" (80). The collision of racial anxiety and fears about crime provided a lasting model for superheroes. The KKK also used hoods, capes, and costumes as a means of hiding one's identity while committing acts of vigilantism. Ben Cameron, the hero of *The Clansman*, not only wears the typical hood, robe, and mask of the KKK but also has superheroic abilities, a secret lair in a cave, and a double identity (80, 82–83). Another important precedent for the masked vigilante was *The Scarlet Pimpernel* (1903), written by the Baroness Emma Orczy, another proponent of eugenics (53–54). Masked heroes proliferated in American culture after *The Birth of a Nation*. The best known is Zorro, first appearing in 1919 and becoming a sensation thanks to the 1920 film *The Mark of Zorro* (Gavaler, "Ku Klux Klan," 197).

Batman represents the clearest example of a superhero influenced by the KKK. Like KKK members, he designed his costume as a means of scaring superstitious criminals. In *The Birth of a Nation*, the idea for the Klan's white hoods comes to Cameron as he watches white children scare Black children by placing a sheet over their heads. Batman's ideology also aligned with the Klan's, at least in part. Both emphasized the constant danger of crime to the fabric of society and the need to remain ever vigilant against it (Gavaler, "Ku Klux Klan," 197). As we have seen, the discourse of eugenics and the Klan associated crime with marginally white southern and eastern European immigrants. Batman comics did not explicitly make the connection between crime and these semiwhite Europeans. Most of the criminals in Batman comics were either of an unidentifiable white ethnic group or were nonwhite. Further muddying the influence of white supremacist sources on Batman, Klan-style regalia was used by Batman's enemies as well as by Batman himself, for example, in a two-part story published in 1939 (Kane, 39–73). Batman's creators likely did not consciously intend to mimic the KKK. As Jews, they were themselves a prime target of the Klan. Batman's resemblance to a Klansman was likely a product of unconscious influence, as his creators absorbed the imagery and ideology of the KKK along with other superheroic influences. The appearance of influences derived from the KKK thus reflects the Klan's ambivalent presence in superhero comics and suggests that Jews could sympathize both with the victims of white supremacy and with whites themselves.

Another key source for the comic book superhero was the supermen who appeared in science fiction and adventure stories in the first decades of the twentieth century. The earliest of these included H. G. Wells's *The Food of the Gods* (1904) and *Men like Gods* (1923), Jack London's *The Sea Wolf* (1904) and *The Iron Heel* (1908), Upton Sinclair's *The Overman* (1907), J. D. Beresford's *The Hampdenshire Wonder* (1911), Edgar Rice Burroughs's *A Princess of Mars* (1911) and *Tarzan of the Apes* (1912), and Varick Vanardy's *Alias* (1913) (Coogan, 129–36, 158–59). The most explicitly racialized of these supermen were Burroughs's John Carter and Tarzan, both of whom were created by Edgar Rice Burroughs, an avowed white supremacist and eugenicist (135, 158–59). Both Carter and Tarzan were important influences on the creation of Superman (Coogan, 158–59; G. Jones, 70–71). John Carter was an aristocratic Virginian who fought in the Civil War on the side of the Confederacy and later grew rich as a gold prospector in Arizona. After apparently dying while hiding from Apaches, he is astrally projected to Mars, where he inhabits a new body identical to his earthly one and defeats aliens of various skin colors. His story is a rather obvious parable of white supremacy. After supporting the Confederacy in its unsuccessful battle to preserve slavery, he recommences his fight for white supremacy in outer space against colored aliens.

Burroughs's other great creation, Tarzan, was the son of a British aristocrat and came to rule over the beasts of the jungle and Black Africans. In his first story, *Tarzan of the Apes*, and frequently thereafter, Tarzan is referred to as a superman (Coogan, 158–59). He was the ideal expression of eugenicist beliefs in the physical, mental, and moral superiority of whites, which, according to Burroughs, resulted from his superior genetic traits, an idea based on the views of eugenicists such as Madison Grant and Lothrop Stoddard (G. Jones, 70–71; Coogan, 159). As Burroughs writes in *Tarzan of the Apes*:

> His straight and perfect figure, muscled as the best of the ancient Roman gladiators must have been muscled, and yet with the soft and sinuous curves of a Greek god, told at a glance the wondrous combination of enormous strength with suppleness and speed. With the noble poise of his handsome head upon those broad shoulders, and the fire of life and intelligence in those fine, clear eyes, he might readily have typified some demigod of a wild and warlike bygone people of his ancient forest. (Nies, 37)

Tarzan is a prime example of the ideal Nordic body, a white man who tames dark-skinned barbarians and savages in the African jungle to protect his white woman, Jane (21).

By the late 1920s, the pulp superman had become a well-worn trope in which a white hero rescues all of society. Buck Rogers, the Shadow, and Doc Savage, who first appeared in 1928, 1930, and 1933, respectively, were all of this type. Philip Wylie's 1930 novel *Gladiator* represented a more intellectual version of the superman genre. Hugo Danner, the novel's hero, attempts to use his powers to aid society, but society's corruption and fear foil his efforts. The world cannot accept or find a place for a human with superpowers (Coogan, 136–37). Danner's attitude of superiority and elitism echoes that of Nietzsche; he mocks junk culture, yellow journalism, and bodybuilding (79). At one point in the novel, Danner considers the use of eugenics to improve humanity (81). *Gladiator* returned the conflict between the superhero and society, a key theme of Nietzsche's Übermensch, to the center of the genre, but whereas Nietzsche believed that the Übermensch would ultimately triumph, Wylie feels that the cause is hopeless. A new spate of philosophical pulp superman novels appeared in the 1930s after *Gladiator* (Coogan, 137–45). As Thomas Andrae puts it, during this period "the superman is a sinister figure who is so obsessed with his power and so contemptuous of mankind that he threatens to dominate and enslave the world; he becomes the evil genius of science fiction cliché.... The message of the superman stories is always the same: whether savior or destroyer, the superman cannot be permitted to exist" (125). The theme of the superman whose great abilities paradoxically cause others to reject him is taken up repeatedly in early superhero comics, casting powerful embodiments of whiteness in a sympathetic light. When Captain Marvel joins his college's football team, his success renders the team meaningless. As exhausted or injured players lie at his feet, the coach tells him, "You run 20 laps around the field in about 2 seconds and then make another touchdown! What are you trying to do, anyway—wreck the team? Get out of here and stay out!!" (Beck and Parker, 155).

The rise of science fiction fandom, pioneered by an ambitious, visionary Jewish immigrant named Hugo Gernsback, was closely related to the pulp superheroes. In 1911, Gernsback published one of his own stories in which he foretold the invention of television, radar, fluorescent lights, tape recording, and jukeboxes (G. Jones, 55). In the early 1930s, science fiction fans debated whether fans represented "a superior order of human" and a higher stage of human evolution marked by "fast imagination and openness to possibility" (33). Jerry Siegel and Joe Shuster, the creators of Superman, were active members of science fiction fandom and created several early superman characters before the iconic Kryptonian. In January 1933, they self-published "The Reign of the Superman" in their own fanzine, *Science Fiction: The Advance Guard of Future Civilization*, with text by Siegel and illustrations by Shuster. The magazine's title captured the utopian faith of 1920s science fiction, but their vision of the superman at this time was quite dark (G. Jones, 29–33). The story features an evil scientist, Professor Ernest Smalley, who uses a new element to give superpowers to a homeless man named Bill Dunn. Dunn gains the powers of telepathy, mind control, mental projection, prescience, and even omniscience, which he uses to amass great wealth and create global chaos. He murders Smalley to prevent him from giving himself superpowers. However, Dunn's powers eventually wear off, and he returns to destitution (Coogan, 138–39).

The Great Depression complicated early versions of Superman as a monolithic instantiation of whiteness, and his various versions during this period exemplified comics' potential as agents of both change and conformity. For example, in late 1933, Siegel and Shuster submitted a story about a new version of Superman to an early comic book publisher called Consolidated Book Publishers. The story was never published, and Shuster destroyed the only copy, but it appears that Superman had now become a prosocial hero, albeit one with no superpowers (Daniels, 17; Coogan, 143–47). According to Thomas Andrae, "One way of understanding this transformation is by interpreting it as a response to the collapse of the Horatio Alger ethos of laissez-faire individualism and its replacement by the experimental collectivism of the New Deal" (125). The evil supermen of the pulps were driven by the economic devastation of the Depression. As Andrae explains, "It is the resentful and downtrodden individuals on the dole who become maniacal, power-mad tyrants" (128). American society has traditionally been highly individualistic, but in the Depression, the negative impacts of capitalism became unavoidable. As Andrae writes, "The social irresponsibility of the entrepreneur, the archetypical hero of laissez-faire individualism, had become oppressively transparent during the Depression" (128). The mad power mongers of the pulps thus had both a sympathetic and an antagonistic aspect. In Andrae's words, they "revealed both the attraction and disillusionment Americans felt toward the success myth during the Depression" (127).

Siegel and Shuster finally succeeded in getting Superman published in 1938 by National Comics, later known as DC. The early Superman stories often cast Superman as the defender of the common man against business owners and the state. In one story, Superman confronts a mineowner whose negligence and lack of safety devices in his mines trap a group of miners, maiming some and endangering their lives. Superman gives the mineowner a taste of his own medicine by stranding him in his own mine, after which the owner agrees to provide the safety devices he had previously spurned (Siegel and Shuster, 32–44; Wright, 11–13). In another story, Superman frees juvenile delinquents from a police paddy wagon because he blames slum conditions for their crimes and then begins tearing down the slum so that it can be replaced by affordable modern housing. Military bombers attack him, but this only serves to complete the demolition of the slum (Andrae, 130–31).

Yet at the same time, Superman was the ultimate individualist, since his superpowers allowed him to take the cause of social reform in his own hands and enforce changes on the powerful with little need for assistance from the masses. These early stories placed Superman outside the power structure of the state and capitalism, but this independence was short-lived. World War II had a lot to do with this shift. As Andrae writes, "By mid-1942, when the war effort demanded unquestioning loyalty to the state and increased collaboration between government and industry, Superman no longer operates outside the law but is made an honorary policeman" (131). Such stories positioned superheroes as representative of the New Deal, with its expansion of labor rights and pro-worker agenda (Wright, 22–23). Superman's alter ego, Clark Kent, reveals a number of contradictions relating to his social position and status. Kent is mistreated by his boss, Perry White, the editor of the *Daily Planet*, and is unable to win the affection of the woman he loves, Lois Lane, who continually bests him as a reporter. Kent is a typical organization man trapped in an unsatisfying, unfulfilling office job that limits his freedom and individuality. As Superman, on the other hand, he escapes all those constraints (Andrae, 132–33). Following Andrew Berman, Andrae argues that

Superman stories "defused widespread feelings of discontent with the system and deflected the potential for revolution by suggesting that the problems of the Depression could be set right within existing institutions" (129).

RACIAL STEREOTYPES IN EARLY AMERICAN COMIC BOOKS

Early superhero comics assumed that superheroes must be white, but whiteness itself was rarely commented on directly or drawn attention to. Non-whiteness, on the other hand, was extremely visible, in the form of racist stereotypes. Ian Haney López writes that racism in the nineteenth and early twentieth century "inseparably conjoined biology and behavior: physical distinctions supposedly corresponded to innate behavioral and cultural deficiencies" (87). This perfectly describes the representation of race in early superhero comics: physical deformity, foreign accents, evil, and stupidity are tightly linked in early American comics. The most common racial stereotype to appear in comic books was the Yellow Peril, a term used to describe stereotypes of East Asians, especially Chinese, Japanese, and Mongolians, as depraved, inhuman monsters, often depicted with long fangs or claws, who sought to invade, overwhelm, and annihilate white Western nations. Black people, primarily Africans, were frequently caricatured as primitive brutes incapable of the kind of sophisticated planning needed for world domination and hence less dangerous than Asians. Racist caricatures of African Americans were less common in early comics than caricatures of other groups, especially Asians, although racist portrayals of "primitive" Africans (as opposed to more "modernized" African Americans) were common in the jungle genre. Latin Americans were also caricatured, usually as scoundrels who would rather steal or rebel than work for an honest living. Black and Latin American characters generally appeared in the context of stories about colonization analyzed in chapter 3.

The most common form of racial stereotyping in early American comics was directed at Asians, predominantly the Chinese and Japanese, who were frequently depicted as monstrous, inhuman villains. These depictions were part of a genre known as the Yellow Peril, which dated back to the 1890s. Some of the most important early examples of the genre were Matthew Phipps Shiel's novel *The Yellow Danger* (1898), H. G. Wells's *The War in the Air* (1908), and Jack London's "The Unparalleled Invasion" (1910) (Frayling, 259–67). Significantly, Wells and London were also pioneers of the science fiction and adventure superman, and the two genres drew on a common stock of ideas about race and modernity. Yellow Peril themes appeared in films as early as 1900 and spread to many other media as well, including comics (286).

The epitome of the Yellow Peril stereotype was Fu Manchu, a Chinese supervillain introduced by the British pulp writer Sax Rohmer in 1912 (Coogan, 159–60; Frayling, 229). Fu Manchu had a massive presence in American mass culture of the early twentieth century. He began to appear in movie serials starting with *The Mystery of Dr. Fu-Manchu* (1923) (Frayling, 286). The first Fu Manchu radio serial appeared in 1931 and was quickly followed by many others (Richards, 34–36). Other celebrated Yellow Peril villains in the 1930s included Ming the Merciless, the main opponent of the science fiction superman Flash Gordon (Frayling, 314–15). Rohmer's famous description of Fu Manchu links the body to race and intellect:

> Imagine a person, tall, lean and feline, high-shouldered, with a brow like Shakespeare and a face like Satan, a close-shaven skull, and long, magnetic eyes of the true cat-green. Invest him with all the cruel cunning of an entire Eastern race, accumulated in one giant intellect, with all the resources of science past and present, with all the resources, if you will, of a wealthy government—which, however, already has denied all knowledge of his existence. Imagine that awful being, and you have a mental picture of Dr. Fu-Manchu, the yellow peril incarnate in one man. (Frayling, 229)

Part of the threat of Fu Manchu revolved around his many attributes that are identical with those supposedly belonging to the Nordic race viewed by eugenicists as being mentally superior. Because Fu Manchu trespasses on territory that supposedly belongs exclusively to whites, he blurs the boundaries between the races, as reflected in Rohmer's description of the villain as having "a brow like Shakespeare," a preeminent symbol of Western literary genius. Fu Manchu's great intelligence and many skills represent the fear that white superiority may be illusory, threatening to topple the whole edifice. The blurring of racial boundaries was also central to Yellow Peril stories in that they often conflated and confused Asian cultures with one another. China was often equated with Mongolia, for instance, although the two groups have historically had different ethnic backgrounds, social structures, cultures, religions, and languages.

The Yellow Peril phenomenon was not driven by any actual threat of Chinese assault on the West. Britain defeated China twice in the nineteenth century in wars instigated by the British. China's state and military were extremely weak during this period, and its society was in a state of fragmentation and upheaval, so it was in no position to challenge the West. Whites' fears of China thus derived not from any actual military threat but from the growing numbers of Chinese immigrants in cities such as London, New York, and San Francisco, each of which became home to Chinatown neighborhoods of significant size. The sight of large numbers of Chinese people speaking their own language and practicing their own customs in the heart of Western cities was a profoundly destabilizing and intimidating experience for many whites, demonstrating how fragile and easily threatened white feelings of supremacy were. The prevalence and intensity of Yellow Peril narratives thus testified to the hypocrisy of whites' racial attitudes, as well as to Western fears that China might return the West's aggression.

The Yellow Peril stereotype was present in comic books from the beginning: the first issue of *Detective Comics* featured a Yellow Peril menace named Ching Lung (Frayling, 296). An earlier action hero created by Siegel and Shuster named Slam Bradley, a kind of proto-Superman, fought a group of absurdly dehumanized Chinese villains in his first story (G. Jones, 120–21). A Fu Manchu comic strip ran in newspapers beginning in 1931 and then was reprinted in *Detective Comics* beginning with issue 17 (Goulart, 106). Comic books regularly featured stories with titles such as "The Terror of the Slimy Japs," "The Slant Eye of Satan," and "Funeral for Yellow Dogs" (Wright, 45). With the American alliance with China against Japan and the Japanese bombing of Pearl Harbor, the main villains of Yellow Peril narratives shifted from the Chinese to the Japanese, but the conventions of the genre otherwise continued unchanged (Frayling, 315). In 1939, Jack Cole created a villain called the Claw, an over-the-top Japanese villain of enormous stature with a mouth full of fangs and long claws on his fingers. In a typical portrayal, the Claw appears on the cover of *Silver Streak Comics* #7 with his daggerlike teeth and claws about to envelop a city as Daredevil leaps nimbly out of his grasp. As in the Ebony White story about Nazi saboteurs, this story was purportedly dedicated to battling the forces of racism but actually perpetuated racist stereotypes in America.

According to J. Richard Stevens, literally every Japanese character in a comic book during World War II was a villain, including Japanese Americans who were American citizens (Stevens, 50). Of the major superhero characters, Captain America's comics were among the most viciously racist. One of his enemies, the Fang, was comparable to the Claw in the degree to which he was dehumanized. This Japanese crime boss based in San Francisco's Chinatown had pointed fangs, an elongated, egg-shaped head, and monkey-like facial features. Captain America comics routinely used slurs such as "yellow

Jack Cole (pencils), cover of *Silver Streak Comics* #7 (January 1941).

monkeys," "dirty Jap," and "dirty yellow Jap" (Stevens, 49). Yellow Peril stories repeatedly suggested that Japanese spies were attempting to undermine the United States from within. For instance, in one 1944 Captain America story (vol. 1, no. 38), a group of Japanese Americans in an internment camp escape and begin planning a surprise attack on the United States (Stevens, 49).

While negative images of Asians predominated in the mass media, other alternatives existed that humanized rather than dehumanized them. The most notable example of a creative work that humanized Asians was Pearl S. Buck's *The Good Earth*. It was the best-selling novel in the United States in 1931 and 1932, won the Pulitzer Prize, and was made into a successful movie in 1937. It presented a hardworking Chinese farming family with humanity, dignity, and empathy, a depiction that resonated with American farmers struggling during the Depression (Frayling, 311–12). *The Good Earth*'s success demonstrates that whites did not unanimously see Chinese people as inhuman monsters and that other representations of Asians were possible at the time. The choice to represent Chinese people in these terms was just that: a choice. This possibility is confirmed by some comic book stories showing East Asian characters in a more positive light. The main example of a positive depiction of a nonwhite character was Kato, the sidekick of the Green Hornet. Green Hornet was the star of a popular radio show before appearing in comics and helped inspire the first superheroes before appearing in his own comic book in 1940. Kato, his valet and chauffeur, is described on the title page of the first issue of Green Hornet's run with Harvey Comics in 1942 as a "trusted Filipino servant who alone shares Reid's secret when he becomes the Green Hornet" (*The Green Hornet Collection: Part 1*, 2). Kato often comes to the aid of the Green Hornet at critical moments, as when Kato shuts off a giant industrial roller that is about to crush the Green Hornet, after which the Green Hornet thinks, "I must remember to thank Kato for this!" (10). Yet, despite his invaluable help, Kato is clearly not the Green Hornet's equal. He is a sidekick, not a partner, and is depicted as being entirely content with this arrangement. The racial hierarchy in which whiteness is supreme is thus preserved, although without the vicious racist hatred found in Yellow Peril stories.

Stereotypical portrayals of Asians were not limited to the Yellow Peril genre. They also partook of the much older discourse known as Orientalism, which applied primarily to the Middle East but could also encompass other parts of Asia. Dating as far back as ancient Greece, the Orient has traditionally been identified in Western discourse as decadent and tyrannical, in contrast to the freedom and rationality of the West.[1] This rhetoric overlaps significantly both with that of the Yellow Peril in the late nineteenth and early twentieth centuries and the Islamophobia of the late twentieth and early twenty-first centuries. Edward Said famously analyzed the history of the contrast between the East and the West in his groundbreaking 1978 book, *Orientalism*. One feature of Orientalism is that it often equates different Asian cultures with one another, ignoring the actual differences between them. We see one example of this in the first appearance of the Green Lantern, in which a Chinese lamp maker and collector of books on sorcery named Chang finds a meteor made out of green metal and fashions it into a lantern. Chang's fellow villagers believe that the meteor was sent by the "evil one," so they murder Chang and burn his books, thereby exemplifying the negative

"The Case of the Murdering Clown." Originally published in *Green Hornet Comics* #7 (June 1942). Reprinted in *The Green Hornet Collection: Part 1* (Classic Comics Library, 2018).

qualities associated with Orientalism (Finger et al., 9). The lamp that Chang produces resembles popular portrayals of Aladdin's lamp, a Middle Eastern form. Yellow Peril stories in comic books and other media rarely show much familiarity with the actual cultures or history of Asia, so it is easy for them to conflate different Asian cultures. Asian cultures, or indeed any foreign cultures, are typically represented in comic books by little more than a traditional costume, a bad accent, stereotypical facial features, and perhaps a single, usually inaccurate reference to a culture's religion or history.

One of the more peculiar aspects of comic books' use of Orientalism is its deployment in relation to German characters, who began appearing as villains years before the United States entered the war in December 1941. We find a typical example of a negative portrayal of a German character in one of Batman's early villains, a mad scientist named Doctor Death, who first appeared in July 1939 and whose real name is Karl Hellfern (Kane, 18). The character has a bald head, large forehead, and short beard and wears a monocle and tuxedo. Variations on this combination often appear in early comic books in mad scientist characters, who are typically identified as German. Germans were occasionally portrayed sympathetically, as when a German American character in a Captain America story declares, "I am of German descent . . . but I'm also a good American citizen! I'll have nothing to do with a [spy] organization that aims to destroy the country that protects me and mine!" (Wright, 48). White ethnics other than Germans were also portrayed in stereotypical terms, but they were comparatively mild compared to portrayals of the Germans. The gangsters Zucco (Kane, 129–36) and Mike Mulgoon (Marston and Peter, 161–71) reflect negative stereotypes about the Italians and Irish, respectively. They speak in heavy ethnic dialects and are violent and cruel, but they are not villainized to the same extent as the Germans, much less dehumanized as nonwhite villains were.

That Germans, who were white, appeared in many comics as villains created a contradiction within the ideology of white supremacy. To reconcile the whiteness of the German villains with their evilness, the comics frequently associated Germans with Asian characters, thereby marking them as tainted by nonwhiteness. Yet their whiteness also moderated their evilness, with the result that German characters were never shown with the same level of malice and dehumanization often applied to Asian villains. They were depicted as bumbling, evil monsters, and sometimes shown with fangs, but their depictions were not as dehumanizing or vicious as those of the Japanese (Stevens, 49–50).

Negative portrayals of Germans did not rest on stereotypes about Germans alone. To buttress the racial otherness and villainy of the Germans, the comics frequently associated them with the Orient in one way or another. For instance, in the first appearance of Doctor Death, the doctor has a brutish henchman named Jabah, whom Batman refers to as a "giant Indian," presumably meaning an East Indian because of his turban (Kane, 23). Batman kills him, but in Doctor Death's next appearance, "The Return of Doctor Death," he has a new henchman named Mikhail, whom Batman describes as "[one] of Doctor Death's Cossacks, such as Jabah" (32). Since Cossacks are from the Ukraine, not India, this appears to be another example of the general confusion of different Asian ethnic groups.[2] In any case, the Cossack henchman serves as a connecting link between Germany and the Orient. Cossacks had a mixture of Slavic and Turkic ancestry and for centuries served the Russian tsar as troops in border regions of the Russian empire stretching from the Caucasus to the Pacific (O'Rourke, xii, 55). They thus literally occupied the frontier between whiteness and the Orient. In any case, both Jabah and Mikhail create an association between Doctor Death and the Orient. On the one hand, the presumed evil of Asian characters rubs off on Doctor Death, making him seem more sinister and evil, while on the other hand, the Asian characters are integral parts of the evil schemes of Doctor Death, validating the negative stereotypes about the Orient. The two ethnic prototypes, the evil German mad scientist and the brutish Oriental thug, reinforce each other.

The use of racial stereotypes in early American comics demonstrates how race could be used to validate gender inequalities. The stories of Wonder Woman, the most prominent female character in the first decade of comics and the only female superhero, were laced with some of the most vicious stereotypes in the industry. A 1942 story, "Wonder Woman Goes to the Circus," provides a typical example of such racist narratives and how multiple

Gardner Fox (script) and Bob Kane (pencils), "The Batman Meets Doctor Death." Originally published in *Detective Comics* #29 (July 1939). Reprinted in *Batman Chronicles*, vol. 1 (DC Comics, 2005). © DC Comics.

overlapping stereotypes could be nested within Yellow Peril narratives. The story features a Japanese saboteur named San Yan who tricks a troupe of Burmese elephant grooms into believing that the elephants in their care are channeling the spirits of the grooms' dead ancestors. San Yan convinces them that "to free our ancestors' spirits we must kill these elephants whom you hold captive, far from their native country" (Marston and Peter, 171). Wonder Woman reveals his deception and accuses him of being a "Jap spy" and of planning the elephant murders to prevent the circus from raising money for the Army Welfare Fund. The Burmese in this story are more gullible dupes than malevolent villains. The implication is that the Japanese San Yan is more treacherous and intelligent than the Burmese he manipulates, setting up a hierarchy of Yellow Perils. Wonder Woman broke gender norms of the time by presenting a female hero who was the most capable and powerful figure in her fictional universe. However, this unusual level of autonomy and independence was accompanied by a virulent white supremacy and racism. Wonder Woman overturns one social hierarchy, the patriarchal power of men over women, but reaffirms another hierarchy, the racial power of whites over other ethnic groups, thereby insulating her from being seen as an outsider or disruptor of social conventions. Her claim to whiteness is further buttressed by the fact that she is an Amazon, a mythical race associated with ancient Greece, commonly seen as the origin of Western civilization and represented as a paragon of whiteness for eugenicists.

Jill Lepore spends only a handful of pages discussing racism in her book on Wonder Woman comics, excusing it with the usual explanation that "the racism of Wonder Woman is the racism pervasive in comic books from the 1940s" before pointing out that what "all villains in Wonder Woman share is their opposition to women's equality" (216–17). Lepore does not say this outright, but the implication is that Wonder Woman's feminism somehow excuses or justifies her racism. Lepore thereby perpetuates the long history of racism within the feminist movement, in which white feminists have minimized or ignored the concerns of Black women and failed to show solidarity with their fight (hooks, *Ain't I a Woman*, 119–96). While this is presumably not Lepore's intent, her analysis of Wonder Woman is a prime example of how well-meaning white liberals have failed to adequately take race and racism into consideration when creating or examining American comics.

Negative portrayals of Black characters could be as virulent as those of Asians but were less frequent. The most prominent Black character in early American comics was Ebony White, who appeared in Will Eisner's *The Spirit*. *The Spirit* was published in comic book inserts in newspapers from 1940 to 1952 and in other venues, including regular comic books. Although Eisner's masked detective is not as well-known today as Marvel's and DC's superheroes, *The Spirit* is considered a classic and an early comics masterpiece. Eisner also contributed to the creation of Sheena, Queen of the Jungle, whose comics, produced by Eisner/Iger Studios for the publisher Fiction House, were filled with racist portrayals of Africans. Eisner thus has a well-established track record of using racist caricatures in his work. Ebony White was the Spirit's sidekick of indeterminate age. It is difficult to tell whether he is meant to be a boy or a man, which plays into the racist trope that Black people have the mental abilities of children, expressed in the social convention of referring to all Black men as "boy," regardless of their age. White was depicted by Eisner and the artists he hired with enormous eyes and round, doughnut-shaped lips that appear more simian than human, all of which conform closely to the standard representation of characters in the blackface minstrel tradition. Blackface minstrelsy is an art form with a long and shameful history in American culture. Dating to the 1840s, blackface minstrelsy was a form of variety theater in which white actors wearing blackface acted out racist stereotypes for the entertainment of white audiences. Alternating between skits and musical performances, minstrelsy was

"Shipyard Sabotage." Originally published in *The Spirit*, August 8, 1943. Reprinted in *Will Eisner's The Spirit Archives*, vol. 7 (DC Comics, 2002). © Will Eisner.

the most popular form of entertainment in the latter part of the nineteenth century and continued to be employed in various forms into the 1960s. It was initially a full-length live performance but was later incorporated into many other media, including sheet music, vaudeville, burlesque, records, film, radio, and television. Blackface minstrels were typically identified visually through the use of absurd, ill-fitting clothing.

Two images from Spirit comics capture the racism and racial contradictions of early American comic books. On the cover of a comic from 1947, the Spirit and Ebony White turn a corner into a darkened alley. The Spirit has a hard, chiseled face and towers above his sidekick, who is unnaturally short, like a child. The Spirit appears unafraid and resolute, leaning almost casually against the wall while looking watchfully into the alley. White, by contrast, appears terrified, with an anxious expression on his face and beads of sweat running down his forehead, making him appear immature and cowardly, serving by comparison to highlight the Spirit's maturity and bravery. A 1943 Spirit story captures the contradiction between comics' vituperative opposition to the Nazis and comics' virulent racism toward nonwhites. As in many American comic books during World War II, the story's villains are Nazi saboteurs. Ebony has just discovered the identity of a group of saboteurs and is on his way to tell the Spirit about them as he submissively exclaims, "Dey's Nazis! Jus' wait until Mist' Spirit heahs 'bout this!" (Eisner, 56). This incident neatly encapsulates early American comic books' racial contradictions, as the accusation of Nazism is put in the mouth of a hideous racial stereotype.

Eisner later altered Ebony White to make him more believable and then eliminated him entirely, partially recognizing the racism exhibited by the character. In his place, Eisner introduced another Black character, Detective

Grey, who was depicted more neutrally. While this change represented an improvement, the semiotics of the characters' names reveals the limits of Eisner's attempt at racial tolerance. Ebony White's name comically juxtaposed the colors black and white. The name is an oxymoron, a denial that anyone with ebony skin could ever possess the attributes of whiteness. Grey's name, on the other hand, is neither white nor Black but rather a mixture of the two. The implication here is that for a Black man to possess the qualities associated with whiteness, he must lose his blackness by mixing it with whiteness, producing an in-between mixture that is neither fully Black nor fully white. While creating a more positive Black character, Eisner undercut this gesture toward racial equality.

JEWISH IDENTITY AND THE AMERICAN MELTING POT

For Jewish cartoonists, the denigration of other ethnic or racial minorities and the suppression of their own Jewishness were the price of entry into the racial "melting pot" of the United States. Jewish writers and artists, mostly from New York City, played a disproportionately large role in the invention of comic books. The creators of Superman were the children of Jewish immigrants, as were the creators of Batman, Green Lantern, Captain America, and many other superheroes. Major figures from the early history of comic books who were Jewish included Jerry Siegel, Joe Shuster, Bob Kane, Gil Kane, Will Eisner, Max Gaines, William Gaines, Harvey Kurtzman, Will Elder, Stan Lee, and Jack Kirby. The predominance of Jews in the comic book industry was in part a legacy of anti-Semitism, as many newspapers and advertising agencies would not hire Jews, so aspiring Jewish writers and artists went into comic books instead (Brod, 2–3).

The melting pot is an apt metaphor for the way in which whiteness was constructed in America in an age of mass immigration. Outsiders who wished to receive the benefits of political and social equality were obliged to shed their own national, ethnic, or racial identities and assimilate into the Anglo-Saxon model of whiteness that dominated American society (Lund, 86–87). This option was open to immigrants from southern and eastern Europe, but not to African Americans, Mexican Americans, or Asian Americans, who were relegated to the margins of US society and the bottom of its racial hierarchy. Jews in the comics industry embraced the opportunity to enter into the melting pot and were willing to mask their own identity and denigrate racial minorities to do so. Many Jewish comics creators changed their names to hide their Jewishness: Stanley Lieber became Stan Lee, Jacob

Kurtzberg became Jack Kirby, Hymie Simon became Joe Simon, Bob Kahn became Bob Kane, and so on. They also embraced the denigration of non-white races and ethnic groups, resulting in the plethora of racist stereotypes in comics they authored.

Superman, the first comic book superhero, is a paradigmatic example of Jewish comics creators' assimilation into whiteness. Superman is a foreign immigrant from a destroyed world who passes for a white American (and human). Superman represented the "little guy" whom Franklin Delano Roosevelt's New Deal was designed to help, but this little guy was invariably white (Lund, 84). Superman comics were largely free of racist stereotypes, not because they depicted people of color as the equal of whites but because they eliminated people of color from their pages almost entirely. No African Americans appeared in Superman stories in *Action Comics* for the series' first three years (Gavaler, *Superhero Comics*, 157). This erasure of Black people parallels the politics of the New Deal, which was intentionally constructed to exclude minorities from most of its benefits. As Ira Katznelson has shown, the New Deal largely excluded African Americans and other racial minorities, thanks to aggressive efforts by southern legislators in the Democratic Party, known as Dixiecrats. A majority of Black workers were either maids or farmers. These occupations were left out of the New Deal's labor protections and did not qualify for Social Security benefits until 1954. New Deal social welfare programs did not include antidiscrimination provisions and were applied in such a way as to avoid challenging segregation and inequality in the South. This disparate treatment continued during and after World War II, when Black soldiers received fewer opportunities for advancement during the war, and Black veterans received fewer government benefits after it. New Deal politics thus provided Superman's Jewish creators with the opportunity to identify as defenders of white workers and assimilate into whiteness by excluding and denigrating racial minorities. However, this disguise resulted in a fragmentation of the consciousness and identity of both the superheroes and their creators.

Superman's story closely mirrors the immigrant Jewish experience, with precedents in both biblical narrative and contemporary history. His story echoes that of Moses, whose mother set him adrift on the Nile to escape the pharaoh's purge of Jewish children, after which the baby Moses was found by the pharaoh's daughter and raised among the Egyptian royal family (Brod, 9). Superman's name also attests to his Jewishness. The name Kal-El sounds like the Hebrew words meaning "all is God" or "all for God" (5). By contrast, his adopted name of Clark Kent is highly English. Note, however, that Siegel claimed in the 1970s that Jor-El was an abbreviation for his father's name, Jerome Siegel (Fingeroth, *Disguised as Clark Kent*, 45). Jerome was killed by a robber, so this origin of the name also refers to a lost father (G. Jones, 38). The use of the suffix *-man* in Superman's name also echoes the common ending of Jewish names such as Lieberman, Kurtzman, and so on (Brod, 9).

The most symbolically laden way in which Superman represents Jewish experience is his adoption of a new identity to blend into an alien environment. Jews immigrating to America left Europe to escape persecution and rising political tensions, which led to two cataclysmic world wars and the Holocaust. Similarly, Superman is a refugee from an alien world in peril who hides his identity on Earth to assimilate into human society. He is an undocumented refugee who creates an alter ego to survive. He then mutes his fragmented, alien consciousness to project and defend a monolithic whiteness, demonstrating the power of whiteness to absorb and eradicate difference. His devotion to upholding the law of the dominant white culture transforms his alien status from marginalized other to guarantor of the white-dominated American melting pot.

Like Superman, American Jews had to maintain a facade that was both real and artificial at the same time, creating an internal mental fragmentation that was a necessary part of survival in white American society. The use of a secret identity reflects the immigrants' desire to avoid scrutiny and not stand out (Fingeroth, *Disguised as Clark Kent*, 25). Danny Fingeroth suggests that Clark Kent and other superhero alter egos provided gentile masks behind which Jewish creators could disguise themselves (34–35). This need to wear a disguise is also evident in the decision of many Jewish comic book writers and artists to conceal their Jewish identities by Anglicizing their names. Superman thus performs both a textual and an extratextual form of assimilation. Within the text, he is an alien from Krypton who must disguise his identity to fool the humans of Earth, but in the real world, Superman also performed an act of disguise and assimilation by masking his creators' Jewishness in a science fiction story about an alien from the planet Krypton.

Other superheroes also displayed signifiers of Jewish identity, although none did so as deeply as Superman. Steve Rogers, Captain America's alter ego, is marked by his name, blond hair, and overall appearance as distinctly Nordic. His origin in New York's Lower East Side, a heavily Jewish neighborhood, is a veiled reference to Jewishness (Fingeroth, *Disguised as Clark Kent*, 102–3). His frail physique and lack of masculinity, which result in his rejection by the military until he receives the serum that grants him superpowers, also align with Jewish stereotypes. Further, a scientist named Professor Reinstein, his name a reference to Albert Einstein, is the creator of the super-soldier serum that gives Captain America his powers (Simon et al., 20). Later versions of superhero comics continued subtly to reference Jewish culture. The name of Barry Allen, the Silver Age Flash, was based on a combination of Barry Gray, a famous Jewish radio host, and Steve Allen, a celebrity entertainer who incorporated Yiddishisms into his material. When Green Lantern was rebooted in 1959, the Guardians of the Universe were given facial features modeled on those of the Israeli prime minister David Ben-Gurion (Fingeroth, *Disguised as Clark Kent*, 88).

Despite this and other indications of the influence of their ethnic background on their creations, most of the key Jewish creators who were there at the founding of the industry felt that religion had no effect on them (Fingeroth, *Disguised as Clark Kent*, 25; G. Jones, 129–30). Joe Simon claimed that religion had no effect on him, Jack Kirby, or Martin Goodman (Fingeroth, 24). Stan Lee similarly claimed that religion never entered his mind when working on comics (Lee, 9–11). Will Eisner said, "I knew I was Jewish in the same sense that any American knows he's Irish-American or Italian-American. It influenced me in that the stories I grew up hearing were the stories told in Jewish families, but I never thought about being Jewish when I did my work" (G. Jones, 130). Many Jewish cartoonists changed their last names to hide their Jewishness. These cartoonists seemed to want to minimize Jewishness as an influence on their work, a hunch confirmed by their decisions to Anglicize their names to hide their ethnicity. Kane did not even mention the words "Jew" or "Jewish" in his autobiography (Fingeroth, *Disguised as Clark Kent*, 51). All of this testifies to the pressure these creators must have felt to conform and assimilate to whiteness.

Although in retrospect this influence seems obvious, in at least some cases, such as Superman, these characters' creators generally refused to see it. This reticence can be interpreted as another symptom of their creators' fragmented identities, which internalized the need to disguise their Jewishness beneath a veneer of whiteness. However, at other times, at least some Jewish creators have acknowledged the possibility that their ethnic background may have influenced their work. Stan Lee has written that "attitudes and emotions that could be called Jewish . . . may have been in the backs of our minds as we were making superhero and all the other kinds of comics—while in the front of our minds we were just trying to make the best action-adventure comics we could" (10–11). Jerry Siegel cited Nazi oppression of the Jews as one of the factors that was on his mind when he was creating Superman (Fingeroth, *Disguised as Clark Kent*, 41). Jules Feiffer, former assistant to Will Eisner, wrote in *The Great Comic Book Heroes* that the Spirit's "nose may have turned up, but we all knew he was Jewish" (Fingeroth, 61).

The approach of World War II added a new element to the impact of Jewishness on superheroes. Much of America had an isolationist attitude toward the growing conflict in Europe. Americans did not want to get involved in another European world war. The rise of the Nazis, however, concerned Jewish Americans directly. They felt connected to the European Jews who had stayed in the Old World, and saw the Nazis as a direct threat to Jews in both the Old and New Worlds. The Kristallnacht pogrom in November 1938 represented an escalation of Nazi persecution of Jews and began the path toward the Holocaust. It may have inspired superhero origin stories by Jewish cartoonists depicting the loss of parents or whole worlds (Fingeroth, *Disguised as Clark Kent*, 55). Jewish comic book artists and writers responded by creating stories that identified the Nazis as a threat to the American way of life and encouraged their readers to support US intervention against the Nazis. Martin Goodman, the publisher of Timely Comics, had already published stories in which Nazis appeared as villains. The Human Torch and the Sub-Mariner had both fought the Nazis, and Goodman was reportedly seeking other characters to continue this battle (Stevens, 25–26).[3] Superman comics had featured villains based on the Axis powers before 1940 but made their opposition to them explicit in a two-page 1940 story published in *Look* magazine, titled "How Superman Would End the War," telling Hitler that "I'd like to land a strictly non-Aryan sock on your jaw" (Bowers, 99–100). The Nazis responded to the superhero offensive by proclaiming Superman an enemy of the Reich, famously declaring in April 1940 in *Das Schwarze Korps* that "Superman is a Jew!" (100). The most aggressively anti-Nazi superhero was Captain America, whose origin and mission were directly related to fighting the Nazis. The first issue of *Captain America* went on sale in December 1940, a full year before the attack on Pearl Harbor and America's entry into World War II. The cover showed Captain America landing a punch on Hitler's jaw.

MORAL CULPABILITY AND RACISM

Critics of superheroes in the 1940s and 1950s were not blind to the racism of superhero comics. Even before Fredric Wertham's criticisms in the 1950s, Gershon Legman wrote in a 1949 book that "the Superman formula is essentially lynching.... Superman glorifies the 'right' of the individual to take [the] law into his own hands.... Superman ... is really peddling a philosophy of 'hooded justice' in no way distinguishable from that of Hitler and the Ku Klux Klan" (117–18). While such charges were hyperbolic, they were not without foundation. Although some superhero comics contained coded references to the trauma suffered by Jews at the hands of Nazi racism, they turned the racial animus of the time on those below them in America's racial hierarchy to better assimilate into the construct of whiteness. The depiction of racial stereotypes directly linked to US nationalism and to wartime fears and anxieties. Marvel's precursor, Timely Comics, created a club for readers of Captain America called the Sentinels of Liberty. Members had to sign a loyalty oath in which they pledged "to uphold the principles of the Sentinels of Liberty and assist Captain America in his war against spies in the U.S.A." (Simon et al., 22). Young fans sent mail to Timely in which they accused people with Germanic names of various acts of treason (Stevens, 27).

Claims of progressiveness are often made for early superhero comics, but such claims rarely acknowledge these comics' frequent racism. Writers often take aim at Fredric Wertham's risible claim that superhero comics were tantamount to Nazism. Despite the racism of early American comics, they stopped far short of espousing mass extermination. These comics' defenders, however, do not acknowledge the extent of their racism or the contradictions between their racism and their anti-Nazi stance. Danny Fingeroth, for instance, acknowledges that "many comic books were racist (which unfortunately was often true, in story and character details, if not in overall intent), with the heroes almost always white Aryan types, whereas the villains were often stereotyped minorities" (Fingeroth, *Disguised as Clark Kent*, 73). It is not clear why the cartoonists get a pass on their "overall intent," and Fingeroth does not pursue the point, changing the subject instead to rebutting Wertham's accusation of fascism. Rick Bowers totally ignores the racism in Superman's comics in his discussion of Superman's progressive achievements and his rebuttal of Wertham's accusations (Bowers, 41, 97). Gerard Jones rightfully dismisses any equation of superhero comics with Nazism but does not address the reality of racism in American superhero comics (G. Jones, 276).

Cartoonists have also generally deflected directly addressing the racism in their comics. Will Eisner, for instance, has acknowledged that his portrayal of Ebony White was racist but has also attempted to excuse it and demonstrated that he still harbors racist assumptions about Black people. Many of Eisner's statements are so equivocal or unclear that they are impossible to interpret, as when he says that "if you go back and examine how I handled Ebony, I was aware that I was dealing with something that was volatile and I had a responsibility" (Eisner and Arnold). At other times, he argues that he was only doing what everyone else was doing or that he later atoned for his mistakes, as when he says, "The only excuse I have for [that portrayal] is that at the time humor consisted in our society of bad English and physical difference in identity. Later I attempted to depart from it by having a black character, a detective, who spoke proper English and I had an airplane pilot that was black" (Eisner and Arnold).

The point at which Eisner comes closest to acknowledging his culpability is when the interviewer asks him how we would react to another author writing a story from Ebony's viewpoint, as Eisner himself had recently done with Fagin, the Jewish villain from Charles Dickens's *Oliver Twist*. Eisner's initial response is that "I would deserve it. . . . As a matter of fact that probably would be a very worthwhile idea" (Eisner and Arnold). However, he then speculates, "[If] I were somebody else and were to undertake that, I would probably do something about his psychology. He lives with the Spirit, his engagement was solely tied up with the Spirit and I would probably touch on the slave mentality that he probably had" (Eisner and Arnold). Even in this quasi apology, Eisner displays racist attitudes in his description of a supposed "slave mentality" that he believes Black people possess. It is not clear what this slave mentality is, but it carries suggestions of Nietzsche's concept of slave morality, W. E. B. Du Bois's concept of double consciousness, or perhaps simply a generalized sense of inferiority. Du Bois argued that Black people living in America internalized the white racial frame, which contradicted and belittled their own experience and identity, resulting in an internally conflicted and fragmented consciousness. Eisner's comment that someone else should do to Ebony White what Eisner did to Fagin suggests that Eisner too recognizes a process of fragmentation at work in his creations, at least when he is forced to account for himself under the questioning of another person. This fragmentation also affected one of the most perennially popular genres in American comic books aside from superheroes, the western.

Chapter Two

THE SOUTHERN OUTLAW AND THE WHITE INDIAN IN WESTERN COMICS

After World War II, superheroes temporarily lost their position as the preeminent genre of American comics. One of the genres that filled this gap was the western. Driven in large part by the myth of the frontier, the western was a prominent feature of the American comic book marketplace from the 1940s through the 1960s. Integral to the myth of the frontier was the belief that progress was defined by the supremacy of pure-blooded whiteness over savagery. Perhaps the most prominent figure in the western genre is the outlaw bandit and gunslinger. Although the gunslinger is a familiar figure to any consumer of American popular culture, most people do not know that its origin can be traced back to the repudiation of government-enforced emancipation and Reconstruction after the Civil War. As the cultural historian Richard Slotkin relates, "The myths of social banditry are symbolic dramatizations of . . . social conflicts. . . . In the South, this kind of conflict [arose] from the northern-imposed 'Reconstruction' of the former Confederacy: a complex of racial, political, and economic conflicts between freed slaves, poor Whites, former masters, and new plantation owners" (129).

A lesser-known western archetype, but arguably one of equal importance, is the white Indian, a white man who absorbs "Indianness" but does not assimilate into it (Chireau, 203). The white Indian occupies an ambivalent and liminal position on the margins of both white and Indian culture. While white Indians typically choose loyalty to white culture over their adopted Indian culture, there are important exceptions to this. To preserve the myth of monolithic whiteness, white supremacy, and the notion of blood purity, many states in the United States adopted the one-drop rule, whereby anyone with at least 1 percent of nonwhite blood was legally nonwhite and could not partake of privileges reserved for white people. The belief in blood purity drew a line between whites and Native Americans that was, at least in theory, uncrossable. However, for whites to survive on the frontier, this line had to be crossed and recrossed time and again. To resolve this contradiction, the figure of the white Indian, or the "man who knows Indians," was created. Slotkin delineates the popular trope of the man who knows Indians or white Indian as a "hero mediator or interpreter between races and cultures but more often as civilization's most effective instrument against savagery—a man who knows how to think and fight like an Indian, to turn their own methods against them" (16). Slotkin traces this trope to the protagonists of James Fenimore Cooper's novels and suggests that Cooper's model was the frontiersman Daniel Boone. The figure of the white Indian is often unequivocally loyal to his fellow whites despite his exposure to nonwhiteness. His dalliance with Native American culture reinforces his whiteness by allowing him to protect the interests of the white American government. The few white Indians in historical texts and comics who did not remain loyal to whiteness were dehumanized and branded as the worst kind of villain.

The white Indian has been a part of western comics from the beginning. Western comics first appeared in syndicated newspapers in the form of strips, beginning in the early twentieth century and booming in the 1930s. In 1933 the popular strip *Whiteboy* featured a protagonist who, after his family was killed by the Sioux, was adopted by a rival tribe and rechristened Whiteboy. The first western comic books were collections of western newspaper strips, which were themselves drawn from dime novels populated by western protagonists such as Kit Carson. Like Daniel Boone and the frontiersman Simon Girty, Kit Carson was an American frontiersman and scout who at one point lived among Native Americans.

Clay Duncan, the central character in Jack Kirby and Joe Simon's *The Kid Cowboys of Boys' Ranch*, which first appeared in 1950, is a man who knows Indians and is referred to as a white Indian but consistently demonstrates his loyalty to white interests and never compromises his mythical white blood purity. Stan Lee's *Rawhide Kid* (begun in 1955) exemplifies the idea of the gunslinger and American outlaw as jilted southerner and white supremacist. The Rawhide Kid is in many ways an archetypal example of the noble gunfighter, albeit one who is unjustly forced into the life of an outlaw. Though small in stature, the Kid is a lethal dynamo who only enacts violence when he is confronted by long odds or defending the powerless, thereby embodying the myth of the United States as a beacon for democracy instead of a nation that colonized and ethnically cleansed its indigenous peoples.

A few decades later, comics creators began publishing revisionist western comics that questioned some of the assumptions and tropes of early western comics, with varying degrees of success. Jonah Hex, first appearing in *All Star Western* in 1971 and then a few years later in *Weird Western Tales*, represents a character whose exposure to nonwhiteness destabilizes his white identity. Clay Duncan, despite being culturally influenced by Native Americans, enjoys a single-consciousness full-blooded whiteness that is never corrupted, while Jonah Hex potentially shatters the concept of racial purity by demonstrating time and again that his Native American cultural influences trump his white "blood," derailing the idea that race is determined by metaphorical blood and instead suggesting that it is driven by socially constructed cultural loyalties. In Jack Jackson's *Lost Cause* (1998), Jackson unapologetically presents John Wesley Hardin as a famous gunslinger oppressed by the Reconstruction era and those who tried to construct a racially egalitarian society in the South, including carpetbaggers, scalawags, and former northern troops, many of them Black. More recently, the comic *Scalped* (2007) presents two white Indians, Dashiell Bad Horse and Diesel Engine, both undercover FBI agents, who while moving within an updated world set on a contemporary Indian reservation, do nothing to transcend the figure of the white Indian prevalent since the beginning of western comics.

HISTORY AND THEMES OF THE WESTERN GENRE

The national fantasy of winning the West depicted the American character as tough, adventurous, resourceful, and exceptional, thus exemplifying American entitlement. America, according to this notion, had a god-given claim to any land west of the Mississippi, all the way to the Pacific Ocean. As Slotkin notes, "The myth of the Frontier is our oldest and most characteristic myth.... According to this myth ... the conquest of the wilderness and the subjugation ... of the Native Americans who originally inhabited it have been the means to our achievement of a national identity" (9). The myth of the frontier pulls double duty in justifying not only westward expansion but also the primary dehumanizing means by which the colonies developed into a powerful country.

Frontier stories were told very early in American history, during the colonial era, when the frontier was still on the eastern coast of North America. The roots of the western go back to this period, when white settlers from Europe began the process of removing the indigenous people of North America from their land so that whites could occupy it. In the 1600s and 1700s, memoirs known as captivity narratives were published documenting the story of whites who were taken captive by Native Americans and lived with them for extended periods of time before returning to white society. The next major iteration of the frontier genre occurred in the 1820s and 1840s with James Fenimore Cooper's series of novels known as the Leatherstocking Tales. Set mostly in the Great Lakes region, they were highly popular in their day and are considered foundational works of American literature. Both captivity narratives and Cooper's novels primarily presented Native Americans as uncultured savages, although both could also humanize Native Americans at times. Cooper in particular did so intentionally, depicting some Native Americans as noble savages who were nevertheless destined to be replaced by the inevitable progress of white American civilization. The western genre as we know it today emerged near the end of the nineteenth century and occupied a central place in American popular culture for much of the mid-twentieth century in film, television, pulp fiction, and comics, among other media.

Androcentrism emerged as a code of behavior that informed a hegemonic heteronormative frontier masculinity predicated on violence and racial purity. In the words of Michael Kimmel, "Violence is often the single most evident marker of manhood" (189). Wallace Stegner described this new law in a new land as having the "blind ethics of an essentially false, imperfectly formed, excessively masculine society" (61). Whether gunslingers or white Indians, the primary characters who populated the western genre were men. Women signified little more than bodies with the potential to taint white blood purity. No female equivalent to the white Indian existed, because no one considered the possibility of a white woman willingly entering into a relationship with an Indian. If a white woman was involved with an Indian, then she was necessarily a captive. Because white women had the power to debase white blood purity, according to the myth, their subjugation was crucial. Similar to the myth of the Black rapist, incorporated to terrorize Black men and their families and limit their political power in the southern United States before, during, and after Reconstruction, so too were captivity narratives propagated that justified Native American genocide. In taming the West, outlaws and gunslingers were charged with ridding the land of nonwhites as well as maintaining the myth of white blood purity by controlling white women.

Masculinity and violence were two of the defining features of the western genre. Slotkin points out that "violence is central to both the historical development of the Frontier and its mythic representation. The Anglo-American colonies grew by displacing Amerindian societies and enslaving Africans to advance the fortunes of White colonists. As a result, the 'savage war' became a characteristic episode of each phase of westward expansion" (11). Violence, consequently, became the defining and necessary characteristic of the development of America as a global power. Unlike the violence of America's foes, who are often people of color, white American violence is characterized by its mythic significance as the driving force toward progress and civilization (13). The archetypal American outlaw's penchant for killing reflects America's belief that only through regenerative violence, primarily directed at Native Americans and African slaves, did America grow into a great nation. Mary Lea Bandy finds that "the leading protagonist of the Western is pretty sure to be a man, but not a kindly, upright sort of guy. . . . He is likely to be a 'good bad man'" (2). Consequently, and perhaps absurdly, the symbol of the gun has developed into a marker of life and freedom instead of death and enslavement. Bandy further holds, "Essential to the figure of the westerner is his weapon. Whether he carries a six-shooter or a rifle, Colt or Winchester, every man of the West has mastered the use of a gun. . . . Killing and avoiding being killed are . . . his principal activities" (3). Westerns are formulaic, repetitious, and redundant, and consumers are addicted to this reliable formula. The gun is one of the most important tools of the trade that defines westerns, making them recognizable as such. It is doubtful that a movie without revolvers could even be considered a western, as the very concept of the gunfighter, whether he be hero or villain, joins together the man and the gun as if they were one (Conway, 28–29).

Another key but often overlooked feature of the western gunslinger is his origin in southern culture after the South's defeat in the Civil War and the abolition of slavery. These features are exemplified by Jesse James, America's most famous outlaw, a southerner whose exploits were first pitted against the American government as it forced southerners to adhere to the new laws of emancipation. The James Gang's postwar attempts to carry on the so-called Lost Cause of slavery, a reference to the heroic plight of southern men to preserve the antebellum southern way of the life that included human bondage, developed into national stories carried by daily papers often depicting "the anti-slavery forces, whose cruelties [drove] Jesse to rebellion and outlawry . . . as 'white trash,' jealous of the Jameses' refinement" (Slotkin, 136). The James Gang's transition from fighting for the Confederacy to robbing banks to robbing trains in 1873–74 catapulted them to national stardom and muted their southern origins (137). Sealing the false narrative of southern men as victims of the Civil War and emancipation was "Frank Triplett's *Life, Times and Treacherous Death of Jesse James*, which appeared just after Jesse's assassination in 1882 [and] was the foundation of the outlaw's literary mythology" (136). Jesse James symbolizes not only the first famous American outlaw, an outlaw whose outlawry centered on his refusal to accept the freedom of Black slaves, but also the first protagonist of an American western and a precursor to the traditional American superhero. Jesse James's extralegal banditry and antagonism against government-sanctioned law and order echoed the Ku Klux Klan, which, as we noted in the previous chapter, represented a model for the first American superhero.

The outlaw gunfighter developed into the single most recognizable figure in the mass cultural genre of the western that perpetuated the myth of the frontier, suggesting that the primary obstacle to progress was Native Americans and freed slaves. As Slotkin further notes:

> The myth of "savage war" blames Native Americans as instigators of a war of extermination.... The accusation is better understood as an act of psychological projection that made the Indians scapegoats for the morally troubling side of American expansion: the myth of "savage war" became a basic ideological convention of a culture that was itself increasingly devoted to the extermination or expropriation of the Indians and the kidnapping and enslavement of black Africans. (13)

By representing Native Americans as the savage aggressors, much as slavery was portrayed as a paternal institution for the betterment of inferior savage Africans, the American army was able to gain public support for what amounted to genocide. In both cases, the threat of miscegenation operated just under the surface, casting white American men as the last membrane between the complete mongrelization of whiteness. Consequently, white men were the able-bodied cisgender protagonist heroes that populated the western genre as upholders of whiteness.

After the gunfighter, the second most common figure in the western genre was the white Indian, or man who knows Indians. This common figure displayed the power and imperviousness of whiteness in relation to other influential ethnicities such as that of Native Americans. Chad A. Barbour points out, "[Daniel] Boone's capture and adoption by the Shawnee in 1778 highlights his significance as a figure of American culture. These few months of his life are not only a standard milestone in the Boone biography ... but a cultural touchstone of national and racial understanding" (38). While Boone knows Indians, his unwavering whiteness remains intact. Barbour writes, "Boone might seem an Indian on the outside, but his interior whiteness remains. In fact, Boone proves himself a natural superior to Indians even in their own culture" (39). His exposure to Native American culture affirms his whiteness by implicitly demonstrating that blood is thicker than culture, a crucial linchpin in maintaining the blood metaphor of race. According to Barbour, Boone's power to blend in with "the Indians" did not change his fealty to whiteness but rather bolstered qualities that he already had (39). In other words, his exposure to Native Americans made him a more powerful white man.

Another deeply influential historical example of a man who knew Indians but whose whiteness was almost never diminished was the legendary American scout Kit Carson. Carson was the prototype western hero and man who knew Indians. He appeared in over seventy books and was beloved for his apparent skill in killing Indians (Sides, 312). Hampton Sides notes that the year 1849 "saw the first publication of *Kit Carson: The Prince of the Gold Hunters*, the first pulp fiction paperback featuring Carson as its swashbuckling protagonist. In this forgettable story, written by a hack named Charles Averill, Carson slaughters Indians by the score and predictably rescues a young girl who has been kidnapped by savages. Carson is presented as a great hero who had never lost a battle" (311). This narrative points to the reason why white Indian characters are always men. Any white woman consorting with a Native American tribe would necessarily be considered a captive and not a willing member of a tribe or wife of a tribesman, just as white women who were in consensual relationships with Black men in the southern United States before, during, and after Reconstruction were automatically considered rape victims. This dynamic empowered white women over Black men and white men over everyone. Ironically, Carson did not despise Indians. His first marriage was to an Indian woman, with whom he had a daughter who was eventually raised by his extended family. Some say Carson lived more like an Indian than a white man despite killing and scalping his first Indian at nineteen years old (21–22). Carson made a living killing Indians notwithstanding his "belief that most of the Indian troubles in the West were caused, as he once flatly put it, 'by aggressions on the part of Whites'" (414). Nevertheless Kit Carson served the American white power structure his whole life, primarily in the role of Native American genocidal killer. He is illustrative of the idea that the man who knows Indians, regardless of what he might think of them, and although his experiences with Indians might belie his commitment to defending white interests, is very often beholden to his white identity.

CLASSIC WESTERN TROPES IN COMIC BOOKS

Jack Kirby and Joe Simon's Clay Duncan from *The Kid Cowboys of Boys' Ranch* represents a great example of the Kit Carson variety of the man who knows Indians. He is like Native Americans but nevertheless loyal to whiteness. When Duncan's family is killed by men who wish to steal his father's trappings, and their house is burning to the ground, Apache chief Running Bear, father of Geronimo, saves Clay, since the chief respected and traded with Clay's father. Running Bear says when he finds Clay, "There is no evil in him! See his gentle eyes.... The little yellow hair shall live in the tepee of Running Bear—and grow to be a sturdy warrior as must my little son, Geronimo" (81). Clay is then raised in the Apache encampment. Eventually he is left with a white scout named Miles Freeman. Chief Running Bear tells Clay, "As your spirit-father I would keep you with me always. As a leader who wants no war for his people, I say you leave, this day, with Miles Freeman ... who will teach you the ways of the great scouts" (84). Running Bear thinks Clay will be able to negotiate advantageous treaties for the tribe and avoid bloodshed, to which Clay responds by saying, "My parents died in the white man's world. I shall make the white man my friend but never my brother" (84).

At times in the comic, Duncan betrays his sympathy for the Indians, such as when he points out, "The Indians never violate a treaty unless it's broken by the white men" (18), but anytime violence breaks out, Clay always sides with the whites. He also vehemently corrects anyone who suggests that he has any Native American "blood" in him. When a corrupt businessman accuses Duncan of being "more Injun than white man," Duncan responds by saying, "I don't like bein' called an Injun the way you mean it" (160). On another occasion, when Duncan is accosted and referred to as "the famous half-breed scout," one of Duncan's boys on the ranch responds by saying, "You heard wrong, mister! Clay was just raised by the Indians! You better get your facts straight before someone straightens them for you!" (190). In both instances, Clay's whiteness is challenged, and he and his boys perceive this as an insult.

We see further evidence of Duncan's white loyalties when Duncan and his boys visit an American government trading post and witness Colonel Chadwick insult chief Crazy Wolf by forcing him and his people to trade outside the fort. Duncan realizes that Crazy Wolf intends to form a war party and attack as retribution for the insult. Although Duncan has no respect for Chadwick, Duncan enlists himself as a scout against Crazy Wolf and warns Chadwick several times that Crazy Wolf is on the warpath. He tells Chadwick, "Crazy Wolf is at Bloody Knife Ridge, Colonel! Twenty miles east.... He has as many braves as I predicted!" (146). Once war breaks out, Duncan without hesitation fights with Chadwick against Crazy Wolf.

Simon Girty represents perhaps the most famous historical frontiersman who rejected white culture in favor of Native American culture: "Simon Girty is the perennial American villain, notorious as the prototypical white

Joe Simon (script) and Jack Kirby (pencils), "Last Mail to Red Fork!" Originally published in *Boys' Ranch* #5 (June 1951). Reprinted in *The Kid Cowboys of Boys' Ranch* (Marvel Comics, 1992). © Joe Simon and Jack Kirby.

renegade. He occupies the same frontier stage as Boone, ever the nemesis to the loyal and brave frontier hero in various historical and fictional narratives. Girty represents treason, turning his back not only on his country but also his race" (Barbour, 54). Girty's primary offense was being a loyalist during the war for independence and fighting with the loyalist Indians whom he adopted as his family. In popular culture, "Girty is a more vicious and dangerous enemy than the Indians. His being a white man turned Indian constitutes part of his heightened threat; the possibility that a white man can become Indian attacks notions of racial purity and essential identity" (57).

In the late 1950s, when the comics industry faced a moral panic over supposed ties between comics and juvenile delinquency, western comics remained strong. This panic culminated in the Comics Code, a self-imposed industry censorship that required comics to bear a seal of approval that ensured their appropriateness for children. However, western comics were not hurt as badly, since the violence endemic to the genre seemed more organic and necessary and less conspicuous than in crime and horror comics. Because the violence endemic to the western genre, primarily aimed at

Native Americans and nonwhites in general, reflected the core beliefs of most Americans, to criticize it would have seemed un-American. As Maurice Horn notes, "The Code had a disastrous impact on most adventure comic books, but in a perverse way it helped sustain the popularity of the western. Because of the traditional, almost ritual, depiction of western violence, the genre was less emasculated by the Code than the more objectionable crime, horror and superhero comics" (99, 101).

In 1955, Stan Lee released *Rawhide Kid*, featuring a bloodthirsty gunslinger who used both a gun and a bullwhip as his preferred weapons. Under the rules of the Comics Code, however, the violence in the comic had to be tempered, and within a year the gunslinger lost his whip and became a rancher in Shotgun City (102). In 1960 the title was reissued with Jack Kirby drawing and Dick Ayers inking and presented a completely different Rawhide Kid, one who was now an orphan named John Bart, living with a retired Texas Ranger named Ben Bart (102–3). That Bart's family is from Texas suggests that his father and his uncle likely fought for the Confederacy in the Civil War and against Mexicans in the Mexican War. The Kid's primary role in Lee's world is that of outlaw. In a story titled "When the Rawhide Kid Turned Outlaw," he finds out that a respected rancher is behind a series of cattle thefts, and shoots him down just before he is shot down himself. As a consequence, the Kid goes on the lam instead of facing his accusers in a court of law and risking being convicted, causing the narrator to suggest, "If the Kid had only stayed to face his accusers, his entire life would have been different!" His role as outlaw aligns him with famous gunslingers such as Jesse James and John Wesley Hardin, who also originated in the South as renegade former Confederate soldiers, or their children who refused to accept the new laws of reconstruction.

The Kid, in addition to being an outlaw, is exceptional and extraordinary in his shooting and riding ability. He is small in stature and only wields his powers to defend himself or the powerless, echoing the way the United States would like to view itself. In a story called "The Rawhide Kid: A Legend Is Born," Lee notes: "For the record: The Rawhide Kid has an unusually low, mild voice! He was five feet, three inches, in his stocking feet, and had never in his life weighed more than one hundred and twenty-five pounds! His hands were normal size, a mite on the small side, maybe, and he carried no more than two regulation .45s!" The Kid can be viewed as a sort of white cowboy superhero gunslinger, a figure crucial in the popular white imagination in the mythology of the western frontier. The gunslinger's racial and southern roots manifest in the Kid's adversarial position to the Native Americans he encounters, usually the Apaches. In early versions of *Rawhide Kid*, in addition to his gun, the Kid wields a bullwhip. This weapon is symbolically freighted because it was the primary weapon used for punishing Black slaves. While in later versions Lee did away with the whip, the Kid still signified white supremacy and the myth of the frontier in his adversarial position to Native Americans and his reputation as a hypermoral outlaw.

Perhaps the most telling story arc regarding the Kid's positioning against the Apaches appears in the "The Rawhide Kid: Beware!! The Terrible Totem!!" A totem represents a spiritual object that symbolizes the Apache people and Native Americans in general. In this story arc, the Kid encounters a living totem: "Can we believe our eyes? Can this actually be a living totem, bent upon destroying the Rawhide Kid? From whence did it come? What is its deadly secret?"

When the Kid joins a group of men working in a mine to escape his pursuers, the men disturb the living totem who dwells deep within. The living totem responds by declaring to the white men: "For- ages- have- I- slumbered- here- in- the- depths! But- now- at- last- I- have- been- awakened!- And- now- shall- I- complete- my- task!—The- conquest- of- the- human- race!" The symbolism here is shockingly obvious in its depiction of Native American culture as a threat to white civilization. As the narrator informs the reader, "That's the secret of the Indian totem poles! Once, years ago, there was a living creature named totem who tried to conquer the human race! He must have been trapped under the earth by the medicine men and kept prisoner here until Ben Bragg freed him by blasting too deep!" Despite the totem being enormous, the Kid bests him by knocking him off balance into a bottomless canyon and thereby saves the white race from the insidious Native American culture.

In a story called "The Rawhide Kid: The Twister," the Kid defends settlers from the marauding Apaches, who marvel at his supernatural powers and gush that "Paleface him ride like the wind. . . . He fires like a man inspired . . . every shell hitting its mark. . . . The guns of the paleface are bewitched!" To the Native Americans, the Kid has supernatural powers superior to their own Great Spirits, including the totem. In response to the Kid's good luck, the Native Americans marvel, "Behold! Even the heavens open to protect the lone paleface! The Great Spirit has spoken! The white warrior must be spared! It is an omen!"

The threat of miscegenation and the corruption of white blood by Native Americans operates just under the surface in a story called "The Rawhide Kid: The Girl, the Gunman, and the Apaches." At one point, the Apaches kidnap a blonde white woman, offering, "Squaw with hair of gold will be worthy prize!" Ultimately, the Kid saves the woman and prevents whiteness from

Jack Kirby (pencils), cover of *Rawhide Kid* #22 (June 1961). Reprinted in *Essential Rawhide Kid*, vol. 1 (Marvel Worldwide, 2011). © Marvel Characters.

being tainted, saying boldly, "No stealer of women is a brave." The Rawhide Kid represents a protector of whiteness on a macropolitical level as well as on a microblood level. This is a prime example of white frontier masculinity operating as an upholder of whiteness by protecting white women from Native Americans. The Apaches refer to the blonde white woman as a worthy prize, since on the frontier, power is sexualized and eroticized. Warfare is likened to sexual conquest, and white women become the spoils. Consequently, control of white women becomes paramount on the frontier if the myth of monolithic whiteness is to be maintained. The Apaches share with their white oppressors destructive and fraudulent notions of white, heteronormative, and sexist hypermasculinities. The Native Americans in the comic enact symbolic warfare that affirms the very white supremacy that oppresses them.

In a story called "There's a Shoot-Out Comin!," linking the Kid to the South and the Civil War, he helps a former Confederate soldier find his long-lost brother, who he fears was killed in the war. The Confederate soldier avers, "I've waited a long time for this moment! At last I've reached me a Yankee town! And now I'll avenge what these ornery carpetbaggers did to my brother!" In a strange chain of events, the Kid realizes that the former soldier's brother is actually the sheriff of the town, having arrived years ago with amnesia. The comic ends on a happy note as the long-lost brothers are reunited.

The exploits of the Kid reaffirm the myth of the frontier as a space where racial violence was necessary to ensure the achievement of the manifest destiny of whites to conquer all lands west of the Mississippi. This is highlighted in the comic "Man of the West," depicting a white pioneer who, along with cultivating the wild land, must kill Apaches. Lee notes, "And so our story ends as it began—with Mark Morgan weary and muscle-sore, making his way thru wild, untamed wilderness, seeking a home site just over the horizon!—But this time there is a difference! This time he has a wife, and a son—and of such sturdy human thread was woven the fabric of the glory of the West!" The story also ideologically underscores the importance of white men like Mark Morgan cultivating the land and populating it with more white people. By staving off the marauding Apaches, Morgan protects his right to procreate with white women like his wife instead of allowing her to be raped and impregnated by Apaches.

THE REVISIONIST WESTERN COMIC

Starting in the 1970s, comic book creators began publishing western comics that questioned the traditional assumptions, stereotypes, and narrative framings of the genre. One of the first and still one of the most interesting examples of these revisionist western comics was Michael Fleisher's version of Jonah Hex, which he wrote in various titles from 1974 to 1987. Jonah Hex is a famous comic book character who occupies a liminal racial space more in line with the likes of Simon Girty than Daniel Boone or Kit Carson. What scant critical attention Jonah Hex has received has been strangely dismissive or inaccurate. In his book *From Daniel Boone to Captain America: Playing Indian in American Popular Culture*, Chad A. Barbour dismisses Hex as "an intriguing character . . . [but] not relevant to this study's focus" (140).

Maurice Horn inaccurately states, "Jonah Hex was an embittered ex-officer of the Confederacy who had had the right side of his face blown away by gunfire on the last days of the Civil War" (110). Jonah Hex's most identifying characteristic, the grotesquely mutilated side of his face, through which one can see his jaw and teeth, was given to him by his Apache father, who enslaved him when he was thirteen years old.

When Jonah's drunken biological father sets off for California during the Gold Rush, he sells his only son as a way to finance the trip, telling him flippantly, "Sorry, boy! Ah tol' yuh ah needed a grubstake fer the gold rush—an tradin' you off seemed the fastest way tuh get it!" (Albano, vol. 2, p. 217). The Apaches exchange supplies for Jonah and plan for him to be the slave of their chief. For a time, "Jonah [becomes] a slave in the Apache encampment... humiliated and abused, forced to work long hours at menial chores, watched constantly lest he make any attempt to escape" (219). When he is still very young, Jonah saves the chief from certain death by killing an attacking puma. As a result, the chief adopts Jonah as his son, announcing to the tribe, "Hear me, Apaches! This boy who was sold to us as a slave is a slave no more! For though his skin is white, the blood of a true warrior flows in his veins.... From this day forth, the boy called Jonah shall sleep in my tepee and eat by my fire! He shall be like a brother to my own blood son! Henceforth, Jonah Hex shall be accorded the respect due a true son of the Apache" (221). Rather than fueling bitterness toward Native Americans, these early experiences as a slave inculcate in Jonah a sympathy for the marginalized that will manifest later in life, especially in the Civil War, and fragment his consciousness as a white man. Before Hex grows into an adult, he is betrayed by the chief's son, who jealously regards him as a superior rival. Hex is taken captive by another tribe and then rescued and left to wander as a displaced and homeless man.

After the Civil War, he finally makes his way back to his tribe to confront his Apache brother and father. The chief decides to have his son and Jonah fight it out to see who is telling the truth. When the chief's son cheats, Jonah violates the rules of engagement and kills him. As punishment for breaking the rules of engagement and killing the chief's son, Hex is branded. The chief himself observes, "Jonah you used your knife! You broke the law! You knew you had no right to use any weapon besides the tomahawk" (235). Before the chief brutally disfigures him, he says, "Henceforth, wherever you wander, the world must know that you are half good and half evil! Henceforth, you shall carry with you for all time—the mark of the demon!" (236).

Hex's second most formative experience, and one that further fragments his consciousness as a white man, occurs during the Civil War. While he initially joins the Confederacy (since he comes from the South and that is

Michael Fleisher (script) and Noly Panaligan (pencils), "Breakout at Fort Charlotte." Originally published in *Weird Western Tales* #29 (July–August 1975). Reprinted in *Showcase Presents Jonah Hex*, vol. 1 (DC Comics, 2005). © DC Comics.

what his friends do), once he witnesses a slave master brutalize his slave, and realizes that the North is fighting to free the slaves, Hex undergoes a change of heart. Hex's moral dilemma causes him to surrender to the Union army and hopefully sit out the war, since he wants neither to fight for slavery nor to kill Confederate soldiers. Once he surrenders, the Union army captures Hex's former unit and takes everyone prisoner, causing Hex's Confederate brothers to think he betrayed them. The Union army tricks Hex into thinking that he and his Confederate unit can escape, all the while planning to massacre them once they do, since the Union army does not want to take rations from their soldiers to feed the prisoners. Once Hex and his unit attempt to escape, the unit is massacred, and Hex barely escapes with his life. Consequently, Hex is accused of high treason against the Confederate States of America and hunted for the rest of his life.

Because of these experiences, Hex harbors no racial loyalties and is reduced to working as a hired gun, which he uses as a sort of veil in what turns out to be a life of fighting for the marginalized, often against the white establishment. For this reason, and because of his face that represents a racially fragmented consciousness, Hex is continually described as "not human" and "some kind of demon" (Albano, vol. 1, pp. 1–11). His disfigurement also positions him as a marginalized and disabled outsider and dehumanized inferior to the townspeople he meets: "Have a savage like that living among civilized people like us? No sir. I guess the poor freak has to live somewhere—but can you imagine what would happen to property values if he ever moved in? I say he should go live with his own kind" (19). Though he never outright fights for a Native American tribe against whites, it is clear that Hex is sympathetic with the Indians despite having been initially enslaved by one tribe. When he encounters a massacre of a tribe by whites, his "stomach slowly sickens as he surveys the gruesome scene of unbelievable carnage" (49). At another point, Hex questions the hypocrisy of US policies concerning Native Americans, causing one man to ask him, "What the blazes are you, Hex—an Indian lover?" (157).

Hex's thin persona as a mercenary gun for hire is belied by actions suggesting otherwise, such as when he gives all his money away to help a sick woman. Most of the time, Hex's selfless actions go unnoticed, but on this occasion, a woman calls him out, chiding him by saying, "Oh, of course! You've got to continue proving what an unfeeling merciless man you are, don't you? Only I'll bet that money you contributed to the children's hospital fund was every cent you had!" (187). Hex's most telling gesture is hiring himself out for the women's suffrage movement against a group of KKK members hell-bent on keeping the women from demonstrating: "Just as the Negro achieved his emancipation in the great war between the states, so will the women of Kansas be emancipated when the legislators in the state capital realize that the time has come to amend the state constitution to give women the right to vote!" (296). Hex's willingness to aid in the fight for women's suffrage indirectly marks him as a race traitor, since the subjugation of white women proves necessary in maintaining white blood purity by preventing miscegenation. This sort of intersectional politics in relation to race and gender echoes similar instances in comics discussed earlier in the chapter where white women are depicted as requiring protection and whose agency is considered a threat rather than a right.

When Hex sees men in white hoods harass the suffragists, he notes, "Mite early for Halloween if'n yuh ask me! Reminds me of them outfits they're startin' to wear in Tennessee tuh frighten black folks! Plain silly, thet's whut it is!" (298). The appearance of the KKK in a comic featuring Jonah Hex references the roots of the contemporary superhero and underscores the importance of counternarratives. In Hex's comic, the hooded men are divested of their power, and Hex dismisses them as "silly . . . Mebbe even worse'n silly" (298), a far cry from their heroic stature in D. W. Griffith's film *The Birth of a Nation* (1915), where they are presented as heroic white saviors. Hex is described as "a man who knows Indians" (Albano, vol. 2, p. 215), but in this case, Hex's Native American influence and racial fragmentation function as a force for good. Hex's heroism is firmly rooted in his defense of the marginalized driven by his disloyalty to white male supremacy, making him the most important white Indian of all time in a genre where the figure has been present from the beginning. The white Indian trope demonstrates that blood is merely a metaphor for institutionalizing racial hierarchies. This was effective for limiting white membership, but what the blood metaphor did not account for were those whom Noel Ignatiev calls race traitors, or those who seek to "abolish the white race," based on the belief that "treason to whiteness is loyalty to humanity." While Jonah Hex does not consciously seek to abolish the white race, throughout his comics, he is shown to be treasonous to whiteness in favor of humanity, demonstrating that cultural loyalties are sometimes thicker than blood.

While Jonah Hex functions as a race traitor, undermining notions of blood purity and monolithic whiteness, in Jack Jackson's graphic novel *Lost Cause* (1998), upholding monolithic whiteness exists as the unabashed raison d'être for the white gunfighter's existence. Jackson notes in the afterword that his "telling of the Reconstruction Era is not 'politically correct'" (286), and his perspective is "from the side of the white Southerners during the Reconstruction period" (292). *Lost Cause* purports to be an accurate depiction of the Sutton-Taylor feud as well as a biographical sketch of the famous gunfighter John Wesley Hardin. Neither of these descriptions of the text is quite accurate. In the case of the Taylor-Sutton feud, as Jackson admits, "Billy Sutton was actually a minor player in the trouble and his death did little toward ending it" (286). The point in implying that Billy Sutton represented one of the families involved in the feud is to lump together a group of mostly white southerners, or "scalawags," who sided against the Taylors in attempting to uphold the laws of Reconstruction after the Civil War.

In this context, John Wesley Hardin, a friend and distant relative of the Taylors', as well as a cold-blooded killer, is offered up as a white victim forced to become an outlaw when the US government unfairly forced white southerners to alter their way of life to accommodate the humanity of Black people. As Jackson notes, "You're talking about a very, very difficult historical period here, Reconstruction. And this is one of the few instances in which the white folks, particularly, those in the South, found themselves the oppressed, as opposed to the oppressor. They were just not ready for it, and could not make the transition to a subjugated people" (291). To Jackson, Hardin was an "American icon" (287) and a "victim" (297). Jackson makes it clear that the comic simply represents the white point of view: "I figure if a black man can tell the story and do it well, from his side—his racist, if you would, point of view—why the hell can't a white man do the same thing?" (296). He admits that although the Black point of view condemns the systematic enslavement and genocide of a group of human beings, he is "not even interested in what happened to the blacks" (293); he is simply lamenting "the passing lifestyle, of which slavery was only one aspect. I mean, here are [white] people being told

Jack Jackson, *Lost Cause: John Wesley Hardin, the Taylor-Sutton Feud, and Reconstruction Texas* (Kitchen Sink, 1998). Reprinted in *Los Tejanos and Lost Cause* (Fantagraphics, 2012). © Sam Jackson.

that they are going to have to live differently and think differently than they have in the past. Nobody wants to be subjected to that kind of domination, especially whenever it's done at the hands of the military" (298).

In addition to detailing the feud between white southerners who resisted Reconstruction and those who attempted to uphold the laws, and the origins of the gunfighter John Wesley Hardin, Jackson makes it clear that in his view emancipation was an unnecessary overreach of power on the part of the federal government. To him, outlawing a practice that was paternal in nature was reckless and politically motivated and merely resulted in freeing a people unfit for freedom. In the comic, Jackson depicts newly freed slaves as reluctant to leave their slave owners: "As word of emancipation spreads, the blacks drift away from their plantation homes—some joyfully, some reluctantly" (160). The slaves who seem to celebrate their freedom, Jackson depicts as obnoxious criminals and rapists, "[congregating] in shanty-towns near cities or military posts, often falling prey to vice and misery" (160). On the other hand, Jackson contradistinctively presents whites as steadfast and determined to maintain their superior position, noting, "Most whites cannot accustom themselves to the altered state of affairs; few even try" (162).

Just under the surface lies the threat of miscegenation and the undermining of white blood purity, as Jackson's narrative voice reports: "That winter is an uneasy one, as Negro soldiers roam about the countryside, keeping people in constant fear. Hey gal, whut you got in thet basket? Sweet taters, I bet!" (163). This panel evokes the scene in *The Birth of a Nation* when the Klan heroically rescues a white woman from a former Black Union soldier who is bent on raping her. While the panel focuses on the Black soldier accosting a white woman, implicit in this dynamic is the need for white men to protect white women by limiting their agency and consequently their humanity. In general, Jackson depicts white southerners as noble and resilient survivors, "beset by hostile Indians, overbearing U.S. troops, gangs of lawless ruffians, and the carpetbagger plague" (165).

The real victims, Jackson argues, are the white southern men like John Wesley Hardin who are forced to become outlaws and are "hunted relentlessly and deprived of making an honest living.... [Some] young men turn to shifty or unlawful means" (214). Jackson argues that the narrative trigger for Hardin's life as an outlaw can be found in his run-in with a former slave named Mage. According to Jackson, the wrestling match gets deadly serious after Mage is scratched. Mage is then completely dehumanized when, despite being shot several times, he does not die, likening him to an inhuman supernatural beast. As a result of killing Mage, "John Wesley Hardin—like many other young Texans—goes on the dodge. His hatred for the oppressors burning white-hot. A man oughta' have th' right to defend hisself!" (220).

Jackson implies that the reputation of the hard-living outlaw stems from being oppressed by an overbearing government. In addition to killing a Native American for demanding a head of cattle in exchange for encroaching on Native lands, (244), Hardin is shown killing several other men, including Deputy Webb, for which he is imprisoned. Jackson relates, "Eventually Hardin becomes reconciled to life behind bars. He teaches Sunday school and joins the prison debating team. My opponent would have you believe that women should enjoy the same rights as men. How ridiculous" (279). Hardin's point of view on gender equality once again indicates the power he feels white women possess to taint white blood purity via miscegenation. In this manner, images of frontier and outlaw masculinities emerge in contradistinction to both women and other races. Kimmel notes that some hypermasculinities emerge from both "sexism and racism." By othering women and other races or sexualities, men ensure that "manhood is only possible for a distinct minority," namely, white American males. Kimmel further states, "By the middle of the [19th] century . . . Native Americans were cast as foolish and naive children, so they could be infantilized as the 'Red Children of the Great White Father' and therefore excluded from full manhood." In other words, hypermasculinities in some cases depend more on what one is not than on what one is. Ironically, to emasculate non-Americans, including Native and Black Americans, white America defined them as "hypermasculine, as sexually aggressive, violent rapacious beasts, against whom 'civilized' men must take a decisive stand and thereby rescue civilization" (192). In presenting the gunfighter Wesley Hardin as a sympathetic figure driven to outlawry by a misguided government interested in freeing human beings not fit for freedom, Jackson underscores the image of the bandit in American western comics and American culture in general as essentially a symbol of the ongoing fight for white supremacy.

Comic book gunfighters proved to be so powerful an image of whiteness that, even in a 2003 reboot of *Rawhide Kid* wherein the Kid is presented as a gay man, his sexual fragmentation does nothing in the comic to undermine his monolithic whiteness. In 2003, Ron Zimmerman and John Severin released a five-issue series called *Rawhide Kid: Slap Leather*, featuring the Rawhide Kid as a gay man. Presenting the Kid as a gay man undermines the obligatory heteronormative whiteness of the gunslinger necessary in preventing miscegenation and the corruption of white blood purity, but overall the comic still positions the Kid as a protector of whiteness, as his primary adversary in this one-off story arc is a diverse group of outlaws called the Cisco Pike gang. As Kimmel notes, "The hegemonic definition of manhood is a man in power, a man *with* power, and a man of power. We equate manhood with being strong, successful, capable, reliable, in control" (184). Very often this man is a white man. By offering the Rawhide Kid as a gay man, Zimmerman and Severin successfully created a white character whose monolithic whiteness is fragmented, but this fragmentation does nothing to alter the events in the narrative in relation to whiteness. When a diverse gang of outlaws threaten Wells Junction, the sheriff enlists the Kid to defend the town. While this comic takes a step forward in complicating images of heteronormative male whiteness as requisite to upholding whiteness and cornering hegemonic masculinity on the frontier, ultimately the racial dynamics of the frontier are left intact.

Through a metatextual historiographic insert in the form of the *Wells Junction News*, Zimmerman and Severin draw on the Rawhide Kid's well-known past, including references to the Living Totem and other villains with whom the Kid has squared off, such as the Raven and the Bat, while establishing his nonnormative sexuality right away. *The Wells Junction News* notes that the Kid "held various jobs and frequently considered setting aside his adventurous life, almost becoming engaged to Marybelle Harte.... Rawhide would embark on several other similarly short-lived relationships, but was later revealed to be gay." Other significant departures from Stan Lee's 1955 version include the Kid's teaming up with the Avengers, being adopted by an Apache tribe, and battling racist night riders in Wyoming, all according to the *Wells Junction News*. The cover of the series features the Kid holding two guns, one in his right hand pointing toward the ground just under his belt buckle, suggesting a penis. References to the Kid's experiences with an Apache tribe, as well as his fight with racist night riders, suggest that Zimmerman and Severin's version of the Kid might be more akin to Jonah Hex in his disloyalty to whiteness, but nothing like this plays out in the comic.

At times, the Kid subtly references his homosexuality to the reader, such as when he tells the sheriff that he could not sleep the night before because he was not used to sleeping in a house full of men. Under his breath, he then adds, "alone." When two young boys find his campsite and ask him about his legendary exploits, the Kid betrays his queerness, unbeknownst to the kids, by admitting that he too would like to meet the Lone Ranger, since he thinks "the mask and the powder blue outfit are fantastic." He also says that he "can certainly see why that Indian follows him around." Later when the Kid confronts Cisco Pike's gang, Pike says to him, "You sure don't act like I would expect from your rep," to which the Kid responds, "Well, if breeding, vocabulary, and sophistication are a crime, please arrest me right now." When the Kid is threatened, he says to Cisco Pike sarcastically, "Oh no. Is this going to be one of those macho tough guy test things?" One of Pike's henchmen refers to the Kid as a "daisyboy." A few members of the gang note that the Kid acts like a woman and is the oddest gunfighter they have ever met, but they all agree that he can fight and shoot. They also note his tight black jeans and "gorgeous shirt."

Despite the Kid's well-established sexuality and alternative masculinity, so unusual on the androcentric frontier, when a group of nonwhites threatens the town, the sheriff enlists the Rawhide Kid as his new deputy, positioning the Kid once again as a default upholder of whiteness. The Cisco Pike gang recruits several nonwhites as they plan to attack Wells Junction, including a Black woman, a couple of Asian men, a Black man, a Latino man resembling Zorro, and a couple of Native Americans. When Pike offers fifty dollars to any man who kills the Rawhide Kid, the Black woman, Catastrophe Jane, says, "You said, 'For any man who kills the Rawhide Kid.' I'm a girl," to which Pike jokes, "Not from what I heard! Haw! Haw! Haw!" The implication of Pike's joke is that Catastrophe Jane is a butch lesbian and so in his eyes not a real woman. Along with the Kid, by virtue of his obviously nonnormative sexuality, the character of Catastrophe Jane positively expands the index of masculinities on the frontier but does nothing to compromise the white/nonwhite binary. The comic is full of cameo appearances by pop culture figures such as "Bernard Phife" from *The Andy Griffith Show* and Hoss and Little Joe from *Bonanza*, giving the comic a spoof-like quality that in some ways undermines the alternative masculinities presented. At one point, the sheriff refers to the Kid as "the most peculiar cowboy I have ever met."

Another comic that seemed to potentially break new ground in comic book tropes in the western genre but ultimately failed to do so was the more recent *Scalped* (2007), by Jason Aaron. *Scalped* was originally released in single-issue form in 2007 and set on a contemporary Indian reservation in South Dakota called Prairie Rose Indian Reservation. The graphic novel offers a contemporary narrative that deals with current issues important to Native Americans, in particular the conflict between reservation leaders who wish to assimilate into US capitalism through the casino industry and traditionalists who still cling to the old ways. However, the text still employs the figure of the white Indian and highlights his loyalty to white interests.

Dashiell Bad Horse and Diesel Engine, both undercover FBI agents with Native American "blood," infiltrate the reservation to take down the chief and leader, Lincoln Red Crow. Dashiell Bad Horse is depicted as a full-blooded Lakota who left the reservation when he was thirteen to live with a relative. Unbeknownst to the rest of the reservation, Dashiell, in addition to joining the army and fighting for US interests, eventually joined the FBI and was chosen by one of his superiors, who holds a grudge against Prairie Rose, to take down Red Crow for the murders of two FBI agents back in the 1970s. Bad Horse is presented as a tough-as-nails criminal who thinks very little of his tribe's traditions and in the first issue refers to his people as "prairie n-----s" and insists that he is "not a member of your fucking tribe. I never gave a shit about any o' this Lakota bullshit before, and I certainly don't care about it now. Not the powwows or the rain dance or your somber little stories about the good ole, bad days. So you can take your Great Spirit and you can blow it out your ass."

Red Crow hires Bad Horse to be one of his reservation police because he is "full-blooded. An I'm sick to goddamn death of half-breeds." The only hint of what drives Dashiell to bring down the leadership of his own reservation is the resentment he feels toward his activist mother for being absent from his life while agitating for Native American rights when he was a child. When Bad Horse learns that his mother is looking for him in the fifth issue, he says, "If that bitch ever wanted to talk to me, she had all the chances in the goddamn world.... [For] my thirteenth birthday, I got to watch her on TV, gettin' arrested at a Redskins game. So the old bitch wants to talk to me now, you say? Well, tell her she's only fifteen fucking years too late."

In part, Chief Lincoln Red Crow's motivation for building the casino has to do with proving that he can succeed in the white world without relinquishing his Native American roots. In a flashback in issue 7, Red Crow is shown enduring terrible abuse as a youth by Catholic schoolteachers, who tell him, "We must kill the Indian inside you in order to save the man! When are you going to learn that?" For him, the casino functions as reparations for white oppression. At one point in issue 6, a corrupt reservation agent says about the casino, "Welcome to the white man's world." For the traditionalists, the casino represents a complete rejection of Native American culture. In issue 1, activists against the casino claim, "We can win this fight only by staying true to the old ways. Red Crow wants to corrupt us with drugs and gambling."

The other white Indian is Diesel Engine. His FBI status is unknown to Dashiell, and the two butt heads throughout the comic. Diesel's motives for taking down the tribe stem from being rejected by a different tribe for not having enough Native American blood required for membership. In issue 7, the tribal council explains to Diesel's mother, "Mrs. Fillenworth, please understand. In light of our current situation, the tribe has no choice but to reexamine our qualifications for membership. And like many other tribes, we're now making blood quantum part of the requirement." Diesel's mother, Mrs. Fillenworth, responds by pointing out, "This is bullshit! This is about you greedy bastards wantin' to keep more of the casino money for yourselves, right?"

Diesel's undercover role is that of leader of the traditionalist resistance group opposing the casino. In issue 7, the other group members question Diesel's legitimacy by telling him, "I didn't sign up to take orders from no white boy," to which Diesel responds, "I'm one! Sixteenth! Kickapoo! Ya cocksucker! Anybody else wanna question my racial integrity!?" One of the conflicts between Dashiell and Diesel revolves around which one of them is a real Indian: Diesel, who embraces his culture but has less blood; or Dashiell, who is full-blooded but cares very little about the culture. The question is somewhat ironic, since both men are undercover FBI agents working against the interests of the reservation. Diesel is shown embracing his cultural heritage early on, proudly offering, "I'm gonna be a great Kickapoo warrior, just like my grand-fathers when they rode with Tecumseh and Quanah Parker." When the two square off, Bad Horse says, "But ya know, there is still just that one teensy little thing where I know I got a leg up on ya and there aint nothin' ya can ever fuckin' do about it. Ya see, me? I'm a real Indian." The truth is that neither of these men is loyal to the reservation; they are white Indians ultimately loyal to white interests. Diesel's homophobic rant also affirms the extremely white heteronormative patriarchal privilege that oppresses Native Americans.

Lost Cause and *Scalped* show that western comics are alive and well in contemporary American culture. They also demonstrate their indebtedness to their predecessors *Rawhide Kid* and *The Kid Cowboys of Boys' Ranch* in their reliance on the tropes of violence and blood purity, the two most important ingredients in the western genre. The western genre and its tropes were central aspects of American popular culture for much of the twentieth century, but the western is just one aspect of America's long engagement with colonialism, which was built into the history of the United States from its earliest origins. The British and other Europeans who settled North America occupied territory that was inhabited by indigenous people, who had to be ethnically cleansed from the land. The western was the cultural expression of the final stages of that long cycle of expropriation, which began with the establishment of the first white settlements in North America. Native Americans were not the only ethnic group to bear the brunt of American colonization, however. The United States became a colonial power in 1898 with its victory in the Spanish-American War. After World War II, the United States became one of the world's two superpowers, a position that it used to intervene in the internal affairs of countries around the world to directly or indirectly install or prop up regimes favorable to American interests. American comic books faithfully portrayed American actions in other countries as morally right and necessary, just as they did the ethnic cleansing of Native Americans, applying many of the same stereotypes and prejudices to foreigners as they had to Native Americans in the western genre.

Chapter Three

COLONIALISM AND PRIMITIVISM IN US COMICS

From the nation's origins as a British colony whose existence depended on the displacement of Native Americans, colonization has been part of American identity from the very beginning. America's colonialism and imperialism abroad influenced its culture as much as the western and shared many of the same ideas and tropes, including the idea that whites represent the forces of civilization, Christianity, reason, and progress, in contrast to people of color, who are savage, primitive, pagan, and childlike. The prehistory of comic book superheroes was strongly rooted in colonialist narratives. Two British characters, Spring-Heeled Jack and Allan Quatermain, whose stories are rooted in British colonialism, are important precursors to the comic book superhero. Spring-Heeled Jack, a widely known character in nineteenth-century British popular culture, first appeared as a theatrical character in 1840 before being featured in penny dreadfuls starting in 1866. In the writer Alfred Burrage's version of Spring-Heeled Jack, he was cheated out of a large inheritance of plantations in the British colony of India. Jack uses a mechanical boot that allows him to leap twenty feet in the air to help him defeat his foes and reclaim his inheritance (Gavaler, *Superhero Comics*, 36–37). The boot and other conjuring tricks were taught to him by "an old Moonshee," a Hindu clerk or secretary under British rule (37). H. Rider Haggard's highly popular 1885 novel *King Solomon's Mines* helped establish many of the key tropes of the colonialist novel. In it, the British hunter and adventurer Allan Quatermain travels from South Africa into the interior of Africa, where he discovers a lost valley containing an ancient Zulu kingdom that is hiding vast wealth. He and his partners are able to capture a small portion of this vast treasure, making them rich men. Many pulp supermen gained their powers through interactions with non-Western cultures. For instance, the Shadow traveled to India, Egypt, and China to learn ancient mysteries that would help him in his mission of fighting crime (43–44).

The classic comics genre dealing with colonialism was the jungle genre, in which a white person protected and ruled over a tribe of primitive, childlike

Africans. The same tropes regarding whites and Africans were reproduced in a wide variety of genres, including superheroes and the "funny animal" genre. Colonialism abroad went hand in hand with racism against people of color at home. Beginning in the late nineteenth century, the United States routinely intervened in the internal affairs of countries throughout Latin America, Asia, and Africa to install or defend regimes that were favorable to US economic and political interests, regardless of the impact on the populations they ruled. These regimes were often brutal dictatorships. When leaders who opposed US interests rose to power, whether through democratic elections, popular revolutions, or some other means, the United States would often lend support to coup attempts, assassinations, or death squads intended to overthrow the ruler and replace them with someone more amenable to US interests. When such tactics failed, direct military interventions, up to and including full-scale wars, could be employed, as in the Vietnam War.

The jungle genre was the primary comics genre through which colonialist ideology was processed into entertainment. The genre ultimately derived from the popular Tarzan novels by Edgar Rice Burroughs, who created Tarzan as a demonstration of his eugenicist views. The jungle genre used racism to defend the need for whites to paternalistically "take care" of Black Africans, much as white nations used the same logic to justify their colonial and imperialist ventures. The classic example of the genre is *Sheena, Queen of the Jungle*, created by Eisner/Iger Studios with the active involvement of Will Eisner, the same cartoonist who created Ebony White, probably the most racist portrayal of an African American in the whole history of American comic books (Webb et al., 1). Like many jungle series, *Sheena* stars a white woman who protects African tribes who are incapable of effectively governing or defending themselves. The idea that whites must paternalistically govern people of color is precisely the ideology of colonialism. This defense of colonialism, combined with the sexual objectification of the white women who serve as the Africans' protectors, merges white supremacy with patriarchy. Sometimes the white protector is a man, but jungle queens are more common than jungle kings. The tropes found in the jungle genre also appeared in many other genres, including superhero comics from Batman to Captain America.

After World War II, the jungle genre took on several added layers by merging with two other tropes, anticommunism and the Yellow Peril. The Yellow Peril trope dated back to the earliest days of comic books, when it was directed mainly against the Japanese, one of America's foes in World War II. In the 1950s, with the victory of Mao Tse-tung's Communist Party and the Korean War, the focus of Yellow Peril paranoia shifted to China and Korea.

Since Red China, as it was referred to in the comics, was both communist and Asian, it posed a double threat. As the Vietnam War became increasingly unpopular over the course of the 1960s, the old narrative about the Yellow Peril and communism became increasingly unsustainable, especially since comic books' main readership—adolescents, teenagers, and young adults—was at the forefront of the antiwar movement. American superheroes, who had previously supported the war, now began to question the conflict's justice, which also necessitated confronting their own pro-war past. An identity crisis thus ensued for many superheroes, in particular Captain America and Iron Man, who were the most closely associated with US imperialism. With the end of the Vietnam War in 1975, this period came to a close, but not before establishing a precedent for the deconstruction of the superhero genre and the whiteness on which it relied.

PRIMITIVISM AND COLONIALISM IN JUNGLE COMICS

In the 1940s, the central focus of imperialist narratives in American comic books was Africa. The primary feature of comic book depictions of Africans is that they were unable to govern themselves and consequently required white assistance and leadership. Whites drive nearly all the action in jungle comics, as both the main heroes and villains. Africans often assist them, but Africans are never the main hero and only rarely the main villain. Whites are presented as the natural rulers of Africa, a concept that is concisely visualized in the final panel of a 1943 Sheena story, "Red Meat for the Cat-Pack," in which Sheena has just rescued the white-skinned people of the Manji tribe, who have been living in a hidden valley unaware of the larger world outside.[1] When the group emerges from the valley, the Manji marvel at the beauty of the continent, "So wide and limitless," "So rich and green," and Sheena's mate, Bob, comments, "It sure looks good to me" (Webb et al.). The group is practically salivating at the prospect of laying claim to the bounteous land below. Standing on a rocky outcropping of the cliffs that separate the hidden valley from the outside world with the sun rising behind her, Sheena is the very image of a white savior, laying claim to "my jungle kingdom." The image, in which no African appears, effectively communicates whites' belief that they were entitled to the status of rightful lords of all they surveyed in Africa.

A corollary of this sense of rightful sovereignty is that any African who disagrees with a benevolent white ruler is evil. Africans and other people of color were not seen as having any intrinsic right to maintain their own autonomy, traditions, or laws. A 1943 Sheena story, "Sky-Altar of the

W. Morgan Thomas (script), "Red Meat for the Cat-Pack." Originally published in *Jumbo Comics* #48 (February 1943). Reprinted in *The Best of the Golden Age Sheena*, vol. 1 (Devil's Due, 2008).

Thunder-Birds," exemplifies this aspect of colonial ideology. Two African tribes travel to visit Sheena so that she can render judgment on a dispute between the tribes over hunting territory. K'haga, the chief of one tribe, addresses Sheena subserviently as "O powerful jungle queen" but finds himself unhappy with her verdict. After he leaves, he complains, "Sheena not fair to K'haga! Someday she pay for this! I get even!," a threat he attempts to make good on. K'haga is infantilized and demonized because of his refusal to obey Sheena, which is the standard treatment of any Africans who show independence from their benevolent white rulers. Conversely, Africans who obey whites voluntarily are presented positively, and such voluntary obedience is depicted as normal. When Sheena rescues a group of Africans, they often respond by immediately pledging to follow her, while in other stories, African chiefs voluntarily offer up their goods or treasure to Sheena.

One of the most typical features of the jungle genre was the use of scantily clad white women as central protagonists. In this, as in other matters, Sheena set the model. It perhaps goes without saying that sexuality was a major part of the appeal of jungle queen stories. Sheena and other women are routinely shown nearly naked, in outfits that look more like bikini swimsuits than anything that would be appropriate or useful for a tropical jungle. The voyeuristic portrayal of female bodies for the pleasure of the male gaze was utterly consistent with the usual practice of American comics, but the demonstration of female power in combat was quite unusual, with Wonder Woman being the only other prominent example of this phenomenon. The normal pattern was for white women to be seen as threatened by Black and other nonwhite villains, and for white men to protect women from these perceived threats; but in jungle comics, women regularly proved themselves to be the most capable fighters in the series. However, this independence did not come without strings attached. Most significantly, women's power and autonomy were only permissible when employed to uphold the racial superiority of whites, and when the white women were available as sexual objects for male gratification.

Another subtle but telling way in which female power was contained appears in the early Sheena stories, which always made sure to present Sheena as not overshadowing Bob, although this imperative was relaxed later in the series. In the early comics, Bob is shown as very active, Sheena's equal if not her superior, and Sheena is only able to undertake feats of heroism on her own when Bob fails. For instance, in "Red Meat for the Cat-Pack," Bob gets his boot stuck in a rocky crevice but urges Sheena to "go ahead . . . I'll work it loose," thereby giving her permission to act heroically without him. Bob's gun, and its potential power or, alternatively, its potential failure, is frequently emphasized in the early stories. In the beginning of "Sky-Altar of the Thunder-Birds," as Sheena hears a stranger approaching, Bob helpfully announces, "Right! I've got my gun handy . . . just in case!" In "Slashing Fangs," after Bob's gun jams during a lion attack ("Darn! My gun is jammed!" he declares), Sheena kills the lion with her knife and then asks to borrow Bob's gun. Why she does not have a gun of her own is not explained, but its meaning on a symbolic level is clear. In this and other cases, the gun can easily be interpreted as a symbolic phallus, which Sheena herself cannot own but can "borrow" from Bob. While Sheena can temporarily act like a man, she cannot come into permanent possession of heroic masculinity, which must ultimately be reserved and protected for white men.

Another aspect of gender relations in jungle comics is the existence of evil queens who counter and balance the jungle queen. Evil queens can be either white or Black, with the latter receiving the most virulent racist abuse of any character type in the jungle genre. Evil white traders and their Black helpers are merely evil, but Black queens are depicted as practically inhuman. As Bob declares in "Spoor of the Dancing Skeletons," the Black queen Hawkina is "not human. . . . She's a devil!" A 1946 story, "The Beasts That Dawn Begot!," takes this simultaneous racism and misogyny a step further, depicting the evil queen as the descendant of prehistoric humanity, complete with a long tail and furry limbs—although she is also scantily clad and seductive. A caption declares, "From the slime-blackened crevices came whisperings of the dawn race, spawned in the evil seed of antiquity. . . . And Darma, the ghastly demon goddess, shrieked a fierce challenge to Queen Sheena, as they danced in death-grip above the yawning torture-pit." The dehumanization of women of color in this scene is obvious and hardly needs additional analysis.

The idea that whites had a right to sovereignty over Africa was grounded in a set of Western beliefs known as primitivism, holding that African and other non-Western societies belonged to an earlier stage of civilization than white societies. This viewpoint was widely shared in Western society by anthropologists, political leaders, the media, and artists, among others. It was integral to the ideology of colonialism because it provided a justification for white rule over other cultures (Richardson and Hena, 1108). Because these cultures were primitive, they needed to be trained in the ways of civilization by whites. Someday they might be ready to rule themselves, but that point was always described by whites as occurring far off in some hypothetical future. The Nigerian novelist Chinua Achebe famously critiqued Joseph Conrad's *Heart of Darkness* for depicting its African characters as primitive and less than human. Achebe describes "the desire—one might indeed say the need—in Western psychology to set Africa up as a foil to Europe, as a place of negations at once remote and vaguely familiar, in comparison with which Europe's own state of spiritual grace will be manifest.... *Heart of Darkness* projects the image of Africa as 'the other world,' the antithesis of Europe and therefore of civilization" (2–3). Conrad all but denies that Africans are human, writing that they "howled and leaped and spun and made horrid faces" but that nevertheless they were not quite inhuman, and "that was the worst of it—this suspicion of their not being inhuman" (6). Conrad emphasizes this mad frenzy repeatedly. Achebe writes:

> The eagle-eyed English critic F. R. Leavis drew attention long ago to Conrad's "adjectival insistence upon inexpressible and incomprehensible mystery." That insistence must not be dismissed lightly, as many Conrad critics have tended to do, as a mere stylistic flaw.... When a writer while pretending to record scenes, incidents and their impact is in reality engaged in inducing hypnotic stupor in his readers through a bombardment of emotive words and other forms of trickery much more has to be at stake than stylistic felicity.... He chose the role of purveyor of comforting myths. (4–5)

Comic books take a simpler approach to depicting Africans and whites than Conrad. Whereas Conrad portrays Africans as inscrutable, comic books depict them as all too easily comprehensible. The main distinction is between good and bad Africans, with the former defined by their obedience to the good whites, and the latter defined by their disobedience, barbaric cruelty, and allegiance to bad whites. Both the good and bad Africans have Black leaders, but only the bad ones, those who disobey white leaders, are given much attention. The good African leaders are generally nondescript, while the bad ones are drawn in lurid detail.

One of the most blatant manifestations of primitivist thinking in jungle comics is the belief that Africans and other so-called primitive peoples were habitual practitioners of cannibalism. In a 1941 Sheena story titled "Slashing Fangs," an evil trader named Gaston de Mond urges a chief to prepare "a real tribal banquet" at which his tribe will eat Sheena and Bob (Webb et al.). The chief replies, "But cannibalism? No! My tribe has given up that practice since the government forbade it." De Mond presses on, offering to pay the chief if he will reinstitute the practice for Sheena. After the chief stipulates that he be paid in "gold and jewels," he readily agrees, and soon "madly the witch doctor whirls into his devil dance.... Wild chants fill the air." This short passage combines a dizzying number of stereotypes, starting with the existence of cannibalism itself, a practice that, according to Nicholas Mirzoeff, was wildly exaggerated if not wholly invented by white explorers, anthropologists, and colonists. After describing how cannibalism was ascribed without evidence to the Mbuti people of Central Africa, Mirzoeff reports:

> Cannibalism has long been used to justify colonization. The British accused the Irish of being cannibals in the seventeenth century, for example.... Cannibalism, understood as the routine eating of human flesh, has been nothing more than an enabling ideology to justify European expansion. For colonists could claim that the formerly prevalent practice of anthropophagy [i.e., cannibalism] had died out as soon as their regime took control, thus taking credit for eliminating something that had not existed in the first place. (137–38)

The passage from "Slashing Fangs" neatly combines the myth of African cannibalism with the equally mythical idea that the practice was eradicated by government decree. It then layers on top of this the idea that the Africans have not actually recognized the evil of cannibalism and are all too ready to revert to it when encouraged to do so, demonstrating that the primitivism and savagery of Africa can never really be erased.

Another common manifestation of primitivism is the belief that African religions are based on superstition, ignorance, and violence, as opposed to Western religions, which are not shown in this light. Giant idols appear regularly in jungle comics as representations of superstitious African religions. The only African culture that has ever used colossal statuary was ancient Egypt, which last produced such objects over two thousand years ago. Further, Egyptian statuary was located in a desert rather than a jungle environment and depicted highly naturalistic images of semidivine human pharaohs rather than abstracted images of gods. However, this lack of accuracy is no obstacle to the colonialist mind-set. The depiction of African idols is linked to the equally inaccurate trope of cannibalism, as any appearance of an idol generally means that a white person is about to be sacrificed to it. "The Beasts That Dawn Begot!," in which "the evil idol, Da-Kaahn leers down terribly upon fresh sacrifices," is a typical example of this motif (Webb et al.).

Another manifestation of primitivism is the belief that Africans are inherently superstitious and thus easily fooled, a weakness that evil whites and Africans regularly use to trick them into obeying their nefarious commands. When a fire mysteriously breaks out just before Bob is about to be executed in "Slashing Fangs," the frightened tribesmen declare, "It is an omen.... The gods forbid us to kill jungle queen! She is free!" After defeating the evildoers, Sheena often warns the Africans who had been tricked into following them not to be fooled in such a way again, but to no avail, as the nameless tribesmen are always ready to be led astray again in the next issue. Africans' superstitious natures cause them to fear or misunderstand modern technology. They call guns "boomsticks" or similar childlike words and run in fear at the mere appearance of modern technology, as in "Slashing Fangs" when "screaming natives scatter as a truck speeds into Sheena's village." This fear is not totally unjustified, as the firepower of modern guns is sometimes given a strong emphasis in jungle comics. In "Slashing Fangs," a white villain manning a machine gun "directs a hail of bullets at the natives. Who fall, dying, in the dust." But this rational fear cannot fully explain the panicked reaction Africans frequently display to technology in jungle comics. They appear to fear the idea of technology as much as its specific destructive powers.

Africa's primitivism is also conveyed through a potpourri of scenery, including ancient ruins, hidden valleys, dinosaurs, and fictional, supposedly prehistoric monsters. Ancient ruins are periodically shown in jungle comics, but they usually appear anachronistically similar to those of classical Greece, with columns and capitals prominently displayed, often alongside animal bones or giant idols. Hidden valleys are a common plot device, communicating the idea that parts of Africa are so remote from the modern world that no one outside them knows they exist, and their inhabitants are equally unaware of the outside world. They convey the same message as descriptions of Africa as "dark Africa," the "dark continent," "darkest Africa," or, in Conrad's famous phrase, "the heart of darkness," commonly used in Western society from the late nineteenth to the mid-twentieth century (Mirzoeff, 128). The primitive, primeval nature of Africa is also expressed through the presence of dinosaurs, monsters, and other prehistoric creatures that inhabit parts of

W. Morgan Thomas (script), "The Beasts That Dawn Begot!" Originally published in *Jumbo Comics* #93 (November 1946). Reprinted in *The Best of the Golden Age Sheena*, vol. 1 (Devil's Due, 2008).

Africa, as in "The Beasts That Dawn Begot!," in which Sheena, Bob, and Professor Craig battle giant spiders, giant lizards, giant crabs, and a sea monster.

While primitivism laid the ideological foundation for colonialism, the underlying motivation for the colonial enterprise was economic. The European powers developed colonies primarily for their access to valuable commodities and natural resources. Secondarily, colonies had the additional purposes of preventing those resources from falling into the hands of rival European nations and of providing foreign markets for the colonizer's manufactured goods. Early Sheena stories could be quite transparent about the economic motivations underlying colonization. In "Slashing Fangs," the evil trader Gaston de Mond declares, "This village has the richest tobacco crop in the territory and I mean to get it at my price. . . . No use letting these dumb natives make a clear profit in the market!" The chief refuses to sell at de Mond's price, which is why de Mond attempts to get rid of Sheena and Bob by having a hostile tribe eat them. After this plan is foiled and de Mond attempts to massacre the tribe who failed to carry out his scheme, the formerly hostile chief tells Sheena, in stereotypically broken English, "You our friends. I give you guides to the tobacco market!" Sheena responds, "I'm glad you came to know your real friends before it was too late," after which a team of African porters provided by the chief carries the bales of tobacco to the market for Sheena and Bob. They arrive "just in time to make the sale," after which Bob gleefully announces, "We got the best price, Sheena!" They then return to the reformed chief and present him with a box of cigars, which Bob hands over with the words "For you, chief! The best cigars in Africa . . . from our tobacco!," to which the chief replies, "Much thanks! Come . . . we have great feast!" This sequence of events reproduces the economics of colonialism quite clearly, albeit with an overlay of morality that was not true to life. With the supposed moral virtue of Sheena removed, what happens here is that whites compete for control of valuable agricultural products, recruiting local leaders to assist them in exchange for a small share of the profits, the bulk of which are kept by the whites. In later Sheena stories, evil white traders continue to threaten the African tribes under Sheena's protection, but she no longer participates in any trading activities herself, instead defeating the evil traders purely out of her concern for the Africans under her protection. Nevertheless, this early story demonstrates that the writers behind the character had some awareness of the real purposes served by colonialism.

COLONIALISM IN EARLY SUPERHERO COMICS

Jungle comics were by definition set in Africa, but they sometimes intersected with American settings and stories. In one story that appeared in *Jungle Comics* in 1940, an African American murderer named Broot (the symbolism of the word's pronunciation as "brute" is quite explicit) escapes from an American chain gang and finds his way to the West African jungle, where he tricks the natives into worshipping him as a god. They call him "massah" and attack their neighbors and white colonists on his orders, until the hero, a Tarzan replica named Kaanga, defeats him. The natives promise Kaanga to behave in the future (Wright, 37). In a 1940 story titled "The Case of the Missing Link," Batman rescues a scientist named Professor Drake from a group of African pygmies. The pygmies try to steal his prize discovery, a giant "'missing link' between man and ape" whom he calls Goliath. Goliath is around twelve feet tall, which Drake explains as "undoubtedly some sort of gland reaction" (Kane et al., 106). He explains:

> While doing research work in the Mabonga country in Africa, I heard of a giant white savage! I found that because of the difference in size, the pygmies worshipped this giant as some sort of god. . . . Needless to say, my scientific interest was aroused, and with the help of some native porters I trapped him! Naturally the pygmies resented our capturing their god, and we had many a pitched battle with him. (107)

Drake tells Batman that he tamed Goliath and was going to "civilize him" and "teach him to speak English" (108). In Drake's words, "I won him over with various psychological methods! He worships me!" (107). Drake rejects an offer from Hackett and Snead, a pair of criminal circus owners, to exhibit Goliath, so they fake Drake's suicide and put Goliath in their circus. Goliath goes on a rampage, killing Drake's murderer, but Batman has to kill Goliath because, "now thoroughly crazed, Goliath reverts back to the beast he is" and cannot be contained (111). At the end of the story, Batman says to Robin that "it's very ironical—Professor Drake wanted to civilize Goliath.... Make a beast into a man ... but he didn't remember there are men who are beasts ... like Hackett and Snead!" (115). In this case, the primitivism of Africa is used as a metaphor for the evil acts of white men, much as in Conrad's *Heart of Darkness*, but this does not fundamentally alter the message that primitivism is the origin of all evil.

Superheroes function as symbolic bulwarks against the perceived dangers of primitivism represented by people of color. For most of their history, superheroes have sought to safeguard the values of white civilization against whatever is perceived to threaten it, but what superheroes and their creators have not seen is that the protection and defense of whiteness are synonymous with the oppression of other ethnicities and races. Captain America is an archetypal example of this phenomenon. He was created by the US military as a weapon to defend American interests and wields a defensive weapon, a shield, rather than an offensive one. This parallels the usual justification for American intervention in foreign countries, that of protecting America's vital interests, or democracy, or some other value, rather than as the acts of aggression in pursuit of self-interest that they frequently are.

Captain America's role in upholding US colonialism can be clearly seen in "The Case of Rozzo the Rebel," a 1942 story from *Captain America Comics*. President Alvaro, the leader of a South American nation called Oroco, visits the United States to attend a diplomatic conference. He is greeted by a crowd of protesters led by Rozzo, an embittered rebel leader who is a "ruthless killer" (Simon et al., 779). While Alvaro is portrayed as a handsome white man with a monocle and nice suit, Rozzo is unshaven and generally unpleasant. The colors of his clothing clash; his hat is rough and torn, and his lips are a bright pink, making him look as if he is wearing lipstick. This last touch calls into question his masculinity, which in the violent world of superhero comics marks him as inferior. His teeth and those of his henchmen often appear to be isolated fangs such as a carnivorous animal would have rather than a human, a feature they share with the most extreme Yellow Peril villains. It turns out that Alvaro had begun his life as a gaucho, a South American cowboy, as had Rozzo, and that the two had been close friends. When Alvaro is broke, Rozzo gives him half his money. Alvaro promises to return the favor when he has money. Alvaro joins a revolution against a

Al Avison (pencils), "The Case of Rozzo the Rebel." Originally published in *Captain America Comics* #12 (March 1942). Reprinted in *Golden Age Captain America*, vol. 1 (Marvel Worldwide, 2014). © Marvel Characters.

"wicked dictator" ruling their country, rising to become an officer and then a general in the revolutionary army (783). Rozzo becomes a general in the dictator's army and becomes Alvaro's prisoner when the dictator is defeated. Rozzo attempts to claim his half of Alvaro's wealth, but Alvaro rebuffs him, telling him that "I do not consider my present position as a profit . . . only a service" (784). Rozzo is then sent into exile in the United States. When Alvaro visits the United States, Rozzo kidnaps Alvaro and attempts to extort him but is eventually killed by Captain America.

The story supposedly takes place in the fictional nation of Oroco, described as having a Pampas, which would place it in the southeastern quadrant of South America. Uruguay is right in the center of this region and, due to its similar phonology to Oroco, is likely the country on which Oroco is based. However, one caption mistakenly calls Rozzo a "Mexican rebel" (789). Rozzo and Alvaro bear a rough resemblance, from their political biographies to their names, to Pancho Villa and Álvaro Obregón, respectively, two key leaders of the Mexican Revolution. Villa was a brash, populist general of the revolution's radical wing, which sought not merely democracy but also economic reform to benefit the poor. Obregón, on the other hand, was a pragmatic moderate who was willing to compromise with Mexico's wealthy elites and the United States (Gonzales, 124–26, 182–84). "The Case of Rozzo the Rebel" presents Rozzo as a greedy stooge of Oroco's dictator rather than as a radical revolutionary. Rozzo is not even presented as a revolutionary, much less a radically democratic and egalitarian one. This judgment is expressed visually as well as narratively, with Rozzo being presented very unflatteringly and Alvaro the opposite. Rozzo has long hair, bushy eyebrows, perpetual stubble, and wears a dull brown uniform, while Alvaro has neatly trimmed hair and an equally neat mustache and wears a bold blue uniform with white, yellow, and red accents. While Alvaro is presented as superior to Rozzo intellectually, morally, and militarily, he still requires extensive help from Captain America, who does most of the fighting against Rozzo's men. The ultimate message that is conveyed is that there are good Latin Americans, such as Alvaro, capable of leading their people, but they require US—that is, white—assistance to maintain power.

THE YELLOW PERIL AND RED CHINA

With the return to popularity of superhero comics in the 1960s, imperialism also returned as an important theme in the genre. Marvel's superhero comics combined the jungle genre with the Yellow Peril and fears of communism. Captain America remained a major protagonist in imperialist narratives and was joined by Iron Man, whose alter ego was Tony Stark, an engineer and manufacturer of armaments. Together, the two characters were the perfect representation of the military-industrial complex, a term that President Dwight D. Eisenhower coined in 1961 to describe what he saw as the dangerous combination of the American military and arms manufacturers. Captain America and Iron Man were closely linked in Marvel comics, costarring in *Tales of Suspense* from 1964 to 1968. From his first appearance in 1963, Iron Man was directly tied to the Vietnam War. On the first page of the first Iron Man story, Tony Stark presents his new transistors, which have the capacity to "increase force of any device . . . a thousandfold," to a general (Lee and Heck, 8). Stark then asks the general, "Now do you believe that the transistors I've invented are capable of solving your problem in Vietnam?" (8). As a weapons manufacturer, Stark was an integral part of the American war effort in Vietnam, a role that was entirely complementary to his other role as Iron Man, who helped prosecute the war on the ground.

Not long after his transistor presentation, Stark is in Vietnam to oversee the implementation of his technology when he is captured by a classic Yellow Peril villain named Wong-Chu, who is described as a "red guerrilla tyrant" (9). Stark hatches a plan to escape from Wong-Chu by building a suit of mechanized metal armor. He is aided in this project by Professor Yinsen, a great scientist who hates the communists but, like Stark, is forced to serve them. Stark calls Yinsen "the greatest physicist of all," but it is Stark who takes the lead in designing the Iron Man suit with his miraculous (and completely implausible) transistors (12). Yinsen declares the Iron Man suit his greatest accomplishment and resolves to sacrifice himself for it (and for Stark), declaring in his final moments, "My life is of no consequence! But I must gain time for Iron Man to live!" (13). Yinsen thus voluntarily sacrifices himself to save Stark, declaring that his own life is utterly disposable, but that of the white Stark is of the utmost importance. While the character of Yinsen appears to place a Chinese character on the same level as a white one, in reality the Chinese character is demoted and rendered disposable.

Interestingly, Iron Man's primary nemesis is a Chinese supervillain named the Mandarin, who is not a communist but rather a foe of both communism and democracy. The Mandarin is a pure version of the self-interested superman from the pre-comic-book days of the pulp superhero, very much like the original Yellow Peril villain Fu Manchu. Although opposed to communism, the Mandarin is constantly described as being embedded deep within Red China. In *Iron Man* #50 (September 1972), a caption notes, "For years men have spoken the name of the Mandarin in hushed whispers! To those of the Western world, he is little more than a fearsome legend! But, in the Orient—in seething, smoldering, secretive Red China, men know—to their sorrow—how real the Mandarin is" (182). The Mandarin borrows the relevance of communist China as a contemporary US foe, but his primary appeal is to the older discourses of Orientalism and the Yellow Peril, which predate the Cold War by centuries and decades, respectively. The centrality of Orientalism and the Yellow Peril to Iron Man comics is further confirmed by the fact that the Mandarin was only one of many Asian villains whom Iron Man fought. Iron Man also fought many non-Asian foes, including Russian communists such as the Red Barbarian, but they did not become recurring villains as the Mandarin did, and they were not depicted with stereotypes as racist as those used against Asian villains. As in World War II, when German villains were depicted as less inhuman than Japanese ones, Russia's identification as white mitigated against the most stereotypical and inhuman depictions.

BLACK PANTHER AND THE CRISIS OF COLONIALISM

After World War II, numerous countries in the Third World won their independence from their colonial occupiers or overthrew rulers who served Western interests rather than their own people. The real-world revolutions against white colonizers challenged the ideology of colonialism and forced comic book creators and publishers to recast the standard white supremacist narratives of the jungle genre and other imperialist discourses. One of the preeminent examples of the reframing of the jungle genre was the creation of the Black Panther, who first appeared in July 1966 in *The Fantastic Four*.

He subsequently appeared as a guest in Captain America and Iron Man comics and as a member of the Avengers before receiving his own comic in 1973, titled *Jungle Action*. The Black Panther's comics continued many of the familiar tropes of the jungle genre but with the crucial difference that instead of a white hero king or queen, the king was now African. The Black Panther thus translated the real-world creation of independent Black nations into a superhero narrative, creating an Afrocentric superhero associated with technological advancement instead of primitivism. While the Black Panther was depicted as powerful, brave, and intelligent in equal measure to white superheroes, the retention of key tropes from the jungle genre undermined this antiracist message. Moreover, his character and relationships with other superheroes were developed so as not to pose too strong a challenge to whites' sense of entitlement and authority.

The first appearance of the Black Panther reinscribed primitivist notions about Africa in several ways. One of the most frequent ways this was done was through frequent comments by the Fantastic Four to the effect that it was surprising that an African would have access to technology such as that possessed by the Black Panther. In the first panel of the first story featuring the Black Panther, as the Fantastic Four ride in a flying car given to them by the Black Panther, the Thing quips, "How does some refugee from a Tarzan movie lay his hands on this kinda gizmo?" (McGregor et al., 6). This quote demonstrates the self-consciousness with which the Black Panther's creators emulated and continued the jungle genre. When they near their destination, Reed Richards exclaims, "The jungle looks so primitive . . . so undeveloped! Are you sure we have reached Wakandan territory?" (12). A similar point is alluded to more subtly through descriptions of Wakanda, echoing the primitivist trope of Africa as the heart of darkness, a place buried so deep in the jungle that it seems impossibly remote from civilization. On the second page of the first Black Panther story, Wakanda is described as being "deep in the heart of equatorial Africa" (7), while in the following issue, Sue Storm says, "I just can't believe we're in the heart of the jungle!" (27). Wakanda is a classic example of a hidden valley, which similarly emphasizes the distance of the African jungle from the civilized world, although in the case of the Black Panther, this meaning is reversed, transforming it into a futuristic rather than a primitive society. Similarly, in Captain America's first full-length encounter with the Black Panther in *Tales of Suspense* #98 (February 1968), he is referred to as dwelling within "the heart of darkest Africa" (Lee et al., vol. 1). Other Marvel comics similarly continued to perpetuate primitivist notions, but without the Afrofuturist element provided by the Black Panther. In *Iron Man* #14 (June 1969), for instance, a Caribbean island is said to be haunted by "the unmistakable rhythm of . . . voodoo drums! . . . Reawakening in everyone superstitions long thought forgotten. . . . Our island has become independent. . . . We struggle to change from an undeveloped colony into part of the 20th century. . . . But, the darkness and the drums deny this, recalling primitive traditions, rituals old and sinister . . . and the evil forces they can summon!" (Goodwin et al.). The reinscription of primitivist tropes begins before the Black Panther even appears in the comic, preparing the reader for his arrival by placing him within a primitivist context. The Black Panther's atavistic primitivism and his technological futurism collide head-on when the hero is eventually revealed. The first appearance of the Black Panther is remarkable for the extent to which these two qualities are held in tension without either of them being definitively given priority over the other. This is due in large part to the extraordinary art of Jack Kirby, which constructs a vibrant image of Afrofuturism, a term that Mark Dery coined in 1994 to describe a cultural work that presents "African-American themes and addresses African-American concerns in the context of twentieth-century technoculture—and, more generally, African-American signification that appropriates images of technology and a prosthetically enhanced future" (180). The first three panels in which the Black Panther appears occupy a full page and present three different approaches to the collision of primitivism and Afrofuturism. In the first panel, the Black Panther appears attired in traditional clothing, sitting on a throne, under an elaborate umbrella held by a servant and surrounded by seminaked tribesmen who carry both rifles and spears. This scene largely conforms to the idea of African society as primitive and traditional but harmonious. In the second panel, the Black Panther appears stripped to the waist, with an intense, threatening expression on his face and a crowd of his cheering subjects behind him brandishing weapons in the air, an image that conforms to imagery of the evil Black rebel or revolutionary. Finally, the third panel shows a giant panther idol being raised from below the ground on a mechanized platform. The Black Panther refers to this as a totem whose appearance signals the beginning of a ritual, reproducing the primitivist trope of an idol to whom the primitive Africans make human sacrifices. While primitivist tropes are used heavily in these images, Kirby's visual presentation of them alters their meaning in significant ways. Rather than depicting Africans as utterly foreign to modern technology and weapons, these images incorporate technology into their vision of Africa. In the first and third panels, this combination appears to be benevolent and even marvelous, but the second panel disrupts this generally positive portrayal with a harsher, more negative image. This montage of images juxtaposes several different visions of Africa, some of them retrograde

Don McGregor (script) and Jack Kirby (pencils), "The Black Panther!" Originally published in *Fantastic Four* #52 (July 1966). Reprinted in *Epic Collection: Black Panther*, vol. 1 (Marvel Worldwide, 2016). © Marvel Characters.

and racist and others progressive and Afrofuturist, without resolving them into a single coherent representation.

The supporting characters in the Black Panther's first appearance serve to further reinscribe primitivist tropes while also insulating the Fantastic Four from any appearance of racism. They perpetuate primitivist ideology while also disguising its presence, a necessary precaution in an era when overt racism was becoming socially unacceptable. The villain of the story, and one of the Black Panther's two primary nemeses, is Klaw, an evil white scientist who seeks to steal Wakanda's vibranium, a rare and powerful metal that is the key to Wakanda's technological advances. As in earlier jungle comics, this white villain serves as a foil for the good whites of the Fantastic Four. Klaw is essentially an evil inverse of Reed Richards, who is also a scientist, but a benevolent rather than malign one.

In the end, the Black Panther is revealed to not be a foe at all and is subsequently integrated and assimilated into Marvel's other superhero comics. He appeared as a guest character in various white superheroes' comics, including Captain America, Iron Man, and the Hulk, and became a member of the superhero team the Avengers in May 1968. This integration paralleled the integration of schools, universities, and other public spaces and institutions that was taking place in the United States at the time. The Black Panther's integration into Marvel's roster of white superheroes was partly a positive development because it established for the first time the possibility of a Black superhero, breaking whites' monopoly on the genre and on the notion of heroism, but it came at a cost. His Afrofuturism was minimized, and he lost the autonomy and independence that his kingship had granted him. He was also relocated from Wakanda, which vanished into the background, to America. To be integrated into Marvel's white power structure, his blackness and Africanness had to be muted, demonstrating that while whites might allow Black people to enter white institutions, they could only do so by shedding the cultural signifiers of blackness.

When the Black Panther received his own series in 1973, it was not under his own name but rather in a title with the telling name of *Jungle Action*. It was launched in October 1972, and shockingly, given how much race relations had changed since the heyday of the jungle genre, it initially featured classic white jungle queen and jungle king heroes. Perhaps realizing that such story lines were no longer politically acceptable, in the fifth issue, the editors gave the title to the Black Panther. The Black Panther continued to star in this series, which only appeared every other month, half as frequently as most comic books, until 1977, when it was canceled and replaced by *Black Panther*. *Jungle Action* returned Black Panther to Wakanda, but it did not restore the

Afrofuturism that had characterized Black Panther's initial story arc drawn by Kirby, and it brought back all the racist stereotypes and colonialist dynamics of the old jungle comics. The hero was now Black, but otherwise the genre was unchanged from its bad old days. In the March 1975 issue, Black Panther travels to Serpent Valley, a classic example of the hidden valley. Fetid oil bubbles up from the ground, and dinosaurs struggle to free themselves from viscous mud. The atmosphere and ambience are turgidly primitive. A caption informs us that "the scent of oil is overpowering, spreading black, leprous fingers. The river struggles to continue its ageless flow—the struggle has been lost! The valley is aptly named. It is evolution denied, time standing as stagnant as the air and water" (186–87). The reference to halted evolution is particularly damning, given the history of white authors, anthropologists, eugenicists, social commentators, and others who diagnosed Black people as subhuman, evolutionarily retarded, and primitive.

This depiction of Black people as not quite human is strongly echoed in the first Black Panther story in *Jungle Action*, in which the villain, a Black character named M'Baku, gains the powers of a white gorilla by eating its flesh and bathing in its blood. M'Baku then dons the fur of a gorilla and takes the name of Man-Ape. This character fulfills many of the worst stereotypes about Africans, including their fictitious penchant for cannibalism and their status as subhuman ape-men. Man-Ape was immediately succeeded by another, equally stereotypical villain, Killmonger, an archetypal example of the stereotype of the brute, a giant, hulking, violent destroyer, whose name testifies to his extraordinary lust for blood. Marvel's white supervillains had names that ranged from the anodyne, such as Magneto, to the sinister, such as the Red Skull and Doctor Doom, but none of them possessed such a repugnant moniker as Killmonger. Killmonger is not even given an origin in this story. He claims to be taking revenge on Black Panther and his father for some past wrong, but it is never stated what this wrong was. Essentially, Killmonger's character, like his name, consists of nothing but a lust for murder as an end in itself.

Whereas in early jungle comics it had been the role of the white jungle queen or jungle king to defeat the bad Black rebel and restore order, that task now shifted to Black Panther, a native African ruler. This exactly paralleled the way that the United States and other Western colonial powers supported African and other Third World rulers who served their interests, many of whom were brutal dictators, while helping to overthrow rulers who challenged US interests. In Africa, the classic example of this was the CIA's support for the overthrow of the independent, democratically elected ruler of the Congo, Patrice Lumumba, by Joseph-Désiré Mobutu (who later changed his name to Mobutu Sese Seko). Lumumba was deposed in 1960, tortured, and executed in 1961 with the support of the US and Belgian governments. After several years of internal conflict, Mobutu organized a second coup with US support, assumed emergency powers, and eventually established himself as a dictator, a position he maintained for decades (Blum, 156–63). The creation of the Black Panther was a step forward in the dismantling of white supremacy, but this dismantling was executed in such a way that limited and constrained its scope and shifted the burden of policing the "bad" Africans from white leaders to "good" African leaders. The Black Panther functioned as a symbol of Black legitimacy and a model for the integration of a muted and tamed blackness into the white power structure, in which "good" Blacks would now police the "bad" Blacks on behalf of the largely intact white power structure.

Ironically, at the same time that Black Panther was being integrated into the white power structure, the questions and issues raised by the civil rights, Black Power, antiwar, and anticolonial movements were causing a crisis in the white identity of Marvel's superheroes. While Iron Man had been created as an instrumental part of the US military-industrial complex and a weapon in the war in Vietnam, by 1970 his young readers had become quite critical of this role. The primary driver of the antiwar movement in the United States was opposition to the draft, which primarily affected young people, so it is not surprising that the young readers of Marvel comics questioned the politics of Iron Man. By 1970, controversy raged in the letter pages of *Iron Man* as fans debated his stance on the war. Marvel created a villain for Iron Man named Firebrand, a leftist radical who first appeared in *Iron Man* #27 (July 1970). Firebrand sides with local Black community activists who oppose the construction of a community center funded by the Iron Man Foundation because the realty firm that owns the land and the construction company that will construct the building are white owned, which means that the funding for the center will not stay within the Black community. It turns out that Tony Stark had been convinced to fund the project by a corrupt city councilman who owns the construction company and realty firm and uses the police to suppress opposition to his project. Firebrand and the city councilman are positioned as twin dangers, preventing the creation of constructive dialogue between Stark/Iron Man and the Black community. In the story's pivotal battle, a race riot triggered by the intransigence of the city councilman and Firebrand, the latter announces:

> I'm just an all-American boy, Iron Man! One of those wide-eyed innocents who started out to make this nation a "better place" . . . ! I sat-in for civil rights, marched for peace, and demonstrated on campus . . .

Bill Mantlo (script) and George Tuska (pencils), "Long Time Gone." Originally published in *Iron Man* #78 (September 1975). Reprinted in *Essential Iron Man*, vol. 5 (Marvel Worldwide, 2013). © Marvel Characters.

and got chased by vicious dogs, spat on by bigots, beat on by "patriots," and choked by tear gas! And blinded by mace, until I finally caught on.... This country doesn't want to be changed! The only way to build anything decent is to tear down what's here and start over! (Goodwin et al.)

Many Iron Man readers felt that Firebrand was right and Iron Man was wrong. One wrote that "while Firebrand was marching, trying to bring about a more peaceful world, Stark Industries was probably building weapons for Vietnam where we 'destroyed a city in order to save it!'"; another reader described Iron Man as a "profiteering, capitalist, war-mongering pig" (Wright, 241).

Iron Man did not travel to Vietnam during this period, presumably because doing so would have been too controversial, but he did deal repeatedly with protesters against the war, racism, pollution, and other causes. His standard response was to decry their "extremism" while admitting that the problems they were protesting were real and then presenting his own solution to them. For instance, in one 1971 story, he defends protesters against a conservative senator who claims they want to destroy the government. On the other hand, when guards at a Stark factory fire at protesters, Iron Man comes to the aid of the protesters but then scolds them for "preaching peace while resorting to violence" (243). This combination was typical of Marvel comics during this period, often sympathizing with the goals of protesters but also condemning them for their supposedly extreme methods. However, shortly thereafter, Iron Man turned decisively against the war, ending Stark Industries' arms manufacturing and focusing instead on consumer goods and environmental protection (243). In a 1975 story, Stark sums up the impact of the war, and the antiwar movement, on him:

> Stark Industries, one of the world's foremost munitions manufacturers, has given way to Stark International—whose business is peace, pure and simple, and a betterment of man through technology! And what about you, Tony Stark? Once you were do or die for America and mom's apple pie! You didn't do much soul-searching back then, did you? As Iron Man you beat the commies for democracy without ever questioning just whose democracy you were serving—or just what those you served intended to do with the world once you'd saved it for them! Viet Nam raised all those questions, didn't it, Tony? Didn't it? Like: "What right had we to be there in the first place?" (242)

Captain America similarly questioned his own existence, soliloquizing in a 1970 story:

> I'm like a dinosaur—in the Cro-Magnon age! An anachronism—who's out-lived his time! This is the day of the anti-hero—the age of the rebel—and the dissenter! It isn't hip—to defend the establishment!—Only to tear it down! And, in a world rife with injustice, greed, and endless war—who's to say the rebels are wrong? But, I've never learned to play by today's new rules! I've spent a lifetime defending the flag—and the law! Perhaps—I should have battled less—and questioned more! (246)

Conversely, Marvel now introduced a number of villains, such as the Hangman and the Tribune, whose missions were to impose traditional social roles under threat of violence (Wright, 238–39, 244). As Bradford Wright comments, "So complete was the cultural transformation of these years that a comic book could feature as its hero a werewolf with extremely antisocial tendencies while casting as its villain a professed champion of traditional moral values" (244). The issues that contributed to this dramatic redefinition of the superhero did not arise solely from the antiwar movement and the anticolonial movement in the Third World. The civil rights and Black Power movements in the United States were taking place at the same time, sharing with these other movements the goal of dismantling white supremacy and contributing to the breakdown of the white superhero persona.

Captain America's questioning of his identity and mission culminated in late 1974, when Steve Rogers briefly abandoned his identity as Captain America, becoming "Nomad, the man without a country" before again taking up the mantle of Captain America in early 1975 (Wright, 245). Steve Rogers's period as Nomad was the high-water mark of superheroes' questioning of establishment morality. After that point, as the antiwar and other protest movements receded, superhero comics likewise placed less emphasis on social and political issues. They did not completely disappear, however, and this period laid the basis for later mainstream comics that took a critical approach to race and other social issues. Captain America himself faced recurrent questions about whether his loyalty to the United States and his commitment to justice and freedom were compatible, as in the run-up to the 1987 "Captain America No More" story line (Costello, 66–69). The comics did not always do so successfully, but even the attempt to critically consider race and whiteness was a step forward for a medium that had previously embraced racist stereotypes without question.

Chapter Four

CIVIL RIGHTS AND THE LIMITS OF LIBERALISM

The white racial frame that ruled comic books without question in the 1930s and 1940s began to show some cracks in the mid-1950s. As the civil rights movement advanced, some publishers with liberal sympathies began to question the tenets of white supremacy in the pages of their comics. EC Comics in the 1950s and Marvel Comics in the 1960s and early 1970s did much to move comic books toward a less racist approach in relation to their characters and American society. Ramzi Fawaz sees this period as ushering in a "radical imagination," arguing that "with a mutant generation of superheroes in the early 1960s, the formerly touted values of the superhero comic book, including law and order, nationalism, and virile masculinity, were increasingly sidelined in favor of producing imaginative fictional universes infused with a democratic political orientation toward the world" (15). However, despite their best intentions, their efforts, along with those of the civil rights activist and anticomics crusader Fredric Wertham, were marred and undermined by their own unexamined assumptions and biases about race, which demonstrated their possessive investment in the white racial frame. After the turbulence of the Depression and World War II, American society sought to crack down on dissent and impose a culture of normality, safety, and conformism. Television shows such as *Leave It to Beaver* (1957–63) presented a tepid, suburban, and extremely white culture as the norm. This sense of normalcy was policed by white authority figures, with any deviations being quickly targeted and isolated. American culture was in the midst of the Cold War, which contributed to a general sense of paranoia and fear of difference. Comics became a scapegoat for any suspect behavior, and an all-out war on them commenced, with the creative freedom of comic book publishers hanging in the balance. In the 1940s and 1950s, nearly all children in the United States read comics (Nyberg, 1). Kids could easily pick up comics at grocery stores, newsstands, and corner drugstores. Due in part to the sheer number of young people who had their hands on them, comic books emerged as low-hanging fruit for parents, educators, and librarians searching for a scapegoat for their children's putative recalcitrant and delinquent behavior.

At the forefront of the war on comics was Fredric Wertham, a psychiatrist who had devoted a large portion of his life to fighting for Black people's rights to proper psychiatric care, and a man who played a pivotal role in the desegregation of schools in the *Brown v. Board of Education* legal battle. Wertham's ultimate goal was to convince lawmakers to regulate comics by instituting an age requirement to buy certain titles. He felt that children under fourteen or fifteen would be harmed by the images of these comics and miss whatever positive message they may have conveyed through dialogue and exposition. The results of Wertham's crusade against comics were three days of congressional hearings that resulted in the Comics Code of 1954, an industry driven, self-regulating system of censorship run by the Comics Magazine Association of America (CMAA) (Nyberg, 110). The Code had an enormous impact on the comics industry, forcing the reconfiguration or cancellation of many titles and the dissolution of a number of comics publishers, including EC Comics, run by William Gaines. One of EC's most popular titles was *Shock SuspenStories*, a slick publication that often featured stories attacking racism and bigotry. Although both Wertham and Gaines had actively fought racism prior to testifying before Congress, Wertham in his psychiatric work and Gaines in his comics, their liberal antiracism was undermined by their egregious sexism and, in the case of Wertham, his homophobia. While both men clearly felt that racial discrimination was wrong, neither understood the intersectionalities of racism, sexism, and homophobia or how their own contributions perpetuated white supremacy. The Achilles' heel of both Wertham and Gaines was their attitude regarding sex and gender. As illustrated in chapter 2, in relation to western comics, racial hierarchies depend on male heterosexual privilege to maintain static power structures by promoting further divisions among the ranks of men and women and preventing alliances further down the chain of privilege. The linchpin of maintaining white supremacy centers on the control and subjugation of white women, for they are seen as essential to maintaining the myth of blood purity.

The Comics Code heavily censored the genres that were the lifeblood of EC, quickly driving most of its titles out of existence. The downfall of EC and the genres it depended on, which had dominated the marketplace after World War II, created an opening for superheroes to return to prominence. The company that developed a new formula to breathe life back into the superhero was Marvel Comics, which had previously been a relatively minor player in the comic book industry. Marvel's most notable creation up to this point had been Captain America, but in the early 1960s, it produced a string of innovative new characters, including the Fantastic Four, Spider-Man, the Hulk, Thor, Iron Man, and the X-Men, among others. Led by Stan Lee, the new Marvel characters were more down-to-earth and relatable than previous DC superheroes such as Superman and Batman. Marvel also introduced a number of characters that showed sympathy to the civil rights movement, evincing a critique of white supremacy and racism that was new and groundbreaking in the comic book industry. However, as with Wertham and EC, the promise of this antiracist message was undermined by unexamined biases that revealed a perpetuation of the white racial frame within Marvel comics.

While little doubt exists that Stan Lee has earned his reputation as one of the "most important creative icons in contemporary American history," the artistic persona that Lee has created for himself is rife with half-truths and self-mythologization (Lee, *Excelsior*, 204). Perhaps the biggest myth of Lee's career is that he was a groundbreaking civil rights advocate who, through works like *The X-Men*, challenged a white supremacist power structure and exposed the machinations of prejudice and racism. While Lee did offer rhetorical support for civil rights in a number of ways, this support was undercut by the persistence of an unexamined white racial frame in Lee's writing, which perpetuated white supremacist tropes even as Lee sought to support the dismantling of white supremacy. Lee is credited, often by himself, with successfully challenging the Comics Code (139) and creating "socially relevant and diverse superhero comic book titles" (2), including what he labeled the first "ethnic comicbook" (161).

The truth of these claims is far more complicated. While Lee did move comic books in a positive direction, there is still much to question in his legacy in relation to race. *The X-Men*, commonly thought to represent a metaphor for American racism and prejudice, presents race as biological rather than socially constructed and features not oppressed characters but rather privileged, whitewashed characters operating in the role of persecuted minorities. Mutancy functions as a stand-in for racial difference, or difference of all kinds, and therefore is offered as a metaphor for systems of prejudice and discrimination in the United States. This metaphor fails, since it posits all difference as being biologically determined rather than socially constructed. On the basis of this questionable metaphor, critics like Amy Nyberg consider *The X-Men* "one of the most socially relevant and diverse superhero comic book titles" of all time (2). This conceit largely fails, since the characters who compose the X-Men have more in common with privileged white Americans than nonwhites. Marvel's other comics also demonstrate a failure to fully recognize or repudiate the white racial frame through the use of racist and sexist tropes.

The subliminal racism beneath Marvel's putative antiracism came to a head in the late 1960s and early 1970s in the pages of *Captain America*. In response to the ongoing civil rights movement, Captain America was given a Black sidekick, the Falcon. The contradiction in acknowledging the demand for racial equality by introducing a Black character as a sidekick, rather than an equal, was obvious. The Falcon was soon promoted to a coequal lead with Captain America, but this only set the stage for further conflict and debate. The Falcon was torn between his loyalty to Captain America and the demands of radical Black activists affiliated with the Black nationalist and Black Power movements. These movements were repeatedly caricatured in the comic as violent, anarchistic, and even racist. They were depicted as fronts for criminal and white supremacist organizations as well as for the Red Skull himself, Captain America's Nazi nemesis. As the Black nationalist and Black Power movements petered out in the mid-1970s, Marvel turned its back on the entire experiment with these politics, whitewashing them by rewriting the Falcon's origin from that of a social worker to a former drug dealer. While Wertham, Gaines, and Lee ought to be lauded for their antiracist efforts, their liberal commitment only went so far. They were ultimately unable or unwilling to fully excavate and root out their assumptions about race, gender, and the intersectionality between them, which limited how far they were willing to go in the fight against racism.

FREDRIC WERTHAM AND *SEDUCTION OF THE INNOCENT*

Fredric Wertham was born in Germany and educated at several universities in Europe, culminating in an MD degree in psychiatry from the University of Würzburg. He counted among his friends Sigmund Freud, whom Wertham cited as a major influence and one reason why he chose the field of psychiatry. In 1922, Wertham accepted a position at the Johns Hopkins Hospital in Baltimore, Maryland. After a decade at Johns Hopkins, Wertham moved to New York and began a crusade to help provide proper psychiatric care for minorities, especially Black people, whom he felt were often falsely accused of crimes they did not commit. Wertham instead pointed the finger at institutional and structural racism as the more salient culprit. Wertham was one of the only psychiatrists who would testify on behalf of low-income Black people accused of crimes, which led him to a friendship with the noted defense attorney Clarence Darrow. In 1946, Wertham opened up a clinic in a Harlem church basement called the Lafargue Clinic. He was known around Harlem as "Doctor Quarter," since the suggested fee for treatment was twenty-five cents. After a decade, the clinic was eventually shuttered, thanks to the retirement of the church's pastor and the application of new government regulations, which sounded the death knell for the revolutionary clinic (Nyberg, 89).

In addition to Wertham's work at the clinic, the psychiatrist devoted much of his time to studying the effects of school segregation. The National Association for the Advancement of Colored People (NAACP) asked Wertham to conduct a study of segregated Black and white students in the state of Delaware. Based on the data, Wertham concluded that segregation was psychologically harmful for both Black and white students. Wertham testified to these findings in 1951, and his thesis would become central to the legal argument in the desegregation case *Brown v. Board of Education of Topeka* (Nyberg, 93). Wertham argued that segregation was pernicious to both Black and white students because it implanted feelings of inferiority in Black students and retarded the development of compassion in white students.

As early as 1948, Wertham began presenting findings that he had gathered at the clinic, suggesting that one of the major factors in the delinquency of children was comic books. At a symposium that took place in March 1948 called "The Psychopathology of Comic Books," Wertham outlined the overwhelming popularity of comics and the need for regulatory legislation (Nyberg, 32–33). In the spring of 1954, the Senate subcommittee on juvenile delinquency held three days of hearings concerning whether or not comics posed a threat to the millions of children who bought and traded them. The result of the hearings was a self-regulatory code adopted by the comics industry itself, representing the ultimate goal of the subcommittee in the first place, since imposing government regulations on the industry itself likely would not have held up to constitutional scrutiny. One of the central witnesses at the hearings was Wertham, who had just published his book *Seduction of the Innocent*, wherein he outlined his beliefs that comics needed regulation, since they were dangerous to children and contributed greatly to childhood delinquency.

One of Wertham's many arguments was that the millions of American comic books exported globally conveyed the idea that American children were being taught to hate other races (100). Wertham illustrated this argument by pointing to racial representations in comic books. Wertham noted that whites and nonwhites were represented very differently in comics. The white men were tall, blond, hard jawed, and often called supermen, and the white women were blonde with large breasts. Nonwhite characters, on the other hand, were drawn with abnormal features, deformities, and dark skin (101). Wertham's central argument was that these images influenced how children thought about themselves and others. He noted that whenever he asked a child to point out the bad guy in a given comic book, the child invariably chose the nonwhite person.

The Senate hearings on comic books and juvenile delinquency featured Wertham prominently, along with the comics publisher William Gaines. According to Amy Kiste Nyberg, "In many ways, these two personified the struggle over comic books in postwar America" (60). William Gaines's father, Max, whom some people regard as the father of the modern comic, was the owner and publisher of EC, or Educational Comics, until he died in a boating accident in 1947, his comics business in debt by over one hundred thousand dollars. His son William, who at that time was an education student at New York University and newly divorced, reluctantly took over the company and quickly turned it into a profitable, industry-changing juggernaut. The younger Gaines changed the name of the company from Educational Comics to Entertaining Comics and introduced several new lines of comics that focused on horror and crime, one of which was *Shock SuspenStories*. Gaines plotted or wrote the preponderance of *Shock SuspenStories* himself, stories that sometimes identified and impugned racism and bigotry (Gaines, *Shock*, vol. 1, p. 7). Informally, Gaines referred to these message stories as "preachies" (Whitted, 18–19). Ironically, Wertham and later the CMAA claimed that the very stories in *Shock SuspenStories* and other titles that condemned racism and bigotry actually promoted racial hatred.

A classic example of the CMAA's upside-down assessment of EC's antiracist stories is the story "Judgement Day" in the publication *Incredible Science Fiction*. The CMAA rejected the story for publication because the coders said it violated the parameter that no ethic group should be ridiculed. The story concerns a society of robots on a planet who had applied for admission to a galactic federation. A federation official is sent to the planet to evaluate the robots and their application and decides to reject them based on their policy of segregating robots based on color. When the official takes off his helmet in a panel near the end of the comic, he is revealed to be a Black man. In an egregious misreading, reviewers rejected the story because the comic presented the character's blackness in a negative light. Nyberg reports:

> The story had an antiracism theme and dealt with a planet of robots who had applied for admission to the pre–*Star Trek* version of a galactic federation, but the society of robots who lived on the planet had a policy of segregation based on what color the robot was. The hero of

the story, who gets back into his spaceship, decides the robot planet is not ready to join the rest of the galaxy. In one panel, the character removes his helmet and the reader discovers the hero is black. Perspiration dots the character's face. The code reviewers, citing the code provision that "ridicule or attack on any religious or racial group is never permissible," apparently decided that a perspiring black character somehow violated code guidelines. (122–24)

Drawing attention to the blackness of a character is not inherently racist, unless one subscribes to the idea that racial harmony means living in a postracial culture where cultural heritage, ancestry, and ethnicity are invisible or totally ignored. Striving for a postracist society does not mean ignoring difference; living in a postracist culture means celebrating difference.

One *Shock SuspenStories* story that particularly drew Wertham's ire was "The Whipping." The story is a fairly simple one about a white man who forbids his daughter to go out with a Mexican boy whose family has recently moved into the neighborhood. When she refuses to quit seeing the boy, the father riles up the community by falsely accusing the boy of raping his daughter in an effort to have the boy murdered by a lynch mob in the style of the KKK. After the lynch mob captures the boy in his bed and beats him to death, the man realizes they have actually beaten to death the man's own daughter, who had been sleeping in the boy's bed before she was inadvertently wrapped up in a sheet in the dark. The boy then tells the men that they were engaged to be married. At the congressional hearings, Wertham claimed the story promoted rather than denounced racial hatred, noting that the story used the derogatory term "spick" twelve times. He began his summary of the story by saying rather sensationally that "Hitler was a beginner compared to the comic book industry. . . . They teach them race hatred at the age of four before they can read" (Nyberg, 63). Wertham's invocation of Hitler is interesting insofar as Wertham's mother was Jewish until she abandoned her faith in favor of her husband's Christian faith. However, as far as the Nazis were concerned, Fredric and his mother were Jewish based on the orthodox view that the mother's ethnicity is what counts. Fear of persecution led Wertham to emigrate to the United States in the 1920s before returning to Europe soon after to continue his studies (Reibman, xi).

Wertham's argument regarding "The Whipping" was that, notwithstanding the overall message, which he glossed over or missed entirely, a child's comprehension of the story could very easily be limited to the idea that a man was justifiably killed because he was different. Wertham maintained that drawing attention to differences such as the religion of the new people in

William Gaines (script), Al Feldman (script), and Wally Wood (pencils), "The Whipping." Originally published in *Shock SuspenStories* #14 (April–May 1954). Reprinted in *Shock SuspenStories*, vol. 1 (Dark Horse, 2016). © William M. Gaines.

the neighborhood was unnecessary and that the only point of this story was the beating of the Mexican man. According to this reading, the fact that the lynch mob accidentally kills the white man's daughter instead of the "greasy Mexican" amounts to a mere accident rather than some sort of poetic justice or moral repercussion (Nyberg, 63–64). Further, the accidental death of the young white girl could still be blamed on the Mexican in whose bed the girl should not have been sleeping. This interpretation provides a sense of how far Wertham was willing to strain credulity to make his desired point.

Wertham argued that even if a story had a positive antiracist moral in it, often related through exposition and captions, children would not get it, because they only looked at the pictures. Wertham was not a racist, but he was also completely obstinate when it came to comics. For him, the end justified the means, even if that meant willful or extremely narrow misreadings of texts. Wertham felt there was absolutely no literary value in comics. He offered:

> By no stretch of critical standards can the text in crime comics qualify as literature, or their drawings as art. . . . [Children] spend a large amount of their time and money on these publications and have nothing positive to show for it. . . . [Crime] comics by their very nature are not only non-educational; they are anti-educational. They fail to teach anything that might be useful to a child; they do suggest many things that are harmful. (90)

Wertham was able to advance the idea that any depiction of race was negative, and this was the tone set for the CMAA reviewers, who themselves focused on the images rather than the narration or dialogue. According to the reviewers, when a panel highlighted the race of a character, possibly to emphasize his identity and subjectivity and justify his point of view, the panel was merely racist. Neither Wertham nor the reviewers gave any credit to the children who read the comics actually being able to comprehend what was on the page, reflecting an extremely low estimation of the intelligence of children in general, as well as of the comic books they loved.

Like Wertham, Gaines's track record of antiracism was beyond dispute, at least on the surface. In many cases, the racial message in his comics is overtly conveyed, condemning bigotry and racism outright. In "The Whipping," the story that Wertham singled out as promoting race hatred, the narrator is a white man who is clearly presented as a bigoted racist: "All the way home, his rage had seethed within him. He'd kissed her! He of the olive skin and the raven hair had dared to touch his white white daughter. By the time they'd reached the house, he'd exploded" (Gaines, *Shock*, vol. 3, p. 58). In this story, the daughter's shapeliness is highlighted, and her whiteness appears to be correlated with her blonde hair and curvaceous body. That the man repeats the term "white" has a powerful contradistinctive effect in relation to the "olive skin and the raven hair" boy she is seeing. One limitation of Gaines's preachies, as Qiana Whitted argues, is that racial and ethnic minorities, such as Louis Martinez in "The Whipping," exist mainly as victims of wrongdoing and are almost never given agency of their own (40). The goal of the preachies appeared to be restricted to furthering the growth of the white characters through shame rather than empowering the characters of color (68). Shaming white characters in the stories extended to EC's larger creative strategy of convincing its white readership about the need for social justice (79).

Another story that focuses on racism, in particular the metaphor of blood purity, as well as shame, is "Blood Brothers," in which a man realizes that his neighbor Henry Williams, who is moving, is considering selling his house to a Black family. When the narrator, Sid, confronts his neighbor, Henry, Sid is horrified to find out Henry's grandmother was African American, making Henry one-quarter African American. Sid reacts by getting Henry, who seems to have been passing for white, fired from his job and blackballed by the community, including the bank where he goes for a loan to pay for medical care for his severely ailing wife. He is unable to procure a loan, and his wife dies as a result. Henry then shoots himself after Sid and some other neighborhood men burn a cross in his front yard. The narrator only realizes his error when a doctor tells him that racial blood is a myth: "There's *no such thing* as *Negro blood*, Sid. *All human blood is the same*, whether it is the blood of an *Oriental*, or an *African*, or an *European* . . . except for *one medical difference* . . . *the blood type. But White, Negro, Mongol, all races* of man have *all the blood types*" (26). The doctor also goes on to relate a story about a boy who had a terrible accident and needed blood to stay alive, and the only available donor was a Black man named George: "*You were that boy*, Sid! *George's blood saved your life*.'*Negro blood*,' pumped into *your veins*, snatched *you* from the *jaws of death*" (27). Upon hearing this tale, Sid is depicted in a blue shadow, racked with guilt and shame, saying, "Oh God . . . sob . . . What have I done . . . ?" (27).

EC's message stories also dealt with anti-Semitism. Since nearly all of EC's writers, artists, and editors were Jewish, this topic directly affected their lives. Unlike the Jewish comic book creators of the 1930s and 1940s, they did not bury their concern with Jewish issues in the subtext of their work but rather drew attention to them and demanded an end to anti-Semitism. In a story similar to "Blood Brothers" called "Hate," a man learns that a family of Jews are about to move into the neighborhood, and worriedly he and some others post a note on their door warning them not to move in. There is some discussion again in relation to the fraudulent metaphor of blood purity: "Did your *father* . . . a small town doctor . . . tell you that, John? Did he list the *genetic differences* between you and them? Did *he* tell you their *blood* was different . . . their *bones* . . . their *hearts*? He was a *doctor*, John! He should have *known*" (Gaines, *Shock*, vol. 1, p. 158). The narrator and the neighborhood leaders continue to harass the newly arrived Jewish family, expressing concern among themselves about diminishing property values. Eventually the bigots burn a cross in the front yard of the offending family, and the house catches fire, causing the inhabitants to leap to their death from the second-story windows. The narrator then learns that he was adopted and is actually Jewish, too, and the story ends as he is enduring a beating for being Jewish by the same men who had helped him terrorize the newly arrived Jewish family. Although Wertham listed Jews as a minority group regularly villainized in comics, he never commented on the EC stories that attacked anti-Semitism, further demonstrating the tendentiousness of his position. Perhaps the fact that he was Jewish himself made him more sensitive to the presence of stories decrying anti-Semitism.

Ultimately, as with Fredric Wertham, there is very little question about whether or not EC comics and William Gaines were antiracist. He certainly was, and many of the comics prove it. Wertham's claim that the stories themselves promote race hatred was simply untrue and actually weakened Wertham's overall argument. Nevertheless, Gaines and EC, like Wertham, are guilty of perpetuating white supremacy in relation to the sexism and misogyny in nearly every story among the eighteen issues of *Shock SuspenStories*. One of the first things one notices while reading *Shock SuspenStories* is that nearly every woman is dressed in red, a symbol of the femme fatale. These women in red dresses are seductresses and temptresses, hypersexual and untrustworthy. Perhaps the second thing one notices is that many of the women are characterized one-dimensionally as out-and-out gold diggers or horribly greedy and deceitful.

EC comics evince a dynamic that Ruth Frankenberg argues is crucial to white supremacy, in which "white women are viewed both as objects of male protection and as people unable to control their own sexuality. In either case, white women and nonwhite men are to be kept apart, by white men" (81). Another of Frankenberg's observations echoed in the pages of EC's *Shock SuspenStories* is that "white women and men [are] placed, respectively, as victim and rescuer in the discourse against interracial sexuality, vis-à-vis the supposed sexual threat posed by men of color toward white women" (237). In "The Whipping" and other EC stories, racism is framed in relation to miscegenation, but the message of these stories does not argue that white women should have the right to be romantically involved with people of color. Rather, the stories superficially condemn the racism of the white actors without arguing for the agency of white women. At no point in the moralistic captions condemning a prejudice that specifically involves interracial sexuality does the narration address the rights of white women. These stories focus on the terrorism of the white men, suggesting that it is their manner of controlling white women that is problematic rather than their right to control them. The men in these stories fall victim to these women because of how they attempt to handle and control them, the apparent message being that men should find better ways to control white women.

In "The Neat Job," for example, a woman in a red dress admits to marrying a man for his money and then attempts to kill him after the marriage does not work out. The girl gets fed up with her husband always complaining about her lack of neatness and poor housekeeping skills, until one day she cuts him up into little pieces and organizes him very neatly into canning jars, telling the police, "In any case, I *did* it! I never *loved* him! I just needed a *husband . . . badly*" (Gaines, *Shock*, vol. 1, p. 14). She then exclaims, "Look for yourselves! I *cleaned up* the blood . . . *every drop*" (20). The detectives respond by saying, "Yeah, Lady! You certainly *did* a *neat job* . . . choke . . . *very* neat" (20). Unlike in the stories about racism, no caption sums up the message. Consequently the message of the story is unclear. The detectives treat the woman's vicious and psychotic murder with a measure of levity, as though there is really nothing out of the ordinary in a woman marrying a man for his money and then dismembering him when things do not work out. The comic's overall structure is a frame story, and the beginning shows her explaining herself to the detective, but we get no indication that the detectives are even surprised by her actions. The message of the story is ambiguous. Who is the villain? The woman, or the man she married for his money?

In this and in many other stories, the message is unclear and seems to suggest that women are habitual liars, thieves, and murderers, and men are justified in hurting or even killing them. Most of these stories seem to suggest that women lack sexual control and need to be controlled by white men. These stories imply that white women's sexuality is to blame for much of the social ills of American culture and needs to be controlled. The notion of needing to control white woman's sexuality is a hallmark of white supremacy. Men who hurt women often go unpunished, whereas in other stories, especially those pertaining to racism and bigotry, the offenders are clearly punished or experience epiphanies. For Gaines, part of the issue seems to be that he wanted some comics to have a message and others simply to be entertaining, and he was willing to ignore the messages communicated in the comics he saw as entertainment.

One of Wertham's primary complaints about comic books was that they encouraged unhealthy attitudes regarding sex and gender. However, while Wertham did point out some of the sexism of comic books, he also faulted comics for encouraging homosexuality and female independence. Wertham noted that white women were often depicted as sexualized prey for rapacious minorities, and only minority women were shown with exposed breasts, resulting in the tacit message that white women should be sexually protected while minority women should not, since they are always already sexualized (Wertham 104–5). Wertham lamented the ubiquity of physical abuse against women in comics and noted that often a man who smacked a woman was glamorized and portrayed as having strength and prestige (110). He also warned that depictions of large-breasted women had deleterious effects on young girls, who were made to feel as though they did not measure up to what men found attractive (210).

Wertham complained that nowhere in comics could be found depictions of "ordinary home life" or a "normal family sitting down to a meal" (236). He made it clear that a normal family life was one of heteronormativity, where very likely a white woman cooked that meal for a white family. His comments betrayed sexist ideologies that contribute to white supremacy, namely, the notion that white women belonged in the home, taking care of the family under the yoke of male domination, rather than enjoying the personal freedom that might bring her into contact with undesirable elements, including people of color. Behind such prohibitions lay, ultimately, a fear that such contact might lead to sexual relations between white women and nonwhite men, which would compromise the racial line of white blood purity.

Wertham clearly found nonnormative sexualities of any kind abhorrent, noting that "only a decent sexual orientation can lead to a decent sex life, for practically all psychological sex problems are ethical problems" (175). He passionately criticized comics for promoting homosexuality. He argued that Wonder Woman promoted lesbianism and presented a "morbid ideal" to young girls (193). Wertham argued that Wonder Woman's powers were also scary for boys, and that Wonder Woman and her gang were essentially man-haters. He found fault in Wonder Woman's valuing the lives of women and rescuing them from male villains. According to Wertham, these sorts of images of female alliance were extremely dangerous for girls in the 1950s and promoted lesbianism, causing terrible unhappiness. Whereas Wonder Woman's feminism came at the expense of her racism, Wertham's antiracism came at the expense of his sexism.

For Wertham, female agency was never the goal. He contended that comics celebrated men abusing women and that women were depicted as sexualized, but then he also lamented images of women fighting against men. He seemed to prefer women in powerless domestic situations. Rather than understanding that the abuse of women was a much larger cultural problem that could not be solved merely by the regulation of comic books, Wertham decided to focus his energies on merely the cultural images of women in comics instead of the overall white power structure that limited female agency and resulted in the kind of domestic servitude that Wertham seemed to point to as ideal. He was correct in his assessment that images of women in comics were dehumanizing, but his argument was terribly undermined by his inability to grant these same women an agency hinted at in characters like Wonder Woman, since that agency would threaten white social hierarchies in which Wertham was clearly invested.

Wertham's most virulent criticism of comics centered on the charge that they promoted homosexuality among men. Despite noting that white women were overly sexualized in comics, Wertham also argued, "A homoerotic attitude is . . . suggested by the presentation of masculine, bad, witchlike or violent women. In such comics, women are depicted in a definitely anti-erotic light, while the young male heroes have pronounced erotic overtones. The muscular male supertype, whose primary sex characteristics are usually well emphasized, is in the setting of certain stories the object of homoerotic sexual curiosity and stimulation" (188–89). Once again, Wertham seemed to be contradictorily criticizing hypersexualized images of women as well as undersexualized images of women, and once again undermining his own ostensible position as a defender of women's rights and furthering white supremacy by arguing for the disempowerment of white women.

Wertham suggested, "In many adolescents the homoerotic, anti-feminist trend unconsciously aroused or fostered by these stories is demonstrable" (191). In addition to misusing the word "feminist," Wertham failed to see that his own homophobia reinforced misogyny. What he seems to be arguing is that sexualized images of male superheroes encourage homoerotic desires in readers, which he equates with misogyny. This point of view is problematic and mistaken on several levels. To begin with, homoeroticism or homosexuality is not antifemale or, as Wertham inaccurately puts it, antifeminist. On the contrary, what actually drives misogyny is not homoeroticism or homosexuality but homophobia. As Michael Kimmel argues, hypermasculinity promotes the fear in men of being seen as having any "feminine" qualities, which are associated with homosexuality (186). In this sense, emotional and physical proximity to "feminine" qualities archetypally represented by the mother undermines a boy's masculine development, potentially marking him as queer and compelling him to reject the mother and devalue all women via homophobia, which in turn operates as a crucial linchpin of white supremacy in its restriction of female agency. The devaluation of women brought on by intense homophobia often results in violence against women, something Wertham claimed comics caused. If Wertham's goal was for boys and men to value women, then he should have fought for queer acceptance rather than queer villainization, since a strong link connects homophobia and the devaluation and abuse of women.

Toward the end of *Seduction of the Innocent*, in which he rarely cited specific story lines in comic titles as evidence for his arguments, Wertham did briefly describe a story that obviously came from the first volume of *Shock SuspenStories* called "Strictly Business." To buttress his argument that comics were dangerous to young readers, Wertham routinely listed a few outrageous plot details from a story without citing the story or offering much detail about where it came from. In this particular passage, Wertham noted, "A very sexy-looking girl tells her husband that she is pregnant. He opens his jacket and the girl looks at him horrified. He tells her: 'You *couldn't* be expecting a child, now, *could you?* Not very well—when your husband is a ROBOT!'" (Wertham, 387). Wertham provided no reference for the story or mentioned who wrote it or published it. Out of context, this passage could suggest any number of plotlines. Is the girl actually pregnant? Is the robot husband actually the husband? If not, did the robot harm the husband? Wertham's goal in briefly delineating this story was merely to shock his readers. The actual story depicts a dandified and closeted businessman named Alec Craven who pays a woman, Diane Masters, ten thousand dollars a year to pretend to be his wife so that he can "assume an air of respectability" (Gaines, *Shock*, vol. 1, p. 134). Masters accepts and successfully performs as Craven's wife, entertaining senators and helping Craven keep up all appearances of heteronormativity. Eventually Masters falls in love with Craven and pretends to be pregnant so that he cannot divorce her. Craven responds by revealing to her that his secret is that he is actually part of a secret cybernetics group that plans to take over the world. In briefly touching on this story, Wertham inadvertently referenced a story that demonstrates how homophobia leads to the devaluation of women. In the story, Masters is merely a homosocial tool used for the benefit of Craven. Her only value is in her objective appearance, her pretty face. His fear of being unmasked as inhuman and sexually nonnormative ironically leads him to dehumanize Masters. One of Wertham's own examples demonstrated that posturing as an advocate for women and being homophobic constitute contradictory viewpoints, since homophobia leads to the devaluation of women.

Further exemplifying Wertham's most notorious scapegoating of purported homosexual tendencies was his claim that superhero comics like Batman not only promoted homosexuality but also pederasty, or the predation of older gay men on young boys. Wertham's queer reading of the dynamic duo asserted:

> They constantly rescue each other from violent attacks by an unending number of enemies.... Sometimes Batman ends up in bed injured and young Robin is shown sitting next to him.... They are Bruce Wayne and "Dick" Grayson.... They live in sumptuous quarters, with beautiful flowers in large vases.... Batman is sometimes shown in a dressing gown. As they sit by the fireplace the young boy sometimes

worries about his partner: "Something's wrong with Bruce. He hasn't been himself these last few days." It is like a wish dream of two homosexuals living together. (189–90)

Wertham's queer reading of Batman and Robin was problematic on many levels and ultimately promoted the brand of hypermasculinity responsible for the abuse of women. According to Wertham, men should not be sensitive to one another or enjoy beautiful artifacts such as vases and flowers. Further, men should not enjoy one another's company without the presence of women. By promoting homophobia, Wertham was in fact putting the lives of women at risk, since, as Kimmel concludes, "[homophobia] is a central organizing principle of our cultural definition of manhood," and "[violence] is often the single most evident marker of manhood" (188–89). For Kimmel, traditional masculinity is driven by homophobia, and this fear results in men enacting violence as conflict resolution and the defining factor of their masculinity. Further, Kimmel warns, "homophobia, the fear of being perceived as gay, as not a real man, keeps men exaggerating all the traditional rules of masculinity, including sexual predation with women" (191). By arguing for an ideology that resulted in the devaluing of women, especially white women, Wertham advanced the aims of white supremacy, which required the subjugation of white women who alone had the power to taint pure white blood.

While Wertham was dead wrong in suggesting that a story like "The Whipping" promoted race hatred, he was correct in arguing that many, if not all, the stories in *Shock SuspenStories* in one way or another were detrimental to the consciousness of readers. But then, so too were Wertham's sexist and homophobic viewpoints expressed on national television during the congressional hearings. In both cases, the comics in *Shock SuspenStories* and the harangues of Wertham, the message that white women represented a threat to the social order and needed to be controlled and subservient to men, aligned with the program of white supremacy. These men were clearly ignorant of the intersectionalities of race and gender, namely, how racism is perpetuated via sexism. Though EC comics published stories that were overtly antiracist, their depiction of out-of-control, sexualized white women who needed protection and control by white men demonstrated the creators' possessive investment in the same white supremacist structure that some of their stories rail against. Consequently, Wertham and Gaines were similar in their somewhat limited antiracist program and overall failure to contribute to the eradication of white supremacy, despite their antiracist track record.

WHITEWASHING—THE MARVEL WAY

After the creation of the Comics Code and the collapse of EC Comics, Stan Lee took advantage of the newly wide-open marketplace to elevate Marvel Comics to the top of the comic book industry. Like Wertham and Gaines, Lee sought to advance an antiracist agenda, but his accomplishments in this regard were even more equivocal than those of Wertham and Gaines. Before 1963, all of Lee and Kirby's heroes, including Spider-Man, the Hulk, and the Fantastic Four, were accidental heroes who through some mishap were empowered for better or worse. Fearing that the public would tire of this origin story, Lee and Kirby decided to create a team of mutants whose powers were congenital or biologically determined (B. Batchelor, 100). Marvel's *The X-Men* is often discussed through a metaphorical prism called the mutant metaphor, which equates mutancy, the possession of a congenital X-gene that produces special powers, with racial minorities. As Danny Fingeroth put it, "The X-Men is the most direct metaphor for tolerance, racial and otherwise, ever to grace the pages of a comic book" (*Disguised as Clark Kent*, 113).

The construction of diversity in the X-Men is problematic on multiple levels, beginning with its location of the root of diversity in biology rather than social construction. Mutants are beings born with a genetic variation that presents as a superpower, resulting in racism and discrimination. The problem with equating ethnicity and biology is that the severe deficits and inequalities that minorities experience in a white supremacist society are all too often ascribed to the individuals themselves and some intrinsic failing on their part instead of to the racist cultural institutions that are actually to blame. In reality, racial divisions are a social and political construct, not a biological one. As Steve Martinot notes, "'Race' names a system of sociopolitical relations in which whites define themselves with respect to others they define as 'non-white' for that purpose. Because whites are the definers, 'race' is inseparable from white supremacy. That is, 'race' as a concept is inseparable from the white hierarchical domination that constructs it" (19). Because the X-Men derive their powers from congenital biological variations, their racial difference affirms rather than destabilizes racial divisions in the United States; that is, what define the X-Men as raced are their biological attributes rather than the social and political institutions that actually create race. The biological differences of the characters in *The X-Men* define their identity completely, thus equating biological difference directly with racial identity. For fans of the comic who view the X-Men's minority status as a legitimate metaphor for race in the United States, biological determinism becomes the most salient characteristic of "race," which reaffirms rather than deconstructs divisions based on regional ethnicities. The mutant metaphor also fails because the figures in the comic who are supposed to represent racially diverse individuals appear white or whitewashed, a term that has increasingly been used in popular websites and blogs to describe how Hollywood often casts white actors in nonwhite roles. Beyond this commonplace usage, the term might also denote the discussion or presentation of racial tableaux untethered from phenomenological or lived racism in relation to either the victim or the victimizer.

The X-Men's supposed antiracism was also undermined by the team's racial composition. As Bob Batchelor writes, "All of the members of the X-Men in this period were white middle-to-upper-class Americans. In short, this was a very WASPish group to be struggling against prejudice within a minority metaphor" (26). Professor X grew up in New Mexico, where his father was a well-respected scientist (Lee, *X-Men*, vol. 2, p. 27). Scott Summers (Cyclops) was an orphan who ran away from his orphanage and became Professor X's first student (vol. 4, p. 166). Warren Worthington III (Angel) came from a very wealthy family who had a $20,000 swimming pool and a butler (vol. 6, pp. 16–17). Hank McCoy's (Beast) father worked at a nuclear plant and was exposed to a damaged nuclear reactor, the implication being that the accident caused a genetic anomaly in his son (vol. 5, p. 184). Bobby Drake (Iceman) came from a small rural town in Nassau County in New York (vol. 5, pp. 37–39). Last, Jean Grey's (Marvel Girl) family cares so deeply for their daughter that once she graduates from Professor X's school, they force her to enroll in a traditional college (vol. 3, p. 41). None of these characters' origins or experiences authentically depict the struggles that minorities in the United States faced in the 1950s and 1960s. As Neil Shyminsky suggests, the predominantly white mutants of the X-Men lack race and typically pass as just people. In spite of their exceptional powers and abilities that mark them as other, most of the X-Men would not be out of place in mainstream white America (162).

Despite the characters in the comic being completely whitewashed and having more to do with upper-class, privileged, white Anglo-Americans in their appearance, social status, and apparent values, critics have continued to draw parallels between the comic and the real-life African American experience in the 1960s. Nyberg notes, "Many have noted this correlation between the X-Men narrative and American historical events, and some have even noted direct parallels between the leaders of the mutant race and civil rights leaders. Professor X . . . is considered to have been inspired by Martin Luther King, Jr. Conversely, Magneto . . . is often seen as reflective of Malcolm X and the black power movement" (30). In using white characters to tell Black stories, Lee replaces the lived historical experience of communities of color in favor of more palatable presentations of America's long history of racial oppression.

The use of the mutant metaphor to stand in for race does not fully emerge until two years into the series. Initially the X-Men are shown to be wealthy, privileged superhumans who are allies of the federal government. A caption tells us, "The band of super-human teenagers are driven to the airport in Professor Xavier's specially-built Rolls Royce, with its dark-tinted windows" (Lee, *X-Men*, vol. 1, p. 17). When the X-Men thwart one of Magneto's plans to enslave the human race, the US military applauds the X-Men for their efforts. A US Army general assures the X-Men, "You call yourselves the X-Men! I will not ask you to reveal your true identities, but I promise you that before this day is over, the name X-Men will be the most honored in my command!" (23). Professor X is shown to have a positive relationship with the FBI, which is problematic, given that at the time, J. Edgar Hoover's domestic counterintelligence program COINTELPRO was busy infiltrating the Black Panther Party, which Hoover considered the greatest threat to America (Grady-Willis, 374). Even the general public in the early issues seems to appreciate the X-Men. As one passerby exclaims to Cyclops, "Say! You're Cyclops, aren't you? One of the X-Men! Never thought you jokers were for real! Put it there, pal!" (Lee, *X-Men*, vol. 1, p. 28). In these early issues, the X-Men in no way represent persecuted or marginalized minorities. The notion of the X-Men being *Homo superior* aligns more with the Nietzschean superman than it does with a persecuted minority. Professor X explains to his students, "You are each more than mere Homo sapiens—you are the forerunners of Homo superior—superior man!" (148). Their difference is unequivocally a power that manifests in the ability to fly, superior agility, laser beam eyes, telekinesis, and profoundly transformative brain power. These were white superheroes who invoked the Nietzschean superman and had nothing to do with any promotion of racial diversity.

More than a year after the first issue, in issue 8 (November 1964), the stories begin to suggest that the public that had once embraced the X-Men in the early issues had now come to mistrust them deeply. One bystander says, "I've heard there are many such mutants in hiding . . . waiting to take over the world!" (173). Another bystander who sees one of the X-Men in public notes the waning trust in the X-Men: "Did you see how he ran past us?? Like he was afraid of us . . . like he knew he's our enemy! He probably saved that kid just to throw us off guard . . . to make us think mutants aren't dangerous. But he can't fool us! C'mon . . . let's get im, before he loses himself in the crowd!" (173). The first X-Men story arc that makes a clear antiracist statement did not appear for another year, in November 1965, in a story featuring a character named Dr. Trask, who begins a public campaign to villainize the X-Men. Trask notes:

> We've been so busy worrying about the cold wars, hot wars, atom bombs, and the like, that we've overlooked the greatest menace of all! Mutants walk among us! Hidden! Unknown! Waiting—!—Waiting for their moment to strike! They are mankind's most deadly enemy! For only they have the actual power to conquer the human race! Even as we speak, they are out there—scheming, plotting, planning—thinking we don't suspect! (Lee, *X-Men*, vol. 2, p. 68)

Trask's fearmongering replicates the reconstruction methodology of instilling fear in the hearts of white women via the myth of the Black rapist: "Dr. Trask warns that the superior abilities and supernatural powers of the hidden mutants will enable them to enslave the human race replacing our civilization with their own.... It is even possible that the superior mutants will consider normal men as little more than savages, suitable only for forced labor and gladiatorial sport!" (71). Trask's diabolical plan involves creating an army of robots called Sentinels that are trained to hunt and kill mutants. While this plotline effectively demonstrates the power of culturally villainizing minorities, the metaphor soon fails because the aspects of the X-Men that render them a minority allow them to rather easily defeat Trask and the Sentinels, suggesting that while the X-Men are vulnerable to persecution, discrimination, and prejudice, their powers are likely to always win the day, a message that minimizes the life-and-death plight of American minorities and their challenges.

In the 1980s, another level was added to the X-Men's role as a metaphor for race. In the 1981 "Days of Future Past" story line, the US government uses Sentinels to exterminate mutants and herd them into concentration camps. This story's connection to the Holocaust is repeatedly made explicit, as when a scientist tells Professor X that she believes the government is planning "registration of mutants today, gas chambers tomorrow" (Fingeroth, *Disguised as Clark Kent*, 127). The next year, Chris Claremont gave Magneto a past as an Auschwitz survivor (Malcolm, 152). Although not stated outright, this suggests that Magneto should be considered Jewish, as does the fact that he later moved to Israel. However, his Jewish origins were not definitively established in the comics until the 2008–9 story *X-Men: Magneto Testament* (Fingeroth, 117; Pak and Di Giandomenico). Claremont reveals that Professor X and Magneto first met in Israel, where Xavier was attempting to heal traumatized

Holocaust survivors, and the two men fought and defeated the Nazi villain, SHIELD foe, and leader of Hydra, Baron Wolfgang von Strucker (128). Claremont has compared Magneto to Menachem Begin, who was considered a terrorist by the British during World War II but eventually legitimized himself politically and became prime minister of Israel (Malcolm, 144). Like Malcolm X, Begin embraced whatever measures he deemed necessary to defend his people. What Claremont does not say is that Begin's defense of his people involved the ethnic cleansing of the Palestinian people from the land that became Israel. The Israeli occupation of Palestine represents yet another example of Western colonialism in action and demonstrates the in-between racial position of Jews. Under the Nazis, Jews were a persecuted minority who were subjected to one of the most brutal campaigns of genocide in human history. However, in response to the atrocity of the Holocaust, within years of the end of World War II, Israel expelled hundreds of thousands of Palestinians from their homeland, thereby transforming themselves in a matter of years from victims of ethnic violence by white supremacists to perpetrators of ethnic violence against brown-skinned people (Pappe). Malcolm X, by contrast, identified his struggle with that of all colonized people throughout the world, especially Africans and Muslims.

Lee perpetuated white supremacy in many of the same ways as EC despite both their claims of being antiracist. For example, the character of Jean Grey, known at the time as Marvel Girl, is initially "treated as an object of love for the male members of the team and has many domestic traits associated with the housewife ideal of the post–World War II America.... Her personality largely remains that of a domestic girl hoping to find meaning in a romantic relationship with Cyclops" (Darowski, 47). As noted in earlier chapters, in the logic of white supremacy, subjugating white women, who alone have the power to taint white blood purity, is crucial. In this manner, *The X-Men* echoed many EC Comics in its failure to address intersectionalities relevant to structural racism like race and gender. Within the first several issues of *The X-Men*, Jean Grey is demeaned, sexualized, and domesticated. For example, she is the default cook for the crew on the cook's day off (122). Even the name of the group, the X-*Men*, marginalizes her. When she first arrives to Xavier's school, she is immediately sexualized and objectified by the other team members. First Iceman asks, "Where did the new doll go? Oh there she is! Wowee!" Then Cyclops adds, "Looks like she was poured into that uniform." Finally Beast chimes in, "Easy, gorgeous! We were just passin' by! Don't go getting' mad!" (16). Lee also sets up a possible love triangle that is eventually dropped among Cyclops, the Professor, and Jean. The Professor considers, "As though I could help worrying about the one I love! But I can

Stan Lee (script) and Jack Kirby (pencils), "X-Men." Originally published in *The X-Men* #1 (September 1963). Reprinted in *Marvel Masterworks: The X-Men*, vol. 1 (Marvel Worldwide, 2015). © Marvel Characters.

never tell her! I have no right! Not while I'm the leader of the X-Men, and confined to this wheel-chair" (51).

For those who have read Lee's autobiography, the treatment of the character Marvel Girl is not surprising. Lee's mostly ghostwritten memoir is filled with tongue-in-cheek sexist comments. At one point he laments, "Today, one of my great regrets is that I cannot remember the name of the daughter of the neighborhood candy store proprietor with whom I lost my virginity" (Lee, *Excelsior*, 15). At another point, he boasts about dating a sex worker without having to pay her, bragging, "We hit it off together and became good friends. The reason I know we hit it off so well is because she didn't ask for any payment. It turned out she was a very high-priced lady who was, to put it as gallantly as possible, in business for herself" (50). Finally, Lee also at one point announces that he forbade his wife to work, admitting that "during those early days as newlyweds, before the age of political correctness, I decided ... to declare myself master of the household.... So I said to Joanie, 'You've got to give up modeling and any thoughts of ever again being an actress. I don't want a wife of mine to work'" (71).

The construction of Jean's identity as a woman raises issues related to white women and second-wave feminism. Her femininity is held up on a pedestal, and she is both protected and sexualized. As noted earlier, her parents, to her surprise, force her out of Professor X's school at one point and make her attend college, where she is pursued by a popular white athlete. These are not issues important to women of color at the time. Third-wave feminism, marked in part by a focus on diversity and intersectionalities, was a response to the previous waves' primary focus on Christian, heterosexual, able-bodied, middle-class, white women within a certain age range. For example, one of the major issues for white women in first-wave feminism was the right to work. For Black women, who largely dominated the domestic worker industry, simply finding a job was not the problem. For white women in the second wave of feminism, sexual autonomy and access to birth control were major issues. Black women looked askance at this goal, since white doctors had been eugenically sterilizing them for decades. Marvel Girl's sexual autonomy and indecision regarding her education were clearly issues central to white women in the sixties. Black women were not yet given these choices. While eventually second-wave feminism would transform into a third wave, Black women in the 1970s and 1980s established a movement of their own called womanism. Because most "women of color ... [found] that their experiences and perspectives were not always reflected in the agendas of feminist organizations, nor reflected in early feminist theorizing" (Launius and Hassel, 116), Black women writers such as Gayl Jones, Toni Morrison, and Alice Walker "[proposed] an alternative ideological frame—womanism—that [could] incorporate and transform the radical elements of black nationalism, as well as enable a fictional creation of a new black femininity that [exceeded] the bounds of Black Aesthetic ideology" (Dubey, 148). As Madhu Dubey notes:

> When, in the 1970s, white women began to seek employment as a means of escaping the confinement of middle-class domesticity, they could not ... strike a sympathetic chord in most black women, who historically had been workers out of economic necessity rather than choice.... Moreover, the Women's Liberation movement targeted the patriarchal family structure as the primary site of women's oppression, but for most black women ... maintaining a stable family

structure was a high priority. Black women greeted with suspicion the Women's Liberation movement's emphasis on sexual liberation, for American patriarchal ideology, in order to preserve the white lady on her pedestal, had always typecast the black woman as a promiscuous sexual animal. (16)

Just as the first and second waves of feminism in the United States alienated women of color who did not identify with the demands white women were making, Stan Lee's depiction of Marvel Girl as a member of a persecuted minority scarcely resembled any of the issues besetting women of color in the 1960s.

In addition to the X-Men, Stan Lee and Marvel Comics created other superheroes and story lines that were racially problematic. The previous chapter examined the use of the Yellow Peril stereotype in the Mandarin, the nemesis of Marvel's Iron Man, and how the Black Panther preserved many of the primitivist tropes of the jungle genre. Many of Marvel's other characters suffered from similar flaws caused by unexamined racial stereotypes. Two of the clearest examples of such stereotypes in a Marvel character are the Thing and the Hulk, white men who are transformed into oversized brutes with colored skin who conform to common stereotypes about Black men. bell hooks has written that Black men have been "seen as animals, brutes, natural born rapists, and murderers. . . . They are victimized by stereotypes that were first articulated in the nineteenth century but hold sway over the minds and imaginations of citizens of this nation in the present day" (*We Real Cool*, xii). The stereotype of the violent Black man relates closely to ideas about people of color that circulated in primitivist and colonialist discourse, which is not surprising, given that Black people were originally brought to the Americas from Africa as slaves, justified by the idea that they were less than human. While the Thing and the Hulk are not Black, they draw heavily on this interconnected set of racist ideas and motifs. They occupy a fictional racial borderland that dramatizes the perils of the color line and the importance of maintaining a clear separation between white and Black, order and chaos, civilization and the beast within. When that border breaks down, as it does in the creation of these characters, problems result. The primary conflict of both these characters, especially the Hulk, is their difficulty in controlling their temper and maintaining their humanity—in other words, of slipping into the realm of savagery represented in white thought by the specter of blackness.

The Thing was a member of the Fantastic Four, a superhero team that has been much praised for ushering in a new era of flawed superheroes and superhero teams. Lee is often credited with creating superheroes that were more like real human beings in their vulnerability to the human condition (Lee, *Excelsior*, 114). First appearing in 1961, *The Fantastic Four* presented a group of individuals who were irrevocably changed due to exposure to cosmic rays on a scientific mission to outer space. However, their mutations based on these rays hierarchized the fighting team along racial lines, led by the older white male, Reed Richards, known as Mr. Fantastic. The most problematic character of the new team was Benjamin J. Grimm, whose exposure to the cosmic rays literally dehumanized him into the Thing. His most salient visible characteristic is that he is no longer phenotypically white, his grotesque orange body marking him as other. Lee claims, "The Thing was perhaps the first superhero who not only wasn't handsome, he was downright grotesque. Also, he had a hair-trigger temper and was always fussing, fighting, and feuding" (117). These qualities of hypermasculine blackness align with entrenched stereotypes about Black men in both the American South and Africa. What makes the Thing even more problematic is that he is the only one who clearly wishes that he could be normal again. While much of this desire can be attributed to the transformation of his physique, it is entirely plausible that his skin color plays a role in this as well. The resulting implication is that nonwhite skin colors are monstrous.

The Thing's racial persona is complicated by the fact that he also displays various signs of Jewish identity. Danny Fingeroth has observed, "Like the classic Jewish use of humor to offset tragedy, the Thing was always cracking sarcastic, self-deprecating jokes worthy of the best Catskills Jewish comedians" (*Disguised as Clark Kent*, 97). The Thing's Jewishness was always left unstated until 2002, when it was definitively revealed in *The Fantastic Four* #56 that he was Jewish. In this issue, Grimm explains the secrecy surrounding his identity by stating, "There's enough trouble in this world without people thinkin' Jews are all monsters like me." Another character in the story, an old Jewish pawnbroker whom the Thing rescues from a supervillain named Powderkeg, compares the Thing to the legendary Jewish protective monster, the Golem. Finally, after apprehending Powderkeg, the latter asks whether he is really Jewish, explaining, "It's just . . . you don't look Jewish" (Waid and Wieringo). Grimm's identity is specifically working-class Jewish, as he was part of a street gang in his youth in a poor, dangerous area of the Lower East Side, a fact that was often contrasted with the intellectual, scientific outlook of the team's leader, Reed Richards. The Thing's Jewishness complicates his identification as primitive and Black. On the one hand, it points to a shared lack of status and perceived rationality between the white ethnic working class and racial minorities. On the other hand, white ethnics, including Jews, always occupied an intermediary position between upper-class WASPs and people of color, from whom they were always clearly distinguished.

If the Thing's racialization is ambiguous, that of the Hulk, his successor as a monstrous superhero, is much less so. Emboldened by the success of *The Fantastic Four* and the Thing in particular, Stan Lee hoped to continue his success with creating new superheroes by creating "a good-looking monster, or at least a sympathetic-looking monster," who also had nonwhite phenotypical skin but was the hero/antihero of his own comic (Lee, *Excelsior*, 121). The Incredible Hulk is exposed to gamma rays instead of cosmic rays and is forever changed from a white man into a hypermasculine beast marked most saliently by his skin color. Lee notes about the Hulk:

> Instead of a colorful costume, I'd give him colorful skin. So I made up my mind to color his flesh gray, which I thought would look kinda spooky. Unfortunately, in our first issue the printer had trouble keeping the shade of gray consistent from page to page. On some pages his skin was light gray, on others it was dark gray, and on some it looked black. Too confusing. So for the next issue I changed his skin color to green, a color the printer had less trouble with.... We now had the Hulk, who was the strongest living human on Earth, plus the Thing, who was almost as strong. (*Excelsior*, 122–23)

In the first few issues of *The Incredible Hulk*, the character's skin is at times iridescent gray, periwinkle blue, sometimes mauve, decidedly nonwhite but not yet green. Contrasted with the culturally, ethnically, and phenotypically white Dr. Banner, the Hulk then becomes an easy metaphor for otherness, particularly stereotypical American male blackness, and the many strains of ethnic masculinity that make up the American male. The Hulk conforms closely to the trope of the primitive brute, a stereotype of the African savage typically depicted as seminude, largely incapable of rational thought, and controlled by his emotions, especially his anger, which contrasts with the whiteness, rationality, and self-control of Bruce Banner. When Banner transforms into the Hulk, it is always against his will initially, but then he is seduced by the sheer physical power of his new body. When he becomes the Hulk, his way of speaking is brutish, uncultivated, and primitive: "Have to reach home! Formula inside home! Must get formula!" (Lee, *Hulk*, 9). In these early issues, the humanity of the Hulk is a regular theme: "Human? Why should I want to be human?" (10). Banner metamorphoses "into that brutal, bestial mockery of a human—that creature which fears nothing—which despises reason and worships power" (15).

Stan Lee (script) and Jack Kirby (pencils), "Enter...the Gargoyle!" Originally published in *The Incredible Hulk* #1 (May 1962). Reprinted in *Marvel Masterworks: The Incredible Hulk*, vol. 1 (Marvel Comics, 2003). © Marvel Characters.

While the Thing shares some of these features with the Hulk, the Thing was far more rational and controlled than the Hulk. The Thing was never a full brute but rather a hybrid of the civilized white man (albeit a working-class white man, who was already depicted as a bit gruff, overdeveloped physically, and underdeveloped mentally) and the brute. In both cases, the whiteness of Grimm and Banner is fragmented dichotomously, the white half symbolizing normativity and the nonwhite half grotesqueness and violent aggression. These identities also have a sexual element that further mirrors the myth of the Black rapist, a myth responsible for perhaps hundreds of thousands of killings of Black men over hundreds of years. The relationships with the women the ineffectual doppelgängers seek are complicated by the shifting identities of the protagonists. The Thing resents Reed for having access to Sue Storm, just as Banner is unable to succeed in his pursuit of Betty

Ross because of his shape-shifting into the Hulk. When the Hulk tries to go after Betty Ross, he is considered a rapist, mirroring the myth of the Black rapist promulgated by white racists to justify the murder of Black bodies.

Marvel's main war comic, *Sgt. Fury and His Howling Commandos* (1963–74), is another example of Lee's use of racial stereotypes. The series was the result of a bet between Lee and Marvel's owner, Martin Goodman. To prove that the success of Marvel's comics came from their style, not their characters, Lee attempted to create an intentionally bad comic and turn it into a success. Lee's example of a terrible comic was, in his words, "the first ethnic comicbook" (*Excelsior*, 161–62). He recalls:

> I'll do a war book with the worst title I can come up with. . . . Then, to make my task even tougher, I gave our hero, Sgt. Nick Fury, the most ethnically mixed platoon I could dream up. It consisted of Jewish Izzy Cohen, Italian Dino Manelli, Irish Dum-Dum Dugan, Gabriel Jones, a black man. . . . There was even a gay platoon member named Percival Pinkerton. . . . So there it was, a comicbook with a terrible title, starring a platoon made up of various minorities—something for every bigot to dislike—and featuring nothing but World War II stories that everyone told me "weren't relevant to today's readers." (162)

Based on this account, Lee saw ethnic and racial diversity as potential marketing weaknesses rather than strengths, which pointed to an ideologically based profit motive that catered to white supremacy. The characters he created were all highly stereotypical, entrenching racial stereotypes rather than combating them. Lee would later say, in the introduction to his autobiography, that he wanted to give the platoon some diversity, since that was what the army was really like.

To make matters worse, the leader of the Howling Commandos is a hypermasculine, able-bodied, cisgender, heteronormative white man, "Sgt. Nick Fury: Six foot two of steel-muscled, iron-nerved fighting man! Fury believes in making his men fear him so much that they would rather face hopeless odds than face his anger!" (2). The one "nonethnic" character besides Fury is "Jonathan 'Junior' Juniper: Fresh out of an Ivy-League college, Junior is the cheerful eager-beaver of the group! But don't let his youthful smile fool you! He's fast as a panther, and just as dangerous!" (2). While all the Howling Commandos are stereotyped, including Fury himself, perhaps the most egregiously stereotyped figure is the Black character "Gabriel Jones: 'Gabe' used to blow the sweetest trumpet this side of Carnegie Hall! Now he gives out with the hot licks on the field of battle . . . but his notes are just as true, and his hand and heart as steady as ever!" (3). Jones often clutches his trumpet even in the heat of battle, reminiscent of Linus and his ubiquitous blue blanket from *Peanuts*, and very often actually plays it as the other men fight the enemy. This is akin to presenting African Americans as minstrelsy, which often included demeaning stereotypes, for the entertainment of white people. The men frequently cajole Gabriel to "play us a little jazz to liven things up, huh?" (6) while they are fighting Nazis and the very white supremacist ideology that the comic reflects.

Stan Lee's whitewashing of race extends to his own name. Like Jacob Kurtzberg, who changed his name to Jack Kirby, and Robert Kahn, who changed his name to Bob Kane, Lee replaced his birth name, Stanley Lieber, with one that was more WASP sounding. All these decisions can likely be explained as a result of the overt and covert anti-Semitism that was still very much pervasive in American culture before and after World War II. What makes Stan Lee's name change puzzling is that Lee claimed his Jewishness had nothing to do with it. Rather, he offered time and again that the name change came about because he had big literary plans for his real name: "I had decided that nothing would stop me from one day writing the Great American Novel. . . . Thus, I was caught up in the fantasy of using a pen name, something suitable for strips, while saving my real name for the saga that would make me immortal" (*Excelsior*, 26). While it is impossible to say whether this explanation was the full story, his denial of race as a factor in this decision would be in keeping with the general whitewashing of race that pervaded Lee's work.

CAPTAIN AMERICA AND BLACK NATIONALISM

In the late 1960s, the racial discourse in Marvel comics made a significant change in direction. It began with the creation of the Black Panther in 1966 and continued in the pages of Spider-Man, Captain America, and other superhero comics. Feeling the pressure from the civil rights movement and its more radicalized successor, the Black Power or Black nationalist movement, Marvel began advocating for various liberal causes, including the civil rights and antiwar movements, while at the same time disparaging the confrontational methods of radicals such as the Black nationalists. In fact, Marvel comics in the late 1960s and early 1970s carried on what amounted to an ongoing smear campaign against Afrocentrist culture and Black nationalism. Marvel's racial rhetoric during this period echoed that of J. Edgar Hoover, who declared the Black Panthers the greatest threat to law and order in the United States and used the COINTELPRO program to attack the Black Panthers and other radical groups using illegal tactics (Grady-Willis, 374). Marvel's overall attitude toward Black characters is well summed up by William L. Svitavsky's description of the period's Black superheroes as comprising "a veneer of streetwise attitude with a core of values comfortable for middle-class readers" (Gavaler, *Superhero Comics*, 164). Anything that exceeded that comfort zone was rendered anathema.

This change in tone related directly to these same comics' changing perspective on the Vietnam War, since both the war and racial injustice were part of the larger political conflict between the youth generation of hippies and radicals and their parents' generation, which upheld the social and political white power structure. Superhero comics responded to the movements by demanding racial justice but sought to limit the extent of those changes and to protect whites from having to accept nonwhites as fully equal. Marvel comics during this period continually emphasized that while the critique of racism and white supremacy was valid, the problem of race relations could only be solved if Black people agreed to work within the system, assimilate into the white power structure, and abandon any tactics that were not approved by the system's white gatekeepers.

These issues surfaced in many Marvel superhero comics, including Iron Man, Spider-Man, and the Hulk, but it was in *Captain America* from 1969 to 1975 that they were developed most fully. A number of developments in *Captain America* that were in tension if not outright contradiction with one another occurred in a complicated chronological sequence that loops, doubles back, reverses itself, rises to a climax, and then collapses. They include the following, not necessarily in chronological order. First, Captain America has an identity crisis in response to the widespread critique of the government and whiteness, both of which he is closely identified with. Second, Captain America trains a grateful Black sidekick, the Falcon, who regards him as a mentor. Third, the Falcon graduates from Cap's sidekick to his partner, and the two attempt to work together within the bounds of law to improve the situation for Black people. Fourth, their main contribution to uplifting the Black community and dismantling white supremacy is to fight Black nationalist groups and reveal them as either criminal gangs, fronts for supervillains, or both. Fifth, the Falcon attempts to create an identity of his own, separate from Captain America, centered on his blackness but without embracing the "extremist" views and tactics of Black nationalism. And sixth, toward the end of this period, racial stereotypes begin to reappear in the comic, signaling the end of this attempt to dismantle Captain America's white supremacy. Each of these has its own ideological content, but the most significant thing about them is that they were all occurring more or less simultaneously. No single ideological position could satisfy all the demands and pressures being put on Marvel and Captain America by various different forces and constituencies, so the end result was inevitably rather incoherent.

Captain America's identity crisis was given dramatic form in a 1970 story described at the end of chapter 3, but this narrative line is curtailed by the addition of the Falcon as Captain America's partner. The Falcon served to forestall Cap's identity crisis, but it reemerged in 1974, when Steve Rogers briefly abandoned his identity as Captain America, becoming "Nomad, the man without a country," before resuming the mantle of Captain America in early 1975. In the Falcon's first appearances, he is essentially a sidekick who is subservient to Captain America, an avatar of whiteness. The Falcon has no superpowers, only a trained hawk who aids him. Stranded on a tropical island, Captain America gives him some abbreviated combat training and convinces him to become the Falcon and join him in fighting the villains on the island. As the Falcon tells Captain America in a 1974 story, "Before we got off that goofy island, you'd molded me into the man I'd always wanted to be! Ignoring your own problems, you'd made me—the Falcon!" (Englehart et al., vol. 4). Captain America often protects the Falcon from his own inexperience, as when the Falcon charges the Red Skull while he is wielding the Cosmic Cube in issue 119, and Cap warns him, "You don't know what you're up against!" (Lee et al., vol. 2). The Falcon's identity as a superhero is thus wholly the invention of Captain America, whom the Falcon looks up to as a mentor and desires the approval of. The Falcon tells Cap in issue 118 that "with a teacher like you, I'll be the greatest!" The Falcon expresses disappointment in issue 132 when Captain America's old sidekick, Bucky, seems to return and takes the place at Cap's side that the Falcon wants for himself. He ponders wistfully, "Man—wouldn't it have been somethin' if only Cap—Awww, nuts! What's the use'a dreamin'?" (Lee et al., vol. 3).

After a few more appearances in *Captain America*, the Falcon and Captain America form a partnership, and the Falcon's name is added to the title of the series, ending his tutelary relationship with Captain America, at least in theory. The two become partners at the end of issue 133, when the Falcon announces his mission to help the people of Harlem, and Captain America unilaterally announces, without consulting the Falcon, that the two are now partners. The next issue reveals that the Falcon, whose real name is Sam Wilson, is a social worker in his civilian identity, a role in which he continues his mission of improving the Harlem community. Like the Black Panther, the Falcon works within the framework of the white power structure. As Captain America puts it in issue 126, "He's not a killer . . . not a criminal! He vowed to work within the law . . . the same as I!" Earlier, in *Tales of Suspense* #97 (January 1968), Captain America goes undercover as a police officer, in the course of which he remarks that "it's men like that—the thousands of unsung cops on the beat—who keep our streets from turning into jungles" (Lee et al., vol. 1). Tellingly, this issue also features Captain America's first encounter with the Black Panther, who is referred to in the next issue as dwelling within "the heart of darkest Africa." The rhetoric of Black ghettos as "jungles" and of Africa as the "heart of darkness" links the racism of colonialism directly to the racism of segregation and uses this shared rhetoric to justify the necessity of using police to control the junglelike and hence savage behavior of urban Black Americans.

One of the critiques of both the civil rights movement and the Black Power movement was that the law is tilted against Black people and other people of color, but this idea remains entirely foreign to Captain America, who assumes that the law is a neutral arbiter rather than part of the mechanism for maintaining white supremacy. Racism and its effects on Black people are not actually addressed in the series. The main evils that Captain America and the Falcon fight are Black nationalism and criminal gangs, which are often one and the same. White police, store owners, and government officials are all shown as good guys who want what is best for Harlem. Various Black characters step forward to vouch for Captain America. At the end of issue 126, the Falcon tells Captain America, "Your skin may be a different color . . . but there's no man alive I'm prouder to call . . . brother!" Similarly, in issue 142, while Captain America is posing as a police officer to solve a string of murders, a sympathetic Black reverend tells a Black nationalist named Leila that she is "creating false tales to suit your own hatreds and prejudices! The policeman Steve Rogers is a friend of this neighborhood!"

Other than run-of-the-mill supervillains, the primary antagonists of Captain America and Harlem during this period are Black nationalist groups, which are always revealed to be secretly controlled behind the scenes by supervillains, either Black or white. The Diamond Heads are a Black nationalist group that is also a street gang, led by a supervillain named Diamond Head, who wears a diamond-like mask in the shape of an African tribal mask. The supervillain Modok creates a huge monster called Bulldozer, who becomes a hero to many in Harlem by demolishing slum buildings. The crime boss Stone Face poses as a Black nationalist to shake down a government official.

The pièce de résistance is a three-part story featuring a group called the People's Militia, the first two parts of which are titled "Power to the People!" and "Burn, Whitey, Burn!" (Lee et al., vol. 3). In the story, the Falcon attends a meeting of the People's Militia with Leila, where he objects to the fact that the group's leader wears a mask to hide his identity (even though both he and Captain America also wear masks to hide their identities). The leader, called the Man, tells the group that they will burn Harlem that night so that "the whites won't be able to make us live in this slum any longer." Supporters in the crowd yell, "This is the start of the black revolution!," "Black is beautiful," and "Power to the people!" Their expressions are wild and frenzied. Captain America then rips the mask off the Man and reveals that he is none other than the Nazi supervillain the Red Skull.

The criticism of Black nationalism as nothing more than race hatred is far from accurate. The Black Panther Party, the best-known and most influential Black nationalist organization, had a wide-ranging political platform that advocated for social justice in many areas and was decades ahead of its time in a number of areas. While the Black Panthers were often accused of fomenting violence and rebellion for their own sake, Charles Jones and Judson Jeffries argue that in reality a

> critical facet of the legacy of the BPP is linked to the organization's commitment to the virtue and dignity of individuals regardless of race, gender, or sexual orientation. Unlike many of the Black Power organizations of the period, the BPP demonstrated a willingness to enter into functional alliances with White leftist groups. Moreover, Panthers were early advocates of the rights of women and homosexuals during the embryonic stage of each of these liberation movements. (31)

This narrative of the bad Black rebels who refuse to follow the rules of the white power structure repeats the classic narrative structure and primitivist, colonialist ideology of jungle comics. In all these stories, Black nationalist criticism of white supremacy and intentions to uplift Black people is depicted as nothing more than racism in reverse. In issue 126, the Falcon explains that the Diamond Heads are "like a black version of the Klan! All they preach is hate whitey! They're dangerous fanatics! They don't care who suffers . . . or who gets hurt! They can set our progress back a hundred years!" (Lee et al., vol. 2).

Although the Falcon rejects the ideas and tactics of the Black nationalists, he is swayed by Leila's criticism of his lack of racial consciousness, as when Leila tells him in issue 143 that she calls him "our friendly, neighborhood Uncle Tom" and says that he is not on "the black side." He responds to the latter accusation by saying that "revolution isn't the answer." After the Red Skull's control over the People's Militia is broken, the Falcon begins to adopt and repeat some of Leila's ideas. When Cap speculates that "all's quiet for now—but who knows what little something it will take to make them explode again!" the Falcon replies, "I don't think I like the way you put that, partner! They—we—got reason to blow up! I got some value reassessing to do! I'll get in touch when I know where I stand!" The Falcon then wonders if he really is an Uncle Tom, but he also recognizes that "on the other hand—I can't go along with the militant methods of the People's Militia!" Starting in the next issue, the two partners temporarily split up, but the break is never complete. In issue 144, the Falcon continues to criticize Captain America, who admits that whites deserve criticism but tells Sam, "Anger and hatred won't help either side." However, the Falcon has embraced the cause of Black Power, at least apparently, telling Cap that "I'm gonna be proud, baby . . . proud to be black," and then unveiling a new costume with elements of soul style. He is not ready to reject Cap, telling him, "Let's just shake and say it's been a gas! I owe you a lot . . . but now I have to get into my own bag!" Soon thereafter, the Falcon tells a crowd in Harlem, "I've split with Captain America—even though he isn't what you call him! I want to devote myself to helping my own people . . . and I can do that best all by myself!" The next issue, he gets a call from Nick Fury, saying that Captain America needs his help, and he tells him, "I've sworn off as Cap's partner . . . yet I can't say no if he's in a jam!"

Brannon Costello has written that Black sidekicks to white superheroes fit into the paternalistic racial paradigm in which "white southerners treated African Americans not simply as inferior but as childlike, as requiring the allegedly beneficent care of a white father figure" (73). Costello points out that superhero sidekicks and African Americans in paternalistic American culture "train at the side of their heroic father-figures . . . but, with some notable recent exceptions, they remain the sidekick, never aging into maturity and becoming superheroes in their own right. The promise that they will one day grow up and fill their masters' shoes is rarely fulfilled, their adulthood endlessly deferred in a fantasy world where characters age incredibly slowly, if at all" (74). *Captain America* comes very close to the point of establishing an independent identity for the Falcon but ultimately shies away from granting him full autonomy. The series never successfully establishes a Black identity for the Falcon that manages to balance his loyalty to Captain America and the white power structure he embodies, the Falcon's desire to establish an independent racial identity, and his hostility to Black nationalism.

DC's team comic featuring Green Lantern and Green Arrow, which ran in *Green Lantern* from #76 (April 1970) to #122 (November 1979), provides an interesting counterpoint to Captain America and the Falcon. Like the latter, Green Lantern and Green Arrow represent conflicting positions, but in this case, both are white. Green Arrow held quite leftist views, especially by the standards of mainstream comic books, and was arguably the most radical character in mainstream comics during this period. Green Lantern was a more moderate liberal who was continually defending himself against Green Arrow's accusations that Green Lantern lacked moral courage and was overly deferential to authority. In turn, Green Lantern repeatedly claimed that Green Arrow was foolhardy and frequently acted without thinking. Nevertheless, the two are presented as best friends who need each other. The series dealt with a number of social issues in addition to race, including labor issues, sexism, poverty, drug use, and environmentalism.

One pivotal moment comes in *Green Lantern Co-starring Green Arrow* #76 (April 1970) when a disheveled old Black man tells Green Lantern, "I been readin' about you . . . how you work for the blue skins . . . and how ona planet someplace you helped out the orange skins . . . and you done considerable for the purple skins! Only there's skins you never bothered with—! . . . the black skins! I want to know . . . how come?! Answer me that, Mr. Green Lantern!" (O'Neil and Adams, vol. 1, p. 15). Green Lantern admits that he cannot answer the man. Later in the same issue, Green Arrow refers to the assassinations of Martin Luther King Jr. and Bobby Kennedy, then declares, "Something is wrong! Something is killing us all . . . ! Some hideous moral cancer is rotting our very souls!" (30). In *Green Lantern* #78, a Native American character delivers a blistering critique of white colonialism, telling the superheroes that "the white-eyes swiped our land, broke treaties, herded us like animals onto reservations. . . . Now, the big-bellies in the capital are talking about taking away our fishing rights! Next, they'll want the marrow from our bones" (68). The villain in this issue is a white supremacist who vows to exterminate all other races.

Despite such strongly worded antiracist statements, the series at times still dealt in racist caricatures. In *Green Lantern* #79, Green Arrow dresses up in stereotypical Native American garb to impersonate the ghost of a tribal elder. The costume includes a feather headdress such as that worn by the Lakota Sioux, although the story is set in the Pacific Northwest. In this guise, he attempts to inspire a Native American tribe to return to their glory days, telling them, "You were once a proud people . . . a great people . . . and you can be again! First, though, you have to stop playing doormat . . . and be willing to fight for your rights!" (98). This is a classic white savior trope and is also absurdly ignorant of the history of extensive Native American struggle against white conquest and domination.

A similar dynamic plays out in *Green Arrow* #87 (December 1971–January 1972) when the Guardians, the source of Green Lantern's power, determine that a new backup Green Lantern must be chosen. They select a Black man, John Stewart, who is first introduced when he stands up to an abusive white cop. Green Lantern is initially predisposed against Stewart, seeing him as too violent and disrespectful to authority, a classic example of racist views of Black people. The Guardians push back against this, telling Jordan, "We are not interested in your petty bigotries!" (106). When Jordan approaches Stewart with the offer, Stewart requests to be called Black Lantern, although this does not appear to actually be put into use (107). Stewart's first adventure as a Green Lantern brings out conflicts between him and Jordan over race, as Jordan orders Stewart to protect a racist senator. Stewart asserts, "He's a racist . . . and he figures on climbing to the White House on the backs of my people!" (110). Jordan defends the senator's right to free speech and orders Stewart to protect the senator. Stewart soon uncovers a false-flag assassination attempt against the senator. The assassination was planned to appear to be the work of Black nationalists but was actually planned by the senator himself to spread fear of racial violence. The racial dynamics of this story are complex. Both Jordan's moderation and Stewart's more radical critique of white supremacy are shown to have merit, but ultimately Stewart is given the last word, as his suspicions about the racist senator are proved correct.

Marvel's and DC's explorations of racial conflict were a response to the specific social and political situation of the late 1960s and early 1970s. When the political context of the United States shifted, so did the politics of superhero comics, which swung back in the opposite direction. In 1973, *Captain America* began a return to outright racism, drawing the comic's engagement with Black nationalism to a close. The most obvious example of this was the 1973 story arc that took place in issues 164 to 167. In the story line's first issue, a villain named Nightshade, who calls herself "the queen of werewolves" and whose costume is S&M wear (Englehart et al., vol. 4), turns the Falcon into a werewolf. As a werewolf, the Falcon is depicted as a giant, hulking monster, a classic brute, "a raging beast," as Cap calls him. Nightshade's boss turns out to be a Yellow Peril villain called the Yellow Claw, who is an evil magician with fangs. His first appearance had been in *Yellow Claw* #1 in October 1956, in which he was depicted as monstrous and inhuman. Another indication of the return to racism and white supremacy for the series occurred in June 1975, when the character of the Falcon was drastically rewritten. This is an example of a retcon, a fan term for "retroactive continuity," in which a character's origin or other history is later altered, creating a new narrative continuity that supplants the previous one. It was revealed that shortly before Sam met Captain America, the Red Skull brainwashed him using the Cosmic Cube to plant a sleeper agent as Captain America's ally. The Red Skull erased

Sam's true history, in which he had been a drifter and a drug dealer, to make him believe that he was actually a socially conscious social worker. So the first African American superhero was turned from a socially conscious do-gooder into a former drug dealer brainwashed by a Nazi supervillain. After two years in which Black nationalists had been repeatedly compared to Nazis and supervillains and tolerance and understanding had been urged as the only solution, the comic brought out a full-on racist caricature. In explaining why he programmed the Falcon the way he did, the Red Skull delivers an incisive critique of Captain America's racial consciousness. He tells Cap, "After so many years, I knew you well, Captain America! I knew exactly what kind of man would most appeal to your sniveling liberalism:—an upright, cheerful Negro, with a love for the same 'brotherhood' you cherish!"

Captain America had gone through his Nomad phase earlier the same year and then resumed the mantle of Captain America. Together, these two events brought this period of Captain America's attempt to grapple with whiteness and race to a close. Marvel's brand of antiracism in this period, like Fredric Wertham's and EC's, failed to fully commit to an anti-white-supremacist program, and while the attempt should be lauded, the ultimate failure also needs to be exposed. These issues were not resolved for superhero comics. They returned in the 1980s and subsequent decades in Will Eisner's stories about the history of the Bronx; in the deconstructive narrative of *Watchmen*, which dissected these questions with surgical precision; in Frank Miller's unapologetic racism and white supremacy; and in the reskinning of white superheroes with new Black characters. Many of the same issues were also raised by Robert Crumb, the leading figure in the countercultural world of underground comix, who pushed racist imagery to the maximum and then beyond. He did so in an effort to demonstrate the absurdity of this imagery, but as with Lee, Crumb's unexamined white racial frame meant that he perpetuated racist stereotypes rather than undermining them.

Chapter Five

ROBERT CRUMB'S CATHARTIC RACISM

Few cartoonists have stirred as much controversy as Robert Crumb. He was the leading member of the underground comix movement of the late sixties and early seventies that rebelled against the mainstream comics of their day. Because of Crumb's centrality to underground comix and the extent to which race was central to his work, this chapter deals extensively with Crumb, only examining other underground cartoonists briefly. Affiliated with the youth counterculture, these comics challenged the values and beliefs of the white establishment head-on, with sex and drugs by far their two most common subjects. Crumb's representations of blackness, central to his work, draw heavily on the same primitivist and colonialist ideology expressed in jungle comics, "funny animal" comics, and blackface minstrelsy. While reproducing the conventions and ideologies of those genres, complete with all their racism and white supremacy, Crumb reinterprets them as an expression and critique of the repressed desires of mainstream white culture. Despite the centrality of blackness to Crumb's work, it has not received the same amount of attention as Crumb's equally offensive representations of women. As Corey Creekmur has pointed out, discussions of Crumb's depictions of women and their sexism vastly outnumber discussions of his depictions of Black people, which have generally been "neglected (if not actively dodged)" (19, 25).

The counterculture is often seen as being allied with the progressive movements of its time, such as the civil rights, antiwar, and feminist movements, but this is a misleading conclusion. As Nadya Zimmerman has written, the counterculture was "pluralistic, not oppositional; it embodied an anything-goes mindset, not an antiestablishment stance; it attracted people who sought, on the whole, to disengage from mainstream society, not to transform it" (5). It was "populated by varied, heterogeneous groups, many of whom had nothing to do with one another, even within the smaller circles of the budding youth culture," and was not "an organized sociopolitical community: they were not oppositional in orientation, not bound by specific

Willie Mendes, "Oma." Originally published in *It Ain't Me Babe* (July 1970). Reprinted in *The Complete Wimmen's Comix*, vol. 1 (Fantagraphics, 2016). © Willie Mendes.

agendas, and not determined to bring about major changes in the system" (3). Consequently the counterculture had little interest in advancing the cause of racial equality. Corey Creekmur writes that the links that had existed between "black and white civil rights advocates in the recent past largely disappeared, and many African Americans found the hippie subculture an unappealing or simply irrelevant alternative; at its worst, the counterculture suggested an escape from rather than engagement with social problems" (28). Underground comix mirrored this stance. As Creekmur writes, with few exceptions, comix had a "limited and ambivalent engagement with race" (19). Race, like other topics in underground comix, was often used to shock the reader and violate mainstream taboos. Underground cartoonists were extremely interested in violating the Comics Code in any way possible. Since the Code forbade comics from ridiculing or attacking any racial group, doing so became one way for underground cartoonists to show their contempt for the Code or for any rules that square society might use to constrain their freedom (Rifas; Creekmur, 19).

One example of an underground comic that repeated traditional stereotypes about people of color was Willie Mendes's "Oma," which appeared in *It Ain't Me Babe* in 1970. *It Ain't Me Babe* was a groundbreaking feminist underground comic, the first of its kind in an underground scene that was overwhelmingly dominated by men who did not accept women as their equals, yet it was not immune from perpetuating racial stereotypes (Robbins, vii). "Oma" is an underground take on the western genre that is set on "a little Pioneer homestead" with a young couple and their infant child (3). Native Americans attack the farm, killing the man and child and kidnapping Oma, the wife and mother. A close-up of Oma's panicked face states: "The Indians rode up and grabbed the baby. What they did to it is best not pictured" (3). The Indians abandon Oma in a desert, where she encounters a radiant goddess in the sky and slays a giant black snake with a magic dagger. She then leaps off a cliff and is reunited with her husband and child. The story provides a narrative of female empowerment through a mystic journey, but this empowerment is clearly racialized as a white experience that uses the specter of evil Native Americans to provide the trauma that Oma must overcome. The cause of pain and suffering in this comic is another racial group rather than white patriarchy. Some later feminist underground comix provide examples of positive, sophisticated, interracial narratives, such as Chin Lyvely and Joyce Sutton's *Abortion Eve*, the cover of which depicts an interracial group of women discussing their feelings about abortion. "Oma" stands as a clear example of many underground cartoonists' oblivious acceptance of traditional white stereotypes about race, but works such as this were comparatively rare in most underground comix. By contrast, Robert Crumb's work is rife with racial stereotypes and violence far beyond anything found in "Oma."

CRITICAL EVALUATIONS OF RACE IN ROBERT CRUMB'S WORK

Robert Crumb's depictions of the absurdly racist character Angelfood McSpade exemplify the counterculture's lack of progressive politics, racist attitudes, and representations and perpetuation of white supremacy. Nearly all of Crumb's comics from the heyday of the underground period, in the late sixties and early seventies, are obscene in some way, but the ones dealing with race are among the worst. In some cases, they seem to have no purpose other than to shock the reader with their over-the-top racism. One of Crumb's most outrageous comics about race, published in 1968, consists of just a single row at the bottom of a page about Mr. Natural, one of Crumb's longest-running characters. It is a mock advertisement for a can of "Wildman Sam's Pure N----- Hearts," with Angelfood McSpade as the spokesperson. Two grinning white kids exclaim, "Hey Mom! Let's have n----- hearts for lunch," while McSpade chimes in, "Sho'nuff! Evvabody loves Wildman Sam's Pure N----- Hearts!" (Crumb, *Complete Crumb*, vol. 5, p. 10). This short strip is so ridiculously inhuman that it cannot be taken seriously or literally. The reader therefore has to search for its actual motivation, with satire being one possibility that springs to mind, but the same extremism and detachment from reality make it hard to see what serious comment or critique it might deliver.

Crumb himself does not deny the racism of his McSpade stories, among others, but asserts that the character is meant to shine a spotlight on the racist stereotypes that have been ingrained in American history, including American comic books. Crumb has said that "I release all that stuff inside myself: taboo words, taboo ideas. It pours out of me as sick as possible" (Rifas). Crumb sees McSpade as the product of his own internalized racial stereotypes, which he hopes to cathartically exorcise through their presentation on the page. He makes the same argument concerning his equally egregious sexist portrayals of women, for which he has also received criticism and which can also be found in his McSpade comics. Crumb asserts that his own viewpoint, marred by the white racial frame, is the controlling viewpoint, and the viewpoints of those who are offended by his comics are irrelevant. However, he ignores the fact that his viewpoint exists within a system of racial framing that normalizes his racist outlook and undermines any satirical elements in the work.

In an essay on Crumb, Corey Creekmur refocuses attention away from the question of whether Crumb was personally a racist and toward "how specific images from underground comix may or may not be described as racist in historical and cultural terms" (24). Comics scholars have generally been reluctant to examine the content of Crumb's racist images too closely. Leonard Rifas, for instance, argues that criticizing "the most extreme images" risks "wasting time by making a cartoonist a scapegoat for a broader social problem." Loath as we are to waste either our time or the reader's, we think that the question of what Crumb was actually communicating through these images, other than outrage, is an important one. We agree with Creekmur that the historical context is important to explore, and that it is more important than the question of whether Crumb was personally a racist. However, the question of the racial logic behind Crumb's comics is also important. Like the question of historical context, it is an analytic rather than an ethical issue.

The central trope in Crumb's racial worldview is that whites repress their sexual appetites and other instinctive drives while Blacks indulge them, a view that is closely linked to the discourse of primitivism. In the primitivist worldview, Blacks and other people of color are childlike and lack the advanced intellectual capacities of white people. They are therefore unable to control their impulses or practice self-discipline and are given to idle play. This is exactly the image of blackness that is put forward in Crumb's comics. Like other underground cartoonists and the hippie counterculture as a whole, Crumb is highly critical of the repression he sees in normative whiteness. He sees Black bodies, identities, and culture as an antidote to this repression, but this does not translate into an affirmative view of blackness. On the contrary, blackness is for him a site of total depravity.

The appropriation of blackness for the recuperation of whiteness fits into a recurring pattern in American culture, beginning with the blackface minstrelsy of the mid-nineteenth to mid-twentieth century, in which Black culture and the white mimicry of Black culture were used by whites to release desires and satisfy urges that were proscribed by the norms of proper white culture (Lott). This process occurred repeatedly in many areas of American culture. The white adoption of jazz, blues, rock, and hip-hop fits into this historical pattern. So did many early animated cartoons, especially Disney cartoons, often featuring Black characters, animal characters, or both, dancing joyfully and goofily to jazz music accompanied by various racist tropes, from jungle savages to minstrel features (Sammond, 18–32, 203–46). The ideal of using Black culture and identity as an escape from whiteness was also a strong feature of Beat culture in the 1950s, which was the direct predecessor and progenitor of the 1960s hippie culture (Creekmur, 28–29) and therefore an important influence on underground comix. Norman Mailer's essay "The White Negro," for example, is the classic statement of the Beats' fascination with Black culture. In his essay, Mailer jubilantly frames African Americans as psychopaths, asserting, "The psychopath, like the child, cannot delay the pleasures of gratification; and this trait is one of his underlying, universal characteristics. He cannot wait upon erotic gratification which convention demands should be preceded by the chase before the kill: he must rape" (590).

Crumb's use of blackness as an escape from the narrow, repressive strictures of whiteness thus fits into a long American tradition in which blackness is both appropriated by whites and denigrated. Crumb absorbed these influences through multiple avenues. The Beats were a formative influence on the hippie culture within which underground comix were embedded. Comics and animation also provided models for the process of white appropriation. As Corey Creekmur notes, the Disney film *Dumbo* (1941) featured "hipster black crows that seem to have directly influenced Crumb's similar characters in his early 'Fritz the Cat' stories" (27). Finally, one of Crumb's seminal influences, dating back to his early years, was the Donald Duck comics drawn by Carl Barks (Rosenkranz, 17). While Barks's comics were not as closely connected to minstrelsy as earlier Disney comics, they did inculcate a view of nonwhite cultures as repositories of resources to be appropriated by whites, as discussed in chapter 3.

While Crumb is undoubtedly correct that the stereotypes evident in his McSpade comics derive from the centuries of racism practiced by white Americans, this does not absolve him of responsibility for his decision to brazenly air these stereotypes. Crumb's assumption that his every thought or feeling deserves to be publicized, regardless of its content or impact, is a classic case of white privilege. Crumb sees such psychic unburdening as a revolt against the repressive nature of mainstream white society, which may well be an accurate description, but he assumes that the virtues of such rebellion outweigh any pain or damage he may cause to Black people (or women, if we consider his sexism rather than his racism). Far from being a rebellion against mainstream white society, this indifference to the welfare of people of other races is completely in line with the history of white America. Crumb sincerely despises and effectively skewers the repressive constraints of white America, but his racial egotism demonstrates that he has not even attempted to imagine how his characters might affect other people. His own privilege as a white man remains entirely invisible to him, a lack of awareness that fatally compromises his attempt to impugn mainstream white America.

Some scholars have argued that Crumb's offensiveness is so universal that it essentially has no meaning. Brandon Nelson, for instance, has written:

> designed to elicit outrage or disagreement from every political ideology, aesthetic preference, and personal taste simultaneously ... content to exist without further explication, representing a borderline nihilistic assertion that all ideology and social persuasion is ruinous and devoid of ethical value. (Nelson, 139–40)

Leonard Rifas and others make essentially the same point. In these readings, Crumb's comics violate the taboos or ideologies of others but have no ideology of their own. According to this line of thought, readers offended by his work are playing the role of cultural policemen, while Crumb is the happy and innocent vandal, smashing their sacred cows. However, Crumb's racial images and narratives are not merely indiscriminate attacks on others' ideologies; they have a racial ideology of their own. When we unpack them, we see that Crumb's criticisms of normative, mainstream whiteness simultaneously reproduce the beliefs, patterns, and stereotypes of earlier formations of whiteness. His shallow critiques mask a deeper agreement with, and reproduction of, whiteness marked by anti-Black racism.

CIVIL RIGHTS IN CRUMB'S EARLY WORK

Crumb's work was not always as virulently racist as it eventually became. The comics he produced as a teenager, in which he was already an accomplished cartoonist, demonstrate an earnest sympathy for the civil rights movement and lack the racist content of his later work. As his work matured over the course of the 1960s, however, racist themes increasingly entered his work, subtly at first and then more explicitly. Crumb's earliest surviving work appeared in *Arcade*, a comic he self-published as a teenager, which mostly consisted of humorous stories containing wry reflections on human nature, but there was occasional political content, especially on the covers. The cover of the fifth issue, published in 1960, is a case in point. It shows a group of well-dressed older white men and women clinging to the mast of a sinking ship or jumping into the water. The ship is labeled "Bigotry and Race Prejudice," and the water into which it is sinking is labeled "Education" (*Complete Crumb*, vol. 1, p. 89). This comic was created during the wave of lunch counter sit-ins that began in Greensboro, North Carolina, and were aimed at integrating lunch counters at drugstores and other venues. The movement made rapid strides after a period of relative inactivity in the late 1950s, and Crumb appears to have been inspired by it.

A journalistic story Crumb created five years later for Harvey Kurtzman's humor magazine *Help!* displays Crumb's continuing sympathy for the civil rights movement, as well as the beginnings of racist imagery in his comics. The story, titled "Harlem: A Sketchbook Report," documents a trip to Harlem in drawings. The title implies that the story will take a kind of ethnographic approach to the subject, like an anthropologist visiting a "primitive" tribe, a narrative device that foreshadows Crumb's later adoption of the tropes of primitivism. It is the view of an outsider bringing a report back to his own people, the whites. The content of Crumb's drawings meet this expectation in every way with their paternalistic brand of liberal politics. They depict Harlem's Black residents as colorful characters who are alternately charming, eccentric, and threatening. The piece draws attention to the city government's neglect of Harlem, including heavy-handed and ineffectual attempts to improve conditions and the presence of police as a hostile occupying

Robert Crumb, cover of *Arcade* #5 (June 1960). Reprinted in *The Complete Crumb*, vol. 1 (Fantagraphics, 1987). © Robert Crumb.

force. In one illustration, a run-down housing project squats behind a chain-link fence topped with barbed wire. A large sign on the fence declares that "another good home of learning" will soon be arriving, featuring "temporary portable buildings" courtesy of the mayor, Robert Wagner. Beneath that is a graffito declaring "Mayor is a mother———" (*Complete Crumb*, vol. 3, p. 8). This illustration effectively identifies the white-run city government as responsible for the lack of adequate school buildings. Several illustrations depict the police as a menacing presence. One drawing shows a group of three police standing outside a movie theater, next to a poster advertising a movie called *The Bloodfeast*, which disturbingly echoes the false charges of cannibalism that white anthropologists leveled against African tribes.

Other vignettes in "Harlem: A Sketchbook Report" poke fun at Black families for having too many children and taking advantage of welfare, common stereotypes used to explain the persistence of Black poverty. Liberals and conservatives alike deployed such stereotypes, as in *Beyond the Melting Pot: The Negroes, Puerto Ricans, Jews, Italians, and Irish of New York City*, published in 1963 and written by two liberals, Nathan Glazer and Daniel Patrick Moynihan. The final image shows two Black men walking down a raucous street at night discussing politics. One of them, gesticulating with his hands, explains to the other, "Mah point is that we, as an ethnic group, have developed paranoiac psychological complexes which, considering subconscious uncertainty of identity, renders us a social enigma" (*Complete Crumb*, vol. 3, p. 12). This mishmash of jargon is largely incoherent. Combined with the mocking use of Black dialect, the panel suggests that Crumb views Black people as incapable of sophisticated intellectual thought, and their attempts to do so as humorous, a stance that is clearly racist and plays off of common stereotypes of Black people as intellectually inferior. It also appears to mock Black attempts to remedy their own condition through social analysis and critique. Thus, while Crumb recognizes and criticizes the impact of white racism, he also indulges in it himself. This mixture of critique and reproduction of white power structures runs throughout his depictions of Black people.

Crumb's reciprocal construction of whiteness and blackness is fleshed out further in a long story that was written in 1964–65 but not published until 1969, titled "Fritz Bugs Out." Fritz is an anthropomorphic, womanizing cat who presents as very friendly and likable but actually has no morals and treats other people as disposable vessels for his own pleasure. Although he is technically a feline, it is clear that Fritz is meant to be a middle-class white college student. His main traits are his easy charm, his serial trysts with women, his hedonism, and his total lack of concern for anyone else's well-being. As such, one can read Fritz as a critique of white male privilege, but Crumb's attitude toward him is a mixture of critique and empathy or, more likely, jealousy. In either case, Fritz is a good example of Crumb's ambivalent attitude toward whiteness, both despising and desiring it.

In "Fritz Bugs Out," Fritz is distraught over his breakup with his girlfriend, Winston, but takes solace by seducing another girl at a party. Frustrated by the exams he has to study for, he quasi-accidentally sets his apartment building on fire. After slinking away, he finds himself sitting at a lunch counter next to a crow. This is a prime example of Crumb's use of crow characters derived from minstrel-like Disney characters. This identification is further confirmed by the crow's use of stereotypical urban Black English. The conversation in "Fritz Bugs Out" goes as follows:

Fritz: I'm hung up ... strung out ... up tight ...
...
Crow: Well, jis don't lose y'coolness, cat, I mean, don't lose y'coolness!
Fritz: Easy for you to talk! You're a crow! Wish I was a crow ...
Crow: Bein a crow aint no bed a roses man ... it sho' ain't!
Fritz: If I was a crow, I'd fly away, man ... I'd fly away from this miserable town for good!
Crow: You think bein' a crow is a big mother fuggin' ball! All you cats th' same!
Fritz: I know it isn't a ball, man! I know! I studied the race problem! I know!
...
Fritz: Listen, this thing affects me very deeply fella! As a cat I have a considerable guilt complex because my kind have brought suffering on your kind ...
...
Crow: I'm gonna buy you a drink, cat, jis' cause I think you got coolness!
Fritz: Great!
I'm telling you the innermost revelations of my soul, man! I'm all screwed up an' sick of this life I'm leading and I'm gonna flunk outa school an' I don't know where th' hell I'm going!
As a writer and poet, I am being stifled by the organization....
My creative mind is bogged down in the socio-political ratrace!
Crow: Listen ... ya in a bag, ya gotta bug out!
Fritz: [looking confused]
Crow: Bug out!
Fritz: By God, man, I'm gonna bug out! (*Complete Crumb*, vol. 3, pp. 23–24)

The two of them go on a bender together in which they steal a car, drive it off a bridge, go to a Black party, get stoned, and Fritz has sex with a female crow. Fritz literally tears her clothes off of her. While they are having sex in a trash pile in an alley, surrounded by abandoned cars and oil drums, Fritz murmurs, "That ol' black magic! mmm ..." (26). But before they finish, he jumps up and declares, "Suddenly it is all very clear! I must tell the people about the revolution!" (26). He runs back into the party and declares, "Revolt, you thick skulled idiots!" (26). He tries soapboxing on the street but is chased off by three cops. Fritz's adventures proceed from there, but this is the key part of the story's depiction of race.

One might draw several conclusions from this passage. Fritz uses the crows as a vehicle for his own personal pleasure and liberation, just as whites had done with blackface minstrelsy and other cultural forms. The use of Black culture and identity as an escape from whiteness was also a strong feature of Beat culture in the 1950s, and it is the Beats that provide the closest analogue for Fritz's desire to "bug out," a phrase that is easy to imagine coming out of a Beat's mouth. This history of whites' racial appropriation of perceived blackness to provide a hedonistic and rebellious, but also safe, escape from the narrowness of white identity is explicit and clear in "Fritz Bugs Out," but Crumb's attitude to this history is not clear. Crumb seems aware of the many problems with Fritz's cultural appropriation, including but not limited to its shallowness, egotism, and exploitativeness; but at the same time, he seems to revel in it. The act of appropriation is itself contradictory, since whites enjoy Black culture and identity while simultaneously travestying it, so perhaps Crumb's appreciation of this tradition is itself contradictory, both critical and celebratory. These contradictory attitudes persisted in the coming years, although Crumb became increasingly uninhibited in his expression of them, generating the absurdly, violently racist imagery he is best known for.

THE HYPERBOLIC RACISM OF CRUMB'S MATURE PERIOD

The relation between whiteness and blackness that is established in "Fritz Bugs Out" laid the foundation for Crumb's further explorations of this subject in the late 1960s. His work from this period practically exploded with exaggerated racialized and racist representations of Black people in the service of Crumb's countercultural agenda. The two key racial figures in these comics are Whiteman and Angelfood McSpade, both of whom first appeared in 1967. Whiteman was created as a critique of the contradictions and failures of the generation of Crumb's parents and the conformist version of whiteness it created in the 1950s after the suffering and chaos of the Depression and World War II. The drawing of Whiteman pictured here shows a barrel-chested, middle-aged man wearing a business suit and glasses walking down a city street; the character bears a close resemblance to Crumb's own father. Crumb had a difficult relationship with his father, who preached a gospel of hard work, discipline, and normality, and was very disappointed with his sons, all three of whom proved to be eccentric and artistic (Zwigoff). Crumb depicts this older model of whiteness in crisis, as indeed it was in the late 1960s. The forces threatening it included the hippie counterculture, Black Power, antiwar protests, and feminism, among others. A caption in the first panel of Whiteman's first appearance informs us, "Poor ol' Whiteman is on the verge of a nervous breakdown! He's a real product of the Great Depression!" while a small note written near the bottom-right corner of the panel reads, "A story of civilization in crisis" (*Complete Crumb*, vol. 4, p. 105).

In this first panel, Whiteman's shoulders are slouched forward as beads of sweat explode from his face. He appears to be propelling himself forward by sheer force of will as he delivers a soliloquy expressing his exhaustion, telling the reader, "I've tried! God knows I've tried! . . . It's such an effort being polite anymore! But if I stop, they'll see. . . . They'll find out. . . . My real self deep down inside. . . . The raging lustful beast that craves only one thing! Sex!" (*Complete Crumb*, vol. 4, p. 104). Crumb reveals that underneath his proper, respectable exterior, Whiteman is driven by primal urges that he struggles to control and his proper exterior is meant to repress and hide. His consciousness is fragmented between the image of the proper white man he presents to the world and attempts to maintain and the inner beast he struggles to contain and control. This depiction of mainstream white society as sexually repressed was one of the main critiques of the youth counterculture, including Crumb, and sexual freedom was one of its primary aspirations. Whiteman attempts to compensate for this intolerable pressure by performing his hegemonic male whiteness, walking in an exaggeratedly upright posture, puffing his chest out, and delivering the following speech:

> Got to get a grip on myself. . . . I'm a grown man! An intelligent adult! With responsibilities! I'm an American! A citizen of the United States! A real hard charger! Step aside, buddy! The man with the know-how! A citizen on the go! I must maintain this rigid position or all is lost! (*Complete Crumb*, vol. 4, p. 106)

After lapsing back into exhaustion, he gets caught in a traffic jam, which primes him to unleash his other repressed drive, aggression, vowing to "kill," "destroy," "cut," "slice," and "maim." He again catches himself and heads to a bar to regain his composure, but it is clear that he cannot stop his fragmented consciousness from revealing itself.

Crumb had obliquely drawn on the history of blackface minstrelsy in his earlier work, such as "Fritz Bugs Out," but in "Whiteman" he makes that connection much more directly. When Whiteman emerges from the bar after his dual outbreaks of lust and rage, he catches the sounds of a parade coming his way. A group of Black men depicted in the style of blackface minstrelsy and racist tchotchkes appear out of nowhere. They have giant, grinning, rubbery

Robert Crumb, "Whiteman." Originally published in *Zap* #1 (November 1967). Reprinted in *The Complete Crumb*, vol. 4 (Fantagraphics, 1989). © Robert Crumb.

mouths, big round eyes, and small skulls and foreheads, and they wave their gloved hands in the air and take big, bouncy steps. Their appearance exactly corresponds to the "circle, black with two hotdogs in the middle for a mouth" that was traditionally used to represent Black people (Johnson, 8). The use of the white-gloved hands relates to the history of animated cartoons as well as blackface minstrelsy. Minstrel performers wore white gloves to represent what contemporaries saw as the absurd pretension of the Black dandy who claimed to be civilized. The gloves were then taken up by early animators, including Walt Disney, and became ubiquitous in early animated shorts. This is the origin for the white gloves of Mickey Mouse and numerous other early cartoon characters. The carefree dancing of the Black characters in "Whiteman" closely mimics Disney cartoons in which Black characters or animals perform in the style of minstrel shows. Crumb's strip "Ooga Booga," in which Black people speak in nonsense syllables, fight with each other, and then dance in the street, is another example of the influence of Disney's minstrel style on Crumb's work (*Complete Crumb*, vol. 6, p. 49).

Rifas points out that "Whiteman" features "minstrelized stereotypes of blacks" but argues that these stereotypes had not been in circulation since the early twentieth century and that "the meanings and struggles over these old images . . . had been largely forgotten." This is demonstrably false. Minstrelized stereotypes continued to circulate widely in American culture, up to and including the present day. *The Amos 'n' Andy Show*, a highly popular radio program, was an updated version of minstrel performance. The show aired from 1943 to 1960 and was adapted as an equally well-known television show from 1951 to 1953. The NAACP and other civil rights groups organized a campaign against the television show, leading to its cancellation, although the radio show persisted another seven years (Turner, 121–22). Other stereotypical images of Black people continued to circulate even more widely, for instance, in the form of commercial products and mascots such as Aunt Jemima, Uncle Ben, and others (20, 24, 49–51, unnumbered plates). So the notion that blackface minstrelsy or its meaning or the struggle against it was somehow "dredged back into circulation" from obscurity is badly wrong. In the words of Charles Johnson, the "relentless agitation" engaged in by civil rights groups in the 1950s succeeded in driving much of this racist drivel from the airwaves and other mass media, only to have underground cartoonists resuscitate it a decade later (Johnson, 13). *Amos 'n' Andy* aired on television in the years when the underground cartoonists were coming of age, and given the show's popularity, it is highly unlikely that any of them were unaware of it.

Whiteman's first response to the minstrels is fear. He bites his hand, and his eyes widen as he complains, "I can't stand it. . . . What if someone sees me like this? In this state of fear!" (107). The minstrels begin by assaulting him. One grabs him by the back of his pants and another by the back of his jacket as one of them says, "Lez pull his pants down!" (108). They do so, and Whiteman hides his head on the ground in shame as the minstrels laugh at him. The Black characters threaten to strip away the privileges of

Robert Crumb, "Whiteman." Originally published in *Zap* #1 (November 1967). Reprinted in *The Complete Crumb*, vol. 4 (Fantagraphics, 1989). © Robert Crumb.

whiteness, leaving Whiteman defenseless as he asks pleadingly, "How could they do this to me.... I'm Whiteman!" One of the minstrels then tells him, "You jis' a n----- like evva body else!" (108). This comment exactly captures Norman Mailer's view of whites as finding spontaneity and authenticity within themselves in the form of an internalized blackness. Earlier in the story, Whiteman calls his inner self a "raging lustful beast," a description that echoes the traditional white supremacist view of Africans and reinforces the idea that blackness represents the instinctive, animalistic self that whiteness represses (105).

However, the minstrels' tone soon shifts as they attempt to coax him into joining them, telling him, "Be cool dad! Liss'n! Hear dat laughin' and singin' comin' down de street?" (108). Whiteman refuses to heed their call, curling into a ball and responding, "I don't hear nothin'! Scram!" (108). But the minstrel characters continue to coax him, appealing to him to release his repressed inner self through music:

Minstrel 1: C'mon n-----! Yo' got music in you' soul! Remember?
Whiteman: I don't know what you'r talking about!
Minstrel 2: Sho' nuff! He plum fergot! (108)

They then invite him to join the parade, and the story ends with Whiteman hesitantly pondering the offer. Just as in "Fritz Bugs Out," the Black characters provide an avenue for the white man to escape the narrow, repressive confines of whiteness.

Angelfood McSpade is an even more absurd and over-the-top racial caricature than the minstrels in "Whiteman." She appeared repeatedly, far more often than Whiteman, becoming one of Crumb's stock characters. McSpade is based on portrayals of Black women from jungle comics, combining the basic character type of the simpleminded, childlike African with that of the Black jungle queen. The general theme of the McSpade stories is that she is an exotic prize that is beguiling to white men, who attempt to discover and capture her for their own purposes. All her stories are some variation on this general theme. Crumb is well aware that his depiction of McSpade is a stereotype. In her first major appearance, he writes in a caption, "She spends her time bopping around in the jungle! Just a simple primitive creature!" (*Complete Crumb*, vol. 5, p. 19), which seems like intentional irony. However, it is also an accurate description of the character as he depicts her. That he is aware that she is a stereotype does not make her any less of a stereotype.

The first long story featuring McSpade begins with her advertising her body parts: "de biggest tits in town," "fahn big laigs," and "mah sweet jelly roll" (*Complete Crumb*, vol. 5, p. 16). Crumb depicts her as eagerly offering her body to any male who desires it: "There she is, all ready, willing, and able, with plenty of what it takes, dying just to give it away" (18). McSpade confirms this description, telling the reader, "Ah don't mahnd a bit, so go ahaid!" (18). The story then shows a scrawny white man tracking her footprints with a magnifying glass in a forest as the caption informs us that "Angelfood McSpade is an extremely elusive creature" (16). In the next panel, the scrawny white man imagines her walking down a city street in the company of a man who bears a general resemblance to Whiteman: white, middle-aged, with a muscular body, wearing a suit and glasses with an upright posture. Everything about their juxtaposition suggests that he is rational and in control while she is feebleminded and "savage," the traditional stereotypes of white maleness and Black femaleness, respectively. He is shorter than McSpade, and his hand rests on her shoulder, guiding her. His expression is sober and serious, while McSpade is grinning absurdly. He is fully clothed in a business suit; her only clothing is a grass skirt and some jewelry.

This image dominates the page, but it is not part of the literal reality of the story. Rather, it is being imagined by the scrawny man, who fits the typical stereotype of the sissy, a man who has been stripped of his masculinity, in contrast to Whiteman, who represents the dominant and normative version of white maleness. The sissy has an expression that appears to be a combination of envy, desire, and hopelessness. The message here seems to be that he has no hope of winning possession of McSpade, who will instead be claimed by Whiteman. McSpade thus becomes a status symbol in this contest between white men. As a caption above the panel tells us, "She's the kind of chick a guy would be proud to walk down the street with" (17).

The humiliation and emasculation of sissies by various versions of dominant white men, whether hip or square, is a frequently recurring theme of Crumb's work. The sissies may be physically beaten, humiliated, or, most commonly, lose a competition for a woman. The scrawny man is sometimes Crumb himself, but even when it is not literally him, the scrawny figures generally resemble him, and as a general rule he seems to identify with them. The humiliation of Whiteman by the blackface minstrels is a rare example in Crumb's work of the dominant white man being humiliated instead of the sissy. This aligns with Crumb's view of Black men as hypermasculine and exposes his fear of racial otherness as perhaps even greater than his fear of white father figures.

Returning to "Angelfood McSpade," the sissy's goal of winning McSpade is made more difficult because the authorities attempt to prevent white men from capturing her. A caption tells us that "she has been confined to the wilds of darkest Africa, the official excuse being that civilization would be threatened if she were allowed to do whatever she pleased" (17). Since McSpade's only feature as a character is her sexuality, the threat presumably is that she would inspire such lust in white men that they would be unable to control themselves. This caption reiterates the traditional description of "darkest Africa" as a benighted place bereft of civilization and a threat that must be contained. It comes across as ironic here because a woman would not typically be considered a threat in imperialist narratives, but the apparent irony masks actual agreement with these sentiments. As in the case of blackface minstrelsy, McSpade represents the primitive desires repressed by whiteness, in this case the sexual desire of white men. Thus what seems like ironic critique or satire is actually agreement on a deep level.

Crumb used stereotypical images of Africans as savages in many instances. In "Ups and Downs," a tribe of Black cannibals wearing bone jewelry attempts to cook two white boys, named Chuck and Bob, in a big cauldron. The boys can readily be interpreted as representing Crumb and his older brother, Charles, who exercised a large influence on Crumb as a child, including by creating comics alongside Crumb. Angelfood McSpade rescues the boys, and they take her home with them. They give her some money to go shopping, and when she returns, she has made herself over into a 1950s-looking young white woman. She tells them, "Not only did I buy some new clothes, but, I also bought a wig, got my skin bleached and got this book on how to speak with perfect diction!!," after which they fall over in disbelief (*Complete Crumb*, vol. 6, p. 93). As a white woman, she appears and acts as a believable human, suggesting that whiteness is a precondition for the possession of humanity, and blackness is its absence. Moreover, the possibility that a Black woman

Robert Crumb, "Angelfood McDevilsfood." Originally published in *Home Grown Funnies* (1971). Reprinted in *The Complete Crumb*, vol. 8 (Fantagraphics, 1992). © Robert Crumb.

could acquire the attributes of "civilization" seems so impossible to Chuck and Bob that it literally knocks them over.

McSpade elicited some of Crumb's most obscene productions. In addition to the advertisement for "Wildman Sam's Pure N----- Hearts," there is "Krude Kut-Ups," a montage of scenes that Crumb created for *Snatch* in 1968. All the scenes were gratuitously crude and sexual, but the one featuring Black characters was far more exploitative than the others. It shows a large-breasted woman sitting on a stool with a bag tied over her head as three children stand around her. One lifts her skirt, revealing her labia, and says "hm" while looking curiously in that direction, as does another boy standing in front of her. A third boy sits on her leg and announces, "My seester she's oggly! Only 3 cents!" (*Complete Crumb*, vol. 5, p. 60).

It should be noted that Crumb did not limit extremely vile scenes such as this to Black characters. One of his most notorious stories, "Joe Blow," from a 1969 issue of *Zap!*, depicts a stereotypical white nuclear family having incest between father and daughter and mother and son (*Complete Crumb*, vol. 6, pp. 35–40). Crumb clarified in 1972 that he was not promoting incest. When asked why he created the story, he replied, "I don't know. I think I was just being a punk" (Maremaa, 70). It is easy to read this strip as an attempt to explode the stereotype of the white nuclear family by simply shocking the reader into submission. Like "Whiteman," the story suggests that repressing sexuality is an integral part of whiteness, and that this repression inevitably fails. "Joe Blow" explores this theme in a completely unbelievable and horrific way, but the underlying idea is the same in both cases. "Krude Kut-Ups," on the other hand, expresses the opposite idea: that Black people are totally unrepressed sexually, to a point of absolute vileness. The two comics present opposite but equally extreme images of whiteness and blackness, total repression and total freedom, with both resulting in a state of barbarism.

Another variety of McSpade story features white men or, more rarely, Black men, using McSpade as a kind of inanimate object for their own purposes. These incidents reproduce the exploitation of people and natural resources that was the raison d'être of colonialism and therefore the underlying context of the jungle genre. In the 1971 story "Angelfood McDevilsfood," a naked Angelfood is washed out of her wooden shack by a flood before falling asleep on the water as it carries her away. As always in Crumb's comics, McSpade (or, as she is renamed in this comic, McDevilsfood) is shown as having no awareness of her surroundings or herself. She does not notice the flood that lifts her body and carries it away. This dehumanizes her by presenting her as bereft of consciousness, not even an animal (which would notice that it was in danger), but rather a kind of living object, alive and mobile but not sentient (*Complete Crumb*, vol. 8, pp. 5–7).

The comic then cuts to the Snoid, one of Crumb's recurring characters, who is walking down a city street. When the flood reaches him, carrying McSpade along with it, the Snoid climbs on top of her and uses her as a raft. This trope also appears in "Ups and Downs," when Chuck and Bob ride on top of McSpade like a raft in the course of their escape. This and all the ensuing events reiterate her status as a living object used by the white Snoid for his own purposes. Throughout it all, she does not feel anything or even realize that she is being used. After climbing aboard her, the Snoid orally rapes her with a ridiculously oversized penis. The Snoid then places her upside down with her head below the water and builds a small cabin on top of her, supported by a pole going into her vagina. The Snoid's rape recalls the habitual rape of Black women by white men during the period of American slavery and after. Black female slaves were the property of their white owners, and their bodies were commodities that could be exchanged without regard for their wishes or desires. Slave owners could do what they wished with their human property, which often included rape. Angela Davis has argued that slave owners' rape of their female slaves was designed to overpower their will to resist and inculcate a sense of passivity in them (23–27).

When McSpade finally wakes up, the pole arouses her to the point of orgasm. The force of the orgasm ejects the cabin from her vagina, and it then lands on top of her head. The final panel shows her peacefully enjoying breakfast with the Snoid inside the cabin. He calls her "sweets," and she treats him familiarly as well (7). Crumb depicts McSpade as consenting to her treatment, albeit retroactively. Rather than experiencing pain and suffering as a result of the Snoid's rape and exploitation of her body, she is revealed to have enjoyed it and to regard the Snoid as her affectionate mate. This representation echoes the claims of slave owners that their human property did not object to their treatment but were happy in their position and grateful for the paternalistic care that their masters showed them. White historians once argued that the sexual relationships between male slave owners and female slaves may have begun through forcible means, in other words rape, but often developed into consensual and loving relationships (Davis, 25–26). Such views attempt to legitimize the systemic rape of Black women by presenting them as willing and consenting partners, which is impossible in a situation in which they were literally the physical property of the men assaulting them. Crumb's "Angelfood McDevilsfood" follows directly in this tradition. Crumb excuses the actions of his character and also his decisions as an artist by making rhetorical claims that are deeply rooted in the history of white supremacy in America.

We should acknowledge that, later in his career, Crumb developed a mode of representing blackness that was not nakedly exploitative. Over the years, he created numerous portraits of old-time Black blues musicians, depicting them with empathy and as fully individualized human beings. However, even these portraits carry an underlying note of cultural appropriation. Whereas Crumb's most controversial depictions of blackness were utterly dehumanized, his portraits of Black musicians have a sense of nostalgia and sentimentality mixed in with heartfelt sincerity and identification. As we have seen, Crumb followed in the footsteps of blackface minstrelsy in his identification of musical blackness as an avenue for the de-repression of white desire. Crumb's attraction to Black blues musicians fits into this pattern, albeit with a far more respectful and humanizing approach than his minstrelized images.

CONCLUSION

Both Crumb and his supporters, critics, and scholars have made many efforts to dismiss or minimize the racism of his work and have used a variety of tactics to this end. As outlined at the start of the chapter, some scholars have argued that Crumb's comics offend everyone, and their various outrages therefore do not have any coherent meaning, in effect canceling each other out. Some have argued that such representations were typical of the period, and therefore Crumb cannot be held responsible for them. Some have argued that he was bravely expressing the real racism of American culture and himself personally, thereby contributing to an honest assessment of the real state of race relations in the United States. Some have argued that the images were satirical, exaggerating common stereotypes to critique them, and anyone who thinks otherwise just does not get the cartoons' true meaning. Some have even argued that Black people themselves, or at least some of them, appreciate and understand Crumb's satirical intent and see in his comics a skewering of white stereotypes about blackness.

The easiest of these justifications to refute is that Crumb passively reflects the racism of his era. First, this was the era of the civil rights movement and the popularization of the idea that "black is beautiful," so the notion that racism was the unquestioned norm is false. Corey Creekmur rightfully questions the idea that "Crumb's controversial images were more acceptable in the context of the late 1960s and early 1970s . . . than they would be 'today,'" given the active civil rights and Black Power movements of the era (24). Racism was most certainly present, but so was its opposite. Crumb himself had been a supporter of the civil rights movement as a teenager, so one could just as easily claim that the struggle for racial tolerance was the true spirit of the times. In the words of Charles Johnson, "I don't buy the idea that an artist is merely a creature of his time, a *tabula rasa* inscribed with the bigoted beliefs of his *Zeitgeist*" (12).

Crumb himself, as well as many of his supporters, has argued that the racist tropes in his work are ingrained in his unconscious and that his airing of them is an act of great honesty. As Crumb has put it, "All this stuff is deeply embedded in our culture and our collective subconscious, and you have to deal with it. It's in me. It's in everybody! It's there!" (Creekmur, 26). No doubt this is true, since psychologists have shown that nearly all members of American society possess an implicit bias in favor of whiteness (Badger). According to this argument, by being brutally honest about his own ingrained racism, Crumb is helping to expose and ultimately defuse racist beliefs such as these.

This argument has several problems. First, while everyone or nearly everyone harbors racial biases, even individuals who are committed to the cause of racial equality, almost everyone also holds contradictory ideas as well. We know that this is true of Crumb, since his early work demonstrated support for civil rights. Second, we are not merely the passive agents of our unconscious biases. We may have relatively little control over our immediate, reflexive responses, but we can and do exercise greater control over our considered, deliberate decisions, and the making of art is the cumulative result of a series of decisions extending over a period of time. Although Crumb drew heavily on his reflexive responses, especially in his work from the peak underground era, comics take too long to draw to be produced in one short burst of energy. Cartoonists may initially be driven by an immediate response or fleeting idea or feeling, but as they continue to work the material, they are forced to make one conscious choice after another, which requires that the initial impulse be shaped, modified, and edited. Blaming everything on the unconscious is therefore a cop-out.

Crumb and many of his white admirers, including Jay Kinney, Les Daniels, Ivan Stang, Alan Moore, and Mary Fleener, have argued that Crumb's comics are meant satirically (Creekmur, 23–26, 32n10). Crumb himself has indicated that he did not mean for the comics to be taken literally, stating, "I was sweating when I was doing [the stories]. I thought, 'Some people are going to take it literally.' I always have gone close to that line" (Rifas). Stang captures the general tone of Crumb's supporters by insisting that "Crumb's depictions of blacks and women . . . were understood by us (fellow white male artists) for what they were—far beyond racism and sexism, and in fact, violent reactions against both, using irony and horror as stylistic tools" (Creekmur, 23). Kinney concurs, although he allows, "that can be a joke that not everyone gets" (23). Ron Turner, publisher of the underground comix company Last Gasp, claimed that a Black radical friend of his, Terry Collins, loved the stereotypical Black character Watermelon Jones from *Radical America Komiks*, where he appeared in "Smiling Sergeant Death and His Merciless Mayhem Patrol" by Gilbert Shelton (Rifas). However, the character of Jones is quite different from those of Crumb. Jones appears only very briefly and is not saturated with racist stereotypes the way that Crumb's characters are. Jones shows no sign of minstrel attributes, and his major contribution to the story is to refuse a command by the hyperviolent titular white sergeant (Shelton).

Creekmur questions these assertions but does so fairly gently, phrasing his objections as questions rather than critiques. He asks, "Do white critics really wish to tell Crumb's offended black readers that their responses are wrong or naïve? If Crumb's images of blacks do not offend white audiences, so what?" (23). Charles Johnson, a prominent Black literary scholar, novelist, and cartoonist, delivers a blistering rebuke to such claims in the foreword to Fredrik Strömberg's *Black Images in the Comics*. The entire foreword is a passionate but also surgically precise critique of racist imagery in comics. Johnson reports, "My visceral reaction to this barrage of racist drawings from the 1840s through the 1940s was revulsion and a profound sadness" (7). Regarding Crumb, Johnson states, "I cannot believe that Robert Crumb's grotesque and pornographic character 'Angelfood McSpade' in the underground comics of the 1960s is avant-garde or provocative in any positive way" (13). Unsurprisingly, such reactions are not unique to Johnson (Creekmur, 22). As Creekmur further points out, "Such images allowed even hip and racially tolerant white readers to indulge in their residual fears and prejudices, protected by the shield of comic, ironic distance" (30). Any satirical effect they may have is balanced, if not overwhelmed, by the permission they give white readers to enjoy racist material under the cover of an extremely thin veil of satire.

Moreover, it is far from clear that what Crumb is doing is satire. At times his comics are so over-the-top and divorced from reality that it becomes impossible to believe that they reflect sincerely held beliefs. However, that is not the same thing as satire. To be effective, satire requires the suggestion of an alternative point of view that differs from the view or views being satirized. Although the level of racism in Crumb's comics is so staggering that it seems impossible to view as sincere, beneath this hyperracism, his underlying views and attitudes are not fundamentally different from those of traditional white racism. He exaggerates the usual white racism against Black people, which makes it seem suspect, but if you dig deeper, he actually agrees with the views that he superficially appears to satirize. In "Whiteman," for instance, Crumb uses blackface minstrels to drive home his critique of the repressive nature of whiteness, a view that he sincerely holds. All of Crumb's racist material, no matter what level of outrage it evokes, revolves around the same fundamental perspective. He never provides any alternate reading of race that might let us see his hyperracist material as satire.

Crumb's weak apology for his racist and sexist comics echoes similar arguments made about forms of internet discourse today that have been described as hipster humor. Alissa Quart reports: "Today, there's a raft of ads, photographs, television shows, films, and T-shirts, which represent young women being defined, but always ironically—and with a wink and a nod—by their sexuality and/or bodies. I think we should call this new strand of culture Hipster Sexism." In other words, hipster sexism, often exemplified in internet memes that are so egregiously sexist that one cannot help but realize that the producer is aware of their sexist nature, is supposed to demonstrate a sophisticated form of satire that indicts sexism even as it ostensibly perpetuates it. Crumb's comics lay bare his inner racist, but they do nothing to critique, counteract, or evolve beyond this primal recognition of his own racism. Crumb thus remains trapped within the same racial construct as the mainstream white society he critiques. In the words of Art Spiegelman, who is both a friend and a critic of Crumb:

> I think he's one of the great cartoonists of all time. Nevertheless, I think there's stuff that he's actually never really examined and doesn't want to examine, and what he wants to do is keep re-expressing a

compulsion—whether that compulsion is to give vent to a racist stereotyped image or to a specific sexual buzz that he gets from certain body types.... I think once you take it on as a subject, you're responsible to do more than just give in to it. That feeling of responsibility isn't something that can or should be imposed from outside. He doesn't feel it. And I think that's where my problem with those aspects of Crumb's work lies, rather than with whether or not he's racist. Not like he's responsible to make the world a better place, but he's responsible to dig deeper into what it means to mess with this particular brand of dynamite. (Groth and Spiegelman)

Spiegelman raises interesting questions about the responsibility of the artist. In his view, the artist's only responsibility is to his or her work, a responsibility that Crumb fails to fulfill by ignoring the implications of his artistic choices. We would argue that an artist's responsibilities are broader than this, not because artists have special responsibilities as artists but rather because they have the same responsibilities as all people. One of the most important of these is to treat other people with respect and dignity. Disrespecting entire groups of people, especially groups that have historically been oppressed and exploited, in precisely the same terms as have been used in the past to justify and profit from their oppression and exploitation, is an act of tremendous disrespect to their humanity.

Crumb's shock tactics reached their apogee in the late 1960s and early 1970s. In 1974 underground comix suffered a major economic and cultural collapse owing to the general decline of the counterculture, police suppression of the head shops where underground comix were sold, a spike in paper prices, and an unfavorable Supreme Court ruling on obscenity standards (Rosenkranz, 185–96). Crumb's comics after this date toned down his racial and sexual provocations while maintaining the same underlying themes. In the years after this date, a number of cartoonists in the later 1970s produced work that replaced the iconoclastic absurdities of underground comix with a greater interest in psychological and historical realism. Chief among these cartoonists was Will Eisner, who had been an important figure in the 1930s and 1940s before giving up comics. He returned to comics in 1978 to pioneer the graphic novel with *A Contract with God* and subsequent works that explored Jewish identity in New York from the 1800s to the 1980s. Eisner presented a view of Jewish identity that promoted Jews as an ideal minority that earned their way into acceptance as whites, a stance known as Jewish exceptionalism, while depicting other racial minorities as undeserving of equal rights and status. Three other cartoonists, Aline Kominsky-Crumb,

Art Spiegelman, and Harvey Pekar also produced important work exploring Jewish identity during this time. All three of these artists had close links to underground comix. Kominsky-Crumb was an underground cartoonist who married and collaborated with Robert Crumb, although she produced most of her work after 1974. Spiegelman was also an underground cartoonist who likewise did his most influential work after 1974, and Pekar was a writer who collaborated with Crumb in the mid-1970s. Kominsky-Crumb, Spiegelman, and Pekar took a different approach from Eisner, questioning the narrative of Jewish exceptionalism and with it the construction of whiteness on which it relied.

Chapter Six

JEWISH EXCEPTIONALISM AND ASSIMILATION IN THE 1970s AND 1980s

Jewish identity played an important though mostly hidden role in early American comics, exemplified in the character of Superman. In the 1970s, Will Eisner, a major figure in the first generation of American cartoonists, dropped the masks and subterfuge and directly addressed his experiences growing up in a Jewish community in the Bronx in the early and mid-twentieth century. His central work on this topic, often considered his masterpiece, is the Dropsie Avenue trilogy, comprising *A Contract with God*, *A Life Force*, and *Dropsie Avenue*. In Eisner's narrative, Jews emerge as the ideal ethnic group, hardworking, community oriented, and sharp-witted. WASPs are privileged but ultimately good-hearted. Italians are hot-tempered and violent, and the Irish are corrupt. However, both the Italians and the Irish retain their humanity. Black people, on the other hand, are either lazy and violent or childlike and in need of paternalistic protection, while Hispanics are basically Italians with less humanity.

Eisner's depiction of Jews as the perfect ethnic group is a position known as Jewish exceptionalism, which has been promoted by writers such as Seymour Martin Lipset and, most influentially, in Nathan Glazer and Daniel Patrick Moynihan's 1963 book *Beyond the Melting Pot: The Negroes, Puerto Ricans, Jews, Italians, and Irish of New York City*. Jewish exceptionalists, including Eisner, do not subsume Jews into whiteness, but they do claim the position of racial supremacy allowed by their provisional proximity to whiteness. Eisner promotes a racial hierarchy wherein Jews and WASPS rank the highest, followed by Italians and Irish. However, all white groups come off as distinctly superior to nonwhites. Eisner's version of whiteness does not collapse white ethnicities into a white monolith. Instead he creates a hierarchy of white ethnicities, all elevated above nonwhites. The racism of Eisner's Dropsie Avenue trilogy has gone largely if not entirely unremarked. Jeremy Dauber has described the ambivalence in Eisner's depictions of Jewish characters in his tenement stories, but he ignores the racism in Eisner's tenement stories toward other racial groups (33–34).

Eisner grew up in the early 1900s, a time when Jews were an in-between ethnic group, according to David Roediger, "neither securely white nor nonwhite" (12), a distinction with the potential to fracture Jewish consciousness. While some Jewish creators addressed their internal fragmentation by making antiracist gestures that unwittingly reinforced the white supremacist power structure, others simply practiced straightforward racism. Will Eisner was a prime example of the ladder approach, thanks to the character of Ebony White, a hyperbolically racist Black caricature who was central to Eisner's *The Spirit*. As Danny Fingeroth has pointed out, Eisner's *The Spirit* paved the way for his later chronicles of Jewish life through the series' chronicling of the ethnic milieu of early twentieth-century New York City (*Disguised as Clark Kent*, 63). The Dropsie Avenue trilogy is like *The Spirit* without the Spirit. The characters in the trilogy are only slightly less stereotypical than those in *The Spirit*. Eisner does not do a good job of imagining either the inner or outer lives of his nonwhite characters, reducing them to stereotypes of good and bad minorities.

In the 1970s, Eisner was a respected elder in the comics industry, but a new generation of Jewish cartoonists was coming of age, including Art Spiegelman, Harvey Pekar, and Aline Kominsky-Crumb, whose work dealt in part with the new position of Jews as assimilated whites in the years after World War II. All three worked primarily in the genre of autobiography, and all three rejected the belief that Jews were the ideal ethnic group. They reflected on the meaning of Jews' assimilation into whiteness, questioning the value of this assimilation and whether Jews had indeed been fully assimilated. They also rejected the racist view that Jews and other whites were superior to nonwhites, and drew attention to the operation of white supremacy within their daily lives.

JEWISH EXCEPTIONALISM IN WILL EISNER'S DROPSIE AVENUE TRILOGY

After more than two decades working in other fields, Will Eisner returned to comics in 1978 with the graphic novel *A Contract with God*. Influenced by the example of underground comix, which he saw as "the renaissance of comics as a literary/art form," he believed the time had come when artistically ambitious comics, which he had always hoped to create, could find an audience and a market (Inge, 129). *Contract*, along with its two sequels, *A Life Force* (1983) and *Dropsie Avenue* (1995), depicted the inhabitants of the Dropsie Avenue neighborhood in the Bronx over the course of multiple generations. *Contract* focuses almost entirely on Jewish characters and is set in an unspecified period in the early twentieth century. *A Life Force* is set in the Depression, and although Jews are again the main characters, WASPs and Italians also make an appearance. *Dropsie Avenue* takes the most sweeping view of the three, with a prequel extending back to the 1800s, but it concentrates more on the period from the 1920s to the 1980s and a cast of characters that includes the Dutch, English, Irish, Italians, Jews, Blacks, and Hispanics.

After World War II, recent European immigrants were granted full status as whites, opening the door to economic and social advancement and leaving behind their prewar status as racially in-between. During this period, a narrative of Jewish exceptionalism was constructed to explain the success of Jews in entering the professions and the middle class and to serve as a model to other, supposedly less capable ethnic groups. This narrative of Jewish exceptionalism was closely linked to that of American exceptionalism, the view of America as a uniquely virtuous nation based on the principles of freedom, individuality, and equality, ignoring the central role that race and racism have played in American history. Seymour Martin Lipset and Earl Raab have written that "Jewish exceptionalism addresses the extraordinary history of the Jewish people and the extraordinary zeal with which American Jews have adopted the American creed and subsequently achieved economic, political, and social success" (7–8), which they attribute to "the congruence between the values and characteristics of the Jewish people and those of the larger society" (3).

Glazer and Moynihan's *Beyond the Melting Pot*, in which they ascribed Jews' success to a "passion for education" (155), did much to help construct this narrative. Stanley Lieberson and Stephen Steinberg have shown convincingly that this explanation was a myth, and Jewish success was mostly based on external factors. Lieberson points out that Jews and other European immigrants were never placed at the very bottom of the American socioeconomic hierarchy with nonwhites, and Europeans were always given more advantageous jobs than nonwhites. Steinberg shows that Jewish success resulted from a close fit between the skills Jews had acquired in Europe because of their exclusion from most occupations and the skills that were in demand in America at the time of their immigration (Lieberson, 383; Steinberg, 82–103). Karen Brodkin adds that after World War II, Jews and other European immigrants benefited massively from what she calls "the biggest and best affirmative action program in the history of our nation," which was "aimed at and disproportionately helped male, Euro-origin GIs" (Brodkin, 27, 38). Jews were upwardly mobile in comparison to other immigrants, but anti-Semitism blocked Jews from many occupations. Consequently, Jews were concentrated in small businesses, the garment and movie industries, and professions serving other Jews but were largely blocked from access to large-scale businesses and academia (Sacks, 399–400).

The flip side of Jewish exceptionalists' praise of Jewish virtues was their denigration of other ethnic groups. Glazer and Moynihan claimed that Blacks' problems were caused by "[broken] homes and illegitimacy," family situations that lacked "defined roles and responsibilities," parents who "refuse to accept responsibility for and resent their children," and so on, a veritable litany of supposed ills of the Black family (50). Glazer and Moynihan admitted that racism contributed to Black poverty, but they laid the heart of the problem squarely on the supposedly dysfunctional Black family. Their analyses of Puerto Ricans, Italians, and Irish were similarly based on racist stereotypes. Lipset and Raab write that "the United States has been open to new citizens who are willing to accept the creed," ignoring the history of brutal white conquest of Native Americans, white enslavement of Africans and subsequent discrimination and violence against them, and white bigotry against new European immigrants (3). They ignore the role of racism in keeping nonwhite groups at the bottom of America's socioeconomic hierarchy, instead describing some groups as merely taking longer to reach the promised land of prosperity than others.

Ian Haney López has written that Glazer and Moynihan's *Beyond the Melting Pot* "effectively laid the groundwork for contemporary reactionary conceptions of race in the United States (94–95). In the *Moynihan Report*, written two years after *Beyond the Melting Pot*, Moynihan takes a harsher tone, writing of the Black community that "a community that allows a large number of young men to grow up in broken families, dominated by women, never acquiring any stable relationship to male authority, never acquiring any set of rational expectations about the future—that community asks for and gets chaos. Crime, violence, unrest, disorder . . . that is not only to be expected, but they are very near to inevitable. And it is richly deserved" (Haney López, 96).

The late graphic novels of Will Eisner exemplify many aspects of the Jewish exceptionalist narrative. Eisner's Dropsie Avenue trilogy presents an image of a Jewish immigrant community that values education, community service, good citizenship, upward socioeconomic mobility, and the preservation of their cultural and religious traditions. One of the main points of Eisner's work is to illustrate the virtues of racial tolerance and cooperation, but as with Glazer and Moynihan, racist, sexist, and classist attitudes lurking below the surface of the narrative undermine this liberal outlook. These attitudes are not mere footnotes to Eisner's call for racial harmony; rather, they structure the entire narrative, imposing biases and preferences that may not be apparent on a surface reading. While not all Jewish characters in Eisner's trilogy are virtuous, on the whole, Jews are depicted significantly more positively than other ethnic groups, who are more likely to engage in reckless, violent, criminal, racist, selfish, and self-destructive acts. This image is highly selective, omitting aspects of the Jewish immigrant experience that do not favor the social and political agenda of those constructing the image, including the large numbers of Jewish labor activists and socialists, the existence of Jewish criminal organizations, and tensions between Jews and other racial groups. This sanitized image allows Eisner to present Jews as the ultimate Americans, a paragon of whiteness and a model for other ethnic groups. These decisions create an image of an idealized, patriarchal Jewish society cleansed of class conflict and criminal behavior and morally elevated above other ethnic groups.

The history of Dropsie Avenue as described in the trilogy's final volume is structured by the successive waves of immigrants who arrive on the street and make it their own, a miniature version of the larger national history. On their arrival, each new wave of immigrants is placed on the bottom rung of the neighborhood's racial hierarchy, scorned and mocked by the previous arrivals, who have managed to raise themselves from their previous position and choose to leave the neighborhood rather than live alongside the new arrivals. The model immigrant groups for Eisner are the Jews, followed by the Italians and Irish. These three groups receive the lion's share of Eisner's attention and sympathy and exemplify the American dream story of huddled immigrant masses arriving at the promised land and working their way to middle-class prosperity. Significantly, Blacks and Hispanics were excluded from this process.

Although Eisner idealizes Jews and slights Blacks and Puerto Ricans, he is at least somewhat critical of WASPs. This indicates that while Eisner embraces American exceptionalism, he is not totally blind to the class and racial disparities of white capitalist America. However, these elements are given much less emphasis than his criticisms of other ethnic groups. The main WASP characters in the trilogy, Rowena Shepard and Elton Shaftsbury II, are depicted as all or mostly good, while minor characters are shown as racist, snobbish, and exploitative, such as Elton's boss at the brokerage house in *A Life Force*. Rowena is presented as a good person from beginning to end, but Elton begins as a prototypical example of an upper-class parasite and has to earn his redemption through work and personal growth. Elton "had been reared in comfort and security. With an unquestioned confidence in his survival that came from the certainty of his social position, he expected his world to go on, as it was, forever. His skills were mainly centered in the art of being accepted and the maintenance of the shallow relationships that were normal for his set" (219). Elton loses his investments and his job as a result of the stock market crash in 1929 and is soon forced to sell his house in suburban Scarsdale and move to a tenement on Dropsie Avenue. He slowly redeems himself by rebuilding his career through personal initiative, falling in love with and marrying a Jewish neighbor, and helping her father and an Italian carpenter buy a lumberyard and turn it into a thriving business. Eisner thus sees whites as benefiting from unearned economic and social privileges but is quite sanguine about their capacity for personal redemption; in his view, individualism trumps structural inequalities, which he largely avoids depicting.

Eisner's commitment to Jewish exceptionalism is not really visible in the trilogy's first volume. *Contract* depicts Jewish characters full of contradictions, conflicts, foibles, and failings, but as the trilogy progresses, the Jewish characters become increasingly idealized. In *Dropsie Avenue*, this growing idealization culminates in Abie Gold, a paradigm of duty, responsibility, patience, and civic virtue. The character remains believable on the page thanks to his grounding in the mundane reality of Dropsie Avenue and Eisner's lack of hyperbole, but Eisner depicts him as an individual who is virtually without flaw or blemish. As a child, Gold faces anti-Semitic hostility from the local Italian boys but proves himself by hitting a home run in a baseball game against a neighboring Irish team. He marries an Italian, Marie Leone, despite the disapproval of some Italians in the neighborhood. Her father, however, who owns a shoe shop next to the tailor shop of Abie's father, Herman, approves of the match. Like second-generation Jews in America, Abie's path upward is accomplished through higher education, in his case law school. He serves as an army defense attorney during World War II, returns home to take up private practice, with the local landlord Izzy Cash as his principal client, and uses his legal skills to assist the community, leading to his election as a city council member. He guides the neighborhood, his political patron, the former prizefighter Polo Palermo, his client Izzy Cash, and his family through one crisis after another, until finally, late in life and with the neighborhood burned out and ruined, he moves to the suburbs of Westchester.

Other Jewish characters are less heroic, and some even have flaws, but we meet no villains among them. The most morally suspect Jew is the landlord Izzy Cash, but even he turns out to have a soft heart that overshadows his implied seedy business practices, which are only hinted at, never made explicit. To maintain the moral elevation of the Jewish community, Eisner minimizes, omits, or distorts elements that he considers discreditable. The most straightforward omission is that of Jewish gangsters, who are erased completely. Following the popular perception that the Italian Mafia had a monopoly on organized crime among European immigrants, Italians perpetuate the majority of the violent crime depicted in the trilogy. In reality, extensive Irish and Jewish criminal networks and organizations existed, including well-known Jewish gangsters such as Arnold Rothstein, Meyer Lansky, Dutch Schultz, Bugsy Siegel, and Louis Lepke (Fried). Gangs were an unavoidable part of the publishing industry in New York City from the 1910s on and were closely involved with the foundation of the comic book industry. Although the details are unclear, Harry Donenfeld, founder of DC Comics, appears to have worked with the mob for many years and used its influence to help launch what became DC (G. Jones, 42–51).

In Eisner's Dropsie Avenue trilogy, men are invariably the primary focus of his stories, both as heroes and villains, while women are relegated to secondary roles as temptresses or nags, and their interior lives largely ignored. The danger posed by women as temptresses is explored in the titular story in *Contract*, where the main character's mistress is described as a "shikseh" and is depicted as malicious, manipulative, and empty-headed. In another story from *Contract*, "The Super," an irritable, anti-Semitic, Nazi-sympathizing building superintendent named Scuggs is seduced and robbed by Rosie, the young niece of one of his tenants. Although Rosie is only an adolescent, Scuggs is depicted as her innocent victim when she offers to show him her underwear for a nickel. After she steals his money and poisons his dog, Scuggs pursues her and is about to attack her in the alley behind the tenement when he is spotted by the building's residents. Realizing what he has done, Scuggs flees the police and commits suicide in his apartment. The story's penultimate page depicts Rosie sitting on the building's stoop and counting her stolen money while humming a tune. Scuggs, a racist brute who treats his Jewish tenants with contempt, comes off in the end as a sympathetic human being, while Rosie is demonized.

Eisner also engages in one of the most persistent female stereotypes of Jewish postwar literature, that of "smothering and emasculating mothers" (Brodkin, 161). In *A Life Force*, Rifka Shtarkah berates and guilt-trips her son over his engagement to a "shikseh," even faking an attack of faintness or high blood pressure while talking with him on the phone (207). Rather than an expression of real emotion, she is shown simulating or exaggerating emotion to manipulate those around her. When her husband Jacob leaves her, he is depicted sympathetically as a man trying to rediscover his zest for living, while she is portrayed unsympathetically as a narrow-minded, henpecking, and castrating shrew who refuses to accept her husband's anguished decision. Throughout the scene, she screams histrionically, more for effect than out of genuine feeling, as when she yells out an open window, addressing the neighbors listening from their windows, "I wash his clothes . . . I make for him a good clean home . . . I give him children. . . . That is by him a prison?" (304). Eisner's Jewish community is a patriarchal construct in which women's voices and subjectivities must be marginalized and denigrated. As Karen Brodkin writes of the intellectual fathers of Jewish exceptionalism:

> Forgotten in the intellectuals' portrayals . . . was the Jewishness that idealized Yiddish mamas as strong, community-centered, and politically activist women (not unlike the African American matriarchs Moynihan later vilified). Forgotten too was the history of very unruly collective action, including rent strikes and meat riots, the Uprising of 20,000—in all of which women figured prominently—and Jewish socialism and Jewish unions. (Brodkin, 150)

In contrast to the idealized image of Jews, all the other ethnic groups in *Dropsie* are some mixture of good and bad, virtuous and villainous. Their character flaws vary, but generalizing somewhat, the Irish are most guilty of corruption, the Italians of organized crime, and the Puerto Ricans of being hot-tempered and violent. The Italians' negative characteristics are balanced by their loyalty, their willingness to befriend Jews, and their general humanity. The overall depiction of the Irish and Puerto Ricans comes off as rather negative. Eisner elevates Jews above the other groups residing on Dropsie Avenue. His depiction of these groups does not follow a simple logic of equating whiteness with goodness. Jews are depicted as morally exceptional, the Irish come off quite badly, and the Italians fall somewhere in the middle.

The trilogy's most problematic depiction of race relations is Eisner's portrayal of Black people. To start with, very few Black characters appear in the trilogy, thereby erasing them from the history of the Bronx. When they are depicted, their only role in the narrative is as recipients of Jewish or white charity. They have no other impact on the story line, and they are not given any role in improving their own condition or fighting their own oppression. The only two significant Black characters are an adult named Jim and his daughter, Ruby. In their first appearance, a Nordic owner hires Jim as a janitor and handyman of a tenement, while Rosie, a Jewish resident of the tenement, befriends Ruby. Rosie feeds Ruby, sharing her ice cream bar and inviting her to lunch. When Ruby enters Rosie's apartment, she tells Rosie's mother, "I'll go eat in the kitchen," explaining that "where I come from, we

Will Eisner, *Dropsie Avenue* (June 1995). Reprinted in *The Contract with God Trilogy* (W. W. Norton, 2006). © Will Eisner Studios.

always eats in the kitchen of folks like you all," but Rosie's mother insists that she "eat in the dining room same as us!" (425). This exchange both indicates Ruby's acceptance of her subservience and Rosie's mother's generosity. After Ruby leaves, Rosie's Irish next-door neighbor opens her door and complains about Ruby's visit, which concludes with the neighbor's husband opining, "I told ya. . . . Let them Jews inta the neighborhood and the blacks will follow!" (426). This scene advocates racial equality and links anti-Semitic and anti-Black racism, but it does not give Jim or Ruby any role in the fight for their own equality, making them passive recipients of others' goodwill. After Jim is injured by an exploding boiler and loses his job, he becomes the recipient of charity once again, this time from a nearby shul (temple school), which hires him as its janitor. While Eisner sees this as a gift, janitorial work was the kind of low-wage occupation that Black workers were restricted to, making economic advancement impossible for many.

Eisner's depiction of Jim and Ruby as accepting their position and being grateful for the charity bestowed on them by their Jewish benefactors enacts one side of a bitter controversy in Black-Jewish relations and also reflects primitivist notions about Black people being childlike and requiring protection and tutelage from whites. While Eisner sees these acts of charity as benevolent and admirable, many Blacks have complained that Jewish assistance was paternalistic and self-serving. Jews gave Blacks charity and hired them in menial positions but exploited them economically and refused to live in the same neighborhood. Jonathan Kaufman has written:

> For their part, blacks growing up in the north had a far more ambivalent view of Jews, shaped by economic contact that almost always put blacks one step below Jews on the urban economic ladder. Whereas Jews often saw themselves reaching out to "help" blacks by extending them credit at stores, giving them jobs as maids, passing on old clothes to their children, blacks bristled at the patronizing attitude that seemed to lurk behind every act of generosity. They chafed at the vast economic disparity between blacks and Jews. (109)

James Baldwin's recollections of his childhood experiences capture the anger that animated this relationship:

> When we were growing up in Harlem our demoralizing series of landlords were Jewish, and we hated them. We hated them because they were terrible landlords and did not take care of the building.... Our parents were lashed down to futureless jobs, in order to pay the outrageous rent. We knew that the landlord treated us this way only because we were colored, and he knew that we could not move out.
> The grocer was a Jew, and being in debt to him was very much like being in debt to the company store. The butcher was a Jew, and yes, we certainly paid more for bad cuts of meat than other New York citizens, and we very often carried insults home, along with the meat. We bought our clothes from a Jew and, sometimes, our secondhand shoes, and the pawnbroker was a Jew—perhaps we hated him most of all. The merchants along 125th Street were Jewish—at least many of them were. (31–32)

Eisner obliterates this side of Black-Jewish relations, avoiding a very sensitive aspect of both groups' history and preserving his idealized portrayal of the Jewish community.

By omitting key facts, Eisner also distorts the reality of how the Bronx was reconstructed after reaching its nadir. The final section of *Dropsie* depicts the collapse of the neighborhood as drug users and dealers begin moving into the area, middle-class whites move out, and landlords stop taking care of their buildings, which become increasingly vacant. Finally, building fires

Will Eisner, *Dropsie Avenue* (June 1995). Reprinted in *The Contract with God Trilogy* (W. W. Norton, 2006). © Will Eisner Studios.

become an epidemic as landlords commit arson for insurance or to evade rent control; tenants commit arson so that they can be relocated to better subsidized housing, and drug users burn down buildings by accident or for sport. All of this accurately depicts what happened in large sections of the Bronx, most famously in the Charlotte Avenue neighborhood, which became a nationally recognized symbol for urban blight (Christie). In Eisner's version, Rowena Shepard returns to Dropsie Avenue to rescue it from its catastrophic decline by constructing single-family homes on its now-vacant lots, which she names Dropsie Gardens. Rowena's plans for Dropsie Avenue closely resemble the actual redevelopment of the Charlotte Avenue neighborhood into Charlotte Gardens (Jonnes, 376–91). Rather than being saved by the intervention of a wealthy white person, the redevelopment was the result of years of community organizing spearheaded by Genevieve Brooks, a Black female resident of the neighborhood. Brooks formed tenant associations, block associations, and an activist group called the Mid-Bronx Desperadoes that cleaned up the neighborhood and lobbied the city for improvements to the neighborhood (Christie). According to former Bronx borough president Fernando Ferrer, "There was a tremendous amount of community action.... That was the secret ingredient. The community refused to give up. They needed allies. They needed people who took the decline of the South Bronx as personally as they did" (Christie). According to Brooks, it took the Desperadoes seven years to obtain funding for Charlotte Gardens because "people view community-based organizations as irresponsible. It's

Will Eisner, *Dropsie Avenue* (June 1995). Reprinted in *The Contract with God Trilogy* (W. W. Norton, 2006). © Will Eisner Studios.

plain and simple racism. We've been here all along. We fought to keep police here, sanitation, a post office. There weren't any street signs or road service; sometimes water was shut off. All those things survived because we wouldn't give up" (Hopkins, 22). Eisner makes precisely the assumptions that Brooks decries about Black and Puerto Rican inner-city residents.

Not only does Eisner assume that the neighborhood's salvation must come from an upper-class white person, but he denigrates the Black political activism of the period. One of the signs of the neighborhood's decline is that what appears to be a radical Black Power group, whom Eisner depicts as menacing slobs, has set up office on the block. The group has signs saying "People Power" with clenched fists hanging in their office, and the group's leader is named Mboto, in keeping with the practice of many Black Power leaders of taking African names (Eisner, 456). Mboto's vaguely threatening attitude and the similarity of his name to that of Joseph-Désiré Mobutu, the military dictator of the Congo, subtly evoke the evil Black rebels in jungle comics, a genre that Eisner played a role in launching. *Sheena, Queen of the Jungle* was a product of the freelance studio Eisner ran with Jerry Iger, and Eisner was directly involved in Sheena's creation (Webb et al., 1). His negative portrayal of radical Black activists is thus continuous with his earlier construction of an entire genre structured by colonialist and imperialist ideology. While Genevieve Brooks's group was not ideologically radical, it falls within the tradition of community self-organization and mobilization that Black Power played a key role in stimulating.

Taken together, Eisner's narrative communicates the idea that minorities can only progress by taking handouts from whites (or Jews), as the Puerto Rican leader and Ruby do, and minorities who make demands and assert their independence are surly and ungrateful. Whites (and Jews) are portrayed as benevolent, paternalistic benefactors whose generosity is not always appreciated by the minorities they generously aid.

ASSIMILATION AND ITS DISCONTENTS

Art Spiegelman, Harvey Pekar, and Aline Kominsky-Crumb belong to the generation of Jews after Eisner's, when Jewishness was becoming mostly assimilated into whiteness. As the cultural scholar Karen Brodkin wrote of her own upbringing in this era, "My parents had no doubt about their Jewishness, and my brother, Henry, and I had no doubt about our whiteness, but the two didn't combine as seamlessly as our public intellectuals said they should" (159). The increasing assimilation of Jewishness into whiteness gave their generation an insider's view of whiteness that their parents never had. It also meant that their relation to Jewishness was typically oriented toward the past, making their parents' generation central for their self-definition as Jews and a site that they explored, questioned, and critiqued to better understand their own identity. While their assimilation was real, it was not complete, making them both Jewish and white, a fragmented condition that they explored in their comics.

One of the key sites of internal conflict in their relationship to Jewishness was the Jewish racism toward other groups, in particular Black people, which they all observed and critiqued to one degree or another. Spiegelman, Pekar, and Kominsky-Crumb grew up with the civil rights movement and the Vietnam War, which gave them a greater sensitivity to racial oppression and the moral failings of white supremacy and led them to question the tenets of Jewish exceptionalism. As Brodkin puts it, "My parents, first-generation U.S.-born eastern European Jews... expect anti-Semitism to be part of the fabric of daily life, much as I expect racism to be part of it. They came of age in the 1920s and 1930s at the peak of anti-Semitism in the United States" (Sacks, 395).

Whereas Eisner tried to tidy up Jewishness, sweeping all the bits and pieces that he found embarrassing or unsightly under the rug, the generation of Jewish cartoonists that followed him did the opposite, exploring the inconvenient cracks and crevices that disrupted the framework of its myth. However, other than rejecting the canonical trajectory of Jewish history in America, these cartoonists have little in common, differing widely in personality, style, and thematic concerns. Spiegelman, Pekar, and Kominsky-Crumb grew up in the postwar period when Jews and other recent European immigrants were being assimilated as whites in suburbia. Although Kominsky-Crumb was the only one of these three cartoonists who grew up in a fully suburban environment (Pekar's residential area of Cleveland and Spiegelman's Rego Park, Queens, were both on the borderlands between the urban and suburban), all three of them rejected both normative whiteness and normative Jewishness, fashioning alternative versions of Jewish and white identity. Spiegelman and Kominsky-Crumb were active in the 1960s counterculture as underground cartoonists, although both were unorthodox members of that already unorthodox group. Pekar was even more of a nonconformist, a cantankerous, self-made, working-class intellectual who was in many ways a throwback to the pre–World War II era when urban, socialist, secular, working-class Jews were common.

Art Spiegelman's acclaimed graphic novel *Maus* depicts his father Vladek's harrowing journey through Nazi-occupied Poland and internment in a concentration camp. The Holocaust had an enormous impact on the consciousness of American Jews, many of whom lost relatives in it. It served to remind Jews of their history of persecution and their continued vulnerability, to renew their consciousness of themselves as a minority group, and to cement their loyalty to the state of Israel, founded in 1948 as an attempt to provide a national home for Jews. Race and nationality are integral to *Maus*, so much so that these features are represented in the graphic novel's visual fabric through the anthropomorphic depiction of different ethnic groups: Jews as mice, Poles as pigs, Nazis as cats, and Americans as dogs. Spiegelman's decision to render his characters as anthropomorphic animals based on their racial identities potentially falls into the same trap as that of the X-Men, in which race is established as a biological reality rather than a social construct. Unlike Stan Lee, however, Spiegelman is aware of this trap and takes steps to avoid it. Spiegelman has explained that "these metaphors . . . are meant to self-destruct in my book—and I think they do self-destruct" (Mulman, 88). One way they do so is through the ways in which Spiegelman plays with the artificiality of the trope of anthropomorphic animals. When characters attempt to disguise themselves or pass as other races, they wear an animal mask of the relevant race. Spiegelman himself wears a mouse mask when appearing as a framing narrator to comment on his adoption of the Holocaust as a subject, and he discusses with his wife Françoise what kind of animal she should be shown as in the comic. Spiegelman thereby acknowledges the artificiality of the animal trope and, by extension, the racial categories it is used to represent. Despite this artificiality, however, Spiegelman believes that the choice of animal species to represent different races still has "a residual force that allows them to work as metaphors" (88).

This force derives in large part from the overdetermined array of iconographic sources that lie behind it. Spiegelman's first mouse comics began with an attempt to do a comic about Black characters and American racism in which the mouse served as a reference to Mickey Mouse, whose first incarnations were based on the tradition of blackface minstrelsy that was deeply embedded in late-nineteenth- and early twentieth-century American culture. Cat characters were to be the Ku Klux Kats. The use of mice to represent Jews became a reference to the Nazis' descriptions and images of Jews as vermin and rats (Spiegelman, *MetaMaus*, 111–22). As Spiegelman explained, *Maus* "was made in collaboration with Hitler.... My anthropomorphized mice carry trace elements of Fips's anti-Semitic Jew-as-rat cartoons for *Der Sturmer*, but by being particularized they are invested with personhood; they stand upright and affirm their humanity" (Doherty, 74). These are just a few of the many parallels and references that Spiegelman discovered in the visual history of American and Nazi racism. Although Spiegelman abandoned the project on American racism in favor of *Maus*, the layering of American and Nazi racist tropes draws a subtextual connection between anti-Black and anti-Semitic racism and between racial oppression by whites in America and Nazis in Europe.

Maus is not simply the story of Vladek's experience in the Holocaust. It is also about Art's relationship with Vladek and, through that relationship, about the process of Jewish assimilation into white America. In many ways, Vladek was an archetypal white father of the postwar period: a stern patriarch verging on the authoritarian, closed off emotionally, who tried to keep his son on the straight and narrow and steer him toward a conventional career and life. Art rebelled, as did much of his generation, joining the counterculture, adopting its alternative lifestyle, and becoming an artist, or rather a cartoonist, an even less respectable profession. Art's rebellion thus testifies to Jews' assimilation into whiteness after World War II, to the extent of undergoing the same generational gaps and rebellions. Vladek was not simply a typical white suburban postwar dad; he was a Holocaust survivor, a legacy that imposed an added weight on his son. When a young Art tells his father, crying, that he fell and his friends skated away without him, Vladek's response is "If you lock them together in a room with no food for a week.... Then you could see what it is, friends!" (6). This already heavy burden was further augmented by the death of Vladek's first son, Richieu, in the Holocaust, and the suicide of his wife, Anja, Art's mother, in 1968. The project of *Maus* was an effort on Art's part to unearth this traumatic past, which had largely been hidden from him as a child. In so doing, he did not shy away from, or attempt to gloss over, its untidy, awkward, and discreditable aspects. Art does not balk at displaying Vladek's personality flaws, even when they play into Jewish stereotypes. As he tells Mala, Vladek's second wife:

> **Art:** He's always been—uh—pragmatic.
> **Mala:** Pragmatic? Cheap!! It causes him physical pain to part with even a nickel!
> **Art:** Uh-huh. I used to think the war made him that way . . .
> **Mala:** I went through the camps. . . . All our friends went through the camps. Nobody is like him!
> **Art:** Mm . . . It's something that worries me about the book I'm doing about him. . . . In some ways he's just like the racist caricature of the miserly old Jew.
> **Mala:** Hah! You can say that again! (133)

Even more problematic than Vladek's emotional and financial miserliness is his racism toward Blacks. When Françoise is driving a car carrying Art and Vladek, she pulls over to pick up a Black hitchhiker, to which Vladek responds, "A hitch-hiker? And—oy—it's a colored guy, a shvartser!" (258) After muttering under his breath in Polish the whole ride, Vladek voices his feelings after they drop off the hitchhiker.

> **Vladek:** I had the whole time to watch out that this shvartser doesn't steal us the groceries from the back seat!
> **Françoise:** What?! That's outrageous! How can you, of all people, be such a racist! You talk about blacks the way the Nazis talked about the Jews!
> **Vladek:** Ach! . . . I thought really you are more smart than this, Françoise. . . . It's not even to compare, the shvartsers and the Jews. (259)

The existence of racism by Jews against Blacks was a topic that Eisner avoided in his trilogy, presenting Jews as having a purely benevolent, paternalistic relationship with Blacks. In the Dropsie Avenue trilogy, other ethnic groups were guilty of racism and interracial conflict, but not Jews.

Like Spiegelman's comics, those of Aline Kominsky-Crumb testify to the tension between assimilation and Jewish identity. Her family too was a combination of the typical and atypical in the white suburban postwar family, although it was a very different version of postwar suburban whiteness from Spiegelman's. Kominsky-Crumb's mother represents the consumption-oriented aspect of postwar suburban whiteness in her desire to keep up with the Joneses by acquiring material possessions and other signs of affluence. Describing the era of her upbringing, Kominsky-Crumb writes:

> America in the 1950s presented an image of prosperity, efficiency, cleanliness, wholesomeness and order, full of well-adjusted, clean-cut productive stress-free citizens. Thanks to modern conveniences, they enjoyed lots of leisure time for Bar-B-Ques with Mom and Dad, Sis and Bro, Spot the Dog, and a few like-minded friendly happy pals.
>
> For my family, and as it turns out for many others, reality was filled with overwhelming pressure to succeed, stress-induced alcoholism, pill-popping, constant fighting and lots of verbal and sometimes even physical abuse—particularly toward us innocent kids. In fact, for most of my generation, growing up in the 1950s in the U.S., and perhaps more so on Long Island, was a horrible nightmare. The bizarre visual and cultural world of the 1950s added a surreal aura to the atmosphere. Objects and motifs from this period still attract and somehow terrify me! (*Need More Love*, 14)

As Karen Brodkin has written of the protagonists of novels by Jewish women from the 1970s and 1980s, "They see their bodies as 'grotesque,' as working against them—because they are too fat or because their nose is too big. The struggle to control a body out of control, or one that always threatens to become so, is a struggle to contain one's Jewishness so that it conforms to whiteness. Mostly it doesn't work" (166). When her family moved to the suburbs,

> This represented a big move up in the world: away with the old-fashioned neighborhood and boring familiar stuff, and on to a cool, new suburban life! It was at this point that my parents' relationship started to deteriorate. The financial and social pressure to keep up was monstrous in the Five Towns. The neighborhood ... was known for gangsters and "JAPs"—Jewish American princesses. Money was sacred, material prosperity was worshipped. (30–31)

In her early stories, such as "Arnie's Air Conditioner" and "Blabette Gets an Afro," Aline depicts her mother, whom she calls Blabette in her comics, as cold and uncaring, preferring material goods and the surface appearance of prosperity and comfort to emotional bonds. She finds her mother's tastes gaudy and tacky and her materialism alienating. Her mother's attempts to cultivate the appearance of success and happiness are all a facade, however, as her marriage is unhappy, her husband is abusive, and she herself is uncaring and oblivious to others' feelings and needs. While Blabette and the other women in her neighborhood attempt to manipulate their physical appearance through plastic surgery and cultivate negative body images, Aline eventually learns to accept and embrace her body as it is (*Need More Love*, 86–88). In another comic, Kominsky-Crumb shows her parents arriving at their new home, a garish ranch house.

> **[Caption]** In 1952 my family moved to a sleek new ranch house in Woodmere, Long Island.... This was a pivotal point in my life.... We no longer lived near my grandparents.
> **Arnie:** I hope you're happy ... I bought this for you.... Ya' like it ??!
> [In a thought bubble] I'll be payin' for it for the rest o' my life!
> **Blabette:** Oh its so gawgeous, spacious + light! We're gonna live a beddah life ovah here.
> **Aline:** I miss my nanny [her grandmother]. (43)

She adds, "Our development was built on a defunct golf course that was part of a private 'restricted' country club. Its physicality was intrinsically boring and suffocating!" (43)

Kominsky-Crumb describes her town as being populated by JAPs, Jewish American Princesses, a cultural stereotype that came to prominence in the 1970s, precisely when Kominsky-Crumb began cartooning. Karen Brodkin has argued that "JAPs are Jewish men's projections of their own nightmares about whiteness onto Jewish women. Such projections of course neatly avoid confronting the thought that men might have the same values themselves" (163). Kominsky-Crumb's comics demonstrate that the JAP was not purely a creation of the male imagination but a nightmare of whiteness to her as well. One could argue that Kominsky-Crumb has internalized the patriarchal perspective by blaming the dangers of assimilation and materialism on women. This reading could find support from the influential feminist cartoonist and comics historian Trina Robbins, who has criticized Kominsky-Crumb for her "supposedly underdeveloped feminist politics—a move that she interprets as punishment for failing to idealize women in her narratives" (Chute, 37). Robbins also criticized Kominsky-Crumb for her marriage to Robert Crumb, whose work Robbins has described as misogynist, going so far as to call her and Diane Noonin "camp followers" for their relationships with male underground cartoonists (Kominsky-Crumb, 153). However, the claim that Kominsky-Crumb has internalized male sexism does not stand up well to the actual content of her work, in which she strongly asserts her independent identity and critically depicts male violence against women and the imposition of unrealistic and monolithic standards of physical appearance on women. As Hillary Chute has written, "Kominsky-Crumb narrates a sexual life that *includes* but is not limited to or determined by an 'objectification' and 'subordination' that she 1. Finds pleasurable and 2. Chooses herself how to represent. Her comics—even those in which Kominsky-Crumb and Crumb battle for space in a frame—are not inscribed by a (male) gaze that subordinates her" (54).

While Kominsky-Crumb's mother stands for a dysfunctional, materialistic version of Jewish whiteness, her grandmother represents a link to the Jewish past that her family was leaving behind. She writes that her mother's family "was neurotic, continually yelling and overeating, but they still held on to old-fashioned family values. They kept a Kosher home, and were clannish, always surrounded by scores of relatives and hangers on for dinner. They suffocated us kids with clinging guilt-inducing love, but still a lot of love!" (15) She sees this Jewish heritage as contributing a key aspect to her art, namely, her satirical, caustic humor, which places her in a long and distinguished line of Jewish comedians. She further notes:

> I was raised on a certain kind of Jewish fatalistic humor, like the stand-up comics of the 1950s, and the storytelling in my family, where you make fun of yourself, to make other people laugh. You exaggerate in a certain way, and it's all to make to a philosophical point, and also to get people to relax and to respond to you. I was raised with that kind of east coast Jewish humor, and it has pervaded my entire life. And certainly, in my comic storytelling, there's my grandpa Joe, who was a great storyteller. And his style comes from a very old tradition of Jewish storytelling, and Jewish writing. So I sort of took that tradition of Jewish self-deprecating humor, and applied it to comics, and perhaps that was unique. (333)

This willingness to make fun of oneself, which Kominsky-Crumb attributes to the tradition of Jewish humor, means that her comics are practically an encyclopedia of the unsavory behaviors that Eisner omitted from *A Life Force* and *Dropsie Avenue* to purify Jewish identity, including racism, crime, violence, and female sexuality. Her father is a deeply unethical salesman, peddling low-quality and defective goods to poor Black customers, whom he despises and calls n-----s. He also sells these same goods to his own neighbors, who complain to the Better Business Bureau, which shuts down their business. Her father Arnie was friends and business partners with Italians involved in organized crime; he may have participated in robberies and fenced the goods with them, and other Jews they knew were involved in similar dealings (Kominsky-Crumb, 32–41, 58).

Harvey Pekar entered the comic book industry for much the same reasons that Eisner returned to it. Like Eisner, Pekar thought that "underground comics have really opened things up" (Pekar, *Bob & Harv's Comics*, 33). As did Spiegelman and Kominsky-Crumb, Pekar's autobiographical *American Splendor* depicts aspects of Jewish experience that Eisner's Jewish exceptionalism excluded, especially those related to leftist politics. Pekar was practically a living fossil of the Depression-era Jew: leftist, a public employee, white-collar but working-class or lower middle-class, living and working in a racially diverse urban area, and an independent, self-taught intellectual. Pekar's family never moved to the suburbs, but their neighborhood of Cleveland was itself practically suburban. Pekar did not join the counterculture and was not interested in marijuana or alcohol, but he was passionate about avant-garde jazz and interested in underground comix.

While identifying as a Jew, he also questioned various beliefs of the American Jewish community, which he enumerated in *Not the Israel My Parents Promised Me*. His mother was an atheistic Marxist, and his father was devoutly religious, but both lost relatives in the Holocaust and shared a commitment to Israel and Zionism. Pekar, like many of his generation, opposed the Vietnam War, which stimulated his sympathy for colonized peoples. Influenced by discussions with Jewish Trotskyists and others in the New Left, he grew disenchanted with Israel's invasion of Lebanon and the construction of settlements in the West Bank. As part of his growing doubts about Israel, he noted that Jews, including his own parents, had racist attitudes toward Arabs. He also noted that Israel was becoming increasingly intolerant and was forming alliances and selling arms to right-wing dictatorships, including fascist regimes and the racist government of apartheid South Africa. He came to believe that Arabs had a right to self-determination and to live in their homeland, and he resented accusations that his criticisms of Israel meant that he was a traitor or a self-hating Jew. Pekar's questioning of the validity of Israel's occupation of Palestinian territories was significant both as a departure from normative American Jewish beliefs but also because support for Israel had been an integral part of the United States' neocolonial effort to dominate the Middle East for the past fifty years. Questioning the nature of Israel's occupation also undermined America's white imperialism in the Middle East. As he wrote, "Nationalism and ethnic pride, in the long run, delay human development, and the misery they cause must be recognized.

If enough people saw that, maybe we wouldn't have so many wars" (*Not the Israel My Parents Promised Me*, 113).

Pekar's representations of race in most of his comics, depicting the everyday events of his day-to-day life, are less dramatic or clear-cut than the narrative of *Not the Israel My Parents Promised Me*. Jewish topics appear frequently in his work, typically presented with a wry skepticism. One example of a Jewish topic that also relates to Pekar's class position and comics history is an exchange he imagines between himself and Superman. Pekar depicts himself jumping up and down on top of a reclining, elderly Superman with receding hair and a large paunch. Pekar exclaims, "Chazzer! Choleria! Fake! A rich Jewish superhero like you—hogs the whole comic book field—won't do a thing for a serious Yiddische writer like me!!!" Underneath him, Superman pleads, "Oy, rachmones, Harvey, please! I ain't got time t'help ev'rybody, do I?? I gotta fight big goyische villains like Luthor. . . . We got the Jewish Welfare Fund for guys like you" (84) As Pekar notes, "I portrayed Superman as Jewish because his creators, Jerry Siegel and Joe Shuster, were, like me, Cleveland Jews" (84). A more realistic example of Pekar's observations about American Jewish culture is a story titled "Standing behind Old Jewish Ladies in Supermarket Lines," in which he complains that Jewish women "will argue forever with a cashier about whether she rung the prices up right, or about coupons, or about the food stamp laws." However, another Jewish woman lets him skip ahead of her because he only has two items, to which Pekar remarks, "Maybe she's the exception that proves the rule. . . . She's taller than most old Jewish women. . . . Maybe she's a mutant!" (*Bob & Harv's Comics*, 12, 15).

The most important character of color in *American Splendor* is Mr. Boats, who works in the same hospital as Pekar. Both Pekar and Boats demonstrate the predicament of the working-class intellectual, while their relationship provides a rare example in comics of a relationship of equals between a white and Black character. Although Boats and Pekar have different tastes—jazz for Pekar, classical music for Boats—both are passionately engaged in music, hold quality and critical standards in high regard, and are critical of conformism and mass culture. They both encounter obstacles in pursuing their interests owing to their modest incomes and lack of formal education and institutional support. Their shared philosophy as independent, working-class intellectuals is epitomized by a story in which Mr. Boats and Jack are standing in a crowded elevator, with the short and rotund Mr. Boats squeezed between a crowd of white passengers towering over him.[1] From the middle of the scrum, Mr. Boats declares, apropos of nothing, "Avoid the reeking herd, shun the polluted flock. . . . Live like that stoic bird, the eagle of the rock," four lines from a poem by Elinor Hoyt Wylie, an early twentieth-century poet

(Pekar, *Bob & Harv's Comics*, 17–18).² The discussion continues to other topics exploring the relative value of high and low culture and the difficulty of maintaining one's integrity in a materialistic world, classic themes of romantic modernism but conducted in a down-to-earth, plainspoken dialogue.

Wylie's lines and the conversation as a whole are emblematic of the romantic modernist quest for artistic isolation, which Boats and Pekar attempt to live despite their very different circumstances from those of Wylie. Unlike an artistically inclined member of the upper class such as Wylie, they had no family fortune to underwrite their artistic endeavors. The scowling and otherwise uncomfortable or unhappy expressions on the faces of those around them indicate the generally tedious and repetitive conditions of office work, precisely what romantics such as Wylie urge the inspired individual to escape from. For Pekar and Boats, this is clearly a practical impossibility, yet they continue to strive for this goal. Mr. Boats's position in the elevator, surrounded by a crowd of whites, suggests the additional obstacle of race that he faces. The diminutive Boats is trapped in the middle of the crowd, surrounded by a ring of whites, including Pekar. Boats appears all but submerged in the crowd, while Pekar has more personal space around him, suggesting the somewhat greater freedom provided to Pekar by his possession of white privilege. As Boats speaks the lines from Wylie's poem, however, the crowd around him parts somewhat as the office workers move away from him while ogling him with surprise and disgust. He remains hemmed in, but he has won himself at least more elbow room.

Although their readings of Jewishness diverge from one another, Spiegelman, Kominsky-Crumb, and Pekar reject the narrative of white supremacy and Jewish exceptionalism put forward by Eisner. They acknowledge the messy reality of Jewish assimilation and Jews' relationships with nonwhites, probing the conditions under which Jews were allowed to assimilate into whiteness, and the continued reality of racial hierarchy and white supremacy in American society. Eisner, Kominsky-Crumb, Spiegelman, and Pekar helped pave the way for what came to be known as alternative comics. The skepticism of the racial myths of Jewish exceptionalism and whiteness that Kominsky-Crumb, Spiegelman, and Pekar displayed were continued in the alternative comics that appeared in the 1980s and 1990s. While some alternative comics, such as Jessica Abel's *La Perdida*, continued to evince an unrecognized white racial frame, others such as Jaime and Gilbert Hernandez's *Love and Rockets* and Chris Ware's *Jimmy Corrigan, the Smartest Kid on Earth* demonstrated an awareness of the white racial frame greater than any previous comics. These comics represented the biggest step forward in racial sensitivity in the previous half century of comics.

Chapter Seven

RACIAL BORDERLANDS IN ALTERNATIVE COMICS

Building on the work of Harvey Pekar, Art Spiegelman, and Aline Kominsky-Crumb, in the 1980s and 1990s, a new generation of cartoonists working outside the mainstream of American comics emerged. In creating the new genre of alternative comics, these cartoonists advanced the artistic boundaries of American comics but had an extremely mixed record regarding race. Some key alternative cartoonists, such as Daniel Clowes and Charles Burns, did not include people of color in their comics at all, a major absence that is rarely if ever discussed in the critical literature. This absence is arguably the most important aspect of alternative comics in terms of race. A handful of alternative cartoonists, however, explored race as a major theme in their work by creating characters and stories that embody what Gloria Anzaldúa has referred to as racial borderlands, spaces where "two or more cultures edge each other, where people of different races occupy the same territory, where under, lower, middle and upper classes touch, where the space between two individuals shrinks with intimacy." Jaime and Gilbert Hernandez's *Love and Rockets*, Jessica Abel's *La Perdida*, and Chris Ware's *Jimmy Corrigan, the Smartest Kid on Earth* are three of the most notable examples of alternative comics that explore racial borderlands. For Anzaldúa, these borderlands are places that are pregnant with the potential to explode governing racial dualities that seek to separate humans into the powerful, whites, and the powerless, nonwhites. She describes this potential as the creation of mestiza consciousness:

> The work of the *mestiza* consciousness is to break down the subject-object duality that keeps her prisoner and to show in the flesh and through the images in her work how duality is transcended. The answer to the problem between the white race and the colored, between males and females, lies in healing the split that originates in the very foundation of our lives, our culture, our languages, our thoughts. A massive uprooting of dualistic thinking in the individual

and collective consciousness is the beginning of a long struggle, but one that could, in our best hopes, bring us to the end of rape, of violence, of war. (80)

Anzaldúa recognizes that the liberatory potential of mestiza consciousness will not be easily achieved. She writes that a "massive uprooting of dualistic thinking" *could* achieve major social transformations "in our best hopes," thereby acknowledging the contingency and difficulty of this outcome. Jaime and Gilberto Hernandez's *Love and Rockets*, Jessica Abel's *La Perdida*, and Chris Ware's *Jimmy Corrigan* all depict racial borderlands in which the potential to deconstruct white supremacy and the white racial frame exists but is difficult or impossible to achieve. This difficulty applies both to the fictional characters who populate these narratives and to the creators of these narratives, who themselves carry the scars and imprinting of white supremacy and the white racial frame.

Jaime and Gilberto Hernandez's *Love and Rockets*, one of the earliest and most influential alternative comics, is a rare example of an American comic told primarily from a Latinx perspective. It is arguably the most successful attempt of any American comic book up to that time, or indeed since, in presenting nonwhite characters as fully developed human beings with the same levels of complexity and empathy as white characters. Gilbert Hernandez uses the character of Howard Miller to exemplify whites' exploitation of other cultures. Miller travels to the small Mexican town of Palomar, where his interactions with the residents occur in a liminal zone in which neither side fully understands the motivations of the other. Miller plans to use the people and location as exotic subject matter for photographs that will launch him to artistic stardom. For him, the people of Palomar are merely tools to use and discard. Jaime Hernandez's Locas story line, on the other hand, imagines a fusion of the punk and Chicanx communities in Los Angeles that creates an ideal racial borderland in which difference is celebrated and racist incursions from the mainstream white world are resisted.

At first glance, Jessica Abel's *La Perdida* appears to offer a similarly sensitive exploration of the racial borderlands between Carla, an American tourist in Mexico City, and the Mexicans whom she becomes involved with there. While the ultimate meaning of *La Perdida* is left open to interpretation, its portrayal of race is problematic, because it actually perpetuates stereotypes about Mexicans as untrustworthy, mercenary, and violent. Carla initially believes that traveling to Mexico can help her reconnect with the half of her ancestry that is Mexican, but the Mexicans she chooses to associate with and place her trust in betray her. Mexico is indeed a borderland for

Carla that is pregnant with possibilities, but in the end, *La Perdida* does more to reinforce racial hierarchies than to contest them. Chris Ware's epic intergenerational graphic novel *Jimmy Corrigan* is in this sense the opposite of *La Perdida*. Whereas Carla's interaction with other races reinforces racial hierarchies, the stories of Jimmy Corrigan and his great-grandfather show the insidious effects of racism on both white and Black characters and how the main characters and their family members are implicated in maintaining white supremacy.

RACIAL BORDERLANDS IN *LOVE AND ROCKETS*

Love and Rockets is arguably the most sophisticated exploration of racial identity in American comics and was one of the first comic book series to explore the lives and personalities of nonwhite characters with depth and subtlety. *Love and Rockets* consists of two independent plotlines, known as Palomar and Locas, which appeared side by side and shared many stylistic and thematic features but followed different groups of characters in different settings. Gilbert Hernandez's Palomar series chronicles the intertwined lives of the inhabitants of a small Mexican village called Palomar, while the Locas series, by Jaime Hernandez, follows a tight-knit group of young Chicanas involved in the Los Angeles punk scene. The most important characters in both Palomar and Locas are women, making *Love and Rockets* a seminal series for its attention to issues of gender as well as race.

All racial categories are artificial constructs rather than biological realities, but this artificiality is especially noticeable in relation to Mexican identity, or Latinx/Hispanic identity more broadly. In Mexico, Mexican racial identity is understood as mestiza/o, or "mixed," referring to a mixture of Spanish and indigenous racial ancestry. This mixture is seen in Mexico as being harmonious and complementary. This conception took shape after Mexico gained independence from Spain in 1821. As a result, racial conflict is not usually seen as a serious problem in Mexico. While attractive, this vision disguises the reality that light-skinned Mexicans of European ancestry have enjoyed status and privileges that have been denied to darker-skinned or indigenous Mexicans throughout Mexican history (Dowling, 79–82).

In the United States, Mexican Americans fall outside the dominant racial binary of white and Black (Foley, 5). The most recent US census asked respondents to state their race and whether they were Hispanic but stated that Hispanic was not considered a race for the purposes of the census. Julie Dowling has shown that many Mexican Americans identify themselves as white when filling out a census form but not in other situations (Dowling, 2). Dowling argues that Mexican Americans variously identify as Mexican, Mexican American, Chicanx, or white, depending on the circumstances in which the identification is made and their views of American and Mexican society. Racism against Mexican Americans, for instance, motivates many Mexican Americans to identify themselves as white to escape discrimination (10). Categorizing Mexicans as a different race from whites is thus inherently problematic and contradictory, but American popular culture and political discourse generally ignore the complexity of this issue and treat Mexican, Hispanic, or Latinx identity as in effect a racial identity. Anzaldúa argues that racial borderlands pose a direct threat to white supremacy by presenting racial liminalities that defy easy categorization:

> Borders are set up to define the places that are safe and unsafe, to distinguish *us* from *them*. A border is a dividing line, a narrow strip along a steep edge. A borderland is a vague and undetermined place created by the emotional residue of an unnatural boundary. It is in a constant state of transition. The prohibited and forbidden are its inhabitants . . . the squint-eyed, the perverse, the queer, the troublesome, the mongrel, the mulatto, the half-breed, the half-dead; in short, those who cross over, pass over, or go through the confines of the "normal." Gringos in the U.S. Southwest consider the inhabitants of the borderlands transgressors, aliens. . . . The only "legitimate" inhabitants are those in power, the whites and those who align themselves with whites. (Anzaldúa, 3–4)

Borderlands that destabilize dominant categories appear everywhere in *Love and Rockets* and undermine the racial categories that divide whiteness from other ethnic and racial identities.

Perhaps the clearest examination of whiteness in *Love and Rockets* occurs in the 1985 story "An American in Palomar." In it, an American photographer named Howard Miller comes to Palomar to photograph the town and its inhabitants for a photo book he is working on, which he hopes will propel him to success and stardom. His strategy is to exploit the picturesque squalor of Palomar. As the narrator informs us:

> The more tragic, humorous, sentimental or wretched the better for Miller, as he has found in the people of Palomar the ideal subject matter for the book he hopes will establish his (self-proclaimed) genius to the art world. . . . With years of experience freelancing for various

geographic magazines behind him, Howard Miller is familiar with his chosen source material while jaded by it as well.... Just another group of Indians and blacks and whatevers to him.... He believes it is his "aesthetic genius," however, that will make all the difference. (Hernandez and Hernandez, 29)

Miller sets out to photograph any examples of squalor or provincialism that he can find. He tries to photograph the local cinema owner, Luba, with her family because he sees Luba covered in dirt after a hard day's work, and he thinks she would be a prime example of squalor. She dresses herself and her family up in their best clothes for their photography session, but when he explains his intentions to Luba, she is furious. She asks him incredulously, "You want . . . a picture of *my* family all sloppy and ragged—to put in a book for the whole world to see—? What the hell do you think we are? A freak show—?" (41). When he tells her that he sees this degradation as a form of beauty, she stomps on his foot with her high-heeled shoe and exclaims, "You're going to make hundreds of dollars by making us look bad and you're talking about beauty?!" (41). As Luba realizes, Miller's goal is to exploit Palomar's exoticism to make himself a superstar. Miller's project presents Palomar as other and offers her otherness up for consumption by the white gaze, reaffirming the duality of nonwhite and white cultures that Anzaldúa seeks to disrupt.

Miller's exploitation of Palomar's otherness resonates strongly with the history of white Western artists appropriating non-Western cultures' art through the discourse of primitivism (Hiller). Hernandez draws attention to this connection through a scene in which a young boy from Palomar leads Miller to a cave filled with large, primitive-looking idols that he enters to photograph for his book. These statues are stereotypical examples of the kind of "primitive" sculpture that was widely appropriated by white modernist artists, and appears frequently in popular culture as symbols of primitivism, including many early American comic books depicting primitive African tribes. While Miller is inside the cave, one or more loud voices ask him a series of questions about his intentions in Palomar, echoing questions that various residents of Palomar have asked him. The questions appear to be Miller's own conscience speaking to him. Primitivist iconography is thus used to represent the white Miller's internal self. This continues a tradition of using appropriated "primitive" imagery of nonwhite cultures to represent the internal life of whites. We see an example of this recurring racial trope in Robert Crumb's use of minstrel images to represent whites' desire to escape the narrow confines of conservative white social mores. The primitive masks in "An American in Palomar" represent Miller's conscience, or superego, rather than his id, or desires, but the larger pattern remains.

One subplot that complicates the primary message of Miller's story deals with his affair with Tonantzín, a young woman of Palomar who believes that Miller will use his connections in Hollywood to make her a star. After Miller ends their relationship, Tonantzín believes that he has taken advantage of her. However, this situation is more complicated than it first appears. It is Tonantzín who hatches the scheme to make herself a star, initiates the relationship with Miller, and decides that she will come to the United States to live with him. Miller warns her that it is unlikely that he will be able to help her start a modeling career, and makes no promises to take her with him to the United States, but she brushes his warnings off, and he does not make too great of an effort to dissuade her. He is also culpable for lying to her when breaking up with her. After Miller breaks off their relationship, Tonantzín's sister Carmen asks her, "Who used who?! Tonantzín, those pictures were your idea! Did he say he was taking you with him?" (44). Thus Miller also becomes a victim, as three local boys beat him up after he dumps Tonantzín, leaving half of his face permanently scarred. In the end, he becomes exactly the kind of deformed "freak," mired in degradation and misery, that he hoped to find and photograph in Palomar.

The final panel of the story recounts, "As time passes in Palomar, the daily rituals of work and play ease the memory of Howard Miller and his proposed book out of the minds of the people. Most folks have already forgotten his name, much less remember his face. Back in the United States, Miller wishes he could be so lucky" (48). This incident suggests several conclusions. First, Miller's quest to find and exploit images of pain, squalor, and degradation ends up turning him into the very thing that he is seeking to find. By extension, this outcome suggests that the whole history of white exploitation and appropriation of nonwhite cultures damages and dehumanizes the white people who undertake this project, as well as those who are subjected to it. Second, it makes the point that whites are not the only ones capable of exploiting others, which has a humanizing effect by creating Mexican characters who have flaws and shortcomings as well as virtues and strengths. While Miller's exploitation of Palomar is the main theme of the story, this subplot makes it clear that manipulation and exploitation are not unique to white people.

Racial identity is a recurring theme in Jaime Hernandez's Locas stories as well as Gilbert Hernandez's Palomar stories. Racial issues are rarely the focus of the story in the Locas story line, but a sophisticated dialogue on race develops through background incidents. The simplest kind of background incident in Locas is the depiction of casual racism from whites against Mexicans and

Gilbert Hernandez, "An American in Palomar." Originally published in *Love and Rockets* #14 (November 1985). Reprinted in *House of Raging Women* (Fantagraphics, 1988). © Gilbert Hernandez.

everyday acts of racial solidarity and community building. One example of casual racism occurs in the "Death of Speedy" story arc. A white janitor hectors a group of young Chicana women standing outside a public restroom, demanding, "How many times have I told you people not to loiter around my restrooms? Now take off!" (49). The reference to "you people" is a subtle indicator of racial otherness, which is then confirmed when he says "damn cholos" as he walks away from them. At the bottom of the page, we see him lying against a wall with stars and spirals floating around his head, the cartoon convention for having been beaten up. It is unclear who has done this to him, but it appears to be the group of tough women whom he has just told to leave the restroom. His attackers were most likely a group of tough girls who have just beat up Maggie, the primary protagonist of the story line, so they are not entirely sympathetic, but their actions in this case are presented as understandable and humorous, thanks to the use of cartoony symbols to indicate his injury.

"Vida Loca: The Death of Speedy Ortiz" also contains an example of racial solidarity and community building. A poster from the Chicanx political movement appears in the background of a meeting of the Widows, a former street gang that is trying to stop a feud between the young men, or "locos," of the towns of Hoppers and Dairytown. One member of the group, Licha, says, "Nowadays, we as a group do things to help the barrio, not hurt. We put on dances, car washes . . ." (44) Behind her, partly obscured by a speech balloon and another character's head, is a poster that says "Raza Unite" around an image of two hands grasping each other. In Will Eisner's *Dropsie Avenue*, a similar poster, saying "People Power" with a clenched fist on it, appears in a scene in which Izzy Cash visits one of his buildings. Both posters use images and symbols associated with ethnic nationalist movements. In *Dropsie Avenue*, the Black nationalists represent an alien threat to the Jewish landlord, but in *Love and Rockets* the poster represents community and the possibility of redemption. The difference in the symbolic framing of the images results from the difference in narrative perspective. In *Dropsie Avenue*, the narrative perspective is that of a provisionally white Jew. In the case of *Love and Rockets*, the narrative perspective is that of a nonwhite.

While the primary plotline of "The Death of Speedy" is not explicitly about race, it emerges as an important subtext of the story. The primary plotline concerns Speedy's romantic relationship with Esther, the sister of Maggie, the main protagonist of Locas, and the feud between his Hoppers locos and the locos of Dairytown, whose leader, Rojo, is Esther's ex-boyfriend. Some of the behavior of Speedy's friends resembles Mexican stereotypes, particularly the stereotypes of macho Mexican men. When Speedy suspects (incorrectly) that Esther has another boyfriend, he walks off in a rage, threatening to kill the hypothetical boyfriend, and promptly has sex with another woman named Blanca. Female characters are also shown suffering from extreme jealousy. Blanca later confronts Esther in a bathroom and accuses her of hitting on Speedy. Maggie intervenes and claims to be the one whom Speedy is sleeping with, after which Blanca and her friends beat Maggie. Speedy's friends are also shown as small-time tough guys through their feud with the Dairytown locos, which escalates from threats to fistfights to a shooting. The "Death of Speedy" story line thus plays into common stereotypes about Mexicans. The story does not exaggerate these stereotypes, and violence of various kinds is a real part of life in many, if not all, communities, so this story line can be seen as an expression of lived experience. Moreover, the story also features a number of events that cut against these stereotypes and complicate the overall depiction of race within the story.

Jaime Hernandez, "Vida Loca 3: The Death of Speedy Ortiz." Originally published in *Love and Rockets* #23 (October 1987). Reprinted in *The Death of Speedy* (Fantagraphics, 1989). © Jaime Hernandez.

One such incident demonstrates how the meaning of racial slurs can be modulated depending on the specific circumstances in which they are used and who is using them. When Ray, an old member of the Hoppers crew, returns to town, he meets a white friend of his named Doyle. They greet each other by trading exaggerated racial slurs. Ray calls Doyle "you crusty poor white trash piece o' shite," and Doyle responds by calling Ray "you greasy wetback shit monger" (9). The closeness of their friendship allows them to use what would normally be highly offensive racial language in a way that they each understand to be affectionate, in the process demonstrating the complexity of racial language.

"The Death of Speedy" also complicates the construction of gender in relation to Mexican identity and stereotypes. The jealous violence and promiscuity of Speedy and Rojo play into stereotypes about Mexican men, but other episodes undercut this message. When Rojo goes to Maggie's home to force Esther to come back to Dairytown with him, Maggie demands that he leave. Rojo threatens her. At that moment, Maggie's aunt, the professional

Jaime Hernandez, "Vida Loca 2: The Death of Speedy Ortiz." Originally published in *Love and Rockets* #22 (August 1987). Reprinted in *The Death of Speedy* (Fantagraphics, 1989). © Jaime Hernandez.

wrestler Rena Titañon, enters the room and confronts Rojo, going toe to toe with him. When Rojo tells Maggie, "I never hit a girl before," Rena responds, "But you're thinking of it, huh, Bozo? Listen. How about if you hit me instead, and then my niece can finally see how two grown men can fit into an aspirin bottle" (39). This scene reverses the presumed physical dominance of the male characters by placing them in a confrontation with Rena, whose fighting prowess, physical strength, and courage have been demonstrated repeatedly in previous stories. Rena's menacing physical presence also undermines and threatens what the Mexican poet Octavio Paz refers to as a Mexican mask of machismo. For Paz, this mask, not unlike for white superheroes, fortifies one's fraudulent masculinity: "The ideal of manliness is never to 'crack,' never to back down. Those who 'open themselves up' are cowards. Unlike other people, we believe that opening oneself up is a weakness or a betrayal" (30). The problem with this psychic structure is that concomitant with the mask is acute sexist thinking. Paz further offers, "Women are inferior beings because, in submitting, they open themselves up. Their inferiority is constitutional and resides in their sex, their submissiveness, which is a wound that never heals" (30). Rena explodes this gender binary and functions as a borderland character that positively undermines sexism.

The image of Mexican male machismo is also undercut by Speedy's relationship with Maggie. The pressures of Ray's relationship with Esther and his feud with the Dairytown boys drive him to feel alone and alienated. Maggie has had a crush on him for years but is currently involved in a complex emotional and sexual relationship with her female best friend, Hopey. Ray seeks solace with Maggie, telling her, "I can't talk to anybody the way I can with you. I probably tell you more shit about me than I've ever told my own family" (34). This confession reveals Ray's emotional vulnerability, contradicting the false persona of machismo that he usually strives to project. Yet Ray can also oscillate in the opposite direction when his masculinity is threatened, revealing its brittleness and potential to fracture. After Maggie sees Ray get hit by Rojo's friend and tries to help Ray, he responds angrily, telling her, "Get out of my fuckin' way! What do you know anyway, with all your punker fag shit!" (38). On the one hand, this is a stereotypical example of machismo, but on the other, it reveals the falseness of the macho persona. It shows Ray's fear of being seen as vulnerable and his inability to accept help, especially from a woman, rendering him incapable of dealing with his pain. In the end, this inability leads to his suicide, which is the ultimate betrayal of machismo, since it confesses a depth of pain that cannot be confronted or dealt with.

Shortly before Ray commits suicide, he has a second heartfelt conversation with Maggie, which results in another exposure of weakness and an unexpected reaction from Maggie that decenters rather than undercuts the construction of machismo. Ray tells Maggie, "I never really wanted Esther, or Blanca, or . . . You're the one I've wanted for along ol' time. You knew that. You did . . . Please, Maggie . . . Keep me going . . . Only you can do it for me. I . . . I—I love you" (56). In their previous conversation, Maggie had responded to Ray's confession with affection, but now she rejects the terms on which he makes his plea for help, telling him, "Oh, stop it, will you?! Don't you dare put this on me! Damn you, Speedy! . . . I don't want to want you any more, Speedy. . . . I can't do it any more. It hurts too much" (56–57). In a male chauvinist society, men presume that when they ask women for help, the women will provide it. Emotional labor in service of men is assumed to be a woman's job. Maggie rejects this arrangement in her response to Speedy, which seems to stun him. He silently departs, and a few panels later, the police find him dead in his car.

While *Love and Rockets* frequently approaches race and whiteness with a probing and critical attitude, in at least one way it evades dealing with an uncomfortable racial issue. A number of characters in Locas are involved in the Los Angeles punk scene, including Hopey, who is on tour with her punk band during the events of "The Death of Speedy." Jaime Hernandez spends little if any time exploring the dialectics of race in punk rock. In Locas, punk rock is a comforting background noise. Race is not totally absent from the punk rock subculture, but it is not seen as problematic either. The antiauthoritarian stance of punk rock is assumed to extend to race, making punks sympathetic to the plight of minorities as victims of the same white power structure that punks are rebelling against. In reality, the place of race in punk rock is considerably more complicated. While punk rock was closely identified with antiauthoritarian, anarchist politics, there were also strains of unconscious racism within the punk movement, much as there have been in even well-intentioned comics by white creators. James Spooner, director of the documentary *Afro-Punk*, has described how he was continually forced to choose between his identity as a punk and as a Black person.

Jaime Hernandez's experience with punk appears to have been somewhat different. He has stated that, in his experience, the Chicanx and punk communities did not overlap or interact much, which was how he preferred it. As he told one interviewer, "I've always lived my life from the outside looking in. While we were growing up Mexican, we were outsider Mexicans because we were rock'n'rollers, and most of the Mexican kids we knew liked funk and soul and stuff like that. . . . I had different factions of friends that liked different things, I kept it all separate on purpose" (Merino, 41). For Hernandez, this separation does not appear to have registered as problematic, which is reflected in how punk rock appears in Locas. In reproducing this experience in *Love and Rockets*, he avoids a difficult and sensitive subject. As Stephen Duncombe and Maxwell Tremblay have written, "From its inception punk rock has tried, in myriad ways, to 'solve' the problems of racial identity in an increasingly multicultural world. But punk didn't deliver, it couldn't deliver. . . . If punk is ever going to be the kind of subcultural form that truly undermines White privilege and develops an alternative way of living race in and against mainstream society, it has to be remade, again" (14, 17). *Love and Rockets* may not have remade punk and its relation to race, but the Hernandez brothers' creation arguably did do so for comics and their own, equally problematic relation to race.

The construction of racial identity is not neat and tidy. The Hernandez brothers explore the messy lived reality of race in borderland spaces between and within whiteness and Latinx identities. The brothers are quite aware of how white supremacy and the white racial frame affect white and Latinx people alike, but they refuse to idealize Latinx identity just because it is oppressed and marginalized by whiteness. Rather, they insist on complicating Latinx identity, exploring its inconsistencies and internal contradictions. The racial borderlands they construct are messy and full of pitfalls as well as liberatory potential.

LIBERAL RACISM IN JESSICA ABEL'S *LA PERDIDA*

While *Love and Rockets* repeats certain racial stereotypes about Mexicans to undermine those stereotypes, the repetition of stereotypes in Jessica Abel's *La Perdida*, which was directly influenced by *Love and Rockets*, is much more ambiguous. In this sense, *La Perdida* creates a textbook example of a borderland, but this borderland does not easily translate into a liberatory deconstruction of the white racial frame, which it reaffirms more so than it dismantles. While this ambiguity is not fully resolvable, and the text leaves space for alternate readings, the comic contains many troubling elements that perpetuate racial stereotypes beneath a veneer of liberal tolerance and concern, thereby demonstrating that racial borderlands can be used to mask a return of old biases as well as to deconstruct them. The main character of *La Perdida* is Carla Olivares, the daughter of a Mexican man and a German American woman from Chicago. Carla travels to Mexico City to discover her lost Mexican roots, aspiring to be what Gloria Anzaldúa has called the new mestiza, who "copes by developing a tolerance for contradictions, a tolerance for ambiguity. She learns to be an Indian in Mexican culture, to be Mexican from an Anglo point of view. She learns to juggle cultures" (79). This ability to bridge two worlds is precisely what Carla is seeking to acquire during her sojourn in Mexico. However, she fails because she approaches the process in a superficial and touristic way, similar to how Howard Miller approaches Palomar in *Love and Rockets*.

One of the main reasons Carla's quest fails is because she has such difficulty responding to critiques of America's imperialist relation to Mexico. Abel's narrative comes across as dismissive of this viewpoint, and the readiest conclusion offered to the reader is that critiques of American imperialism and white privilege are false and hypocritical. Race and racism are very much central to the book, but Abel only considers them through the opinions of a central character, a Mexican man named Memo, whom Abel discredits from his first appearance to the book's conclusion. This allows Abel to dismiss his ideas by discrediting his character, creating a situation in which the existence of racism and white privilege appears to be little more than the ravings of an unsavory zealot. Abel does nothing to provide any alternative to this impression. In this sense, Carla and Abel fail to capitalize on the potential for borderlands to, as Anzaldúa puts it, "[make] a new *mestiza* consciousness . . . a consciousness of the Borderlands" (77).

Carla's decision to travel to Mexico stems from her feeling little connection to the nation or its culture. Her parents separated when she was young, and she was raised by her white mother, having little contact with her father, unlike her brother, Rod, who was raised by their father. She is thus split between whiteness and nonwhiteness. Initially she opts to embrace the former and banish the latter. With her father out of her life, she tries to erase her Mexican heritage. However, after an exposure to Frida Kahlo in a college art class piques Carla's interest in her Mexican ancestry, she decides to discover the meaning of this aspect of herself and her history. It is clear to the reader, if not initially to Carla herself, that her embrace of Frida Kahlo, and of Mexican culture generally, is uninformed, naive, and reified. As Carla tells the reader, "She was more than my ideal of an artist, she was my ideal woman. All I wanted was to be more like her" (Abel, 20). While Carla exalts Kahlo, this worship also distorts her, transforming her from a living, flawed human being into an idol, and suppressing any realities about Kahlo's life that do not fit with Carla's conception of her, such as her communist politics and her troubled marriage to the abusive artist Diego Rivera. Carla's other main interest in Mexico is *folklórico*, the trappings of "authentic" Mexican folk culture, which in urban Mexico City are almost exclusively tourist fodder. Carla is a classic gringo tourist, an American who has an idealized and false vision of Mexico. As Memo describes her, she is a "bourgeois dilettante in the lovely aesthetics of a Mexico that isn't now and probably never was" (103). This is but one example of the accuracy of Memo's critiques, despite Abel's attempts to render him an unreliable narrator. Carla does eventually come to recognize the naïveté and romanticism of her quest, telling the reader, "I wanted to find my Mexican roots. Somehow it seemed I would like them better than my Anglo ones, which makes no sense when you think about it" (11).

This lesson in the pitfalls of racial self-discovery is taught through the characters whom Carla encounters in the course of *La Perdida*'s story. When Carla first arrives in Mexico, she moves in with her ex-semi-boyfriend, Harry, who is an archetypal depiction of the rich, spoiled American. Harry is rude and privileged and, rather ridiculously, fancies himself a bohemian poet when in fact he is actually a frat boy slumming it south of the border. He is an extreme version of Howard Miller. Carla is aware of the white privilege inherent in Harry's Mexican sojourn and, by extension, her own. At one point, she accuses him of occupying "the First World Zone" (Abel, 24) and later says to him, "What a novel idea: travel to foreign lands, meet exotic

Jessica Abel, *La Perdida* (Pantheon, 2006). © Jessica Abel.

people, and look down on them and write about how corrupt and stupid they are.... You come in here with your fat wallet, order people around, rent a beautiful apartment then trash it, breeze in and out like it doesn't fucking matter, but you're completely a colonialist asshole" (57). Carla also seems aware that a lighter version of this critique could apply to her as well. She wishes to avoid occupying this position and consequently overcompensates in the opposite direction.

Harry is a quintessential example of the ugly American, but other characters who are decent, caring people, who do not flaunt their white privilege and are able to assimilate at least somewhat into Mexican society, balance him out. One of these is a friend of Harry's named Sylvia, who is kind, caring, intelligent, and levelheaded, all things that Harry manifestly is not. Sylvia's main role in the story is to serve as a foil to Carla. Whereas Carla becomes increasingly callous to the feelings of those who do not share her belief in the importance of Mexican authenticity, Sylvia remains kind and compassionate. Carla's brother, Rod, offers another positive American model. Although younger than Carla, Rod is both more successful and more authentically Mexican than she is, since he was raised by their Mexican father rather than their white mother. Rod is depicted in glowing terms. He has become quite successful at a young age, thanks to a thriving website he owns that sells skateboarding gear, but he is not conceited and is consistently generous, kind, empathetic, and helpful. Through his online network of skater friends, he actually knows Mexico City better than Carla does despite never having visited it before, and he quickly finds out about a number of cool local places of which Carla is unaware. The final American character is Ray, an American who is part of a criminal gang run by an ex-cop called El Gordo. When Carla first meets Ray, she starts speaking to him in English, but he snaps at her to stop because, as Carla later explains, "One expat gringo in a crowd can be the exception to the rule, the cool American who proves everyone's lack of prejudices. But two gringos, speaking English, and suddenly your Americanness becomes notable, and neither of us wanted that" (Abel, 98). Ray is a repulsive character who is always rude and, as we find out later, dangerous as well. It is significant and typical of *La Perdida* that the American who is most fully immersed in Mexican society is also a boorish, violent criminal.

All these white Americans function as foils of one kind or another for the character Memo, who dominates the entire story. Like Ray, Memo is extremely rude and abrasive, but rather than simply being a thug, he is an outspoken, self-proclaimed Marxist and a harsh critic of the United States and everything associated with it. Memo poses the question of white privilege bluntly, at one point telling Carla, "You don't see the advantages your white skin and your American accent give you" (105). Along the same lines, in their first conversation, Memo asks Carla, "How can you be Mexican when you grow up with the dollar who rides on the backs of the poor people of the world, and guns in every closet, and Hollywood that tell you you are right!" (26). These views are never given a fair hearing. Abel tells us right from the start that Memo is a phony. Before he even says a word, Carla tells us in a text box, "In retrospect, he must have been ridiculous, but I couldn't see it in him. He put me on the defensive right off" (25). Sylvia's intervention in the conversation serves to further discredit Memo. Sylvia interrupts the conversation to defend Carla, telling Memo that "you take out your aggressions on one little tourist" (27). She interprets Memo's critique of whiteness and the United States as merely personal aggression, not a viable political or social critique. This move occurs throughout the book. At no point does any character actually consider the content or validity of Memo's arguments, either to agree or to disagree with them. Nor does Abel provide any events or context for his views, other than the petty antics of Harry. We are not shown anything that would either confirm or deny Memo's assertions of the negative impacts of American imperialism or racism.

The most effective way in which Abel discredits Memo is through his personal behavior, especially his womanizing. Memo initially hits on Carla aggressively, but she rebuffs him. After Carla begins dating a younger friend of Memo's named Oscar, Memo temporarily drops his pursuit of her. Eventually he does make one final duplicitous pass at her, offering her "the best of both worlds. Sexy boy toy upstairs, an intelligent man of the world here in front of you" (Abel, 92). Memo later dates Carla's roommate, Liana, but cheats on her. When Carla confronts Memo about this, he uses his politics as an excuse for his behavior, telling Carla, "You think you can hold me to your bourgeois standards? . . . I'm a free man! I act as an agent of my own will in the world!" (85). This represents a recurring pattern for Memo: he behaves terribly and justifies his behavior with a superficial and self-serving Marxist critique. While it is still possible for the reader to agree with Memo's criticism of the United States and white privilege despite his unsavory behavior, the dice are loaded against these points. In contrast to Memo, Carla's boyfriend, Oscar, is apolitical and focused entirely on having a good time. He is a small-time drug dealer who has an unrealistic dream of becoming a globe-trotting, successful DJ. He is consistently shown as being unrealistic, incapable, impractical, and weak willed. Although good-looking and fun, he has low status among his friends and extended family. Oscar's cousin Ricardo is his drug supplier and is considerably more dominant, aggressive, and violent than Oscar. Ricardo is El Gordo's son and a member of his gang. Together, they represent the corruption and violence that Abel repeatedly portrays as endemic to Mexico, which the kidnapping of Harry that dominates the second half of the graphic novel epitomizes.

Rather implausibly, about halfway through the narrative, Oscar and Memo come up with a plan to kidnap and ransom Harry to his wealthy father, and they bring Ricardo, Gordo, and Ray in to actually execute the kidnapping. This fits with what we know about Ricardo, Gordo, and Ray, who are consistently portrayed as thugs, but it is very much against the characters of Oscar and Memo as they have been portrayed up to that point. While both of them have significant character flaws, they are never shown as being capable of violence until they suddenly concoct a plan to kidnap someone who had previously been a friendly, albeit resented, acquaintance of theirs. Any sympathy that the reader may have felt for Memo or Oscar vanishes as a result of this decision, and in the end, Memo sinks even lower. When Oscar attempts to pull out of the kidnapping and take Carla with him, Memo betrays him to Ricardo, who murders Oscar.

These are the versions of American and Mexican identity presented by Abel. All the Mexicans are criminals and are either violent, lazy, dishonest, hypocritical, or all of the above. Any political critique they might offer of American imperialism can easily be explained as a hypocritical rationalization for their own pose of victimhood that masks their amoral, self-serving, criminal interests. To be sure, a handful of "good" Mexicans appear as background characters, such as the journalist whom Harry and Carla visit near the beginning of the story, or the anonymous neighbors in Carla's apartment building. The narrative focuses, however, on the bad Mexicans who conform to the worst American stereotypes about Mexico. The Americans, by contrast, come off as significantly better, although not flawless. Harry is depicted as being self-indulgent, pampered, and lazy, and Carla herself is naive and self-centered, but others, such as Sylvia and Rod, are decent people, even saintly ones. Rod's near perfection as a human being serves as an implicit but powerful refutation of Memo's criticisms of American capitalists as evil and terrible human beings. It is telling that the only fully decent person in the story is, as Memo puts it, an American capitalist.

Abel has indicated that she sees authenticity as the key theme of *La Perdida*. In a 2005 interview in the *Comics Journal*, Abel said that Carla "sees Memo's intractability about issues of authenticity as indicating that he is authentic" (Abel and Stump, 87). It is interesting and significant that although Abel wrote all of Memo's dialogue, her understanding of what it means differs significantly from what the character actually says. While Abel describes Memo's statements purely in terms of authenticity, in fact this is only one part, and not the most important one, of his critique. Authenticity is Abel's way of redirecting the actual content of Memo's critique in a direction that can more easily be debunked. The main lesson that Abel wants readers to take away from *La Perdida* is the pitfalls of this quest for false authenticity. This is the realization that Carla herself comes to at the end of the story. In Abel's words, "If she hung out with somebody like Liana who didn't give a crap that Carla was American, she would probably have not gotten into the situation she got into. . . . She had an opportunity to be friends with all these [other] people. She wouldn't have been able to feel this rush of anger and superiority that she felt all the time with Memo. Nor would she be with a bunch of idiot criminals" (Abel and Stump, 90–91). This statement makes clear that in Abel's mind, the best way to deal with race is by ignoring it; Carla should have chosen friends who did not care about race, which would have allowed her to avoid confronting the reality of white privilege and America's exploitative relationship to Mexico. Moreover, this quotation indicates that for Abel, critiques of the United States are at the least associated with criminality, if not synonymous with it. Readers can easily infer from *La Perdida*'s narrative that any criticism of the United States leads directly and inevitably toward violence and crime. In this way, *La Perdida* has much in common with American Cold War comics, in which communism was demonized and equated with crime, as well as with female independence and autonomy—comics that in hindsight appear absurd, paranoid, and sexist. It is surprising to see such dated, discredited ideas resurfacing in the twenty-first century, especially in an alternative comic that has the trappings of racial tolerance. Abel does not appear to have intended to embed this message in her book. If this were the case, *La Perdida* would stand as yet another American comic that imposes a white racial frame despite the conscious intentions or desires of its creators. Like many other American comics creators, Abel's unexamined assumptions about race and her own position of racial privilege end up doing more harm than good.

THE COST OF WHITENESS IN CHRIS WARE'S *JIMMY CORRIGAN*

If *Love and Rockets* tends to understate the complexities of racial identity and conflict in American society, Chris Ware's *Jimmy Corrigan* obsessively works over those issues. The comic follows four generations of a white Chicago family and a Black family whose history is intertwined with theirs, although neither family is aware of this ongoing connection. The relation between the two families is a prime example of Anzaldúa's concept of a racial borderland. The graphic novel takes place in two parallel stories, the first of which is set in the present and follows the titular character, a lonely man who makes contact with the father who abandoned him and his mother when he was little. The second story line is set in 1892–93 and follows Jimmy's grandfather, James, as a child and his relationship with his abusive father, William. Race is entwined in the story in several ways. In addition to emotionally and physically abusing his son, William is also a racist with violent tendencies, suggesting a link between white supremacy and other forms of violence. In Jimmy's story, his father, James William, has a loving and nurturing relationship with his adopted Black daughter, which causes Jimmy to further question why he was not worthy of receiving his father's love. The relationship between Jimmy and his newfound sister is complicated and deftly intertwines complex personal issues dealing with vulnerability, love, and insecurity with equally complex social ones regarding race.

The story's emotional core centers on fathers and their cruelty to their sons. Both William and James William abandon their sons at a young age,

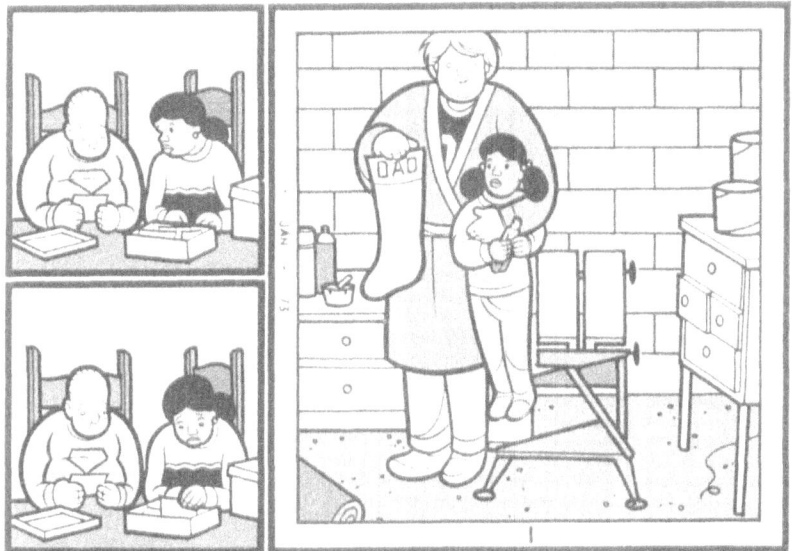

Chris Ware, *Jimmy Corrigan, the Smartest Kid on Earth* (Pantheon, 2000). © Chris Ware.

with William doing so in dramatic fashion by leaving James on the roof of a building at the 1893 World's Columbian Exposition. William is also the most overtly cruel, waking James up at one point with the words "get up you goddamn little son of a bitch." He is mildly physically abusive and repeatedly tells James that he did not want to have a child and does not want James around. James William's cruelty is more subtle and is the result of insensitivity and disinterest rather than anger or malice. For instance, when he picks Jimmy up at the airport, he pays a stranger to find him, is watching boxing when Jimmy first meets him, and is very cold and mildly aggressive. He asks Jimmy how his mother is, as if it is no big deal, and is continually nonchalant about the fact that he abandoned Jimmy and has not seen him in decades. He never attempts to explain why he did so or acknowledge the pain he has caused. He also talks casually about his daughter, Amy, and introduces Jimmy to his grandfather as if these were ordinary events, thereby dismissing the pain and other emotions Jimmy experiences. The feelings behind these omissions are later elucidated when James William expresses a hostile and dismissive attitude toward the notion of family. When Jimmy asks his father about his sister, his first response is "What . . . you thought you were the only mistake I ever made?" He later makes other comments about how he did not like raising children. When Jimmy finally mentions something about how James William was not around when he was growing up, the father lets loose a litany of complaints, beginning with the statement "What a load of whiny woman talk show shit.... Photo albums, turkey dinners, 'family vacations.'... All that's crap as far as I'm concerned."

William and James William's cruelty to their sons is mirrored by their cruelty to, and disrespect for, people of other races. For instance, in the contemporary story line, after hearing a report on the radio about a Hispanic man being murdered, James William says, "Stupid goddamn spicks . . . let 'em all shoot each other dead for all I care." In the 1892 story line, William calls a newsboy he buys a paper from a n-----, and when he and James are riding through a Black neighborhood, his father says, "We give them their freedom and look at how they waste it." One of the most chilling instances of racism is a story that William tells James one night over dinner. William describes a Black person he had known as a child, whom he calls N----- Barney. He was an old Black man, a former slave, who promised William's father, a doctor, that in lieu of payment he could have his skeleton when he died to keep as a kind of medical reference item or status symbol. When he dies, William's father has to steal the corpse and hide it to deceive Barney's friends. William tells James that "he'd been the source of many a 'prank' for us, and he was almost like a member of the family." The most obvious feature of this sequence of events is the extreme dehumanization of Barney, but it has a number of less obvious lessons. It depicts William's father as a calculating, heartless individual, which helps shed light on where the family traits of coldness and casual cruelty originate. The comment that Barney's skeleton was almost a family member is a telling description of the kind of family life William experienced, as is the statement that playing pranks, quite possibly cruel ones, was a regular part of their lives and their treatment of one another. This is just one example of the repeated implication that an individual who uses race as an opportunity to inflict pain and make oneself feel superior is likely to do the same things to one's own children. Further, the idea that Barney's skeleton would be the property of William's father invokes the white racist tradition of obtaining a souvenir at a spectacle lynching. As Amy Louise Wood reports, "Mass spectacles of morbid amusement . . . drew thousands of spectators, who traveled long distances, collected souvenirs, and took photographs" that would often be passed down through the generations as family heirlooms (29).

The 1892 story line also depicts racism between whites. A girl James meets at school calls another of their playmates, an Italian named Antonio, a Wop. James befriends Antonio but refuses to speak to him at school and later says while feeding his father's horse that he hates the boy and repeats the epithet. Later James meets Antonio's family, who are all very friendly to him, and he says it is the first time he has met any adult who was kind. Sexism is another recurrent theme. After Jimmy first meets his father, they go out for lunch, where his father insults a teenage cashier with a child for no reason and tells Jimmy she has nice breasts. He is astoundingly cavalier and continually talks about sex, advising Jimmy to withhold emotion as a way of seducing women: "Never tell 'em you like 'em until you've 'done' 'em."

In these white families where an overbearing father lords over his hapless children, Black women are often a source of unexpected kindness. In the contemporary story, we learn in a flashback that it was Amy who convinced her father to contact Jimmy. In the 1892 story line, one night James's father punishes him by denying him dessert, but their Black maid takes pity on him and gives him two cookies. When William discovers them, he fires the maid. Sometime later, she returns to the house looking for William but instead finds James. She appears to be pregnant but leaves without telling William of this. Later, in one of Chris Ware's signature full-page diagrams, we find out that her and William's child is in fact Amy's great-grandmother, making her related by blood to William, James William, and Jimmy, unbeknownst to any of them. This revelation advances the recurring theme of a connection between racism and abuse by showing that there is not simply a shared power dynamic and emotional payoff connecting them; they are literally the same thing. One could also read, as a broader implication, that all people are part of one larger family, humanity, and we are all interrelated and interdependent and therefore have an obligation to care for one another.

These conclusions are given one further wrinkle through the unexpected behavior of several individuals. The greatest inconsistency in the story is James William's relationship with Amy. Although James William is repeatedly shown to be a cruel, uncaring, racist, and sexist, he is very loving to Amy, who feels the same way about him. James William married the woman who adopted Amy, and although he did not intend to start a second family, he became close to Amy and raised her after Amy's mother passed away. This relationship demonstrates the possibility that people can change for the better, although whether James William achieves redemption is debatable, since his kindness only seems to apply to Amy and does not extend to Jimmy or anyone else he encounters. James William's inconsistency is epitomized by the fact that he criticizes his father for saying racist things about Amy but continues to say similar things to other people he encounters.

Amy herself is also inconsistent, although her inconsistency is more understandable and forgivable than James William's. She is solicitous of Jimmy's needs and sensitive to the turmoil he is going through, but she also gives him space and does not demand answers from him, although she is clearly curious about what kind of person he is and what his life has been like. Ware avoids the pitfall of turning her into an idealized source of healing. In his depiction, she is still a person with needs and issues of her own. Thus, when James William dies, Jimmy tries to comfort Amy by touching her hand, but she pushes him away. In that moment, her own grief overwhelms her ability to remain sensitive to Jimmy's needs. While she can hardly be blamed for this reaction, it represents the end of her newfound relationship with Jimmy, as he quickly retreats to the hospital lobby. A series of errors and mistakes then transpires that Jimmy passively goes along with, resulting in him being put on a train back to Chicago. The possibility of rebuilding their family, which Amy had created by convincing James William to reach out to Jimmy, collapses as a result of James William's death and Jimmy's emotional passivity. Redemption is possible, at least in theory, but it is fragile and difficult to achieve.

The Hernandez brothers, Jessica Abel, and Chris Ware all explored the racial borderlands of whiteness in their work. Their specific subjects, their thematic concerns, and their conclusions vary, but all display a conscious interest in exploring liminal racial spaces, something that few previous American cartoonists had engaged in. Mainstream comics of all genres, including superheroes, westerns, and jungle comics, had typically operated within a white racial frame that portrayed whites as superior to other ethnic and racial groups. Racial borderlands are anathema to this frame because they blur the boundaries between whites and other ethnic and racial groups. Only by maintaining these boundaries can the framework of white supremacy be maintained. In the late 1960s, some cartoonists had begun questioning the white racial frame and exploring the racial borderlands of whiteness in their work. For a time, mainstream white characters such as Captain America, Iron Man, and Jonah Hex displayed an awareness of the history of racial injustice and their own implication in the maintenance of white supremacist ideology. Among underground cartoonists, Robert Crumb began exploring his own racial borderlands in the late 1960s, followed by Aline Kominsky-Crumb and Harvey Pekar in the 1970s. In the 1980s and 1990s, the number of cartoonists interested in exploring the racial borderlands of whiteness expanded significantly. The Hernandez brothers' *Love and Rockets* and Art Spiegelman's *Maus* both appeared during this period, as did Alan Moore's *Watchmen*, which reopened the critique of superheroes' white racial frame with a vengeance.

Chapter Eight

THE DECONSTRUCTION OF THE WHITE SUPERHERO IN *WATCHMEN*

The late 1960s and early 1970s, superheroes reached a moment of racial crisis, but it was a short-lived one. By 1973 this moment was in clear decline, and by 1975 it was over. However, the white superheroes' destabilization would prove difficult to dispel. It reemerged in the mid-1980s in Alan Moore's *Watchmen*, Frank Miller's *The Dark Knight Returns*, and a series of "reskinnings" in which white superheroes handed over their identities and powers to successors of color. The first of these manifestations of racial crisis, and arguably the greatest superhero comic of all time, Alan Moore's *Watchmen*, reinvigorated the superhero genre by employing postmodern techniques such as deconstruction and metafiction to defamiliarize the tropes of the white superhero and expose them as a fraudulent construction of heteronormative whiteness. Historically, superhero comics have validated discourses of power by presenting white heterosexual men who defend a white heteronormative culture from villainous agents of change and disruption. In *Watchmen*, Moore deconstructs the superhero as perpetuating and defending a fraudulent version of whiteness predicated on masking splintered consciousness and sexual borderlands, both of which constitute monolithic whiteness. Moore draws attention to the mechanisms by which superheroes are constructed, to wit, by masking their fragmented consciousness and sexual borderlands. In doing so, he exposed whiteness as the prevailing social barometer that superheroes employ and require to mete out justice, and thereby freshened a genre that had grown somewhat stale. Despite *Watchmen* appearing on *Time*'s list of the greatest English-language novels since 1923, the extant published criticism of the graphic novel has been relatively narrow in scope. Articles by Michael J. Prince, Jamie A. Hughes, and Adnan Mahmutović predominantly focus on politics and ideology or the graphic novel's internecine narrative structure. Two articles by Mervi Miettinen and Yen-Lian Liu discuss the hyperbolic and destructive masculinity of the superheroes, but no discussions of race or sexuality are available.

From World War II to the 1960s, comic books had sown fear of the racial other and validated US imperialism, but the moral tragedy of the Vietnam War and its unpopularity forced American superheroes into a moment of moral reckoning and self-awareness in the late 1960s and early 1970s. Arguably the most influential, artistic, and psychologically complex comic book of the past forty years, *Watchmen* is the heir to these self-questioning superhero comics of the previous two decades. For Moore, the Cold War instilled paranoia about the imminence of another nuclear war, causing him to create "an obituary for the concept of powerful heroes in general and superheroes in particular" (Wright, 272). After the popular upheavals of the 1960s and early 1970s, conservative leaders such as Ronald Reagan in the United States and Margaret Thatcher in England reestablished social hierarchies, including white supremacy, that *Watchmen* sought to deconstruct. "To place faith in such icons," Moore argued, "was to give up responsibility for our lives and future to the Reagans, Thatchers, and other 'Watchmen' of the world who are supposed to 'rescue' us" but all too often merely make decisions that are in the best interests of the white elite (273).

Hooded Justice, the first documented superhero in *Watchmen*'s fictional world, represents a construct of white male heteronormativity that functions as a closet, masking what W. E. B. Du Bois calls a fragmented or double consciousness and Gloria Anzaldúa describes as an internal borderland. Both theorists identify internal identity fragmentation, the idea of an individual identifying with multiple social groups and categories, as a characteristic of marginalization. We would take these theories one step further and suggest that identity fragmentation is actually the normative social state of being for a preponderance of Americans, if not all human beings. In drawing attention to the hidden borderlands of identity, both Du Bois and Anzaldúa align with queer theorists such as Eve Kosofsky Sedgwick who highlight the closet, which can pertain to any hidden identity, as a result of both individuals and society as a whole dichotomizing sexual identity. The obvious messiness of sexual desire notwithstanding, the human species "has come more and more to be divided" between homosexual and heterosexual, just as it is often divided between white and nonwhite (912). Consequently, one can view sexuality and race on a macro level as marked by a cultural closet inhabited by people masking splintered internal identities to fit into constructed sexual and racial binaries. Hooded Justice's political whiteness denies his fragmented consciousness and internal borderland. Both Du Bois and Anzaldúa identify the source of their fragmented consciousness in the heteronormative white gaze. For the superheroes in *Watchmen*, hiding their broken consciousness is part of the foundation of their whiteness.

Symbolically related to the Ku Klux Klan by his hood and the noose he wears around his neck, Hooded Justice overcompensates for his closeted sexual identity by openly aligning himself with Nazi white supremacist ideology and embracing hypermasculinity, laying the foundation from which other hooded vigilantes emerge, such as Captain Metropolis, Rorschach, and the two Nite Owls. In *Watchmen*, the ostensible raison d'être for the hooded vigilantes' existence, to protect and defend the citizenry, camouflages the more important goal of masking normative insecurities and defending political whiteness, something of which superhero comics have long been guilty. On the other hand, Dr. Manhattan represents the only nonwhite superhero, the only superhero who has given up his secret identity, and the only one with actual superpowers, who by virtue of his racial otherness and inability to project a monolithic whiteness faces a bewildered public that resents his unique and amazing power in part because of his nonwhiteness. Eventually he loses interest in the dominant white culture that rejects and alienates him, much like the fate of the Nietzschean superman who finds it difficult to harmonize with a culture that he has transcended. Comics possess a long history of insidiously promoting racist and imperialistic ideologies and villainizing nonnormative or nonwhite identities—a history that *Watchmen* reveals, critiques, and deconstructs.

The effectiveness of *Watchmen* centers on its power to lay bare the contradiction of superheroes defending unjust laws. *Watchmen*'s profound influence on the superhero genre can be seen in story arcs like "Captain America No More" (1987–89) and Marvel's *Civil War* (2006–7), wherein, similar to the conceit of *Watchmen*, superheroes face government regulation or risk criminalization. In *Civil War*, the emphasis is on the gray area in which superheroes exist in relation to the law. The superheroes in *Civil War* must choose to either exist as law enforcement or be criminalized. In a racist state, a superhero is either an agent of the state or a criminal. There is no in-between. While other comics such as *The X-Men* and *Uncanny X-Men* pit superheroes against the government, *Watchmen* takes great pains to imagine superheroes within actual contemporary culture. The realism in *Watchmen* distinguishes it from other comics. Even after the 1975 reboot of *The X-Men* called *Uncanny X-Men*, featuring characters such as Storm and Wolverine, noteworthy story arcs such as "Days of Future Past" in issues 141–42 (1981) relied on classic science fiction tropes like mutant-hunting robots to present metaphors for marginalization. While *Watchmen* certainly contains fabulist elements, Alan Moore spends a great deal of time melding elements of realism with fabulism to deconstruct the superhero, a strategy later adopted by comics like *Civil War*.

COMICS AND AMERICAN IMPERIALISM

The central symbol of the white power structure in *Watchmen* is the Comedian, who signifies imperialism posing as American exceptionalism and freedom. The Comedian displays an unabashed will to power that exploits white supremacy and the great American fiction that positions the United States as a beacon of freedom rather than a self-appointed global authority and targets anyone who threatens monolithic whiteness or America's global dominance. The Comedian has a vested interest in superheroes masking their internal fragmentations and adopting a white supremacist ideology masquerading as justice, as that is the source of his power. As Michael J. Prince notes, the Comedian resembles Captain America in both his mission and his costume. He "is draped in stars and stripes from the American flag, and, like Captain America, he uses his skills and costumed hero persona . . . as a tool of American foreign policy," which reflects an American exceptionalism predicated on white hypermasculinity (819). Prince further notes, "Blake displays racial intolerance, abusive behavior to women, and a gleeful appreciation of carnage" (819). In Vietnam, Blake impregnates a Vietnamese woman and kills her after she demands that he acknowledge his child: "That's right. Pregnant woman. Gunned her down. Bang. . . . You watched me" (Moore and Gibbons II, 15). To him, the woman merely represents a nonwhite country in which he can wield his murderous energies with no regard for human life. After the woman cuts his face with a bottle and right before he shoots her, he calls her a "bitch" and a "whore" and refers to Vietnam as a "cruddy little country" (II, 14–15). Although lacking the Comedian's bloodthirsty viciousness, Dr. Manhattan also functions as an agent of US imperialism. He describes both his and the Comedian's involvement in Vietnam, confessing that "Blake is interesting. I have never met anyone so deliberately amoral. He suits the climate here: the madness, the pointless butchery. . . . As I come to understand Vietnam and what it implies about the human condition, I also realize that few humans will permit themselves such an understanding. Blake's different. He understands perfectly . . . and he doesn't care" (IV, 19). Dr. Manhattan then describes how his intervention in Vietnam has tipped the balance of power there: "The Vietcong are expected to surrender within the week. Many have given themselves up already. . . . Often, they ask to surrender to me personally, their terror of me balanced by an almost religious awe" (IV, 20).

The Comedian is more than just a tool of US imperialism; he also functions as a sort of vigilante of masculinity among the other superheroes. As Michael Kimmel notes, "[Men] are under the constant careful scrutiny of other men. Other men watch us, rank us, grant our acceptance into the

Alan Moore (script) and Dave Gibbons (pencils), *Watchmen* (DC Comics, 1987). © DC Comics.

realm of manhood" (186). The text strongly suggests that the Comedian kills Hooded Justice as revenge for his intervention when Blake attempts to rape Sally Jupiter. To Blake, this intervention and Hooded Justice's queerness betray the social hierarchies on which Blake's identity depends. Adrian Veidt, the civilian name of the superhero Ozymandias, known as "the world's smartest man," reports: "Researching my masked predecessors I investigated the mid-fifties disappearance of Hooded Justice. An operative, government sources revealed, had tried unearthing him back then, reporting failure.... Unearthing the operative, tracking him to dockland proved easier. Edward Blake.... Had Blake found Hooded Justice, killed him, reporting failure?

Alan Moore (script) and Dave Gibbons (pencils), *Watchmen* (DC Comics, 1987). © DC Comics.

I can prove nothing" (Moore and Gibbons XI, 18). After Hooded Justice defends Sally, Blake says to him, "I got your number, see? And one of these days, the joke's gonna be on you" (II, 7), strongly suggesting that ultimately he makes good on his promise. Blake feigns interest in protecting the public; his real agenda is to protect America's right to global domination, a domination that starts with maintaining social hierarchies at home that prop him up as a paragon of power. Blake realizes that if social hierarchies were dismantled, his elite status would crumble. His elite status requires that identity fragmentations remain hidden and delegitimized. When the public riots and lashes out at the self-appointed authority of the superheroes, Blake cites this uproar as the ironic fruits of a fraudulent American dream: "What's happened to the American Dream? It came true. You're lookin' at it" (II, 18). Blake understands the American dream as a mirage necessary to keep the public in check and the prospect of its reality total chaos.

WHITENESS, DOUBLE CONSCIOUSNESS, AND SEXUAL BORDERLANDS

In the *Watchmen* universe, Hooded Justice represents not only the first superhero to emerge but also the first masked crusader to inhabit a fragmented sexual closet and present himself as monolithically white. In Hollis Mason's book *Under the Hood*, a metatextual insert in *Watchmen*, he notes that news of Hooded Justice's adventuring emboldened him to assume the role of masked vigilante and subsequently inspired a whole slew of superheroes to "[escape] from their four-color world and [invade] the plain, factual black and white of the headlines" (I, I *Under the Hood*, 6). Mason, who became the first Nite Owl, describes Hooded Justice as "a tall man, built like a wrestler, who wore a black hood and cape and also wore a noose around his neck.... The first masked adventurer outside comic books" (6). Nite Owl explicitly maintains that Hooded Justice represents the first superhero from which all the other superheroes derive: "Within twelve months of Hooded Justice's dramatic entrance into the public consciousness, there were at least eleven other costumed vigilantes operating on or around America's West Coast" (8). The significance of Hooded Justice as harbinger lies in his open Nazi sympathies and closeted sexuality, the former operating as fortification for the latter. He pretends to have a heteronormative relationship with the hypersexualized Silk Spectre, setting the tone for other racist, homophobic, and hypermasculine superheroes such as the Comedian and Rorschach to follow in his closeted footsteps.

If W. E. B. Du Bois and Gloria Anzaldúa define otherness by pointing to its internal fragmentation in a world where normativity is constructed as a binary and then privileged, then one can define white male heteronormativity as the internal false denial of double consciousness and sexual borderlands. Du Bois observes, "One ever feels his two-ness,—an American, a Negro; two souls, two thoughts, two unreconciled strivings; two warring ideals in one dark body, whose dogged strength alone keeps it from being torn asunder. The history of the American Negro is the history of this strife,—this longing to attain self-conscious manhood, to merge his double self into a better and truer self" (8–9). Hooded Justice and other vigilantes in *Watchmen* attain their self-conscious manhood by denying and masking their twoness and then targeting others who threaten the myth of monolithic whiteness, not unlike nineteenth-century Irish immigrants, who had to earn their whiteness by brutalizing Black people, oftentimes in the role of law enforcement. Noel Ignatiev writes, "The Irish cop is more than a quaint symbol. His appearance on the city police marked a turning point in Philadelphia in the struggle of the Irish to gain the rights of white men. It meant that thereafter the Irish would be officially empowered (armed) to defend themselves from the nativist mobs, and at the same time to carry out their own agenda against black people" (189). Similarly, Hooded Justice, Captain Metropolis, and Rorschach primarily target socioeconomically disadvantaged citizens, minorities, or generally those who threaten imperialist white supremacist patriarchy. For example, Captain Metropolis spends much of his time "eradicating organized crime in the inner urban areas" (Moore and Gibbons I, II *Under the Hood*, 8). Nite Owl asserts that what the hooded vigilantes are up against are "social evils . . . promiscuity, drugs, campus subversion, you name it!" (II, 10). Additionally, he writes that they are at odds with "the beatniks, the jazz musicians and the poets openly condemning American values whenever they opened their mouths. . . . With all these sudden social upheavals just when we thought we'd gotten everything *straight*" (II, III *Under the Hood*, 13; italics mine).

Like Du Bois's notion of double consciousness, Gloria Anzaldúa describes a borderland as a "vague and undetermined place created by the emotional residue of an unnatural boundary. It is in a constant state of transition. The prohibited and forbidden are its inhabitants . . . the squint-eyed, the perverse, the queer" (3). *Watchmen* is replete with references to sexual borderlands that indicate the centrality of sexuality in the text. For example, the metatextual inserts that provide much of the commentary, such as *Treasure Island Treasury of Comics*, a book of criticism about comic books, allude to the treatment of sexuality in *Watchmen*:

> The stories that came from his pen in this period are uniformly dark and sinister, balancing metaphysical terrors against an unnerving sense of reality, particularly when applied to matters of mortality or sexuality. Readers who came to the series expecting a good rousing tale of swashbuckling were either repulsed or fascinated by what were often perverse and blackly lingering comments upon the human condition. Tales such as "The Figurehead," which deal unflinchingly with male homosexuality, and the harrowing "Marooned" spring most readily to mind. (Moore and Gibbons V, *Treasure Island*, 61)

The lesbian relationship between Joey the cab driver and Aline, a member of the Knot Tops gang, underscores the theme of nonnormative sexualities that some of the heroes attempt to mask, as well as the powerful pull of normativity. When the two women are fighting, Joey, the more masculine of the two, says, "I wanna go to *bed* with you, and . . . and I wuh-wanna be *straight* . . . and I wanna be *dead*" (XI, 9). Joey, rather than feeling comfortable as a masculine gay woman, performs destructive hypermasculine behavior, such as purchasing *Hustler* magazine, despite Aline's disapproval, and eventually beats her.

The symbolism of Hooded Justice's superhero moniker and the noose he wears around his neck directly invoke the Ku Klux Klan. The noose represents not only victims of lynching but also Hooded Justice himself, whose life has been strangled by masculine fear and insecurity. The symbolism of the noose in relation to Hooded Justice's fear of being outed as a gay man underscores the intersection between race and sexuality, namely, that whiteness assumes heteronormativity. In the novel, the right-wing magazine the *New Frontiersman* articulates the connection between the hooded vigilantes and the KKK:

> Nova Express makes many sneering references to costumed heroes as direct descendants of the Ku Klux Klan, but might I point out that despite what some might view as their later excesses, the Klan originally came into being because decent people had perfectly reasonable fears for the safety of their persons and belongings when forced into proximity with people from a culture far less morally advanced. No, the Klan were not strictly legal, but they did work voluntarily to preserve American culture in areas where there were very real dangers of that culture being overrun and mongrelized. (VIII *New Frontiersman*, 2)

By comparing closeted masked superheroes in *Watchmen* to the Ku Klux Klan, Moore offers readers an insight into the construction of monolithic political whiteness as an essentially closeted identity that masks double consciousness and internal sexual borderlands. Hooded Justice, with the help of the gossip writers interested in the "hooded [vigilantes]" (II, III *Under the Hood*, 11), goes to great lengths to hide his nonnormative sexuality to project a monolithic whiteness:

> Over with the cape-and-mask crowd, lips are buzzing and tongues are wagging about cheesecake crime-crusher Sally Jupiter, alias SILK SPECTRE. It seems that she and veteran vigilante HOODED JUSTICE are something of an item.... Can wedding bells be too far away?... Just look whose arm our Sal is hanging onto in the recently released publicity photographs of that tights-and-trunk-clad team, the Minutemen.... Does he keep that hood and noose on all the time? (IX *Daily World*)

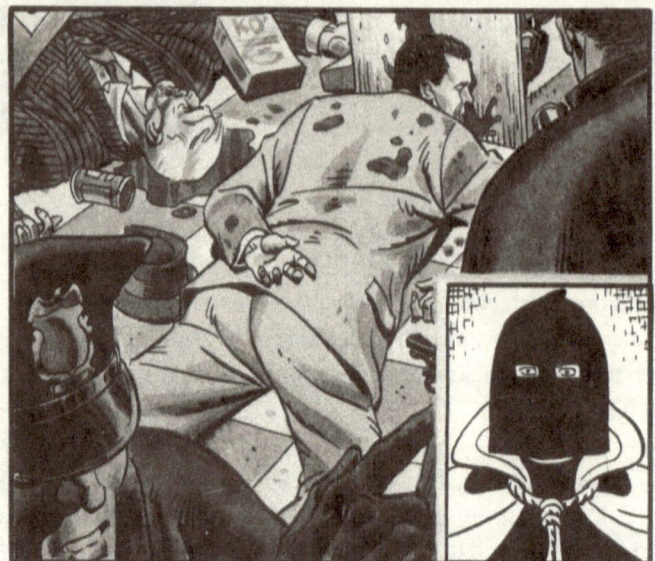

Masked adventurers make the front page. (New York Gazette, October 14th, 1938) Note artist's impression of "The Hooded Vigilante."

Lamont Cranston with his slouch hat and blazing automatics
Alan Moore (script) and Dave Gibbons (pencils), *Watchmen* (DC Comics, 1987). © DC Comics.

Along with pretending to be romantically involved with vigilante sex symbol Silk Spectre, Hooded Justice "openly [expresses] approval for the activities of Hitler's Third Reich" (I, II *Under the Hood*, 8) and struggles to hide his gay relationship with Captain Metropolis, evidenced by a letter from Silk Spectre's agent and eventual husband Laurence Schexnayder: "Those two are getting worse. The more they . . . act like an old married couple in public, the harder they are to cover for. I know that you've provided a pretty steady alibi for H.J. up to now . . . but it can't last much longer. Nelly says he's always . . . out with boys, and apparently there's a lot of rough stuff going on" (IX, letter from Larry to Sally).

While Captain Metropolis's and Hooded Justice's sexually closeted personae are presented to the reader through metatextual inserts, Rorschach's sexual closet is much less obvious but no less insidious. As Prince notes, "Alan Moore has aligned Rorschach . . . with what may be termed 'the lunatic right-wing fringe . . . [which believes] Jews, Negro drug dealers, organized crime, and the liberal press are in league to destroy America. . . . Antisemitic, homophobic, a paranoid millennialist who routinely breaks the fingers of those he interrogates, there is little in Rorschach to inspire empathy and identification" (822–23). Despite Rorschach's character flaws, fans of *Watchmen* seem to love him. According to Sara J. Van Ness, "Moore [was] baffled by the vigilante's popularity among his readers: 'I originally intended Rorschach to be a warning about the possible outcome of vigilante thinking. But an awful lot of comics readers felt his remorseless, frightening, psychotic toughness was his most appealing characteristic'" (121). Rorschach's popularity indicates that readers identify with him and the unabashed white racial frame through which he views the world. Further, his popularity suggests that his closeted sexuality has been completely missed by readers and critics alike.

Rorschach creates a double persona to mask his sexual borderlands and thereby maintain his superhero status. Like Hooded Justice, Rorschach compensates for his sexual insecurity by adopting a Manichaean worldview and punishing those who operate outside of heteronormative whiteness, including minorities. His belief that "there is good and there is evil, and evil must be punished" (Moore and Gibbons I, 24) guides his worldview, along with his belief that everyone has "a choice . . . [especially] all those liberals and intellectuals and smooth-talkers" (I, 1). One choice Rorschach seems obsessed with centers on sexuality. Time and again, he references good and evil in relation to sexuality, thereby revealing his sexual insecurities, as when he refers to unidentified people engaging in "child pornography" (I, 16), "the accumulated filth of all their sex" (I, 1), "fornication" (I, 14), and "[homosexuality]" (I, 19). Homosexuality hangs over the narrative threateningly whenever Rorschach appears. When the authorities incarcerate him, the other inmates threaten to "tear this guy a new hole" (VIII, 7) and make him "our woman first" (VI, 6). The specter of nonnormative sexuality lurks about Rorschach, causing him to vigilantly suppress it in himself and root it out in others. Rorschach proves especially brutal to sexual deviants, like a masochist "who pretended to be a super villain so he could get beaten up? . . . Captain Carnage . . . Rorschach dropped him down an elevator shaft" (I, 26).

Perhaps the most telling aspect of Rorschach's character is his origin story. After Rorschach's father leaves him and his mother, she engages in sex work, which leads to Rorschach being "regularly beaten and exposed to the worst excesses of a prostitute's lifestyle" (VI, New York Psychiatric Hospital). While institutionalized as a youth, he documents a dream in which he feels sexually aroused after encountering an androgynous figure:

> [They] were squashed together like Siamese twins, joined at the face and chest and stomach. They didn't have any face, you could only see their ears, two on either side of the head facing towards each other.

Their hands were growing into each other as well, but they had all four legs free and they were sort of dancing sideways towards me down the dark hall like a crab, and there was something tripping 'em up, wrapped around their feet, and I looked down and I saw it was trousers and underwear and stuff. They were coming towards me, and then I woke up. I had feelings when I woke up. Dirty feelings, thoughts and stuff. The dream it sort of upset me physically. I couldn't help it. I feel bad just talking about it. (VI, Charlton Home)

The dream likely stems from seeing his mother and one of her johns having sex, but his drawing of the dream that accompanies his essay transforms this image into an androgynous figure that arouses sexual desire. Rorschach's suppressed arousal in relation to an androgynous dream figure points to a hidden sexual borderland and consequently a fragmented whiteness, since monolithic whiteness assumes heteronormativity.

Rorschach fashions a disguise that he refers to as the actual "skin from my head" (V, 11) from "the remains of [an] unwanted dress" (VI, 10). He notes, "When I had cut it enough, it didn't look like a woman anymore" (VI, 10). Rorschach's self-loathing due to his disguised sexual borderlands indicated in his dream compels him to transform the symbolic feminine skin of his body into something that no longer resembles femininity. As he tells his psychiatrist, "We do it because we have to. We do it because we are compelled" (VI, 15). In this sense, Rorschach feels compelled to rid his self of his sexual borderlands, adopting a version of hypermasculinity defined by homophobia and flight from femininity and targeting anyone not of a piece with monolithic whiteness.

Rorschach shares many similarities with Batman. As Alan Moore once noted, "[Gibbons and I] thought about superhero types like Batman, so I thought, 'What would he be like in the real world.' And he'd be very much like Rorschach" (Surman). Both are orphans working as super-detectives above the law, and both possess horrific origin stories. Batman "was one of the first fictional characters to be attacked on the grounds of presumed homosexuality by Fredric Wertham in his book *Seduction of the Innocent*. Secondly, the 1960s TV series was and remains a touchstone of camp" (Medhurst, 150). Batman's link to homosexuality centers on his companionship with his younger sidekick Robin. As Andy Medhurst notes, "Denied even the remotest possibility of supportive images of homosexuality within the dominant heterosexual culture, gay people have had to fashion what we could out of the imageries of dominance, to snatch illicit meanings from the fabric of normality, to undertake a corrupt decoding for the purposes of satisfying

Alan Moore (script) and Dave Gibbons (pencils), *Watchmen* (DC Comics, 1987). © DC Comics.

marginalized desires" (153). To homosexuals, "Batman was a particular gift on the grounds of his relationship with Robin" (156). Both Rorschach and Batman exhibit a supposed monolithic whiteness that exists in tension with either their internal subjectivity or how readers interpret them. In either case, they both signify characters whose heteronormative whiteness proves shaky at best. In Frank Miller's graphic novel *The Dark Knight Returns*, Miller, the subject of the next chapter, avoided visual tableaus of the sexually ambiguous duo by presenting Robin as a young girl.

Like Rorschach, both Nite Owls demonstrate a link between masked whiteness and heterosexual identity that operates as a form of monolithic whiteness and manifests as antiwhite hostility. Hollis Mason, the first Nite Owl, notes in his book *Under the Hood*:

> They've called us fascists and they've called us perverts and . . . there's an element of truth in both those accusations. . . . Captain Metropolis has gone on record as making statements about black and Hispanic Americans that have been viewed as both racially prejudiced and inflammatory. . . . Yes, I daresay some of us did have our sexual

hang-ups.... Yes, we were crazy, we were kinky, we were Nazis, all those things that people say. We were also doing something because we believed in it. We were attempting, through our personal efforts, to make our country a safer and better place to live in. (Moore and Gibbons I, II *Under the Hood*, 8)

Hollis's admission that some of his fellow superheroes were Nazis undermines the often-cited polar opposition between superheroes and Nazis, who shared common roots in eugenics, white supremacy, and the idea of the superman dating back to the 1920s and 1930s. His equation of Nazism with sexual hang-ups further emphasizes the intersection of sexuality and race by suggesting that part of the impetus for becoming a masked hero had to do with masking his sexual borderlands by adopting an ethos of white supremacy.

Hollis Mason never marries or ever mentions having a girlfriend. When he calls Sally Jupiter about Dan and Laurie's masked reunion, Sally says, "All this time you had my number; you wait till we're both in our sunset years to use it?" (VIII, 1). Despite the apparent opportunity, Hollis never made a play for Sally. Mason begins *Under the Hood* with an objective correlative that sheds light on the nature of disguises. He tells a story about his father's boss Moe Vernon discovering that his wife has run off with his head mechanic Fred Motz. The interesting part of the story centers on Vernon's peculiar sexual behavior. Mason relates:

> Moe had one of the largest collections of tasteless novelty items that I had seen up until that point or have seen any time since. They were all risqué little toys and gadgets that Moe had picked up from gag shops or on visits to Coney Island ... every ballpoint pen with a girl on the side whose swimsuit vanished when you turned it upside down; every salt and pepper crewet set shaped like a woman's breasts.... Every time anybody went into his office he'd try to startle them by displaying his latest plaything.... What I found funny was that for no apparent reason, a grown man should have a desk drawer full of such ludicrous devices. (I, I *Under the Hood*, 2–3)

The garage where Mason's father works is a decidedly male space wherein Moe's behavior is homosocial and designed to prove his heterosexuality but winds up pointing to his fragmentation. Moe finds out about his wife "in his office ... sitting wearing an artificial foam rubber set of realistically painted ladies bosoms.... There was a letter from Moe's wife Beatrice, informing him that for the past two years she'd been sleeping with Fred Motz, the senior and most trusted mechanic employed at Vernon's Auto Repairs" (3). Moe then tells the rest of the men in the shop that his wife has run off with Motz, after which they laugh at him because of the foam bosoms. He then kills himself in his office. Moe's sexual insecurity drives him to try to prove himself to his peers with his toys and costumes, but the costume itself winds up emasculating him and marking him as a cuckold. Once his insecurities are out of the closet, the costume becomes not a means by which to hide his fragmentation but rather its biggest indication. Notably, Mason says after relating this story, "I'm crazier than Moe Vernon ever was" (I, I *Under the Hood*, 4).

Like Hollis, Dan Dreiberg, the second Nite Owl, has sexual insecurities that stem from impotence and manifest as hostility toward racial otherness. The blackness of the people whom Dan and Laurie save from a burning tenement building and to whom they are hostile and abusive allows them to feel racially superior and helps stimulate their libidos by exoticized racial proxy. Their ostensible raison d'être, to fight crime and protect the citizenry from villains, functions as a ruse to mask their true purpose of constructing their whiteness by dissembling their own twoness and internal borderlands. When Dan and Laurie rescue the group of mostly African Americans from the burning building, whose race has the layered effect of contrasting with the whiteness of the superheroes, Laurie says, "There's a bunch of people still need their *asses* hauled out of the fire, remember?" (VII, 24). Also, while saving the desperate people, she verbally abuses them: "Listen, I don't *care* about your '*allergies*' or your '*medicine*!' Just get in the *ship*, you asshole" (VII, 25). Saving the tenants from the burning building inadvertently masculinizes Dan. Before the rescue, he had been unable to perform sexually with Laurie, but immediately after the rescue, they make love on Dan's ship, stripping out of the costumes that have inspired him to recapture his sexual potency. After successfully having sex with Laurie, Dan says, "I guess the costumes had something to do with it. It just feels *strange*, you know? To come out and *admit* that to somebody.... To come out of the *closet*" (VII, 28).

Only after Dan and Laurie don their costumes can Dan perform sexually, hearkening back to Mason's point that "I can remember a lot of hooded vigilante jokes coming into circulation during the early fifties. The mildest was one that suggested we were called the Minutemen due to our performance in the bedroom" (II, III *Under the Hood*, 11). For both Nite Owls, adventuring equals white heteromasculinity; for Hollis, adventuring may have covered up his homosexuality. For Dan Dreiberg, adventuring exists as his only remedy for impotence. In both cases, masked identities cover sexual borderlands that might potentially compromise both characters' monolithic whiteness, which also expresses itself as racial hostility.

THE EMERGENCE OF A NONWHITE SUPERHERO

Dr. Manhattan signifies a cataclysmic change in the *Watchmen* universe because he emerges as a nonwhite superhero with boundless superpowers and a singular identity. Rather than masking his fragmented whiteness by using a costume and pretending to be white like Superman, Manhattan flaunts his otherness and thereby exposes the other superheroes as inauthentic, causing widespread fear and distrust among them. Manhattan's appearance reveals the fault lines in the other characters' attempts to mask their internal fragmentation and present themselves in the guise of monolithic whiteness. His blueness contrasts with that of all normal human beings, cutting across the false racial categories created by whites.

Dr. Jon Osterman, a white, Princeton-educated nuclear scientist, dies in a tragic accident in an "intrinsic field chamber," only to be reborn and restructured as an immensely powerful blue-skinned being capable of mastering all matter. Like Superman, Dr. Manhattan's superhero persona is his real self, but unlike Superman, Manhattan does not employ a secret identity and is not white. Mason notes, "Dr. Manhattan's appearance was certainly one of the factors that led to my own increased feelings of obsolescence and my eventual decision to quit the hero business altogether" (III, V *Under the Hood*, 13). Manhattan affects not only the white world's technology and balance of power but also America's internalized white supremacy and its association of power with whiteness. Mason further notes, "If I had to boil it down into three words, those words would be, 'We've been replaced'" (13). Mason's basic sympathy and agreement with his grandfather's belief that "country folk were morally healthier than city folk and that cities were just cesspools into which all the world's dishonesty and greed and lust and godlessness drained and was left to fester unhindered" (I, I *Under the Hood*, 4) suggest his alignment with racist white culture.

Manhattan's arrival on the scene sends a shock wave through the *Watchmen* universe because of his superpowers, but one can easily read the responses as racialized. Although Mason says that his consternation stems from Manhattan's ability to "rearrange things completely with a single thought" (III, V *Under the Hood*, 13), his fear also seems tied to Manhattan's blue skin. Mason notes, "The first time you meet him your brain wants to scream, blow a fuse and shut itself down immediately, refusing to accept that he exists. This lasts for a couple of minutes, at which time he's still there and hasn't gone away, and in the end you just accept him because he's standing there and talking to you and after a while it almost seems normal. Almost" (14). Manhattan's appearance as much as his power elicits Mason's latent hostility: "If you accept that floating rifle parts are real you also have to somehow accept that everything you've ever known to be a fact is probably untrue" (13). Like Mason, Captain Metropolis reacts to Manhattan's existence mostly with fear: "We asked those costumed vigilantes remaining from the 1940's masked hero fad how they felt. Well, uhh, we're pleased obviously" (IV, 13). Though Metropolis does not admit it—simply expressing approval regarding Manhattan—the image in the text suggests his deep masculine insecurity. Mason offers, "It became gradually easier to accept the dream-like unreality of those first newsreel images: a blue man melting a tank with a wave of his hand" (13). The dreamlike unreality centers on Manhattan's nonwhiteness as well as his immense power.

Unlike the Thing or the Hulk, Osterman embraces his transformation into Dr. Manhattan and does not spend his time lamenting his nonwhite skin and wishing that he could return to the comfortable folds of whiteness. Eventually Manhattan's racial isolation and marginal status due to his blue skin alienate him from the dominant culture that, like the Übermensch, he has transcended. He notes, "Their *bleached* faces stare up at me, *pale* and insubstantial in the sudden flare of the ultraviolet" (IV, 10; italics mine). He even feels like an outsider among the other masks, noting that they are "friendly middle-aged men who like to dress up. I have nothing in common with them" (IV, 14). Manhattan's character development involves his slow withdrawal from a culture that he no longer feels a part of and that no longer trusts him. The more he presents his powerful nonwhiteness, the more the dominant culture turns on him. First he decides to shed his costume and reveal his nakedness: "I'm informing the Pentagon that I'll be no longer wearing the whole of my costume" (IV, 16). Then he disavows any inkling of a dual persona: "I've revealed my true name to the public. After Father's death, there seems little point in concealing it" (IV, 19). Consequently the dominant culture, including other superheroes, loses its trust in him: "I do not believe that we have a man to end wars. I believe we have made a man to end worlds" (IV Dr. Manhattan I). Eventually the press accuses Manhattan of spreading cancer and posing a threat to civilization:

> The suggestion that the presence of a superhuman has inclined the world more towards peace is [repudiated] by the sharp increase in both Russian and American nuclear stockpiles since the advent of Dr. Manhattan.... Our entire culture has had to comfort itself to accommodate the presence of something more than human.... The safety of a whole world rests in the hands of a being far beyond what we understand to be human. (IV Dr. Manhattan III)

Manhattan no longer views humanity as something worth saving, offering, "A live body and a dead body contain the same number of particles. Structurally, there's no discernible difference. Life and death are unquantifiable abstracts. Why should I be concerned?" (I, 21). He explains to Laurie that he can no longer find value in a culture that marginalizes him: "Don't you see the futility of asking me to save a world that I no longer have any stake in?" (IX, 8). Laurie rightly points out, "To him it's like walking through mist and all the people are like shadows" (III, 9). At the end of the graphic novel, Manhattan kills Rorschach to prevent him from informing the dominant culture that its respite from world war is a scam, but Manhattan also knows that it does not matter, that Rorschach's journal will be discovered, and "nothing ever ends" (XII, 26), including racial prejudice, white supremacy, and the public's distrust of a godlike leader who does not look like them.

DECONSTRUCTING THE WHITE SUPERHERO AFTER *WATCHMEN*

Watchmen initiated a new period of deconstruction of the white superhero. One of the first series to follow in its footsteps was the "Captain America No More" story line, which ran from 1987 to 1989. In this story arc, Steve Rogers resigns as Captain America when the federal government demands that he place himself under its authority rather than acting as an independent vigilante. White vigilantism has roots in the post–Civil War KKK, but in this case, Captain America's objection to obeying the federal government is rooted in his reluctance to be involved in military missions that would compromise his morals, such as assisting the right-wing Contras in Nicaragua (Costello, 68). While on hiatus from his Captain America persona, he takes on the guise of USAgent to continue his heroic mission. His replacement as Captain America is John Walker, a conservative from the town of Custer's Grove, Georgia, a name that immediately invokes white violence against people of color (69).

Walker's replacement of Rogers as Captain America was the culmination of a conscious campaign on his part to challenge Rogers's status as the superheroic embodiment of the United States. Walker sees Rogers's (alleged) restraint and respect for human rights as unnecessarily deferential and weak and wishes to project a more aggressive vision of American power. After becoming Captain America, Walker shows himself to be cocky and careless, narrowly escaping disaster several times in his early adventures. An adult Black man named Lemar Hoskins, taking the name of Bucky, assumes the role of his sidekick. Bucky was also the name of Steve Rogers's sidekick in his initial run as Captain America. As readers wrote in to point out, the name of Bucky holds strong racist meanings, since a "buck" was a traditional racist epithet that describes African Americans as animals (71–72). As Donald Bogle has written, "Bucks are always big, baadddd n-----s, over-sexed and savage, violent and frenzied as they lust for white flesh" (13–14). Hoskins's identification as a buck is buttressed by the cover story he is given in his first adventure, as a talent scout recruiting models for nude photos in a men's magazine (Costello, 77). Brannon Costello comments:

> If "buck" suggests threatening power . . . then "Bucky," with its juvenilizing, familiar suffix, suggests the containment and deflation of that power. Bucky's visual design generates the same effect as his moniker. Although physically larger than new Captain America and just as super-strong, he nonetheless looks faintly ridiculous in a dated costume designed for a teenaged white boy. (72)

Although Walker himself is inexperienced and impulsive, Hoskins is portrayed as being deferential toward him and needing guidance and correction (73). In response to fan criticisms of his name, Bucky eventually renames himself Battle Star and designs a new costume. In the story, this is explained as Bucky's response to a prison guard who suggests to him that "the government stuck you with that name to keep you in your place" (78). However, he remains Walker's sidekick, and their relationship continues largely as before (79). This version of Bucky never gets as close to establishing an independent identity as the Falcon did in the early 1970s. Walker's identity is further complicated by his implication in white supremacist violence in his hometown. He is sent to infiltrate a racist vigilante group called the Watchdogs, who "believe themselves to be arbiters of the public good" and are "against pornography, sex education, abortion, and the teaching of evolution" (76–77). Walker agrees with all these positions, and a number of his old friends are now members of the group, but he has been assigned by the government to infiltrate them, giving rise to many mixed feelings on his part. Walker poses as a potential recruit for the group and uses Hoskins as bait to lure the Watchdogs. The Watchdogs plan on lynching Hoskins, which Walker does not attempt to prevent from happening, although Hoskins manages to survive anyway (76–78). In a later story, the Watchdogs kidnap Walker's parents in revenge for his betrayal, and Walker is unable to prevent their deaths. Walker is relieved of his duties as Captain America and takes on the identity of USAgent, which Rogers had used during his hiatus from Captain America.

Rogers and Walker are contrasted throughout "Captain America No More," with Walker expressing sympathy with white supremacy and the aggressive use of military force, and Rogers representing a more measured application of American power. Yet, as we have seen in previous chapters, Rogers himself has a long history as a symbol and enforcer of white supremacy. Unlike Captain America's writers in the early 1970s, Mark Gruenwald, the author of "Captain America No More," accepts the character's persona as a defender of freedom and equality at face value. This Captain has no identity crisis over his past deeds, which are washed clean in this story line. This historical amnesia is paralleled by Rogers's actual amnesia after the death of his parents, when the government erases his memory of their deaths so that he can continue to be an effective super-soldier. He eventually regains his memories after Hoskins shows him their graves, after which the government restores his memory (81). Whether intentionally or not, this story arc acknowledges the uncomfortable similarity between Rogers and Walker through the ease with which they trade identities, as Walker repeatedly adopts identities vacated by Rogers. Walker is very similar to *Watchmen*'s Comedian. Walker first appears in *Captain America* #323 in November 1986, shortly after *Watchmen*'s debut two months earlier, making this a case either of rapid and direct influence or parallel thinking. Walker and the Comedian are both exaggerated versions of Captain America's patriotic mission backed up by the use of force, but Gruenwald's critique is far more mild than Moore's. Gruenwald leaves implied and ambiguous many things that Moore states explicitly and forcefully.

Appearing two decades after *Watchmen*, the Marvel miniseries *Civil War*, like *Watchmen*, imagines a world where superheroes face governmental regulation. Instead of the Keene Act, the law in the *Watchmen* universe that bans vigilantism, in *Civil War* public outcry forces the government to institute the Superhero Registration Act, forcing superheroes to choose to defend white supremacy or become criminals. The Keene Act sought to corral superheroes operating extralegally, suggesting that in a society of laws designed to sustain conformity and the white power structure, the existence of traditional superheroes is unviable. The name of the series *Civil War* alone invokes race and the battle for the emancipation of African American slaves. In the world of *Civil War*, the superheroes must prove their whiteness or their allegiance to whiteness manifested in the law to literally keep their freedom or be imprisoned in the Negative Zone. The superheroes are forced either to become agents of a racist state in the form of an elite law enforcement group or to operate as criminals. Essentially no scenario exists wherein superheroes can be morally viable in a racist society ruled by a white power structure, whether they are sanctioned law enforcement or not. Either they become a part of the white racial frame that brutalizes minorities or dissidents of any kind, or they operate above the law totally unregulated and pose a threat to society as potential criminals. This element in the comic also implicates the existence of superheroes in other comics and in our collective cultural imagination.

In part 1 of *Civil War*, public support wanes fast for superheroes due in part to "the Hulk trashing Vegas" and "Wolverine saying he was going to kill the president" (Millar). The final event that pushes the public over the edge occurs when a group of young superheroes called the New Warriors instigates a fight with several powerful villains to garner ratings for a reality TV show. The fight results in an enormous explosion in the town of Stamford, killing hundreds of children at a nearby elementary school. In addition to the media's widespread attack and condemnation of superheroes, they also sustain a rash of violent attacks by public citizens. At a nightclub, a club-goer attacks Johnny Storm, the Human Torch, calling him a baby killer and breaking a bottle over his head. The drumbeat for superhero reform is under way and intense.

Without public support, superheroes encounter serious pressure to offer themselves up to the state as tools of law enforcement. Immediately several superheroes, including Iron Man and Mr. Fantastic, begin to consider ways that superheroes can gain back the public trust, including registering as SHIELD agents. SHIELD, which originally stood for Supreme Headquarters, International Espionage and Law-Enforcement Division, represents an elite law enforcement cell led by Nick Fury. Iron Man offers, "Why shouldn't we be better trained and publicly accountable? As far as I'm concerned Stamford was a wake-up call. What alcoholics refer to as a moment of clarity. Becoming public employees makes perfect sense if it helps people sleep a little easier." Several other superheroes, including Captain America and African Americans Luke Cage and Falcon, bristle at the idea. Luke Cage quips in part 4, "What you gonna do . . . pull on those nice little jackboots and smack whoever they tell you to smack? Superheroes are supposed to be volunteers." Captain America also voices their concern poignantly in part 1 when he notes, "Superheroes need to stay above that stuff or Washington starts telling us who the super-villains are." Luke Cage's and Cap's comments highlight the gray area in which superheroes exist in relation to the law. If superheroes are beholden to the law, then they are no more than a cog of the state; but if they operate above the law, then as far as the public is concerned, superheroes are criminals, completely out of control, and pose a threat to the public good. Alternatively, as in the case of a character like Rorschach in *Watchmen*, they simply defend white supremacy outside the law.

The plot of *Civil War* seems to overtly condemn the Registration Act as one of the first events that takes place after its inception is the killing of

Goliath, an African American superhero. Iron Man and Mr. Fantastic, along with the US government, create the Superhero Registration Act, requiring all superheroes to work for SHIELD or be imprisoned in a state-of-the-art prison located in the Negative Zone. Additionally, Mr. Fantastic and Tony Stark intend to create new groups of cyborg superheroes in all fifty states to be led by one legitimate noncyborg superhero. Two factions for and against the Registration Act develop, one led by Iron Man and the other by Captain America with Black Panther and the X-Men initially agreeing to remain neutral, but the tides soon turn in favor of the resistance when, during the first major battle, Goliath, Bill Foster, an African American superhero, is killed by a clone of Thor created by Mr. Fantastic and Iron Man, a sort of prototype of the cyborg superheroes they intend to create to police the entire country. This tragedy causes several superheroes working for Stark and SHIELD to join Captain America's resistance. A leading citizen activist named Miriam Sharpe, who lost one of her children in the Stamford incident, says to Stark at Goliath's funeral in part 4, "Goliath knew what he was doing. He was breaking a law designed to save people's lives. If he'd only gone legitimate, he'd still be alive. This is no more your fault than a cop could be blamed for shooting a punk who pulls a gun on him."

The death of Goliath shifts the narrative of the comic and brings into focus the subtext of the story, namely, that superheroes are only as good as the racist laws they defend. Highlighted by Ms. Sharpe, the registered superheroes, including the nonhuman ones like cyborg Thor, represent the police, whose task is to defend the law regardless of what that law is. The fact that Thor, a white superhero with his signature long, blond hair, kills an African American whom Sharpe refers to as a punk simply because the law grants Thor the right to do so, calls into question laws that facilitate police brutality, especially against minorities. As a result of Goliath's death, Black Panther and the X-Men, both of whom are associated with antiracist politics in the Marvel universe, decide to join Captain America. To make matters worse, and to also underscore the notion of the folly of superheroes defending unjust laws, SHIELD decides to release the worst villains from prison to catch the superheroes fighting for the resistance. Spider-Man decides to leave Stark and join the resistance, but not before he is captured by a group of supervillains in part 5, including Scarecrow, who nearly kills him. Scarecrow asserts, "This gig seemed like such a bum deal at first. Working for SHIELD forced to do what they said—but when word from the top says kick the crap outta Spider-Man . . . well, what can we do? We're only obeying orders." The only difference between the police and criminals is that police are given the power of the law.

Although the resistance led by Captain America is poised to defeat the superheroes on the side of the government led by Iron Man, Captain America realizes that their most important goal is to win over public opinion that is on the side of the government. Cap realizes, perhaps naively, that their only chance to remain superheroes who operate outside the law is to regain the public's support. In the comic's final battle, the resistance is on the brink of defeating Iron Man and his team of SHIELD agents when a group of citizens attacks Captain America. It is then that Cap realizes the resistance has already lost. He says in part 7, "We're not fighting for the people anymore.... Look at us. We're just fighting." He gives up and allows Iron Man to arrest him.

Civil War is compelling insofar as it positions superheroes as either agents of the state or criminals. Unlike *Watchmen*, which presents an entirely conceived and closed world, *Civil War* relies on the reader's knowledge of the extensive mythologies of each of the characters. For example, the fact that all the Black characters side with the resistance is never broached. This lack of focus on the part of *Civil War* separates it from the more overt treatment of race and sexuality offered in *Watchmen*. That the billionaire weapons manufacturer Tony Stark and the consummate patriarch Mr. Fantastic side with the government is never really discussed either. Like *Watchmen*, to which *Civil War* owes a significant debt, *Civil War* seeks to lay bare the artifice of superheroes and demonstrates their instability in a postmodern world. By the end of *Civil War*, readers are left with the idea that crime fighters, whether they be police or superheroes, are mere tools of the governing law, and anyone who tries to operate outside the law or change the law is criminalized and vulnerable. That all the Black characters in *Civil War* side with the resistance implicates the racist government and its attendant laws and suggests that the Black characters would benefit more from the destruction of that law rather than its defense.

CONCLUSION

Alan Moore's deconstruction of the superhero both weakened the genre by revealing its contradictions and hidden agendas and strengthened it by exposing new creative possibilities for the genre based on a recognition of the genre's origins and biases. *Watchmen* highlights and deconstructs the superhero persona as a racial construct predicated on masking a divided consciousness in tension with American monolithic heteronormative whiteness. This construct, apparent since Superman, transforms the superhero into a defender and champion of political whiteness who is compelled to hide his or her origins and insecurities and target others who exist outside the dominant culture. Hooded Justice represents a figure from whom the other masked characters descend. His racist and closeted persona, echoing the KKK, demonstrates that political whiteness often masks what W. E. B. Du Bois and Gloria Anzaldúa characterize as double consciousness and internal borderlands. The hooded vigilantes' struggle to conceal their normative insecurities and personal reasons for adventuring reflects the destructive tendency in comics to promote imperialist white supremacist patriarchy in a medium that emphasizes reader identification with the albescent, putative heroes while eschewing or villainizing difference. In *Watchmen* as well as in "Captain America No More" and *Civil War*, the moniker of "hero" itself becomes a construct dependent on the law. Particularly in *Civil War*, whose debt to *Watchmen* is unavoidable, the liminal space in which the superhero exists in relation to the law is exposed as the heroes must either register with the government and defend racist laws or operate as criminals.

Moore is often paired with Frank Miller because they published their most important works simultaneously, Moore's *Watchmen* and Miller's *The Dark Knight Returns*. Both were brilliant reimaginings of the superhero genre that depicted superheroes in a dark light, but in the end, they pointed in opposite directions as far as their racial frameworks went. The deconstruction of the white superhero that began in the early 1970s reached an artistic and political pinnacle in *Watchmen*. Miller reacted to this deconstruction by insistently retrenching and fortifying white supremacy in increasingly hysterical terms, culminating in the bitterly racist *Holy Terror*.

Chapter Nine

FRANK MILLER'S HYPERMASCULINE WHITENESS AND THE DEFENSE OF WESTERN CULTURE

Like Robert Crumb, Frank Miller is one of the most controversial, as well as one of the most influential, figures in American comics. Miller's comics depict white male heroes defending civilization against bloodthirsty people of color. His heroes are paragons of hypermasculine, hyperviolent, monolithic white men who defend Western civilization against its various enemies, both internal and external. Paradoxically, in Miller's view, the only way to salvage the supposedly rational and freedom-loving civilization of the West is for it to become more violent and irrational than those threatening it. When deployed against enemies hailing from the Middle East, these heroes function as unequivocal agents of white supremacy. When confronting internal enemies of Western civilization, however, they often fight against white villains with the aid of nonwhite allies. On a surface level, Miller's comics about internal threats to Western civilization are color-blind, but this color blindness breaks down when one begins examining his specific choices concerning characters of different races and the racially charged images and subtextual ideas he deploys. For example, one can identify a convergence, although somewhat muddled, between crime and Black men in Miller's comics. Further, Miller has attempted on several occasions to create heroic female characters of color, but these attempts are undercut by their recurrent subordination to stronger white men.

Miller's heroes are fiercely independent and frequently find themselves in opposition to official institutions and authorities. This stance differs from the classic superhero role as defender of the white power structure. Like the pulp supermen that preceded the creation of Superman, Miller's heroes struggle against the constraints imposed on them by the limited vision and mediocrity of social norms and institutions, which encourage mediocrity, conformity, dependence, and decadence. Ayn Rand, a libertarian philosopher and novelist whose work was closely related to the broad stream of pulp superheroes and who has become a major figure in the contemporary libertarian movement, influenced this vision. In Miller's view, the positive qualities of Western culture are undermined from within by liberalism's dangerous permissiveness of crime and terrorism and attacked from without by dangerous Middle Eastern fanatics and terrorists. Miller's highly influential miniseries *Batman: The Dark Knight Returns* presents Batman as an exemplar of the simultaneously authoritarian and libertarian hero who reconstructs society in his own image. The dangers of street crime have always been a central theme in Batman comics, written into the character's origin in the murder of his parents by a mugger. In Miller's version of Batman, however, the dangers of street crime assume unprecedented proportions as a threat to all of Western civilization, a threat that is subtly but repeatedly associated with African Americans.

In *300* (1998) and the later, exponentially more hysterical *Holy Terror* (2011), Miller portrays the cultures of the Middle East as unreasoning, violent, and incapable of civilized behavior. His position continues the history of Orientalist thought from early American comic books while adding a new element, Islamophobia, the fear and hatred of Islamic cultures, especially those of the Middle East and North Africa. Miller's Orientalism is extremely similar to the Yellow Peril tropes of early American comic books, but with the geographic and cultural focus shifted from East Asia to the Middle East. In early American comics, the Middle East was used primarily as a source for exotic costumes and disguises. It was mildly threatening, but not terror inducing in the way that East Asian villains were. Middle Eastern villains in Frank Miller's are every bit as demonic and subhuman as the earlier Yellow Peril villains, but Miller contrasts these barbaric Asians with equally violent but freedom-loving and usually white Western heroes. Miller thus emerges in *300* and *Holy Terror* as an unapologetic advocate of white supremacy on a global scale.

MILLER'S HYPERMASCULINE WHITE HEROES

The prototypical Miller hero is Batman, the hero of the miniseries *Batman: The Dark Knight Returns*, which was later collected as a graphic novel. Arguably the most influential comic book of the past forty years, it follows an older Batman who comes out of retirement to combat Gotham's slide into chaos. Although older and less physically capable, he uses his sheer willpower to overcome enemies physically more powerful than he is. In addition to old enemies such as the Joker, Batman also faces the Mutant, a giant, semihuman creature, and his eponymous gang. Miller's Batman differs from previous versions of the character in his alienation from the institutions of mainstream white society, which Miller presents as weak and decadent. Batman's mainstream society and authority are dramatized by his conflict with Superman, who has become a pawn of the US government. The story concludes with Batman faking his own death to literally go underground and found a new society, an ending that is reminiscent of the conclusion to Ayn Rand's *Atlas Shrugged* (1957), in which America's business leaders abandon a society they see as hostile to them to found a new society.

Most of Miller's later heroes are essentially exaggerated versions of the *Dark Knight* Batman. In his *Sin City* series, Dwight and Marv are bitter loners shunned by society who use acts of extreme violence to take revenge on the people who have hurt them or their loved ones. The *Sin City* stories depict these hypermasculine characters as under siege by a world that seeks to rob them of their freedom, safety, and loved ones. The hero of *Holy Terror* is another hyperviolent white male hero who defends a collapsing Western civilization against the onslaught of barbaric terrorists, as do the Spartans and their king, Leonidas, in *300*. Although strong and powerful, Miller's white male heroes are frequently depicted as aggrieved victims. Miller's Batman is one example of this character type in Miller's work, but the protagonists of the *Sin City* series are even more archetypal and extreme in this regard. This sense of powerful white men as victims exemplifies the belief among many whites that they have been victimized by minorities and demands for equal rights. A 1984 study by Stanley Greenberg found that "many whites had come to understand *themselves* as victims of racial mistreatment," a trend that has only grown more intense in the years since (Haney López, 71). Their victimization justifies the extremes of violence and brutality to which they go. Miller celebrates brutality in his white men, such as the kindhearted psychopath Marv in *Sin City*, but decries it in people of color.

Not all of Miller's representations of whiteness are positive. He is highly critical of white-dominated institutions that he views as discouraging individualism and freedom, either by fostering dependence in others or by using force to control them. In his view, such institutions include the state, the military, and corporations. This is in keeping with the libertarianism that Miller espouses, at least some of the time. Miller's commitment to freedom is highly inconsistent, but it is nevertheless a major factor in his work. In *Dark Knight*, politicians are weak and ineffectual; the wealthy are corrupt and indifferent, and the military is casually destructive. In the *Sin City* series, the main villains are the wealthy and politically connected Roark family. In *Give Me Liberty*, Erwin Rexall, the president who is murdered near the beginning of the book, is an authoritarian, whereas his successor, Howard Nissen, is a pampered liberal, both of whom Miller depicts critically.

Miller directly connects the violence and masculinity of *Sin City*'s modern white heroes to the foundations of Western culture, represented by the Spartans in *300*. Miller makes this connection in the final chapter of *The Big Fat Kill*, which he opens with a one-page summary of the battle of Thermopylae. On the next page, Dwight shifts the scene to the present day with the words, "Two millennia and a whole bunch of centuries later, I'm rattling around in the cab of a beautifully restored 1940 Ford coupe" (Miller, *Sin City: The Big Fat Kill*, 136). Later in the chapter, Dwight and the Old Town prostitutes ambush their foes in a narrow alley, harking back again to the battle of Thermopylae and reinforcing the connection between them. Miller underlines the comparison with an image of Dwight in the alley that parallels the image of a Spartan warrior in the narrow pass of Thermopylae from the initial splash page. He thus connects Sparta not only to the present day of Sin City but also to the earlier period of 1940s and 1950s America, both here and elsewhere in the series. This was the era of the original hard-boiled pulp crime fiction and noir film on which *Sin City* is based. Both the time in general and the hard-boiled and noir genres in particular are commonly associated in popular memory with images of masculine strength. It was a time when white men dominated society. The racial component of the era for Miller is made clear in a brief reference later in the series. After stealing a car, Marv tells the reader, "The Mercedes hums and handles like a dream. She may look like some Jap designed her, but the engine's a beauty" (Miller, *Sin City: The Hard Goodbye*, 83).

The larger significance of the connection between the Spartans and the vigilantes of Sin City is that Miller views the Spartans and the Sin City vigilantes as basically the same, except that the contemporary whites have been unfairly constrained by the changes in the modern world around them. In *A Dame to Kill For*, the highly violent hero Dwight says of the even more violent Marv, "There's nothing wrong with Marv, nothing at all—except that he had the rotten luck of being born at the wrong time in history. He'd have been okay if he'd been born a couple of thousand years ago. He'd be right at home on some ancient battlefield, swinging an ax into somebody's face. Or in a Roman arena, taking a sword to other gladiators like him. They'd have tossed him girls like Nancy back then" (Miller, *Sin City: A Dame to Kill For*, 97). These men's raw physical power no longer guarantees the preservation of white male power.

THE RHETORIC OF CRIME AND DOG WHISTLE RACISM

Crime is central to Miller's work, where it is presented as a pervasive problem that threatens to bring about the collapse of society. This theme also plays out in *Ronin* (1983–84), *The Dark Knight Returns*, and the *Sin City* and *Martha Washington* series. Miller ties the theme of crime to Orientalism with his use of the story of Sparta and Thermopylae in *The Big Fat Kill* when he compares the Spartans to the story's homicidal antihero, Dwight McCarthy. Not coincidentally, in the 1980s, at the same time that Miller was starting his career, politicians were using crime as a way to invoke racist stereotypes without mentioning race directly, appealing to white voters who harbored resentments toward minorities. This strategy, dating back to Richard Nixon, was further developed by Ronald Reagan, and reached new heights (or depths) with Donald Trump. Dominant racial narratives in America have long associated Black people with crime, creating a narrative that people of color are more likely to commit crimes than whites, and accusing people of color who demand equality of being criminals. The association of crime and race goes all the way back to the Reconstruction period after the Civil War, when prison was used as a substitute for slavery to reenslave large numbers of Black men and profit from their labor under appalling conditions. Whites spread a narrative that Black people were inherently animalistic and violent and that, without slavery, their criminal natures were given free rein (Haney López, 38–40).

The stereotype of Black people as criminals continued to be propagated during and after the civil rights movement. Ian Haney López writes, "From the inception of the civil rights movement in the 1950s, Southern politicians had disparaged racial activists as 'lawbreakers,' as indeed technically they were. . . . Dismissing these protesters as criminals shifted the issue from a defense of white supremacy to a more neutral-seeming concern with 'order,' while simultaneously stripping the activists of moral stature" (Haney López, 23–24). As a result, calls for law and order became racialized:

> By the mid-1960s, "law and order" had become a surrogate expression for concern about the civil rights movement. . . . FBI Director J. Edgar Hoover denounced the advocacy of nonviolent civil disobedience by civil rights leaders as a catalyst for lawbreaking and even violent rioting: "Civil disobedience," a seditious slogan of gross irresponsibility, has captured the imagination of citizens.". . . Exploiting the growing panic that equated social protest with social chaos, one of Nixon's campaign commercials showed flashing images of demonstrations,

riots, police, and violence.... As Nixon exulted after watching one of his own commercials: "Yep, this hits it right on the nose.... It's all about law and order and the damn Negro-Puerto Rican groups out there." (Haney López, 24)

After the civil rights movement of the 1960s, using racial slurs in public was no longer acceptable, so politicians and other public figures who wanted to continue invoking race had to do so more subtly. As Lee Atwater, an aide to Ronald Reagan, put it, "By 1968 you can't say 'n-----'—that hurts you. Backfires. So you say stuff like forced busing, states' rights and all that stuff" (Haney López, 57). Drawing on the long history of stigmatizing Black men as inherently predisposed to violent crime, crime easily became one of the issues used to invoke race without having to mention it explicitly. Since race was never directly mentioned, politicians were able to deny that they were using racial code words. This use of racially loaded terms without directly mentioning race is often referred to as a "dog whistle" because it is "inaudible and easily denied in one range, yet stimulating strong reactions in another" (3). Reagan's rhetoric created an image of a hardworking, law-abiding white America located in the suburbs and rural areas, in opposition to a dishonest, lazy, morally weak urban population of nonwhites (Alexander, 48–49).

Criminals in Miller's comics are not exclusively or even mainly people of color, but people of color, especially men, are mainly either criminals or otherwise decadent and violent individuals, such as Xerxes in *300*. Examples of threatening Black male criminals include Manute in *Sin City* and Ice Man in *Give Me Liberty*. Manute is a hulking, massive Black man who chauffeurs the wealthy couple Damien and Ava Lord and helps Ava murder Damien and frame Dwight, the story's hero, for the crime. In the *Martha Washington* series, Ice Man is a gang enforcer whose name evokes the rappers Ice-T and Ice Cube, both of whom were objects of a racially motivated moral panic about rap music in the 1980s that repeated and updated stereotypes of Black men as violent criminals. While Miller's work includes white criminals as villains who are at least as evil and vicious as these characters, Miller gives us no heroic images of Black men to counterbalance these, whereas a plethora of white heroes balance negative images of white criminals

Miller's depiction of urban crime is uncannily similar to that of Donald Trump's, a resemblance that one can see in Trump's involvement with the 1989 Central Park jogger case that served as a model for his later use of race-baiting in his presidential campaign and then as president. After a white woman was raped while jogging in Central Park, four young Black men and one Latino man were arrested, pressured into making false confessions, and sentenced to prison. Trump took full-page ads out in four major New York newspapers describing crime as having taken over New York City and calling for the restoration of law and order with a vengeance. Trump wrote that New Yorkers were witnessing

> the complete breakdown of life as we knew it. . . . a world ruled by the law of the streets, as roving bands of wild criminals roam our neighborhoods, dispensing their own vicious brand of twisted hatred on whomever they encounter. . . . Mayor Koch has stated that hate and rancor should be removed from our hearts. I do not think so. I want to hate these muggers and murderers. They should be forced to suffer and, when they kill, they should be executed for their crimes. . . . I am not looking to psychoanalyze or understand them, I am looking to punish them. . . . I no longer want to understand their anger. I want them to understand our anger. I want them to be afraid.

Trump did not mention the case by name in his ad, but his rhetorical question about the beating and rape of a helpless woman was taken by everyone as a reference to the Central Park jogger case. In 2002, the convictions were conclusively shown to have been false after a convicted murderer and rapist confessed to the crime, and DNA evidence confirmed his guilt. The five men were released and eventually received a major settlement from the city. Trump continued to insist that they were guilty and has never to this day apologized or admitted to any error, and his speeches as a presidential candidate, most notably his speech to the Republican National Convention, used the same language and ideas as in his 1989 advertisement.

Trump's description of the city could have been taken directly from Frank Miller's depiction of Gotham in *The Dark Knight Returns* three years earlier. In a speech to his followers, the Mutant, the leader of a massive and vicious street gang that has been terrorizing Gotham, exhorts his followers by telling them, "They call us a gang. They call us a mob. They think we just noisy kids. Only when they die by our hands and see their women raped will they know. . . . We have the strength—we have the will—and now we have the guns. Gotham City belongs to the Mutants!" (Miller, *Batman*, book 2, p. 17). The Mutant's speech depicts an inner city ruled by crime, similar to Trump's vision but even more dire and lurid. The disorder of the urban environment is given literal form in *Ronin* and *The Dark Knight Returns* in the form of disfigured, semihuman creatures who live in the sewers beneath the city. In *Ronin* this is a society of monstrous cannibals who prey on those above, while in *The Dark Knight Returns* it is a single creature, the gigantic and monstrous Mutant, who becomes leader of a criminal gang bearing his name, the Mutants. The Mutant's race is not identifiable, but he resembles primitivist stereotypes of savage Africans. He has sharpened teeth longer than any human's, and although his skin usually appears white, in one sequence it has a distinctly greenish tinge. It is tempting to speculate that he may in fact be a mutant, as his name suggests, but Miller never tells us one way or the other. If we take his name literally and place it within the lexicon of comics, then his character inevitably evokes comics' most famous team of mutants, the X-Men, a group that is widely understood, if undeservedly, as a metaphor for the civil rights movement. This reading thus aligns the despicable Mutant with African Americans.

In addition to the rich and powerful from above and street criminals from below, another threat that besets society in Miller's vision consists of liberals who attempt to explain, sympathize with, or rehabilitate criminals. The most archetypal example of this kind of character is Dr. Bartholomew Wolper, the psychiatrist in *The Dark Knight Returns*, who blames Batman for triggering the Joker's madness and crimes. Wolper believes that he has cured the Joker and arranges for him to be interviewed on a talk show, which the Joker uses as an opportunity to escape, murdering Wolper, the talk show host, and the entire audience in the process. Similarly, in the *Martha Washington* series, the liberal president, Howard Nissen, uses the increased powers of the presidency created by Rexall to forge a liberal agenda cheered by liberals, environmentalists, feminists, and ethnic leaders, but Nissen's concessions only fuel further demands from ethnic and other minorities. For Miller, as for Donald Trump, the authorities have become too permissive, too soft on criminal evildoers, and harsher forms of punishment need to be reinstituted. In Miller's logic, attempts to satisfy minority demands for equal rights are dangerous and should be avoided. The same point applies to criminals and to protesters, indicating again Miller's view of the two groups as basically the same.

At one time, Miller acknowledged the legitimacy of concerns about the use of racial and other stereotypes while also registering resentment at how these concerns limit his freedom. In 1991, he stated, "When I write my stories I honestly try to avoid targeting anyone. Working in Hollywood recently I've come to realize how many prohibitions there really are against even touching one group or another, to a point where the villain can't be female, can't be gay, can't be black. I understand this, but I still don't like the limitations placed on how you can go about creating characters" (Sharrett, 37). At least in *Dark Knight*, Miller is careful not to depict Black people as criminals, for instance, by making the members of the Mutant gang all white. He also deserves recognition for attempting to create Black female heroes in his comics at a time when heroes of color were rare in American comics. However, the comics spend little time exploring how race actually affects these characters, and Miller opts not to confront any of the difficult realities of race in the United States. Whatever positive impact Miller's female heroes of color make, they are undermined by other factors such as his equation of minority demands for equal rights with crime and urban collapse.

STRONG BUT SUBMISSIVE: WOMEN OF COLOR IN MILLER'S COMICS

While Miller's depiction of men of color is overwhelmingly negative, his depiction of women of color seems at first glance to be far more positive, even heroic in some cases. On closer inspection, however, he turns out to undermine these characters' independence and render them subservient to more powerful white characters. The most direct way he accomplishes this is by making these characters sidekicks to white men. This is Miller's strategy in *Ronin*, *Holy Terror*, and *Sin City*, all of which feature female heroes of color who assist white male protagonists.[1] In each case, the nonwhite female character begins fiercely and defiantly independent, but as the series progresses, she becomes increasingly subordinate to the white male hero. This narrative subordination is accompanied by a sexual relationship, although these relationships have little or no emotional component, as the attraction is based primarily on the male's strength and fighting ability. The relationship between the Fixer and Stack in *Holy Terror* is a prime example. Stack repeatedly praises the Fixer's power but shows no sign of an authentic emotional relationship with him. Miller does not develop their relationship outside of physical combat, and their first sexual encounter occurs while they are actually fighting each other. The white male's strength is the central fact about these relationships. The attraction is based solely on power and results in the woman of color giving up her independence to the man and admitting his superiority. Miller depicts these situations with the assumption that it is the powerful white man who automatically has the right to lead and give orders, much as whites were shown as the natural leaders and rulers in the jungle genre.

Sin City exemplifies the dynamic of strong white men dominating Black female characters. The prostitutes of Old Town are supposed to be tough and fiercely independent, but the white male characters Marv and Dwight easily gain control over them. Both characters are initially captured by the heavily armed prostitutes, but both manage to escape and subsequently take command of the situation, relegating the prostitutes to the status of foot

Frank Miller, *The Big Fat Kill* (Dark Horse, 1995). © Frank Miller Inc.

soldiers. Dwight's control over the armed prostitutes of Old Town is shown in a panel in *The Big Fat Kill*. Dwight's face is twice the size or more of the two women whose faces are crowded behind and below his, emphasizing his greater prominence and importance. Although their faces are visually conjoined, Dwight's is also enlarged and elevated, positioning him as the dominant one among the trio. The implication that, in Miller's view, women ought to know their place, is confirmed in a comment by Marv in *The Big Fat Kill* that his accomplice, Wendy, "doesn't ask any questions. Class dame" (Miller, *Sin City: The Hard Goodbye*, 162).

Old Town's fighting women include Miho, a deadly Japanese fighter who wields katana swords but never speaks. She demonstrates how Miller's Orientalism manifests itself in his crime comics as well as in *300* and *Holy Terror* through the stereotype of the submissive Asian woman. Although she occasionally demonstrates her deadliness in combat, she is generally subservient to Dwight and does not show much if any agency of her own. Whereas Batman and Leonidas possess iron wills that allow them to bend others to their goals, Miho has no will of her own whatsoever and serves only to advance the goals of others. She is an archetypal example of the Orientalist stereotype of the submissive Asian woman. When Dwight reveals that, unbeknownst to her, he once saved Miho, the revelation causes her to abandon her initial hostility to him and serve him silently and unquestioningly (Miller, *Sin City: A Dame to Kill For*, 159–60). As Dwight tells her and the other women who control Old Town, "When I give an order, it will be obeyed" (156). Similar to how Dwight is able to dominate and lead the Asian Miho despite her greater lethality, the white villain Ava is able to dominate and command her powerful Black bodyguard, Manute, calling herself a "goddess" and him her "slave" (176). Manute again invokes the language of slavery when he returns in a later miniseries, stating, "I serve a new master, now," referring to a mob boss who wants to take over Old Town (Miller, *Sin City: The Big Fat Kill*, 110). Like Miho, Manute has no will of his own and only exists to serve his white mistress.

The *Martha Washington* series features a woman of color as the protagonist rather than a supporting character, but even here, Miller strips her of any will of her own and finds ways to diminish her. He makes her a model minority who does not challenge white supremacy. White characters control the flow of events, and she is extremely slow to stand up for herself or fight back. She is ultimately shown to be vastly inferior to a white male superhero. She is extremely hesitant to confront the villains of the series, and she is not the one primarily responsible for defeating them. Whereas most protagonists of action comics end up defeating their enemies and stopping the injustices they perpetrate, Washington is primarily a survivor rather than a victor. If one line sums up Washington's overall narrative, it is the vow she makes after her fellow soldiers are slaughtered in Brazil: "This won't kill me. I won't die here. This won't kill me" (Miller and Gibbons, 51).

Washington's status as a bystander and her secondary position in relation to whites are made clear in a short 1995 story titled "Insubordination," featuring a white superhero named Captain Kurtz. The character visually and thematically resembles Captain America, a reference that is confirmed by the fact that Dave Gibbons, the artist for *Martha Washington*, states that the story was an homage to Jack Kirby, whose last name resembles the character's (Miller and Gibbons, 234). Miller presents Kurtz, who is only a minor guest character in the series, as an absurdly heroic individual who is superior in every way to Washington. As Miller writes, Kurtz is "the kind of man they tell you doesn't exist. People aren't supposed to be good at more than one thing. He's not just a soldier. He's an inventor. A geneticist. A physicist. And a genius at everything he's ever done" (242). Like Batman and Leonidas, Kurtz is the very embodiment of a powerful, cohesive consciousness who can order the world around him at will. The story often appears to be so corny it cannot be taken seriously, and part of it is probably a reference to the corniness of many of Kirby and Lee's stories, but this is also clearly an homage, in which the corniness is supposed to be appealing. In a sense, this is appropriate, since Kirby's early Captain America stories were indeed viciously racist, but Miller pays no attention to this inconvenient reality.

In the story, Kurtz has single-handedly broken through Nazi lines to rescue the Liberty Bell so that it does not fall into their hands. Washington does not even know what the Liberty Bell is, a sign of the suppression of American history, but also of Kurtz's knowledge of the truth and Washington's ignorance. Washington is exaggeratedly wide-eyed when she meets him, emphasizing the awe in which she holds him. She tells him, "You're the only hero I ever had, except for my mom" (Miller and Gibbons, 244). Kurtz's face is located above hers, while she looks up at him with eyes spread wide in amazement and admiration. In the end, Kurtz sacrifices himself to save Washington, ordering her to save herself while he holds off the Nazis. Again, the images convey his superiority to her. Their faces are shown in adjoining panels, with his panel larger and his head above hers. His expression is brave and cheerful, while she can only cry and frown. Kurtz is adorned in the bright and patriotic colors of red, white, blue, and gold with an eagle on his forehead, while Washington is dressed in the olive drab of an ordinary soldier.

It is unclear if Miller intended this, but the choice of Kurtz as a name recalls Joseph Conrad's celebrated novella *Heart of Darkness* (1899), whose hero and/or villain is named Kurtz, as is the equivalent character in Francis Ford Coppola's film adaptation, *Apocalypse Now* (1979). In both stories, Kurtz is a senior white official who "goes native" in a remote region of the jungle (the Congo in the novella, Vietnam in the film), where he has committed unspecified atrocities against the natives. In both stories, a younger white man (Marlow in the novella, Willard in the film) has to go out and retrieve Kurtz, whom the proper authorities consider to have gone mad. This situation fits the plot of "Insubordination" fairly well, as Washington, standing in for Marlow/Willard, travels to the center of a combat zone where Kurtz is surrounded by enemies, the Nazis, standing in for the Congolese/Vietnamese. If the overall scenario fits, however, the message has been reversed. In Conrad's novella and Coppola's film, Western man's exposure to the barbarity of "primitive" cultures results in the barbarization of the West and the fragmentation of the white heroes' consciousness. This narrative contains both a racist, white supremacist component, the view of non-Western cultures as barbarous, and a critique of Western imperialism for its inhuman atrocities and madness. Miller's version, on the other hand, changes the mission of Kurtz from one of imperialism to that of anti-Nazism and removes any sense of madness or barbarism from Kurtz. Given Miller's wholehearted embrace of American imperialism in the Middle East, it is not surprising that

Frank Miller (writer) and Dave Gibbons (pencils), "Insubordination." Originally published in *Happy Birthday, Martha Washington* #1 (March 1995). Reprinted in *The Life and Times of Martha Washington in the Twenty-First Century* (Dark Horse, 2017). © Dave Gibbons and Frank Miller.

his version of *Heart of Darkness* casts the Western man as an unambiguous hero and expunges any negative reference to the imperialist project. If the reference to *Heart of Darkness* and *Apocalypse Now* is in fact correct, then Miller turns a figure who is meant to call Western imperialism into question into an absurdly overinflated symbol of Western greatness.

James Braxton Peterson has argued that Washington is a Black nationalist figure, but his analysis is unconvincing. It hinges on the appearance of a black cat early in the narrative, when Washington is a child, and the later repeated appearance of a black panther, first in the Amazon, and later in visions she receives (209). This can indeed be taken as a reference to both the Marvel character Black Panther and the historical Black Panther Party, but it hardly makes Washington an icon of Black nationalism, as when Peterson claims that "the black panther is both Martha Washington's avatar and the visual articulation of her Black Nationalist persona" (209). Peterson does acknowledge that Washington's creation by two white men is problematic (206), her Black nationalism is "uncanny" (206), and "Martha is a nationalist in the most traditionalist sense" (210). In the end, he states that her depiction as a black panther is "dense" and that she "is never separate from the history of Black Nationalism" (210). While it may be true that she cannot be separated from this history, Miller uses her character to undermine Black nationalism as a threat to society, not to uphold it. As Peterson himself notes, in *Give Me Liberty*, Miller presents "a version of America where nationalist ideology is unchecked, out of control" (209).

ORIENTALISM AND THE DEFENSE OF WESTERN CULTURE

Miller's view of the Middle East as a threat to white Western culture is the subject of *300* and *Holy Terror*. As Ian Haney López has pointed out, after 9/11 the "figment of a threatening Middle Eastern figure" moved from "the periphery of America's racial imagination" to its center (117). President George W. Bush made the war on terror the central theme of his presidency, calling it "the decisive ideological struggle of the 21st century" and "a clash of civilizations," the latter phrase borrowed from the controversial political scientist and historian Samuel Huntington (119). Miller's *300* was published three years before 9/11, but it uncannily prefigures the anti-Islamic rhetoric, also known as Islamophobia, of the post-9/11 war on terror. In 2006, George W. Bush described the conflict with radical Islam in the following terms:

> Since the horror of 9/11, we've learned a great deal about the enemy. We have learned that they are evil and kill without mercy, but not without purpose. We have learned that they form a global network of extremists who are driven by a perverted vision of Islam—a totalitarian ideology that hates freedom, rejects tolerance and despises all dissent. And we have learned that their goal is to build a radical Islamic empire where women are prisoners in their homes, men are beaten for missing prayer meetings, and terrorists have a safe haven to plan and launch attacks on America and other civilized nations.... This struggle has been called a clash of civilizations. In truth, it is a struggle for civilization. We are fighting to maintain the way of life enjoyed by free nations. (Haney López, 119)

Miller repeatedly uses freedom, civilization, humanity, and reason to justify the militarized, hypermasculine, hyperviolent defense of Western, white supremacist society while simultaneously celebrating brutal white warriors as heroes and mocking whites who lack sufficient masculinity or show empathy for their putative enemies. This Islamophobic rhetoric has continuities with both the long history of Orientalism in Western culture and the history of Yellow Peril themes in early comic books, the pulps, and turn-of-the-century mass culture in general.

Miller's *300* comments on relations between the West and the Middle East through a retelling of the battle of Thermopylae in 480 BC that was fought between an alliance of Greek city-states and the Persian empire of the Achaemenid dynasty. The title is derived from the force of three hundred Spartan soldiers who defended a narrow pass against a Persian army numbering in the tens of thousands. Although the story is set in antiquity, Miller uses the Spartans to stand for white, Western civilization as defenders of freedom, civilization, and reason, and to represent his ideal society, which he contrasts with the irrational, despotic hordes of the Middle East, represented by the Persians and their king, Xerxes. In Miller's portrayal, Xerxes appears draped in layer upon layer of gold chains, bands, rings, bracelets, and piercings, painting a picture of him as vain, pampered, and effeminate. His perpetual sneer indicates excessive pride, while the weblike forms of the gold chains recall spiderwebs and make him seem insectoid, predatory, and inhuman. While Leonidas's willpower, ability to dominate his environment, and even his brutality are all presented as positive attributes, the same qualities in Xerxes are shown in a negative light. The other characters in Miller's work whom Xerxes most closely resembles visually are the mostly white female prostitutes from his *Sin City* series (1991–2000) and a Black male gang member named Ice Man in *Give Me Liberty*. Dark skin, criminality, tyranny, and sexual profligacy are all brought together in this recurring visual trope. The Spartan king Leonidas, by contrast, is depicted as minimally adorned and resolutely masculine.

The Persians function throughout *300* as foils to the Spartans, with the negative qualities of the Persians highlighting the positive ones of the Spartans. Miller repeatedly depicts the Persians as not merely cruel but animalistic, barely even human, and links their animalism to their disdain for freedom, describing the Persian army as "snorting, snarling desert beasts. Howling barbarians. The armies of all Asia—pledged to crush the impertinent republics of Greece—to make slaves of the only free men the world has ever known." The Persians are repeatedly depicted wearing black, a color associated with darkness and evil. It is the color of the skin and uniforms of many of the Persians, the color of the wolf that Leonidas must kill to pass his rite of initiation into manhood, and also the color of the uniforms of the elite Persian soldiers, the Immortals (Proszek, 42–43, 54–55). As James Proszek writes, this creates "a false binary in which blackness becomes [a] moral type of darkness that exists only in the Persian people," in contrast to the heroism and virtue of the white Persians (45). Proszek also points out that the Spartans are typically depicted as individuals, often accented by their red capes, whereas the Persians frequently meld together into a seamless, formless mass. As Proszek points out, "Each soldier's dark, fully-clothed body is indistinguishable from his neighbor and lacks individually identifiable features. By making the Persians unrecognizable and/or indistinguishable, *300* effectively erases their humanity" (40–41, 54). When the Spartans enter battle, they are fused together into a solid mass, but the individual bodies remain

Frank Miller, *300* (Dark Horse, 1999). © Frank Miller Inc.

distinct and evident, in large part because of the visual prominence of their shields. This gives them a strong sense of group strength without sacrificing their individuality. The elite Persian warriors known as the Immortals, on the other hand, are shown blending into one another without borders, visually denying their individuality and humanity. Similarly, the Persians' masks are snarling and animalistic, discouraging the reader from thinking of them as human beings, whereas the Spartans' are more recognizably human. The tropes of the faceless horde and the snarling beast are both reminiscent of the Yellow Peril racism of early superhero comics.

Miller depicts Sparta as his ideal society, so it is worth examining this depiction and actual Spartan society in some detail. According to Miller, Persia's invasion sought to "vanquish tiny Greece, to crush her impertinent invention of democracy and extinguish the only light of reason in the world" (Miller, *Sin City: The Big Fat Kill*, 135). Miller expands on the meaning that Sparta and Thermopylae hold for him in *300* in a speech Leonidas gives to his troops before the battle against the Persians:

> Come tomorrow, we light a fire that will burn in the hearts of free men for all the centuries yet to be. No retreat. No surrender. This is Spartan law. And by Spartan law, we will stand and fight and die. The law. We do not sacrifice the rule of law to the will and whim of men. That is the old way. The old, sad, stupid way. The way of Xerxes [the Persian king] and every creature like him. A new age is begun. An age of great deeds. An age of reason. An age of justice. An age of law. And all will know that three hundred Spartans gave their last breath to defend it.

To justify the Spartan violence he glorifies, Miller presents the Spartans as the defenders of freedom, reason, and civilization, but these assertions are hollow and hypocritical because Miller's portrayal of Sparta twists Sparta's actual history into its opposite, making a mockery out of his claims for it. Miller's depiction of Greek civilization follows a long Western tradition of portraying ancient Greece as the beginning of the putative Western tradition of reason, individualism, and democracy, which supposedly form the cornerstones of Western culture. Miller's account differs from most of its predecessors by associating Sparta with these accomplishments. Sparta was a militaristic society that placed a high value on obedience, strength, and duty and was not known for its philosophy, art, literature, or democracy. Miller's choice of Sparta as his ideal society actually undermines the values he claims it stands for, embedding a contradiction at the core of his conception of Western society, and hence of whiteness.

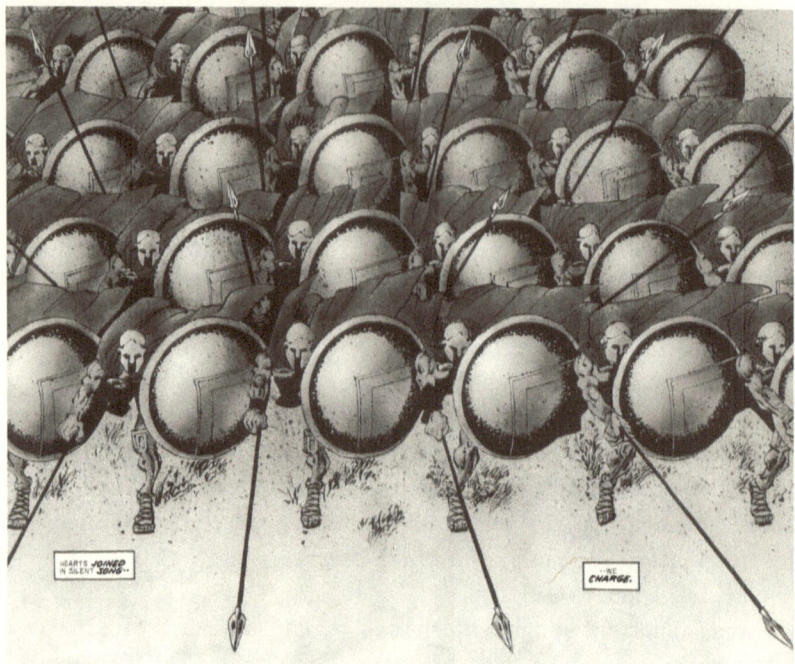

Frank Miller, *300* (Dark Horse, 1999). © Frank Miller Inc.

Freedom is central to the racial rhetoric of *300*, but it bears no resemblance to the actual conditions of Spartan society. As Dan Hassler-Forest asks, "What was Sparta if not a military dictatorship?" (124). To begin with, the Spartan freedom that Miller praises rested on the lack of freedom of the helots, neighboring Greeks whom the Spartans had enslaved. Although all Greek cities owned slaves in varying numbers, Sparta was the only one that held a large number of fellow Greeks as slaves (de Ste. Croix, 190–91). Sparta's mistreatment of the helots, whom Spartans were conditioned to view as subhuman animals, was quite brutal (Whitby, 92). Even to Spartan citizens, Sparta was a militaristic society that emphasized strength, discipline, and unity above all else, which Miller portrays as virtues, but can easily be seen as sinister. As Leonidas tells the reader, "We are born. We are inspected. If we are small or puny or sickly or misshapen, we are discarded. We are starved. Driven to steal and fight and kill. We are tested. Tossed into the wild. Left to pit our wits and will against nature's fury. By rod and lash, we are punished. Trained to show no pain. Our training never ends." It is tantamount to an ancient version of eugenics. The Spartan training regimen was extreme and seen by many of Sparta's contemporaries as barbarous. The philosopher Aristotle, a

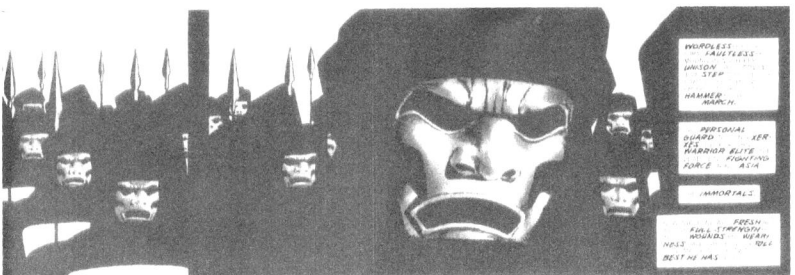

Frank Miller, *300* (Dark Horse, 1999). © Frank Miller Inc.

harsh critic of the Spartan system, believed that this extreme training made the Spartans "beast-like" (de Ste. Croix, 192–93).

While Miller and the Spartans worship strength and discipline, they find democracy distasteful. When a Spartan soldier attempts to offer his loyalty until death to Leonidas, the king responds contemptuously, "I didn't ask. Leave democracy to the Athenians, boy." To facilitate the illusion that Sparta was a democracy, Miller also distorts the Spartans' and Persians' respective views of the divinity of kings. Miller repeatedly has the Persians, including Xerxes himself, state that he is a god-king, which makes him seem arrogant and tyrannical, but in reality the Persians were monotheistic Zoroastrians who saw their emperors as representatives of their god, not as gods themselves, while the Spartans believed that their kings were divine, claiming descent from the mythical demigod Heracles (Parker, 161–62; Bridges, 81, 195; Boyce, 55).

Another quality Miller misleadingly associates with Sparta is reason, as when Leonidas implores Spartan religious leaders to let him lead the army against Persia during a religious festival by telling them, "I'd prefer you trusted your reason." Miller's characterization of Sparta as supporting reason over superstition rings hollow. Unlike Sparta's main rival, Athens, Sparta never produced any great philosophers, nor did it have any institution that could compete with Plato's academy in Athens. In fact, Sparta was known among Greek cities for the extent to which it followed religious traditions to the letter, rather than breaking with them in the name of reason (Parker, 163–70). Miller also distorts actual Spartan society by erasing its ubiquitous practice of homosexuality. Leonidas is not shown to have any homosexual partners, and he makes several comments disparaging the Athenians for their homosexuality. In fact, homosexuality was as prevalent among the Spartans as among the Athenians, if not more so. Judging by surviving texts, homosexual relationships were at least as important in Sparta as heterosexual marriages (Powell, 93–94). The distinguished classical historian

Paul Cartledge has written that the "average Spartan male" had a "strongly homosexual orientation" (Cartledge, 142). Miller's omission of the Spartans' homosexuality displays his homophobia, since he sees the Spartans' supposed heterosexuality as superior to the homosexual Athenians and the sexually ambiguous Persians.

Miller's *300* was heavily criticized as racist, both in its original comic book form and in its adaptation as a film. This brought Miller a significant amount of controversy, but this was nothing compared to what he faced in response to his 2011 graphic novel *Holy Terror*, which earned him unanimous censure. Set in the present day, *Holy Terror* follows a superhero named the Fixer and a cat burglar named Natalie Stack who quickly becomes his sidekick. Miller initially planned *Holy Terror* as a Batman comic, but DC never made an official announcement about the project, and it was eventually published by Legendary Comics instead (Kovacs, 387). The connection between *300* and *Holy Terror* is indicated in one panel in which two strands of Greek helmets appear without explanation, meandering across the page over a drawing of the terrorists' underground lair. In *Holy Terror*, the xenophobic paranoia of *300* goes completely off the rails, verging on incoherence. It reads like a parody of *Batman: The Dark Knight Returns* (1986) and *Sin City* and was panned by critics (Hassler-Forest; Bridges, 193–97; Proszek, 33–39). The plot is a succession of rapid-fire events with little or no attempt to build a coherent narrative, explain why things are happening or who is doing them, or indicate the characters' motivations.

What is clear is the existence of an absurdly exaggerated white hero desperately trying to stem the tide of Islamic fanaticism that threatens to overrun America. *Holy Terror* does not identify the specific ethnic origin of its villains, which is in keeping with its practice of reducing all Muslims to a single characteristic, that of violent, extremist terrorism. Miller's lack of differentiation between ethnicity, culture, and religion is itself part of his racism, since he collapses all these categories into a single, monolithic identity. The confusion created by this cultural amalgamation is nowhere more evident than in the terrorists' headquarters in a mysterious underground ruin, which includes non-Western, primitivist-looking dinosaur heads mounted on the wall. Their narrative purpose is unclear, but they recall the idols and prehistoric creatures that appeared periodically in jungle comics. Here they link the terrorists to fearsome carnivorous animals and the Western trope of primitivism.

Holy Terror is powered almost wholly by a bloodthirsty rage that is so overwhelming it almost appears to be satirizing itself. Miller not only endorses torture as a means of fighting terrorism but revels in it. As the Fixer says after terrorists blow up a police helicopter, "Let's get us some killing done"

(Miller, *Holy Terror*). Before they kill the final terrorist in one battle, the Fixer says, "Leave one of them alive. To talk. . . . We'll have to torture him," to which Stack replies, "Torture. Okay. I'm down with that." There then follows a grisly scene in which the Fixer and Stack taunt their victim with racist insults while torturing him, asking him, "So Mohammed, pardon me for guessing your name, but you've got to admit the odds are pretty good it's Mohammed—what's the plan?" After some torture, the Fixer extracts the necessary information and then kills the terrorist by throwing him off a building and detonating his suicide belt. Stack comments, "Yeesh. That's a lot of chunks of terrorist." The Fixer responds, "At least we know they're the same species," although how exactly they deduce that fact from a pile of meat is unclear. The whole comic is a love letter from Miller to carnage and pain. When the Fixer rescues Stack and takes out the terrorist headquarters, Stack narrates approvingly, "He brings hell to earth," as the Fixer attacks the terrorists with their own chemical weapons, the same ones whose use he has previously decried as barbaric.

The violence in *Holy Terror* is heavily sexualized; it gives the impression that for Miller, violence is the ultimate aphrodisiac. When Stack first encounters the Fixer, after several minutes of intense fighting, she inexplicably jumps on him and begins kissing him, telling us in the caption, "You are mine, you do-gooder prick," after which they resume fighting, before returning to sexual interaction (Miller, *Holy Terror*). The panel showing the Fixer using chemical weapons also features him straddling the bound and tied body of Stack in a sexually suggestive pose, while the enormous gun the Fixer holds is likewise sexually loaded. The terrorists have tied up stack, but as drawn by Miller, her restraints emphasize her weakness and passivity in comparison to the Fixer's power and control of the situation. The orgasmic attraction to violence displayed in this image is exactly what he criticizes the Muslim terrorists for. *Holy Terror* makes sure to show that the male Fixer is in every way superior to the female Stack, as when Stack complains of pain but the Fixer remains stoic. The Fixer's greater strength and capacity for violence are made clear in Stack's narrated statement to the reader that "the Fixer holds me up. He's got a tremble running through him, too. But his is angry. Like he wants to start killing people. Me, I'm just plain scared." At one point Stack calls the Fixer "boss," to which the Fixer replies, "'Boss.' I like the sound of that." Although Stack tells him not to get used to it, Miller's desire for a strong white male to take control and give orders is obvious. However, while Miller attempts to construct yet another hero with an unbending will who can control the people and environment around him, he can no longer render this effort plausible. The Fixer seems to be a consciousness on the verge of fragmentation and collapse, much like the narrative and visual structure of *Holy Terror* itself, which are practically incoherent.

Miller's condemnation of fundamentalist Islamic terrorism does not include any consideration of Western actions that might have caused the crisis that give rise to terrorism, such as the history of Western colonialism, imperialism, invasion, and support for coups and military dictatorships in the Middle East. Terrorists make an easy target, since attacking civilians is clearly atrocious, but Miller ignores the fact that the West is guilty of its own atrocities. The idea that the West, and America in particular, may have caused massive pain, death, destruction, and social fragmentation in the Middle East is not considered for even a passing moment. In fact, Miller goes further than simply ignoring Western atrocities; he revels in them, celebrating the Fixer's thirst for blood while decrying the terrorists' identical urges.

It is even clearer in *Holy Terror* than in *300* that Miller believes that the only way to defeat what he sees as the barbarian enemies of Western civilization is to become like them, but even more so. This need to employ the violent, uncivilized methods of the enemy to preserve freedom and civilization echoes the justifications for torture and preemptive invasion espoused by the George W. Bush administration and to many statements made by Donald Trump, such as his wish to return to the use of torture as an interrogation technique. *Holy Terror* also makes it clear that, in Miller's view, liberals are allied, whether intentionally or unintentionally, with the terrorists. Miller expresses this point with a montage in which Democratic politicians, including Barack Obama, Joe Biden, and Hillary Clinton, are interspersed with portraits of Third World dictators and terrorists, effectively equating all of them as enemies of democracy and human rights. Significantly, only two of these villains, Clinton and Biden, are white, the latter of whom is positioned behind Obama, suggesting his subservience to the Black President. The view that all government programs represent dangers to freedom has become universal on the right. This view is based on the idea that liberal programs intended to help the poor are giveaways to racial minorities. As Ian Haney López has written, "Dog whistle racism has helped convince many whites, arguably even a majority, that the greatest danger they face comes from a liberal government in hock to minorities, rather than from concentrated wealth and its plutocratic agenda" (167). One of the main ways this has been done is by linking minorities with the abuse of government-funded services and with crime, a tactic that Donald Trump continued to pursue throughout his presidency.

In the Trump era, Islamophobia continues to be a major force in American politics. Trump proposed banning all Muslims from entering the United

States, and as president he imposed a series of travel bans on majority-Muslim countries. He "embraced a deeply suspicious view of Islam that several of his aides have promoted," such as his former senior adviser Steve Bannon, who has said, "Islam is not a religion of peace—Islam is a religion of submission" (Shane et al.). Such views of Islam and the Middle East as a whole as inherently hostile and dangerous form the centerpiece to two of Miller's comics, *300* and *Holy Terror*, which use these views as a foil for the supposed love of freedom and reason of the white Western world.

CONCLUSION

Miller repeatedly uses Nazis as villains in his comics, but in ways that reinforce racism rather than undercut it. This contradiction is reminiscent of early superhero comics in which anti-Nazi propaganda stood shoulder to shoulder with blatant racism, to which Miller adds his own idiosyncratic twists. To begin with, Miller often combines Nazism with social groups that the Nazis reviled. Miller has a habit of making feminist and LGBT characters Nazis, thereby turning straight people into victims. A spokesman for the Aryan Thrust announces on television, "the Aryan Thrust cannot be stopped—America's future is white—and male—and gay" (Miller and Gibbons, 98). Another villain Miller creates along the same lines is a group of blonde, genetically engineered female warriors who kill their billionaire creator and become soldiers of PAX. The absurdity of these situations can hardly be exaggerated, and they serve to paint various disenfranchised and oppressed groups as villains rather than heroes, as perpetrators of oppression rather than its victims, thereby turning the tables on those groups who would call for equal representation and treatment.

Miller does more than just demonize his political foes as Nazis, however. In fact, Miller's worldview has a great deal in common with the Nazis, including his worship of strength and violence as a cleansing force, his belief in the fundamental corruption of Western society and white supremacy over other races, his adoration of Sparta, and his extreme hostility to liberalism, the Left, racial minorities, women, and LGBTQ people. The militarism, discipline, and total control over its citizens made Sparta a model to the most white supremacist movement in history, the Nazis, who saw the Spartans as belonging to a different and superior race than the helots, with Hitler calling Sparta "the first racialist state" (Chapoutot, 220, 223). For Miller and the Nazis, Sparta represents the superiority of whites over other races, of militarism and authoritarianism over democracy, and of the construction of the ideal male body. The Nazis traced the perfection of the Aryan body back to the Greeks, and their eugenics program was designed to recapture this lost ideal. In *300*, the character of Ephialtes, who betrays the Spartans because he cannot become one of them, functions as an antithesis that contradistinctively defines the ideal. None of these views belong exclusively to Nazi ideology, and it would be an exaggeration to describe Miller as an actual Nazi; but taken together, they indicate that he has far more in common with Nazi beliefs than he would care to admit. Like the first generation of American comic book creators, Miller frequently uses Nazis as villains while propagating racist stereotypes.

Miller's politics are not consistent. He poses as a defender of freedom and an opponent of state power over the individual, but he also embraces the quasi-totalitarian society of Sparta and the imperialist, militaristic rhetoric of the war on terror. These contradictions in Miller's thought are not unique to him. Trump and much of the contemporary libertarian-tinged Right share them. The Tea Party, for instance, combined a putative support for individual freedom and opposition to big government with a racist attack on the United States' first Black president that questioned whether he was a legitimate American citizen. Known as the birther movement, this line of thinking provided Donald Trump's first major entrée into US politics. Miller shares Trump's rhetorical hostility to white elites but also his xenophobic hostility to Islam, his sense of white victimhood, his passion for violent vengeance and punishment, his apocalyptic vision of American cities as overridden with crime to the point of chaos and collapse, and his sense that white supremacist Western civilization is on the point of collapse (Thrush and Davis). In fact, Miller did much to help pioneer this vision of urban collapse in *The Dark Knight Returns*. This vision entered mass consciousness through a plethora of movies. Miller's Hollywood career started with *RoboCop 2* and *RoboCop 3*, which he cowrote, films that presented a grim vision of lawless American cities in need of aggressive policing. This vision also pervades the many Batman movies made since the 1989 *Batman*, all of which were heavily influenced by Miller's *Dark Knight*. In addition, this vision is also expressed in the many film adaptations of Miller comics, including *300* and *Sin City*. Miller has declared Trump a "buffoon" and does not seem to share Trump's animus toward Hispanic immigrants, but these differences do not negate their overall similarity (Kit). For Miller, the brutal white men of Sparta and Sin City are one and the same: strong, willful, dominant heroes defending Western culture against an onslaught of enemies who are also all basically the same, whether ancient Persians or modern-day terrorists or criminals.

Miller resisted the deconstruction of the white superhero by retrenching white supremacy in a variety of genres, including war, crime, and science fiction comics. His racial rhetoric drew on the same sources as the politics of resentment that Donald Trump was developing in the same years. White anxieties about the progress of civil rights also found expression in those years in another phenomenon, the reskinning of white superheroes as Black characters, beginning with the 1982 replacement of Hal Jordan with John Stewart as Green Lantern. Although these reskinnings sought to broaden racial diversity in the ranks of major superheroes, most of them inadvertently demonstrated their creators' inability or unwillingness to fully abandon white supremacy and the white racial frame. Miller's work contrasts strongly with that of a number of alternative cartoonists working at the same time, such as Gilbert and Jaime Hernandez and Chris Ware, whose comics thoughtfully probed and critiqued the meaning of whiteness at the same time that Miller's comics were indulging in Orientalism, primitivism, and dog whistle racism.

Chapter Ten

RESKINNING NARRATIVES

Taking Off the Mask

Over the past several decades, a recurring plot device has emerged in Marvel and DC comics in which canonical white superheroes are replaced by Black and Brown characters, a phenomenon that we label reskinning.[1] Major characters who have undergone reskinning include Iron Man (1982), Green Lantern (1984), Superman (1993), Captain America (2002), and Ms. Marvel (2014). On the one hand, reskinning narratives acknowledge the existence of white privilege and attempt to provide a counterweight by replacing white superheroes with Black or Brown ones, often as a result of some personal failure, life choice, or tragedy on the part of the white superhero. On the other hand, reskinning narratives often present the Black or Brown version of the superhero as a glorified sidekick who frequently fails without the assistance of the white hero or needs to be rescued by the white hero. The most telling aspect of reskinning narratives is how they often trigger the white fragility of the departing superhero. Robin DiAngelo defines white fragility as "a range of defensive moves" triggered by race-based stress, including "the outward display of emotions such as anger, fear, and guilt, and behaviors such as argumentation, silence, and leaving the stress-inducing situation," which together "function to reinstate white racial equilibrium" (54). In reskinning narratives, the superheroes' white fragility is often triggered by their Black replacements, resulting in some or all of the responses described by DiAngelo. Most white superheroes in reskinning narratives only give up their power and role unwillingly and quickly begin trying to reclaim it from their Black replacement, which they eventually succeed in doing. Their former replacement is often allowed to continue as a spin-off character, but one who is of distinctly secondary importance.

Reskinning narratives present a dramatic example of the emotional, social, and political investment that American society has made in white supremacy, and the difficult struggle that is required to divest from it. As George Lipsitz notes, "White Americans are encouraged to invest in whiteness, to remain true to an identity that provides them with resources, power, and opportunity.... This whiteness is ... a delusion, a scientific and cultural fiction," and yet it is "a social fact, an identity created and continued with all-too-real consequences for the distribution of wealth, prestige, and opportunity" (vii). Reskinning narratives demonstrate the investment that the fictional white superheroes and their creators have placed in the powers they possess, which have previously been denied to people of other races and are thus examples of white privilege. The persistence of this investment is demonstrated by the fact that in the 1980s and 1990s, the writers of reskinning narratives ultimately refused to transfer the powers and identities possessed by white superheroes to their Black successors, choosing instead to restore them to their original white owners. As Joel Olson notes, "Abandoning one's white privilege to join the rest of humanity is usually a fleeting temporary thing.... When whites abandon white privilege it is always temporary.... We whites always eventually grab our white privilege back" (Ignatiev, 141).

The 2002 miniseries *Truth* represents a dramatic and important departure from the earlier pattern of reskinning. Instead of a Black character replacing a white one, it emerges that Isaiah Bradley, the Black Captain America, was actually a member of the original group of Black soldiers who were used as test subjects for the super-soldier serum. Even more recently, the Hugo Award–winning *Ms. Marvel: No Normal* (2014), featuring Kamala Khan, a Pakistani American born in Jersey City, completely avoids the pitfalls of previous reskinning narratives, first by barely including the former Ms. Marvel, Carol Danvers, in the narrative, and second by dramatizing Khan's transcendence of her white predecessor as she embraces her own nonwhite cultural superhero identity. While several websites catalog superheroes who have undergone racial transformations, mostly in film, little scholarly output has dealt with the trend. Adilifu Nama devotes a chapter to the discussion in his book *Super Black: American Pop Culture and Black Superheroes* (2011), noting that most of the reskinnings amount to little more than "watered-down replicas of white superheroes" (98) and calling for Black versions of traditional superheroes to embody more of a "black racial identity and worldview" (125), a call that the creators of *Ms. Marvel: No Normal*, at least, seem to have heard.

WHITE SAVIORS AND WHITE FRAGILITY

Perhaps the earliest example of reskinning is Jim Rhodes's run as Iron Man. Suffering from alcoholism in the 1980s, Tony Stark proves incapable of maintaining his role as Iron Man, leading to a plotline in 1982 wherein his pilot and best friend Jim Rhodes takes over the armor. Rather than expanding the symbol of the armor beyond its locus of white imperialism, this merely sets up a white savior narrative wherein Captain America swoops in to convince Stark that he is the rightful owner of the armor and his country desperately needs him. The white savior narrative is a popular trope in American culture that often presents Black characters in films, television shows, and comics in need of white saviors. This dynamic is particularly pernicious, since it operates under the disguise of selflessness on the part of the white savior. The message is that the white hero ought to be celebrated for coming to the aid of the Black character. The ideological underpinnings of this trope, however, reaffirm white supremacy and the disempowerment of nonwhites. The obvious alternative narrative would be for the Black character to help herself or himself or be rescued by another nonwhite character.

Leading up to Stark's alcoholic breakdown, Rhodes is mostly depicted as needing rescue, such as when he is captured and tortured in Scotland by a Scottish villain who refers to Rhodes as "the black" (Lee, *Invincible Iron Man*, 204). Iron Man successfully saves Rhodes and spares no expense in helping him recover. Fearing recapture, Rhodes disappears from his hospital bed and eventually tries to escape by passing as white. "The worst part was this disguise," he reflects, "this gunk I put on my face . . . flour and egg-yolk—ugh! Had to be done, though. My black skin would've stood out like a camel in a swimming pool" (284). Having to negotiate his blackness after being tortured by a Scot acknowledges the challenges presented by Rhodes's racialized bodily signifiers in a globally racist world. In another plotline replete with racial symbolism, Tony Stark saves Rhodes while the two are in Wakanda, the technologically advanced African country under the rule of the Black Panther. Iron Man and Rhodes visit Wakanda to meet with the Black Panther and inspect a "research plant operated by Wakanda in conjunction with Stark International" (102). When they arrive, the Wakandans appear nearly naked and extremely primitive and are all drawn exactly the same shade of color, broadly defining the African tribe as a monolith of primitivism. The presentation of the Wakandans functions in a manner ideologically similar to the presentation of the Mandarin as an exotic other that simultaneously normalizes whiteness.

Rhodes is tricked and held captive by Killmonger, who attempts to gain control of the tribe, compelling Iron Man to save his pilot and friend once again. Presenting a white savior narrative in the African country of Wakanda, replete with racial stereotypes of Black primitivism, as a precursor to the reskinning of Iron Man forecasts the potential narrative limitations of Jim Rhodes as Iron Man as likely to be filled with stereotypes and limited in scope. In no way does the comic prepare the reader for Rhodes as a capable replacement or a natural successor to Tony Stark. Rather, he is merely shown as a liability, and the setting of Wakanda, with its primitive symbolism, pulls double duty in presenting Stark and white imperialism as superior.

Rhodes's run as Iron Man also demonstrates Stark's ultimate reluctance to relinquish his white privilege and his deep investment in the white privilege that aided in the creation of his superhero identity, namely, his father's business, which allowed him to become a wealthy arms dealer and create his signature armor. As a lead-up to Rhodes taking over the armor, Stark undergoes an identity crisis that is perhaps responsible for his alcoholism, and considers whether or not his authentic self is Stark or Iron Man, noting, "Sometimes I wonder which is the real me . . . this splendid metal skin I've created . . . or the frail thing of flesh that wears it" (185). Stark aptly equates his armor to his skin, since without his whiteness, he would have no armor and thus no power beyond his money and influence.

Tony soon descends into an alcoholic vortex. He is shown flying around in the armor, drunk and crashing through billboards in a blackout. A television announcer reports, "Good morning. Our top story: Apparently, Anthony Stark's mysterious bodyguard got mad at midtown last night—or at least at the advertising in Manhattan's busiest neighborhood. Our Channel Three news team got this exclusive footage of Iron Man destroying billboards high above Times Square." When Stark sees the footage of himself drunk and out of control, he notes, "I was here all night . . . just sitting around, relaxing, having a few drinks. . . . I don't remember going *anywhere*" (302). When Tony is once again drunk and completely incapacitated, Rhodes realizes he must be the one to continue Stark's crime fighting, admitting that he knows that Iron man is actually Stark. When Rhodes finally dons the armor, he notes, "I just realized . . . I'm putting on the suit, me—*Jim Rhodes*! Soon as I drop this helmet on I'll actually *be* Iron Man!" (318). The moment underscores the idea that Rhodes assumes the armor only because Tony is out of his mind with drunkenness. Rhodes does not aggressively or confidently take over as Iron Man, and Tony Stark does not willingly give up his power. The shift in the power dynamic is due to Stark's disease. Rhodes is a reluctant hero, and

Tony's downfall is filled with pathos that elicits sympathy. At no point is Tony Stark decentered as the real or authentic Iron Man. Consequently, Rhodes's empowerment does nothing to undermine white supremacy.

Rhodes feels impelled to put on the armor when Tony cannot, but never really controls the armor as Tony does. Moreover, the story highlights Rhodes's role as surrogate or replacement. When Tony sees another person controlling the armor, he mutters, "Imposter . . . wearing my armor—fighting Magma" (328). Here Tony's unhappiness at losing the armor to another, even his best friend Rhodes, is on display. Tony never willingly gives up his power and privilege. The remainder of the comic is predicated on him getting better and taking his privilege and power back. Rhodes notes, "The tin-suit is probably *loaded* with gadgets . . . but I don't know what they are" (329). Although he is an ace pilot, Rhodes employs a young, Harvard-educated white engineer to help him with the suit: "Without you to figure out how the various gadgets work the tin suit would be no more to me than a set of chrome long johns." The engineer offers, "It's been an incredible pleasure to work on such *beautiful* circuitry. Whoever designed it is a *genius*" (345). The genius the engineer is referring to is, of course, Tony Stark.

Rhodes feels like a surrogate hero who has little chance of mastering Stark's technology: "Feel a twinge of guilt when I think like that. After all, I'm Iron Man for a real bum reason—because Tony is drinking his life away" (370). The thrust of the narrative is not so much about Rhodes occupying the armor as much as it is about Stark self-destructing, and considering Stark's symbolism as American imperialistic capitalist, his rehabilitation appears crucial to the health of America.

In another white savior narrative, the man sent in to rehabilitate America's imperialistic position as global power is none other than Captain America, whom we might think of as the strong arm of the American military. Captain America appears in the comic as a deus ex machina who attempts to jar Stark out of his funk and acts as the ultimate white savior:

> Tony! Tony! Why? Just tell me why. You're an intelligent man. You must know what you're doing to yourself. You must realize that you're destroying yourself—with every single drop of that stuff you drink. You have everything, man—you own your own company, you have plenty of money, you're an electronics genius. . . . Women find you attractive, you're respected in the community, you have a brilliant future ahead of you . . . and I find you in here, in a rundown hotel in the worst section of the city . . . swilling cheap liquor wrecking your life. (376)

Meanwhile, Rhodes flounders in the armor, feeling inferior and self-conscious. Captain America's appearance in the comic is rather bizarre, given that he had not been a part of the plot before showing up at Stark's rundown hotel. Cap is not interested in helping Rhodes at all, and his appearance does more to diminish Rhodes by comparison than add to the narrative.

To demonstrate that Rhodes has no designs on usurping Stark's playboy image or tainting so-called white blood purity, Rhodes encounters and rejects a white woman with supernatural seductive powers, admitting, "It's easy to understand why Tony fell so hard for the lady. Kind of woman I usually don't go for . . . too perfect, too *symmetrical* somehow. I generally like 'em more human" (403). Rhodes also proves that he is not interested in financially benefiting from Stark International by deciding instead to hire himself out as a strong man and seeking out the advice of other superheroes of color, namely, Power Man and Iron Fist: "You guys still call yourselves 'heroes' for hire? . . . Well, it's the '*hire*' part that interests me. I'd like to know how you do it. . . . I want to get paid big bucks for superheroing like you guys" (485).

Rhodes never escapes the symbolism of a Black man replacing a white man. Aside from haphazardly wearing the armor and ineffectually fighting villains, Rhodes remains a tier below his predecessor, both technologically and financially. He proves a weak symbol for American imperialism, implying the importance of Stark as the true owner of the armor. Rhodes's narrative highlights that the whole time he is in the armor, he exists in the shadow of Tony. This is why Rhodes rejects the advances of the white woman, why he does not financially capitalize on the armor and Stark Industries, and why he is a reluctant hero rather than one who feels comfortable within a space of power and privilege. Rhodes's run as Iron Man merely demonstrates to readers the folly of replacing Stark with Rhodes. Rhodes is simply unfit to be the hero, and the sooner Tony can reassume his rightful place within the hierarchy of white supremacy, the better.

Although John Stewart first appeared in the early 1970s as a substitute Green Lantern, it was not until 1984 that he replaced Hal Jordan full-time as the primary member of the Green Lantern intergalactic police force responsible for the planet Earth. Stewart's replacement of Hal Jordan stemmed from Jordan's decision to give up the ring to pursue a relationship with Carol Ferris, the daughter of Jordan's old boss at Ferris Aircraft. The reskinning of Green Lantern draws attention to Hal Jordan's run as Green Lantern, which began in 1959, as essentially the embodiment of a recursive white savior trope, as well as presenting Hal Jordan as a good example of white fragility and how white people often feel as though Black empowerment is a zero-sum game that simultaneously diminishes white people.

Right from the start, Hal Jordan's run as Green Lantern included an element of race insofar as his one weakness was, rather oddly, the color yellow. In the version of Green Lantern's origin that was created for the character's revival after World War II, a dying Green Lantern, Abin Sur, crash-lands on Earth, desperately trying to pass on his power to another deserving being. Abin Sur's wine-colored skin suggests that the Green Lantern Corps is a diverse body of intergalactic beings. Abin Sur tells Hal Jordan that the only thing in the world that the Green Lantern ring is powerless against is the color yellow or any yellow object. No explanation beyond Sur's initial warning is offered for why the color yellow has this amazing power against which the ring is powerless. In many of the first issues involving Hal Jordan, Hal is confronted with objects that are yellow, so that he must adapt in some creative fashion to thwart them. As discussed in chapter 1, the color yellow was closely associated in American culture with the so-called Yellow Peril, supposedly represented by the invading hordes of China, Japan, Mongolia, or East Asia more generally. For readers in the 1950s, the source of the Yellow Peril, which had been identified with Japan during World War II, would have shifted back to China, the original source of the Yellow Peril, which had now become a communist country and therefore an enemy of, and perceived threat to, the United States.

Along with trying to avoid any object that is yellow, Hal Jordan spends much of his time chasing after Carol Ferris, the boss's daughter who takes over the company that he works for as a pilot. When Hal is not busy chasing Carol and lamenting her infatuation with Green Lantern, who she does not realize is Hal Jordan, his duties as Green Lantern often call on him to act as the white savior to nonwhite primitive beings, such as a group of "blue-skinned humans—living in caves! They're primitive—as your cavemen on earth were—millions of years ago" (Broome, 37). Hal Jordan is summoned through his lamp and told that "an emergency has arisen on the world called Venus in the solar system in which you live! You are the only lamp possessor who can reach there in time! You must hurry" (34). In this capacity, Green Lantern's whiteness is on full display in his role as white savior: "I see now why I was sent here . . . to prevent this band of humans from being wiped out! Humans everywhere are important for all other humans!" (41). Jordan realizes that the blue-skinned primitive humans are being threatened by yellow pterodactyls, so he creates a green counterpart to thwart the yellow beasts. The color green in this context is a facile symbol for American capitalism.

Additional racially problematic stories include one where Green Lantern tracks down a villain with no other description than "he was a small, dark-faced man" (60). The man ends up being part of a spy ring that Hal Jordan stops. Another story centers on Green Lantern's sidekick Pieface, a native Alaskan and the only person on the planet who knows Hal Jordan's secret identity. Pieface, with his strange, somewhat emasculating name, is clearly the lesser of the two men and depends on Green Lantern to save his family. In all these instances, nonwhites seem to merely demonstrate the need for a white superhero. The existence of helpless nonwhite beings and nonwhite sidekicks does the work of empowering the traditional white superhero and perhaps more perniciously suggests that the white superhero is being magnanimous in his selflessness by helping out the nonwhites. The narrative presents a sort of tableau of racial interaction that serves whiteness rather than promoting equality.

A quarter century later, in 1984, with the emergence of the Black Green Lantern John Stewart as a full-time member of the intergalactic police force, we find almost no mention of the color yellow being a threat to the ring, since the Yellow Peril tropes and racial stereotypes stemming from Orientalism and the threats from the East were not as in vogue. Stewart's emergence as the new Green Lantern is a result of Hal Jordan resigning so that he can pursue a relationship with Carol. Stewart becomes the natural choice, since he has already subbed for Hal Jordan in the past. When Stewart shows up as Green Lantern, both villains and other members of the Green Lantern Corps meet him with incredulity because he is Black.

Like Jim Rhodes, John Stewart is initially reluctant to take on the mantle of the ring, even though the Green Lantern galactic council deems him worthy. Stewart objects to the idea that he must accept the honor and technological power bestowed on him: "What about *my* honor? What about *my* rights? Why should I go out and risk my *life* for people I've never even *met*?" (Englehart, 47). As a consequence, he must deal with overt racism by the Green Lantern council: "This one is like all the others of his race . . . selfish . . . *self-serving*" (47). Although it is unclear whether one of the council members is referring to humans in general or to African Americans specifically, Stewart takes the comment at least in part as a slight against his blackness, indignantly responding, "I've spent a *lifetime* listening to garbage like that—and frankly, I'm *sick* of it! All *black* men do not have *rhythm*—and all *earth* men aren't cowards!" (47). It is here that Stewart first hears about the ring's vulnerability to anything yellow, but unlike Hal Jordan, Stewart never winds up confronting any yellow threats. The Black Green Lantern never has to fight against anything that is yellow, similar to the way that Rhodes as Iron Man does not face off with the Mandarin. As nonwhite versions of traditional superheroes, nonwhite villains lose their relevance.

Stewart's run as Green Lantern is not without its stereotypes and limitations, which has the effect of diminishing his character and at the same time drawing attention to Hal's choice to abnegate his power, as well as to Hal's white fragility, as he is at times moved to outrage when confronted with his Black counterpart. Unlike Hal Jordan, Stewart seems to wield his power carelessly: "Okay, I'm out . . . now where do I wanna play? Guess I'll just have to *cruise* the neighborhood" (89). To the amazement of Jordan, Stewart reveals his identity by taking off his mask, implying that his blackness is the most salient characteristic of his character and causing Jordan to exclaim, "He can't do that! He can't reveal his secret identity!" (101). Stewart's decision to reveal his identity as John Stewart, architect for Ferris Aircraft, underscores the double consciousness that Stewart already feels as a Black man in a racist, white-dominated culture. In Stewart's mind, a Green Lantern mask is redundant. Stewart's blackness already operates as a sort of mask, insofar as his skin color affects how people view his identity. His blackness is abnormalized in the same way someone's would be who was wearing a mask. Where Hal Jordan, and former Green Lanterns such as Guy Gardner, can take off the mask and blend in with the rest of the white population, Stewart must always be on guard, since his blackness always already makes him a target. He is no more a target for having revealed his identity as Green Lantern than he is as a Black body moving through a dominant and hostile white culture.

Despite his past experience as Green Lantern, Stewart is reluctant to control the ring and its power full-time, further diminishing his hero status, explaining, "See, what you have to *understand* is I never *wanted* the job! I saw myself more as the *backup quarterback*—you only play when the *real guy's* hurt—and only until he gets better! That's the attitude you *have to* have. If I'd sat around *chafing at the bit*, with *months between call ups*, I'd have gone *crazy!*" (108). Like the white savior narrative, which masquerades as white selflessness and sacrifice, John Stewart's reluctance to take on the role of hero reflects positively on Hal, who has given up his power magnanimously for love. The idea is that readers will likely wish that Hal could both find love and maintain his role as Green Lantern. In this sense, Hal is still the hero of the comic even though he no longer is the primary Green Lantern in the narrative.

As a result of Stewart's hesitation and general failure to be an effective hero, he is given a senior adviser from the galactic Green Lantern Corps to help him through the transition process in the form of a female Green Lantern who has the same skin color as Abin Sur. To blend in, or perhaps not to offend readers by creating an interracial relationship, Katma changes into a phenotypical Black woman, saying to Stewart, "I thought I would draw *stares*

Steve Englehart (script) and Joe Staton (pencils), "Macho!" Originally published in *Green Lantern* #191 (August 1985). Reprinted in *Green Lantern: Sector 2814*, vol. 2 (DC Comics, 2013). © DC Comics.

with *crimson skin*, so I used my ring to match color" (108). Though Katma does not normally wear a mask, as Stewart points out, she does so when she is accompanying Stewart. She essentially dons the mask of blackness once she understands that Stewart's blackness is a permanent mask. Rather than drawing attention to that mask and his already precarious position as a Black man in a white-dominated culture, she shares in the mask and demonstrates her loyalty to him not only as a Green Lantern member but also as a sentient being with a precious life.

Meanwhile Hal Jordan's white fragility is on full display as he witnesses Stewart control the power of the ring; at one point, Jordan declares, "I still count, dammit! Hal Jordan still counts!" (169). His uneasiness at relinquishing his power to a Black man is front and center as the comic cannot help but tacitly imply that Stewart's run as Green Lantern is a zero-sum game wherein Stewart's power automatically diminishes Jordan's despite Jordan's decision to give up that power in the first place. Toward the end of the comic, the "Black

Green Lantern" faces off with Hal Jordan in the form of the alien Replikon, satisfying the implied white desire to gaze at Stewart fighting against his white counterpart.

At one point, Stewart and Kat discuss their goals for the ring, and Stewart says, "Why couldn't we all get together—heck, why couldn't the guardians get together—and wipe prejudice off the map? It's held me and every other minority back all our lives. . . . Wash people's minds you mean?" (213). His idea is merely to mask the problem rather than root out its origin, not unlike his own reskinning. Like Tony Stark, Hal Jordan is a reluctant participant in his own displacement and clearly responds negatively to his own disempowerment, echoing the idea that white people do not give up their privilege easily, and often when they do, it is only temporary and triggering to their white fragility.

As noted in previous chapters, Superman, despite being an alien, represents the pinnacle of whiteness and white supremacy, even more so because his whiteness was earned through assimilation. Consequently his "death" in 1993 was replete with symbolism that could have indicated the death of white supremacy or at least its thorough deconstruction or decentering. With the death of Superman, a gap appears in the cultural landscape, only to be filled with several supermen who either claim to be some form of Superman returned from the dead or a replacement Superman who is ready to don the mantle. There is a fascist, a clone, a cyborg, and a Black man by the name of John Henry Irons, also known as Steel, who is a weapons manufacturer like Iron Man. Steel shares the stage with three other supermen who claim to be the Man of Steel, which has the effect of disqualifying all of them as frauds and suggesting that what the world really needs is the return of the authentic Superman.

Due to a weapons-manufacturing malfunction at a clandestine military complex, Doomsday emerges as a nearly indestructible force bent on wreaking havoc on an unsuspecting public. When Superman gets involved, he soon realizes that he is up against his most formidable opponent ever. Doomsday's moniker, as well as his origins, suggests that his evil power is somehow linked with America's out-of-control military-industrial complex and its ability to destroy the world, something against which even Superman is powerless. At the end of the comic, Superman and Doomsday square off, and the two beat each other to death. When Superman is finally destroyed, his legacy is quickly memorialized in the eyes of a worshipful public: "Most will remember this sad day . . . as the day the proudest, most noble man they ever knew—finally fell . . . for this is the day that a superman died" (Jurgens, *The Death of Superman*).

In a subplot toward the beginning that positions Superman as a white savior, a secret society of underground monsters plans to take over the city. Echoing the same dynamic in earlier reskinning efforts, a young Black boy becomes privy to the plan and thinks about Superman in savior-like terms, wishing that there was some way to contact him, since Superman has "saved me two times now. Superman is my friend" (Jurgens, *The Death of Superman*). The boy wonders whether the monsters are holding his mother, who abandoned him as a baby, hostage. The boy buys a can of glow-in-the-dark spray paint and draws a big circle with an *S* in the middle in an attempt to get Superman's attention. Superman sees the boy's signal, and the boy tells him about the monsters. Instead of Superman rescuing the boy's actual mother, Superman saves Lois Lane, who has been captured. The boy notes, "He's so awesome!" While this subplot represents just a small portion of the overall plot of Superman's death, it sets the table for a limited story line.

At the beginning of *Reign of the Supermen*, the follow-up to *The Death of Superman*, in an issue called "Busting Out," Steel is immediately racialized and contradistinctively shown talking to some kids in "the worst section of Suicide Slum. Even the fast money of Easy Street doesn't trickle down here. Shark Enforcers, toting Toastmasters, stalk the Man of Steel through alleys shadowed by the bombed-out shells of ancient tenements" (Jurgens, *Reign of the Supermen*). Soon a gang guns one of the children down with weapons that Steel manufactured, causing him to create a full-body iron suit and fight against the gang, for which he in part feels responsible. Steel's decision to create the powerful iron suit and hammer to use as a weapon and a symbol of his blackness tied to the mythic John Henry aligns him with the other supermen who claim to be Superman's replacement or a version of Superman himself. However, Steel is the only Superman replacement who does not claim to be Superman and attempt to rekindle the flame with Lois Lane. This is important, as it prevents any indication of miscegenation and the undermining of white blood purity, a hallmark of white supremacy discussed in several previous chapters. In the issue "Iron John vs. the Metropolis Kid: Title Bout," Lane notes, "Hold it right there, buster! The others have been falling all over themselves trying to convince the world they're Superman! What about you?" "I never said I was Superman," Steel replies (Jurgens, *Reign of the Supermen*). Steel creates his own steel Superman suit, using his own technological prowess, his superhero identity stemming from African American cultural legend John Henry, a legend that he shares with the neighborhood kids in the issue "Busting Out":

Ya see back in the old days, men called steel drivers used ten-pound hammers to pound steel drills into rock to make holes for blastin' explosives. Then, one day, the managers brought in an experimental steam-driven steel drill. They claimed the engine . . . could out-pound any man alive. Well, John Henry laughed at that an bet he could beat that . . . in a race. He lifted a 20-pound hammer in each hand an' he started poundin'! Half an hour later he'd drilled two 7-foot holes, almost twice as far as the steam engine. . . . He pounded so hard a blood vessel in his brain burst and he died!

While Steel is steeped in African American myth and is presented as wielding technological prowess, he still relies on the myth of Superman, a consummately white and heteronormative myth, as one gets the impression that Steel is merely keeping the bed warm for the real Superman's return, whose own origin is left unbesmirched. Further, Steel's competition with other replacement supermen who claim to be the Man of Steel situates him as simply one more fraud among frauds who represent lesser versions of the authentic Superman whom the world mourns.

RESKINNING AS CRITIQUE AND TRANSCENDENCE

Despite the failure of reskinning narratives to undermine white supremacy in the 1980s and 1990s, the new millennium brought with it two reskinning comics—*Truth: Red, White & Black* (2004), written by Robert Morales; and *Ms. Marvel* (2014), written by G. Willow Wilson—that highlighted the white supremacist cultural landscape out of which white superheroes emerged, as well as presenting a reskinned character who operated independently of her predecessor. In 2004, Marvel released *Truth: Red, White & Black*, which deconstructed Captain America as a construct of white privilege. Morales accomplishes this significant feat by positing a Black equivalent to Steve Rogers, Isaiah Bradley, who is one of three hundred Black soldiers called on to test the super-solider serum in its early stages before it is successfully administered to Rogers. Several of the Black soldiers die as a result of the untested drug, but a few, including Bradley, successfully undergo the treatment that Dr. Reinstein admits in part 2 is "necessary to see if our methods apply to the inferior races" (Morales). Bradley and his team are soon sent to Germany on a mission to destroy a shipment of the serum and other medical supplies meant for the Nazis. Only three survive, including Bradley. Army headquarters then orders the three surviving members to assist Steve

Rogers, who has now become Captain America after successfully receiving the serum, on a mission to Germany to intercept the replacement shipment of serum. Before the team can be assembled, a white racist lieutenant kills two of the Black soldiers, and Steve Rogers is delayed by a monsoon in the Pacific theater. Consequently Isaiah Bradley is sent alone on a suicide mission, but not before stealing Captain America's uniform. Bradley winds up successfully infiltrating a concentration camp but is eventually captured by Hitler and ultimately imprisoned in the United States for stealing the uniform. Meanwhile the white Captain America, Steve Rogers, is worshipped as the quintessential American hero.

Truth: Red, White & Black represents one of the most devastating indictments of white privilege in the history of comic books and an excellent example of how reskinning a traditional superhero can do important work in deconstructing the white supremacy found in popular cultural production. What makes Captain America so intriguing a subject for deconstruction is his unabashed symbolism for American whiteness, including white American imperialism and individual white privilege. Captain America's role as an embodiment of America reflects the position America wishes it had in the world, or tries to promulgate: that of a global power with the optics of defense rather than force. Those optics are instantiated by Captain America's shield, which operates as both an offensive and a defensive weapon as Cap throws it around, inflicting great destruction on his enemies. A sleight of hand is at play in his weapon of choice, similar to America's propaganda myth of spreading democracy or defending powerless nations while invading countries and exploiting foreign resources.

Captain America's origin story offers a telling example of how white privilege operates in relation to individual success. Captain America notes in a 1959 issue of *Tales of Suspense* called "Captain America," "You think you *prepared* for this fight? There's one bit of preparation you missed—a lifetime of athletic training such as *I* had" (Lee, *Essential Captain America*). Captain America's power never stemmed from any sort of training but rather came from the serum cocktail that instantly empowered him mightily. Steve Rogers is chosen among many other sickly looking white boys unfit to join the military. One caption in a 1963 issue of *Tales of Suspense* called "The Origin of Captain America" notes, "With obvious nervousness, yet with a firm, fearless tread, a thin, somewhat sickly-looking youth enters the lab—walking slowly, silently, towards—the *unknown*." The American military plucks the young man from a limited pool that represents the highest echelons of a racial hierarchy wherein white Anglo Saxons are at the top and everyone else who is nonwhite is at the bottom. Rogers's good fortune is explicitly stated, as one panel makes clear: "*Steve Rogers*! Too puny, too sickly to be accepted by the Army! *Steve Rogers*! Chosen from hundreds of similar volunteers because of his courage, his intelligence, and his willingness to risk death for his country if the experiment should fail! You must drink this quickly, before the chemicals lose their potency. Good luck, my boy!" In this manner, Captain America symbolizes the machinations of white privilege that undermine the myth of the American dream, a dream only available to white men like Steve Rogers. Captain America is to specifically be a weapon of war, a sort of dehumanized machine for global imperialism in the shape of a defense, equipped with a shield rather than an offensive weapon like a sword or a firearm. If successful, the plan would be to create an army of these eugenically created white fighting men hearkening back to the origins of the original superheroes discussed in chapter 1.

Conversely, in *Truth: Red, White & Black*, three hundred Black soldiers, of which Bradley is one, merely represent exploited and disposable test subjects for the benefit of white soldiers like Steve Rogers. The use of Black people for scientific experiments recalls atrocities such as the Tuskegee syphilis study, wherein some Black volunteers suffering from the disease were given placebos and allowed to die. In Morales's comic, some of the Black soldiers who test the serum literally explode due to an overdose, and several are grotesquely deformed as a result. After one test subject explodes in part 3, and his blood and guts cover the walls, a doctor notes, "Subject A-23 expired at 1718 hours. Now it is certain that 5 cc's of the serum is too much." Bradley and several other Black soldiers survive the experiment and, like Steve Rogers, are changed forever; but unlike Steve Rogers, the unit of Black super-soldiers is expendable, and their lives do not matter. One of Reinstein's colleagues notes in part 2, "What I'm saying is, we don't need all these Negro men."

In part 4, when Bradley and the two other remaining Black soldiers are waiting to assist Steve Rogers on another mission to Germany, Bradley metatextually reads a Captain America comic book and realizes that he and the other Black soldiers were guinea pigs for Steve Rogers, setting in motion his run as the Black Captain America. Bradley muses, "Don't it make you curious? I mean, this comic came out more'n a year ago, but it pretty much got our whole story—it has Doc Reinstein, the drug we got, and this Steve Rogers fella the brass is so high on." One of the other Black soldiers, Maurice, realizes that no matter what happens, Steve Rogers will get the credit for their military accomplishments. Maurice also notes, "I saw his costume.... We'll look like minstrels led by a Confederate circus clown into battle." After Bradley is captured in part 6, he is interrogated by Hitler himself, who questions why Bradley fights for a country that "[denies] you the glory of this

Robert Morales (script) and Kyle Baker (pencils), *Truth: Red, White & Black* (Marvel Comics, 2004). © Marvel Characters.

other soldier." Bradley escapes and is hidden away and fed by Black Germans before he is passed on to the Belgian underground and then to some Black GIs, who bring him back to the States. It is notable that other Black men—not a white savior, as in previous reskinning narratives—save Bradley.

Decades later, in part 7, Steve Rogers finds out, to his chagrin and consternation, about Bradley and the stolen uniform. An FBI agent whose Afro-German grandfather saved Bradley in Germany tells Steve Rogers, "Don't tell me you haven't heard of Isaiah Bradley—the Black Captain America!?" Rogers is shocked and mortified, his white fragility thoroughly triggered, by the realization that he is not the only Captain America. The agent tells Rogers, "Every black person in America's heard of Bradley—although what happened to him is pretty much a mystery." The truth of the serum that gave Rogers his power is revealed to him by a top American operative, who explains, "Before the First World War, eugenicists from around the world—primarily the Brits, the Germans, and us—routinely met to effect racial hygiene policy. The U.S. and British government took the early lead in the sterilization of undesirables, for instance.... As a result of those meetings... Project Super Soldier was born." On the basis of this admission, the top-level government operative reveals to Rogers that the super-soldier serum responsible for his power was really a mechanism for white supremacy designed to empower white men and ultimately wipe out other races. Bradley's wife also tells him that while he has been worshipped as a god, Bradley has been treated like an animal and destroyed for wearing the Captain America costume. Bradley's wife informs Rogers that the Black Captain America was arrested and court-martialed for stealing the uniform upon returning to the United States from Germany, where he not only heroically infiltrated a Nazi concentration camp and destroyed serum samples but was also held as a prisoner of war. She further reveals to Rogers that "Isaiah served seventeen years in solitary confinement at Leavenworth. He received less than rudimentary medical care, and I could only afford to see him three times a year.... The early stages of what made you? It left my husband *sterile*, and after so many years of confined neglect, his brain slowly *deteriorated*." Rogers finally meets with his Black counterpart, apologizes, and returns the tattered Captain America uniform to an infantilized Bradley.

What distinguishes *Truth* from other comics that have reskinned superheroes is that it not only presents Isaiah Bradley as capable of carrying the mantle of Captain America but also deconstructs the original Captain America, Steve Rogers, as emerging from a racist culture where Black lives do not matter. Bradley's success in infiltrating the concentration camp and destroying the serum demonstrates that anyone can be Captain America if only he or she drinks the serum. Nothing about Steve Rogers is special other than his whiteness. At the end, the narrative is bittersweet, if not completely bleak, as an infantilized Bradley meets with Steve Rogers, who, as Osvaldo Oyola points out, is recentered in the Captain America narrative and never really holds the US government accountable for its treatment of Bradley (21). However, the comic itself represents an important chapter in the superhero reskinning trend.

Perhaps the best example of a nonwhite superhero embracing a nonwhite racial identity and worldview is the character Kamala Khan, a Pakistani American girl living in New Jersey who first appeared in the comic *Ms. Marvel: No Normal* in 2014. Much of the plot of *Ms. Marvel: No Normal* revolves around Khan struggling with her own internalized white racial frame, which invariably associates power with whiteness. Kamala miraculously transforms into a white version of Ms. Marvel with blonde hair and a tight-fitting suit and struggles with the inauthenticity of her new identity. She fears that the public is "expecting *Ms. Marvel*. Ms. Marvel from the news. With the hair and the spandex and the *Avengers swag*. Not a sixteen-year-old brown girl." By the end of the comic, Kamala embraces her cultural roots and fuses them with her newfound powers, deciding, "I'm not here to be a watered-down version of some *other* hero.... I'm here to be the best version of *Kamala*." Unlike in previous reskinnings, Khan is the central hero of the comic rather than a temporary replacement for Carol Danvers. Further, instead of returning the Ms. Marvel mantle to Carol Danvers once she has her run, Khan sheds Danvers's white superhero signifiers and embraces a new, nonwhite, culturally authentic version of Ms. Marvel that aligns more with her cultural identity.

In the comic's first panel, Kamala stares hungrily at a BLT sandwich through a glass case at a convenience store called the Circle Q, wistfully remarking, "Delicious infidel meat," her double consciousness as a hyphenated American on full display (Wilson). This initial panel immediately calls attention to Khan's Muslim orthodoxy, as well as her struggle to adhere to it, and inches dangerously close to perpetuating the stereotype of Islamic culture as restrictive in comparison to the normalized, freedom-loving Christian culture. Kamala's friends tease her for being a fangirl, particularly of the Avengers. Very soon in the comic, Kamala defies her strict parents by sneaking out of her house to attend a high school party where alcohol and boys are present. Khan's nemesis, her very white and very blonde classmate Zoe Zimmer, immediately teases Kamala when she sees her at the party, rudely quipping, "I thought you weren't allowed to hang out with us *heathens* on the weekends! I thought you were like, *locked up*." Kamala realizes her mistake in defying her parents to ingratiate herself with girls like Zoe and quickly leaves the party alone, admitting to herself, "I can never be one of them, no matter how hard I try. I'll always be poor Kamala with the weird *food rules* and the *crazy family*." Kamala's struggle in these early panels directly relates to her nonwhiteness. She views her culture as an obstacle to fitting in, and though she sees the flaws in a girl like Zoe, she nevertheless wants to be like her as well as be liked by her. It is clear that, along with her fragmented consciousness, Kamala has internalized the white racial frame, viewing her own culture as different, weird, crazy, and inevitably inferior.

The implicit message from the beginning of the comic is that Kamala ought to embrace her own culture and not worry so much about fitting in with her white counterparts, especially once she is granted the powers of Ms. Marvel. Just after Kamala leaves the party, a strange mist that seems to engulf, sedate, and physically surround Kamala envelops the neighborhood. While Kamala is tranquilized, Captain America, Iron Man, and the former Ms. Marvel, now Captain Marvel, Carol Danvers, visit her. Captain America chastises Kamala for sneaking out, pointing out, "You thought that if you disobeyed your parents—your culture, your religion—your classmates would accept you. What happened instead?" Kamala responds by saying, "They *laughed* at me." Kamala also admits to Captain Marvel, "I want to be beautiful and awesome and butt-kicking and *less complicated*. I want to be you," meaning Carol Danvers. This admission is noteworthy, since Danvers looks more like Zoe Zimmer than Kamala Khan. When Kamala finally emerges from her slumber and bursts out of the cocoon that has somehow enveloped her, she finds that she has transformed into Ms. Marvel, with flowing blonde hair and a form-fitting costume. Khan has become white, except her whiteness does not remedy her fragmentation, illustrating that monolithic whiteness is out of her grasp, just as it is out of everyone's grasp. Kamala soon realizes that she has the power of shape-shifting. That she has turned into the white Carol Danvers betrays her internalized white supremacy and desire to be white instead of a Brown Muslim girl.

The first event that empowers Kamala to give up her inauthentic whiteness is when she reveals her secret identity to her friend Bruno. This occurs after she stops someone from trying to hold him up while he is clerking at the Circle Q. The robber is actually Bruno's brother Vick, who has gotten mixed up with a villain named the Inventor. While struggling with Kamala in the Circle Q, Vick accidentally shoots her while she is still in the form of Carol Danvers. After transforming back into Kamala, completely healed, she explains to Bruno what has happened. Bruno is shocked but supportive, and this empowers Kamala to give up her Carol Danvers form for good. Kamala's rejection of her whiteness in favor of her own authentic supernonwhite self calls attention to the history of superheroes as embodiments of white power to the exclusion of Black and Brown people. Kamala realizes, "I always thought that if I had amazing hair, if I could pull off great boots, if I could fly—that would make me feel strong. That would make me happy. But the hair gets in my face, the boots pinch, and the leotard is giving me an *epic wedgie*." Kamala then agrees to investigate Vick's involvement with the Inventor, but instead of shifting into Carol Danvers, she creates a costume that barely conceals her real identity, Kamala, a Pakistani American girl from Jersey City. Her rescue of Vick, who is being held captive by some flunkies of the Inventor at an abandoned house, fails because, as Kamala notes, "I thought I could just charge in—isn't that what heroes do?" Kamala realizes that even though she has divested herself of white superhero signifiers, she is nevertheless copying a white hypermasculine superhero formula based solely on blind power. She realizes that she must be smarter in her strategies. With the help of Bruno, who is a science whiz, Kamala learns more about her powers, underscoring her need to learn more about her authentic identity.

Her second rescue attempt succeeds in part because she breaks into the house as a smaller version of herself, admitting, "Mastering bigness is easy. It's mastering smallness that takes work." After rescuing Vick and swearing to defeat the inventor, Kamala creates a brand-new costume with a small mask, declaring, "I can change my face, but I wear a mask instead. There are layers of unpackable crazy up in here. I am a shape-changing, mask-wearing, sixteen-year-old super 'moozlim from Jersey City." In owning her fragmented consciousness and not letting it diminish her ethnicity, Kamala realizes her potential as a superhero.

The character arc of Kamala Khan in *Ms. Marvel: No Normal* is an important one. She transforms from a girl who literally becomes a white superhero despite her internal racial fragmentation to an authentically Brown female superhero who celebrates her fragmentation and uses it to her advantage. Indeed, as she notes, "There are layers of unpackable crazy up in here." Her acknowledgment of her fractured racial and sexual consciousness within a white supremacist patriarchal culture positions her as a powerful twenty-first-century superhero and a champion of multiculturalism, pointing the way forward for a new brand of superhero whose powers do not mask their differences.

Presenting the world with superheroes of color is a step in the right direction. There have certainly been missteps along the way, as many Black superhero comics are still rife with stereotypes that are often difficult to shake loose, such as the white savior narrative. One ought to consider what actual progress is being made when superheroes are reskinned as heroes of color. The danger in a superficial reskinning is that the heroes operate on a substratum beneath the real superheroes, which does nothing to decenter or deconstruct the original and in many cases reaffirms white supremacy rather than undermines it. *Truth* depicts Isaiah Bradley as a highly capable superhero and recontextualizes Captain America as the beneficiary of white privilege gleaned from the dominant white racist cultural landscape that dehumanizes and literally kills Black people, sometimes for the express benefit of whites like Steve Rogers. *Ms. Marvel: No Normal* dramatizes Kamala Khan's triumph over her internalized white racial frame as she realizes that she can be both a Muslim and a superhero. The other three reskinned superhero comics do nothing to decenter the traditional superheroes, and the Black figures never really lose their status as inferior replacements.

CONCLUSION

We might think of the history of American comics and graphic novels as a genealogy of false heroes. While putting forward an endless succession of putative heroes in brightly colored costumes, American comics have often catered to white men's basest desires, instincts, and fears of progressivism and multiculturalism by simultaneously villainizing difference and exulting in heteronormative whiteness. Oftentimes, comic book creators have sought to undo white supremacy, only to further reinforce it as a result of their unexamined racial biases and framing. American comics and graphic novels symbolize ideological cultural dreamscapes where far too often what appears on the page is sublimated white supremacy. While we should have reason for hope, as comics like *Ms. Marvel: No Normal* have managed to shatter these dreamscapes, and nonwhite creators like Ta-Nehisi Coates now have narrative control of flagship characters like Captain America, we still have much work to do, especially when one considers that an extremely dangerous false hero, Donald Trump, a kind of caricature of a comic book white supremacist villain, became the leader of the "free world."

While one can trace Superman's powers to the sun, Green Lantern's to his cosmic ring, and Captain America's to the super-soldier serum, that of whiteness can be traced to structural racism and its power of invisibility. Its origin story lies in its self-designation as the state of normality, contrary to nonwhiteness, which has been rendered supposedly abnormal. While nonwhites were racialized, whites themselves, even as their ranks changed and absorbed formerly racialized folks like the Irish and Italians, were considered raceless, their ethnicity a lacuna, a blind spot, a lack. Consequently, the existence of the power structure driven by white supremacy, which has been responsible for so much destruction and dehumanization, has generally been denied by its very perpetrators and left to operate unbeknownst to those who benefit most from it.

Our central conclusion in this book is that comic books have existed for most if not all of their history as an instantiation of white supremacy, and the power of invisibility by which whiteness operates has rendered its cultural agents mostly unaware of their own complicity in its operation. These chapters cover many industry giants, publishers and creators alike, who have unwittingly perpetuated white supremacy even as they have publically denounced it. Titans such as Jerry Siegel and Joe Shuster, EC Comics, Stan Lee, Robert Crumb, Will Eisner, Frank Miller, and many artists who have reskinned superheroes over the last several decades have all in one way or another perpetuated white supremacy in their respective comics, very likely without a clue that they were doing so. In this book, we hope that we have made visible what has been invisible, even to the cultural producers themselves, and especially to the millions of fans of comics and their cultural permutations. We hope that we have demonstrated that whiteness exists as a destructive cultural and political force in America that can be identified and analyzed within our most powerful cultural artifacts with the hope that if we can see it, then we can destroy it. On this score, there is reason for optimism when one considers two fairly recent comics publications, the Marvel release *Captain America: Winter in America* by Ta-Nehisi Coates and the indie comic *Your Black Friend* by Ben Passmore. Both of these titles demonstrate the way forward for comics as a medium with the unique power to help dismantle white supremacy.

We have focused a lot in this book on Captain America. While he is just one character among a multitude of superheroes, we feel our approach is justified because Cap functions as the ultimate paragon of American whiteness, which makes focusing on him both appropriate and necessary. He represents not only how privilege operates in the US domestic sphere but also how global whiteness weaponizes itself in the form of imperialism and exploitation disguised as defense or the propagation of democracy. In the first six-issue collection of *Winter in America*, published in March 2019, Coates sets his story during the aftermath of the previous Secret Empire story arc written by Nick Spencer, wherein Cap was appropriated as a fascist Hydra agent. The United States has slipped rather easily into a fascist state, losing both Captain America and its symbolic weight as a beacon of freedom. In the first issue of *Winter in America*, Hydra has been defeated and Captain America restored to his former self, although without the full trust of his country. America has become a weakened, fragmented shell, barely holding on to its former identity located in, as Captain America calls it, "the dream," an allusion to the American dream, the only thing to which Cap says he is loyal. In Coates's hands, Captain America is a conflicted hero, a "warrior who hates war." America has been torn asunder and has lost its monolithic symbolic weight, revealing the fragility of our cherished democracy. Cap is the authentic, if weakened, symbol of America, still bearing the unearned privilege of the super-soldier serum given to him in the 1940s.

Captain America attempts to make sense of today's political landscape by harking back to some vaguely defined historical moment when both America and Cap were good and noble. In an introductory insert, Captain America wistfully remembers that "Captain America was right, because America was right. And Captain America was good, because America was good." What emerges in the comic is the idea that the impetus for Captain America, the desire to strengthen the US Armed Forces for total domination by eugenically creating superhuman white male soldiers, has been replicated and employed by dictatorial groups such as Hydra and the Power Elite and exposed as a dangerous racial strategy that was terribly flawed to begin with. Early in the comic, Cap faces and defeats several Hydra super-soldier cyborg "nostalgists." Like Cap, they are well-built, blond "Aryan" archetypes with the American flag seemingly tattooed on their faces. Captain America underscores his own complicity by noting, "I became the first in a line of super-soldiers—a line that also ended with me. That's the story we tell. The truth is that the world keeps churning out super-soldiers. Cyborgs and clones. Mystic spawn of the Cosmic Cube. And every time I see another of them ... I see another part of me." Captain America realizes that the threat he now faces is a mirror of himself, just as Donald Trump reflects the American white racial frame. Regrettably, Trump is who we are as a nation.

In the wake of Hydra's reign, the public can no longer identify who has its best interests in mind. The result is a comic that not so subtly comments on the rise of Donald Trump, a narrative that Coates has written about in an article in *The Atlantic* in October 2017 called "The First White President: The Foundation of Donald Trump's Presidency Is the Negation of Barack Obama's Legacy." In this article, Coates argues, "There is a kind of theater at work in which Trump's presidency is pawned off as a product of the white working class as opposed to a product of an entire whiteness." For Coates, singularly ascribing Trump's presidency to a particular voting bloc, the white working class, whose bleak economic reality and sense of abandonment provided the impetus for Trump's victory, allows white America as a whole to ignore the foundational white supremacy at "the very core of his power." Coates implores readers to accept that white supremacy, rather than the alienation of the white working class, ushered in the era of Trumpism. He warns that simple explanations such as this evade the existential reckoning required to understand the rise of Trump.

The character Joe Evers, whose name seems to denote his status as a white Joe Everyman, represents the sort of blue-collar, white, salt-of-the-earth men who have often been held responsible for the rise of Trump. In the comic, Evers cannot distinguish between any of the splinter groups who employ super-soldiers, be they clones or human beings or both. He is only interested in which group benefits him most. Like Americans in 2016, just under the surface of Evers's economic concerns lies a virulent racism and white nationalism, underscoring Coates's point that the most salient quality of the white working class is not so much their economic alienation as their internal racism, which exists as a microcosm of the country's internal racism. Captain America relates, "There's a story I've heard all over small-town America. The story Joe Evers is telling me right now. It's the mine closing, the church shuttered and schools gone to seed.... The wife on disability. The kid on dope. And it's Joe watching a way of life disappear." As Evers himself explains, "I didn't like Hydra's methods, but they kept us safe." This attitude allows first Hydra and then the Power Elite, both controlled by the Red Skull, to gain control of America.

Evers's reaction to Captain America working with Black Panther illustrates his white racial frame and, for Coates, the white racial frame responsible for Trump. Despite warnings from the US government to stand down, Captain America insists on investigating who is behind a group of murderous super-soldiers. He enlists the help of Black Panther, and together they subdue the super-soldiers. When Joe Evers is shown footage confirming that Captain America has been working with the mysterious Black Panther, Evers says, "I don't know why he'd do this.... Ain't Captain America supposed to stand for us little guys? Is he Captain America or Captain Wakanda?" Evers's comment reflects the racism and white nationalism lurking just under his economic concerns and reflects Coates's belief that working-class whites, along with feeling left behind or ignored, are also virulently racist, and that racism is largely responsible for Trump. For Coates, white male economic dissatisfaction and racism go hand in hand. For whites, economic blight is difficult to bear largely because they feel that their whiteness ought to inoculate them from poverty or struggle.

In addition to comics creators of color deploying flagship, traditionally white superheroes under the banner of Marvel, independent publishers such as Silver Sprocket are doing their part to publish provocative comics that complicate the messy world of race in the United States on a smaller but no less meaningful scale. For example, in 2016 Ben Passmore released a minicomic with Silver Sprocket called *Your Black Friend* that deftly illustrates how well-meaning white people, such as many of the comics creators in our book, struggle, often unwittingly, to effectively support Black people but often wind up perpetuating the very racism they wish to undermine. The comic announces at the beginning, "*Your Black Friend* is an open letter from your black friend to you about race, racism, friendship, and alienation."

The comic is addressed to a general white reader, but within the comic, the white character is a woman, and the Black friend is a man. At the beginning of the comic, Passmore employs a quote by Frantz Fanon: "My body was given back to me sprawled out, distorted, recolored, clad in mourning in that white winter day." The quote suggests that whites impose blackness on Black people for the purpose of white self-definition, and even antiracist white allies impose blackness on Black people rather than granting them agency and access to blackness as they wish to define it.

The narrative revolves around the relationship between an unnamed Black character and his white female friend, but the use of the second person suggests that the letter is addressed to any white person who has a Black friend, or really any white person who cares about race, especially those who consider themselves racially woke. The comic suggests that even woke allies of the struggle can easily fall into deleterious racist patterns that demean and dehumanize their Black comrades. The comic's narrative structure is a frame story that pays off at the end and illustrates the uphill climb involved in shattering the white racial frame. The narrator is first shown at a coffee shop with his white friend, eating a sandwich from another establishment and overhearing a woman who is described as a "white lady w/ eat, pray, love, vibe," a sort of new-wave neohippie. He overhears the lady talking to a barista, telling her that she has just called the police because she saw "this sketchy guy coming out of this backyard with a bike." The barista alerts the customer that the sketchy guy actually lives at the house and the bike is his. The narrator then notes:

> Your black friend has seen this many times: a white person unaware of their racism, blunders into a moment in which it is undeniable. He knows that this woman will still not see it, she is both afraid of black people and the realization of that fear. It will take the barista, seemingly race savvy and familiar to the rich lady, to clarify what has just happened. But, your black friend knows the barista will say nothing. What white ppl fear most is "making things awkward." Your black friend would like to say something but doesn't want to appear "angry." He knows this type of person expects that from him and he will lose before he begins. . . . He wishes he could make you understand this, and many other things.

The rest of the comic delineates a list of microaggressions of which the narrator wishes that his white friend were aware. In many cases, the examples reflect moments the white friend imposes a form of blackness on her Black friend. For example, he notes, "He sees white friends wanting to participate in 'blackness' like it was a costume, but knows they wouldn't want to live with the consequences of actually *being* black." In another example, the narrator offers, "Your white friends . . . express their undying love for the 'Black Lives Matter Movement.' Your black friend thinks wannabe politicians hijacked the BLM, but your white friends ignore him." In these two examples, the narrator points to white allies attempting to take part in a commodified blackness irrespective of the lived blackness of actual Black people, and this act feels threatening to the narrator, as well as inauthentic. These examples are reminiscent of Stan Lee's and Marvel's X-Men representing persecuted minorities even though they appear to be white. The narrator poignantly notes, "Your black friend doesn't think that 'black' is a performance, isn't earned through association, he believes it is an existential reality."

The comic ends with the barista exploding at the customer whose clear racism provoked her to call the police on a man for nothing more than being Black, but the rich white lady is unfazed by the barista's criticism. When the narrator attempts to comment on the exchange, the barista tells him that he is not supposed to eat the po'boy that he has purchased from another establishment in the coffee shop, something he knew that he was not supposed to be doing in the first place but was relying on "white guilt [to] keep the barista from confronting him about it." While the narrator is wrong in thinking that the white barista will not say anything to the offending customer, the result is disappointing, as the censure appears to have no effect on the rich white lady or the racial frame through which she sees the world. However, the narrator is right in that his own point of view concerning the incident is ignored and silenced as he is scolded for bringing a sandwich into the shop from another establishment. The takeaway is that even among the woke, much work remains to be done, including heavy involvement from the marginalized as well as allies.

Passmore's comic exposes the mechanisms of white supremacy that often go unnoticed and encompass our lives as water surrounds a fish. Our assumption, as well as Passmore's, is that highlighting racism, even microaggressions perpetrated by woke white allies, will destabilize petrified behaviors that marginalize people of color. As we have noted throughout the book, one of white supremacy's greatest strengths is its invisibility. By casting a light on the white supremacy of comic books, we hope to provide tools for readers to use in identifying white supremacy in other areas of human life. We are humble in our project, but we are also passionate, and we think it is possible and more necessary than ever to arm ourselves for the fight.

NOTES

CHAPTER ONE

1. I use the term "Orient" throughout this chapter to describe Asian cultures as viewed by Western whites who used an Orientalist framework. This is meant not to describe what these cultures were actually like in reality but rather to reflect how they were perceived through the Orientalist ideology of the West.

2. It is possible that the writers were attempting to use "Cossack" as a general description for an armed henchman, although this seems a rather odd usage. It could also simply be a badly worded sentence, or the writers may have forgotten that Jabah was East Indian and mistakenly believed him to be a Cossack. Even if one or more of these alternate explanations are correct, however, this description still demonstrates that the writers were highly careless in their representation of nonwhite ethnic groups.

3. DC, on the other hand, initially blocked its artists and writers from taking on the Nazis in its comic books, out of fear of alienating isolationists, Italians, and Germans (G. Jones, 165).

CHAPTER THREE

1. The Manji are an odd group. Their skin is white, but their clothing appears to be inspired by ancient Egypt, suggesting that they have been living an isolated existence in their valley since arriving there somehow from ancient Egypt. Their white skin is perhaps due to the fact that ancient Egypt has often been considered part of Western culture, thanks to Egypt's strong artistic and intellectual influence on ancient Greece. In primitivist logic, civilization is inherently tied to whiteness, so any great civilization such as that of ancient Egypt must somehow have been created by whites. This interpretation is speculative, since the story does not provide an explanation for the Manji's origins, but it fits within the ideological structure of primitivism that pervades jungle comics.

CHAPTER SIX

1. This early story is technically not autobiographical, since the main character is named Jack rather than being Pekar himself, but the story is thinly veiled autobiography, and Boats continued to appear in *American Splendor* once it became fully autobiographical, so we are treating this character as Pekar.

2. Oddly, Mr. Boats does not interpret Wylie's lines in terms of the individual's relation to society as a whole; rather, as he tells Jack/Harvey, "It means get away from your family! Your family ain't gonna do you no good!" (Pekar, *Bob & Harv's Comics*, 18). This interpretation is disputed by Harvey, who argues that "maybe it just means stay away from crowds of common ordinary people an' do yer own thing" (18). This is a prime example of Pekar's frequent habit of inserting messiness into his dialogue, undermining the communication of any stable message. Despite the confusion over the line's exact reference, its general thrust remains clear.

CHAPTER NINE

1. In *Ronin*, the male protagonist initially appears to be a Japanese samurai warrior, but it turns out that this character is actually a projection created by Billy Challas, a deformed but extremely powerful white male psychic who has been trapped and controlled by the corporate owners of the Aquarius Complex, a utopian techno-city. The samurai warrior is Billy's subconscious attempt to free himself from the control of the Aquarius Corporation. The samurai warrior functions as an Oriental screen for the power fantasy of a victimized white male.

CHAPTER TEN

1. As far as we know, the term "reskinning" has never appeared in print in reference to traditional white superheroes appearing as nonwhite characters. We first heard the term from an audience member at the PCA/ACA 2018 National Conference in Indianapolis, March 28–31, 2018, and have been using it ever since.

BIBLIOGRAPHY

Aaron, Jason. *Scalped Book One*. DC Comics, 2015.

Abel, Jessica. *La Perdida*. Pantheon, 2006.

Abel, Jessica, and Greg Stump. "The Jessica Abel Interview." *Comics Journal*, no. 270 (August 2005): 68–106.

Achebe, Chinua. "An Image of Africa: Racism in Conrad's *Heart of Darkness*." In *Hopes and Impediments: Selected Essays*, 1–20. Doubleday, 1989.

Albano, John. *Showcase Presents Jonah Hex*. Vol. 1. DC Comics, 2005.

Albano, John. *Showcase Presents Jonah Hex*. Vol. 2. DC Comics, 2014.

Alexander, Michelle. *The New Jim Crow: Mass Incarceration in the Age of Colorblindness*. Rev. ed. New Press, 2012.

"All-Time 100 Novels." *Time*, December 28, 2018.

Andrae, Thomas. "From Menace to Messiah: The History and Historicity of Superman." In *American Media and Mass Culture: Left Perspectives*, edited by Donald Lazere, 124–38. University of California Press, 1987.

Anzaldúa, Gloria. *Borderlands / La Frontera: The New Mestiza*. San Francisco: Aunt Lute, 1987.

Badger, Emily. "We're All a Little Biased, Even If We Don't Know It." *New York Times*, October 5, 2016. https://www.nytimes.com/2016/10/07/upshot/were-all-a-little-biased-even-if-we-dont-know-it.html.

Baldwin, James. "Negroes Are Anti-Semitic Because They're Anti-White." In *Blacks and Jews: Alliances and Arguments*, edited by Paul Berman, 31–41. Dell, 1994.

Bandy, Mary Lea. *Ride, Boldly Ride: The Evolution of the American Western*. University of California Press, 2012.

Barbour, Chad A. *From Daniel Boone to Captain America: Playing Indian in American Popular Culture*. University Press of Mississippi, 2016.

Batchelor, Bob. *Stan Lee: The Man behind Marvel*. Rowman & Littlefield, 2018.

Batchelor, John. *H. G. Wells*. Cambridge University Press, 1985.

Beck, C. C., and Bill Parker. *The Shazam! Archives*. Vol. 1. DC Comics, 1992.

Bloom, Harold. "Introduction." In *George Bernard Shaw's Man and Superman*, 1–13. Chelsea House, 1987.

Blum, William. *Killing Hope: U.S. Military and C.I.A. Interventions since World War II*. Updated ed. Common Courage, 2004.

Bogle, Donald. *Toms, Coons, Mulattoes, Mammies, and Bucks: An Interpretive History of Blacks in American Films*. 4th ed. Continuum, 2002.

Bowers, Rick. *Superman versus the Ku Klux Klan: The True Story of How the Iconic Superhero Battled the Men of Hate*. National Geographic, 2012.

Boyce, Mary. *Zoroastrians: Their Religious Beliefs and Practices*. Routledge, 2001.

Bridges, Emma. *Imagining Xerxes: Ancient Perspectives on a Persian King*. Bloomsbury, 2015.

Brod, Harry. *Superman Is Jewish? How Comic Book Superheroes Came to Serve Truth, Justice, and the Jewish-American Way*. Free Press, 2012.

Brodkin, Karen. *How Jews Became White Folks and What That Says about Race in America*. Rutgers University Press, 1998.

Broome, John. *The Green Lantern Chronicles*. Vol. 1. DC Comics, 2009.

Brühwiler, Claudia Franziska. "'A Is A': Spider-Man, Ayn Rand, and What Man Ought to Be." *PS: Political Science and Politics* 47, no. 1 (2014): 90–93.

Butler, Christopher. *Postmodernism: A Very Short Introduction*. Oxford University Press, 2002.

Cartledge, Paul. "Spartan Wives: Liberation or License?" In *Sparta*, edited by Michael Whitby, 131–60. Edinburgh University Press, 2002.

Chapoutot, Johann. *Greeks, Romans, Germans: How the Nazis Usurped Europe's Classical Past*. Translated by Richard R. Nybakken. University of California Press, 2016.

Chireau, Yvonne. "White or Indian? Whiteness and Becoming the White Indian Comics Superhero." In *Unstable Masks: Whiteness and American Superhero Comics*, edited by Sean Guynes and Martin Lund, 193–211. Ohio State University Press, 2019.

Christie, Les. "The Greatest Real Estate Turnaround Ever." *CNN Money*, November 25, 2009. https://money.cnn.com/2009/11/09/real_estate/greatest_neighborhood_turnaround/.

Chute, Hillary L. *Graphic Women: Life Narrative and Contemporary Comics*. Columbia University Press, 2010.

Coates, Ta-Nehisi. *Captain America: Winter in America*. Marvel, 2019.

Coates, Ta-Nehisi. "The First White President: The Foundation of Donald Trump's Presidency Is the Negation of Barack Obama's Legacy." *The Atlantic*, October 15, 2017.

Coogan, Peter. *Superhero: The Secret Origin of a Genre*. MonkeyBrain, 2006.

Conway, Christopher. *Heroes of the Borderlands: The Western in Mexican Film, Comics, and Music*. University of New Mexico Press, 2019.

Costello, Brannon. "Southern Super-patriots and United States Nationalism: Race, Region, and Nation in *Captain America*." In *Comics and the U.S. South*, edited by Brannon Costello and Qiana J. Whitted, 62–88. University Press of Mississippi, 2012.

Creekmur, Corey K. "Multiculturalism Meets the Counterculture: Representing Racial Difference in Robert Crumb's Underground Comix." In *Representing Multiculturalism in Comics and Graphic Novels*, edited by Carolene Ayaka and Ian Hague, 19–33. Routledge, 2015.

Crumb, Robert. *The Complete Crumb Comics, Vol. 1: The Early Years of Bitter Struggle*. Edited by Gary Groth with Robert Fiore. Fantagraphics, 1987.

Crumb, Robert. *The Complete Crumb Comics, Vol. 3: Starring Fritz the Cat*. Edited by Gary Groth with Robert Fiore. Fantagraphics, 1988.

Crumb, Robert. *The Complete Crumb Comics, Vol. 4: Mr. Sixties*. Edited by Gary Groth with Robert Fiore. Fantagraphics, 1990.

Crumb, Robert. *The Complete Crumb Comics, Vol. 5: Happy Hippy Comix*. Edited by Gary Groth et al. Fantagraphics, 1990.

Crumb, Robert. *The Complete Crumb Comics, Vol. 6: The Crest of the Wave.* Edited by Gary Groth et al. Fantagraphics, 1991.
Crumb, Robert. *The Complete Crumb Comics, Vol. 8: The Death of Fritz the Cat.* Edited by Gary Groth and Robert Boyd. Fantagraphics, 1992.
Daniels, Les. *Superman: The Complete History.* Chronicle, 1998.
Darowski, Joseph J. *X-Men and the Mutant Metaphor: Race and Gender in the Comic Books.* Rowman & Littlefield, 2014.
Dauber, Jeremy. "Comic Books, Tragic Stories: Will Eisner's American Jewish History." In *The Jewish Graphic Novel: Critical Approaches,* edited by Samantha Baskind and Ranen Omer-Sherman, 22–42. Rutgers University Press, 2008.
Davis, Angela. *Women, Race and Class.* Vintage, 1983.
Dery, Mark. "Black to the Future: Interviews with Samuel R. Delany, Greg Tate, and Tricia Rose." In *Flame Wars: The Discourse of Cyberculture,* 179–222. Duke University Press, 1994.
de Ste. Croix, G. E. M. "The Helot Threat." In *Sparta,* edited by Michael Whitby, 190–95. Edinburgh University Press, 2002.
DiAngelo, Robin. "White Fragility." *International Journal of Critical Pedagogy* 3, no. 3 (2011): 54–70.
Dobratz, Betty A. "The Role of Religion in the Collective Identity of the White Racialist Movement." *Journal for the Scientific Study of Religion* 40, no. 2 (June 2001): 287–301.
Doherty, Thomas. "Art Spiegelman's *Maus*: Graphic Art and the Holocaust." "Write Now: American Literature in the 1980s and 1990s." Special issue, *American Literature* 68, no. 1 (March 1996): 69–84.
Dowling, Julie A. *Mexican Americans and the Question of Race.* University of Texas Press, 2014.
Dubey, Madhu. *Black Women Novelists and the Nationalist Aesthetic.* Indiana University Press, 1994.
Du Bois, W. E. B. *The Souls of Black Folk.* 1903. Penguin, 2009.
Duncombe, Stephen, and Maxwell Tremblay. "White Riot?" In *White Riot: Punk Rock and the Politics of Race,* edited by Stephen Duncombe and Maxwell Tremblay, 1–17. Verso, 2011.
Eisner, Will. *The Contract with God Trilogy: Life on Dropsie Avenue.* W. W. Norton, 2006.
Eisner, Will. *Will Eisner's The Spirit Archives.* Vol. 7. DC Comics, 2002.
Eisner, Will, and Andrew D. Arnold. "Never Too Late." *Time,* September 2003. http://content.time.com/time/arts/article/0,8599,488263,00.html.
Engle, Gary. "What Makes Superman So Darned American?" In *Culture: An Introductory Text,* edited by Jack Nachbar and Kevin Lause, 331–43. Bowling Green State University Popular Press, 1992.
Englehart, Steve, et al. *Essential Captain America.* Vol. 4. Marvel, 2010.
Fawaz, Ramzi. *The New Mutants: Superheroes and the Radical Imagination of American Comics.* New York University Press, 2016.
Feagin, Joe. *The White Racial Frame: Centuries of Racial Framing and Counter-Framing.* 2nd ed. Routledge, 2013.
Finger, Bill, et al. *The Golden Age Green Lantern Archives.* Vol. 1. DC Comics, 1999.
Fingeroth, Danny. *Disguised as Clark Kent: Jews, Comics, and the Creation of the Superhero.* Continuum, 2007.
Fingeroth, Danny. *Superman on the Couch.* Continuum, 2004.

Foley, Neil. *The White Scourge: Mexicans, Blacks, and Poor Whites in Texas Cotton Culture*. University of California Press, 1997.
Fox, Gardner, et al. *The Golden Age Flash Archives*. Vol. 1. DC Comics, 1999.
Frankenberg, Ruth. *White Women, Race Matters: The Social Construction of Whiteness*. 5th ed. University of Minnesota Press, 1993.
Frayling, Christopher. *The Yellow Peril: Dr. Fu Manchu and the Rise of Chinaphobia*. Thames & Hudson, 2014.
Fried, Albert. *The Rise and Fall of the Jewish Gangster in America*. Rev. ed. Columbia University Press, 1993.
Gaines, William. *EC Archives: Shock Suspense Stories*. Vol. 1. Dark Horse, 2016.
Gaines, William. *EC Archives: Shock Suspense Stories*. Vol. 2. Gemstone, 2007.
Gaines, William. *EC Archives: Shock Suspense Stories*. Vol. 3. Dark Horse, 2016.
"Gates, Henry Louis, Jr." In *The Norton Anthology of African American Literature*. Norton, 2004.
Gavaler, Chris. "The Ku Klux Klan and the Birth of the Superhero." *Journal of Graphic Novels and Comics* 4, no. 2 (2013): 191–208.
Gavaler, Chris. *Superhero Comics*. Bloomsbury, 2018.
Gibbons, Dave. *Green Lantern: Sector 2814*. Vol. 2. DC Comics, 2013.
Glazer, Nathan, and Daniel Patrick Moynihan. *Beyond the Melting Pot: The Negroes, Puerto Ricans, Jews, Italians, and Irish of New York City*. MIT Press, 1963.
Gonzales, Michael J. *The Mexican Revolution, 1910–1940*. University of New Mexico Press, 2002.
Goodwin, Archie, et al. *Essential Iron Man*. Vol. 3. Marvel, 2008.
Goulart, Ron. *The Funnies: 100 Years of American Comic Strips*. Adams, 1995.
Grady-Willis, Winston A. "The Black Panther Party: State Repression and Political Prisoners." In *The Black Panther Party Reconsidered*, edited by Charles E. Jones, 363–90. Black Classic, 1998.
Grant, Madison. *The Passing of the Great Race*. Arno, 1970.
The Green Hornet Collection: Part 1. Classic Comics Library, 2017.
Groth, Gary, and Art Spiegelman. *Art Spiegelman Interviewed by Gary Groth Excerpted from the Comics Journal #s 180 & 181*. https://web.archive.org/web/20071015220338/http://tcj.com:80/2_archives/i_spiegelman.html. Accessed December 16, 2018.
Haggard, H. Rider. *King Solomon's Mines*. Open Road, 2016.
Haney López, Ian. *Dog Whistle Politics: How Coded Racial Appeals Have Reinvented Racism and Wrecked the Middle Class*. Oxford University Press, 2014.
Hassler-Forest, Dan. "The 300 Controversy: A Case Study in the Politics of Adaptation." In *The Rise and Reason of Comics and Graphic Literature: Critical Essays on the Form*, edited by Joyce Goggin and Dan Hassler-Forest, 119–41. McFarland, 2010.
Hernandez, Gilbert, and Jaime Hernandez. *House of Raging Women*. Fantagraphics, 1988.
Hernandez, Jaime. *The Death of Speedy*. Fantagraphics, 1989.
Hiller, Susan, ed. *The Myth of Primitivism: Perspectives on Art*. Routledge, 1991.
hooks, bell. *Ain't I a Woman*. South End, 1981.
hooks, bell. *We Real Cool: Black Men and Masculinity*. Routledge, 2004.
Hopkins, Ellen. "6 Rooms, Bubble View." *New York* 17, no. 11 (March 1984): 18–22.
Horn, Maurice. *Comics of the American West*. Winchester Press, 1977.
Hughes, Jamie A. "'Who Watches the Watchmen?': Ideology and 'Real World' Superheroes." *Journal of Popular Culture* 39, no. 4 (2006).

Ignatiev, Noel. *How the Irish Became White*. Routledge, 1995.
Ignatiev, Noel, and John Garvey, eds. *Race Traitor*. Routledge, 1996.
Inge, M. Thomas, ed. *Will Eisner: Conversations*. University Press of Mississippi, 2011.
Jackson, Jack. *Jack Jackson's American History: Los Tejanos and Lost Cause*. Fantagraphics, 2012.
Jacobs, Will, and Gerard Jones. *The Comic Book Heroes: From the Silver Age to the Present*. Crown, 1985.
Johnson, Charles. "Foreword." In *Black Images in the Comics: A Visual History*, 6–19. Fantagraphics, 2003.
Jones, Charles E. "'Talkin' the Talk and Walkin' the Walk': An Interview with Panther Jimmy Slater." In *The Black Panther Party Reconsidered*, edited by Charles E. Jones, 147–53. Black Classic, 1998.
Jones, Charles E., and Judson L. Jeffries. "'Don't Believe the Hype': Debunking the Panther Mythology." In *The Black Panther Party Reconsidered*, edited by Charles E. Jones, 25–55. Black Classic, 1998.
Jones, Gerard. *Men of Tomorrow: Geeks, Gangsters, and the Birth of the Comic Book*. Basic Books, 2004.
Jonnes, Jill. *South Bronx Rising: The Rise, Fall, and Resurrection of an American City*. Fordham University Press, 2002.
Jurgens, Dan. *The Death of Superman*. DC Comics, 1993.
Jurgens, Dan. *Reign of the Supermen*. DC Comics, 2016.
Kane, Bob. *Batman Chronicles*. Vol. 1. DC Comics, 2005.
Kane, Bob, et al. *The Dark Knight Archives*. Vol. 1. DC Comics, 1992.
Katznelson, Ira. *When Affirmative Action Was White: An Untold History of Racial Inequality in Twentieth-Century America*. W. W. Norton, 2005.
Kaufman, Jonathan. "Blacks and Jews: The Struggle in the Cities." In *Struggles in the Promised Land: Towards a History of Black-Jewish Relations in the United States*, edited by Jack Salzman and Cornel West, 107–21. Oxford University Press, 1997.
Kimmel, Michael S. "Masculinity as Homophobia: Fear, Shame, and Silence in the Construction of Gender Identity." In *Feminism and Masculinities*, edited by Peter F. Murphy, 182–99. Oxford University Press, 2004.
Kit, Borys. "A Rare Interview with Frank Miller: 'Dark Knight,' the Unmade Darren Aronofsky Batman Movie, and Donald Trump." *Hollywood Reporter*, March 2016. http://www.hollywoodreporter.com/heat-vision/a-rare-interview-frank-miller-871654.
Kline, Wendy. *Building a Better Race: Gender, Sexuality, and Eugenics from the Turn of the Century to the Baby Boom*. University of California Press, 2001.
Kominsky, Aline. "Arnie's Air Conditioner." *Arcade*, no. 7 (Fall 1976): 25.
Kominsky, Aline. "Blabette Gets an Afro." *Arcade*, no. 6 (Summer 1976): 49.
Kominsky-Crumb, Aline. *Need More Love*. MQP, 2007.
Kovacs, George A. "Truth, Justice, and the Spartan Way: Freedom and Democracy in Frank Miller's *300*." In *Classics in the Modern World: A "Democratic Turn"?* Oxford University Press, 2013.
Launius, Christine, and Holly Hassel. *Threshold Concepts in Women's and Gender Studies*. Routledge, 2015.
Lee, Stan. *Essential Rawhide Kid*. Marvel Comics, 2011.

Lee, Stan. "Foreword." In *Disguised as Clark Kent: Jews, Comics, and the Creation of the Superhero*, by Danny Fingeroth, 9–11. Continuum, 2007.

Lee, Stan. *The Invincible Iron Man: The Enemy Within*. Marvel, 2013.

Lee, Stan, and Steve Ditko. *The Amazing Spider-Man #96*. Marvel, 1963.

Lee, Stan, and Don Heck. *Epic Collection: The Invincible Iron Man*. Vol. 1. Marvel, 2014.

Lee, Stan, and Jack Kirby. *Essential Captain America*. Vol. 1. Marvel Comics, 2001.

Lee, Stan, and Jack Kirby. *Marvel Masterworks: Sgt. Fury and His Howling Commandos*. Vol. 1. Marvel, 2017.

Lee, Stan, and Jack Kirby. *Marvel Masterworks: The Fantastic Four*. Vol. 1. Marvel, 2011.

Lee, Stan, and Jack Kirby. *Marvel Masterworks: The Incredible Hulk*. Vol. 1. Marvel, 2003.

Lee, Stan, and Jack Kirby. *Marvel Masterworks: The X-Men*. Vol. 1. Marvel, 2015.

Lee, Stan, and Jack Kirby. *Marvel Masterworks: The X-Men*. Vol. 2. Marvel, 2004.

Lee, Stan, and George Mair. *Excelsior! The Amazing Life of Stan Lee*. Simon & Schuster, 2002.

Lee, Stan, et al. *Essential Captain America*. Vol. 1. Marvel, 2001.

Lee, Stan, et al. *Essential Captain America*. Vol. 2. Marvel, 2010.

Lee, Stan, et al. *Essential Captain America*. Vol. 3. Marvel, 2010.

Legman, Gershon. "From Love and Death: A Study in Censorship." In *Arguing Comics: Literary Masters on a Popular Medium*, edited by Jeet Heer and Kent Worcester, 112–21. University Press of Mississippi, 2004.

Lepore, Jill. *The Secret History of Wonder Woman*. Vintage, 2014.

Lieberson, Stanley. *A Piece of the Pie: Black and White Immigrants since 1880*. University of California Press, 1980.

Lipset, Seymour Martin, and Earl Raab. *Jews and the New American Scene*. Harvard University Press, 1995.

Lipsitz, George. *The Possessive Investment in Whiteness: How White People Profit from Identity Politics*. Temple University Press, 2006.

Liu, Yen-Lian. "The Masculine Masquerade of Superheroes in *Watchmen*." *Gender Forum: An Internet Journal of Gender Studies* 62 (2017): 39–65.

Lott, Eric. *Love and Theft: Blackface Minstrelsy and the American Working Class*. Oxford University Press, 1993.

Lund, Martin. "American Golem: Reading America through Super-New Dealers and the 'Melting Pot.'" In *Comic Books and American Cultural History: An Anthology*, edited by Matthew Pustz, 79–93. Continuum, 2012.

Lyvely, Chin, and Joyce Sutton. *Abortion Eve*. Nanny Goat, 1973.

Mahmutović, Adnan. "Chronotope in Moore and Gibbons's *Watchmen*." *Studies in the Novel* 50, no. 2 (Summer 2018): 255–76.

Mailer, Norman. "The White Negro: Superficial Reflections of the Hipster." In *The Portable Beat Reader*, edited by Ann Charters, 582–605. Penguin, 1992.

Malcolm, Cheryl Alexander. "Witness, Trauma, and Remembrance: Holocaust Representation and X-Men Comics." In *The Jewish Graphic Novel: Critical Approaches*, edited by Samantha Baskind and Ranen Omer-Sherman, 144–60. Rutgers University Press, 2008.

Maremaa, Thomas. "Who Is This Crumb?" *New York Times Magazine*, October 1972, 12–13, 64–73.

Marston, William Moulton, and H. G. Peter. *Wonder Woman Archives*. Vol. 1. DC Comics, 1998.

Martin, Waldo E., Jr. "'Nation Time!' Black Nationalism, the Third World, and Jews." In *Struggles in the Promised Land: Towards a History of Black-Jewish Relations in the United States*, edited by Jack Salzman and Cornel West, 341–55. Oxford University Press, 1997.

Martinot, Steve. *Machinery of Whiteness: Studies in the Structure of Racialization*. Temple University Press, 2010.

McCloud, Scott. *Understanding Comics: The Invisible Art*. HarperCollins, 1993.

McGregor, Don, et al. *The Black Panther: Panther's Rage*. Marvel, 2016.

Medhurst, Andy. "Batman, Deviance and Camp." In *The Many Lives of the Batman: Critical Approaches to a Superhero and His Media*, edited by Roberta E. Pearson and William Uricchio, 149–63. Routledge, 1991.

Mendes, Willie. "Oma." In *The Complete Women's Comix*, vol. 1, 3–8. Fantagraphics, 2016.

Merino, Ana. "The Impact of Latino Identities and the Humanizing of Multiculturalism in *Love and Rockets*." In *Representing Multiculturalism in Comics and Graphic Novels*, edited by Carolene Ayaka and Ian Hague, translated by Elizabeth Polli, 34–48. Routledge, 2015.

Middleton, Stephen. "The Battle of Racial Identity in Popular and Legal Cultures, 1810–1860." In *The Construction of Whiteness: An Interdisciplinary Analysis of Race Formation and the Meaning of a White Identity*, edited by Stephen Middleton, David R. Roediger, and Donald M. Shaffer, 11–43. University Press of Mississippi, 2016.

Miettinen, Mervi. "Representing the State of Exception: Power, Utopia, Visuality and Narrative in Superhero Comics." In *Images in Use: Towards the Critical Analysis of Visual Communication*, edited by Matteo Stocchetti and Karin Kukkonen, 269–90. Discourse Approaches to Politics, Society and Culture. John Benjamins, 2011.

Millar, Mark. *Civil War: A Marvel Comics Event*. Marvel, 2007.

Miller, Frank. *300*. Dark Horse, 1999.

Miller, Frank. *Batman: The Dark Knight Returns*. DC Comics, 1986.

Miller, Frank. *Holy Terror*. Legendary Comics, 2011.

Miller, Frank. *Sin City: A Dame to Kill For*. Dark Horse, 2010.

Miller, Frank. *Sin City: The Big Fat Kill*. Dark Horse, 2010.

Miller, Frank. *Sin City: The Hard Goodbye*. Dark Horse, 2005.

Miller, Frank, and Dave Gibbons. *The Life and Times of Martha Washington*. Dark Horse, 2010.

Mirzoeff, Nicholas. *An Introduction to Visual Culture*. 2nd ed. Routledge, 2009.

Moore, Alan, and Dave Gibbons. *Watchmen*. DC Comics, 1986.

Morales, Robert. *Truth: Red, White & Black*. Marvel, 2004.

Morrison, Toni. *Playing in the Dark: Whiteness and the Literary Imagination*. Vintage, 1992.

Mulman, Lisa Naomi. "A Tale of Two Mice: Graphic Representations of the Jew in Holocaust Narrative." In *The Jewish Graphic Novel: Critical Approaches*, edited by Samantha Baskind and Ranen Omer-Sherman. 85–93. Rutgers University Press, 2008.

Nama, Adilifu. *Super Black: American Pop Culture and Black Superheroes*. University of Texas Press, 2011.

Nelson, Brandon. "'Sick Humor Which Serves No Purpose': Whiteman, Angelfood and the Aesthetics of Obscenity in the Comix of R. Crumb." *Journal of Graphic Novels and Comics* 8, no. 2 (2017): 139–55.

Nielsen, Kim E. "What's a Patriotic Man to Do? Patriotic Masculinities of the Post-WWI Red Scare." *Men and Masculinities* 6, no. 3 (January 2004): 240–53.

Nies, Betsy L. *Eugenic Fantasies: Racial Ideology in the Literature and Popular Culture of the 1920's*. Routledge, 2002.

Nietzsche, Friedrich. *Beyond Good and Evil / On the Genealogy of Morality*. Translated by Adrian Del Caro. Stanford University Press, 2014.

Nietzsche, Friedrich. *Thus Spoke Zarathustra: A Book for None and All*. Translated by Walter Kaufmann. Penguin, 1954.

Nyberg, Amy Kiste. *Seal of Approval: The History of the Comics Code*. University Press of Mississippi, 1998.

O'Neil, Dennis, and Neal Adams. *The Green Lantern / Green Arrow Collection*. Vol. 1. DC Comics, 2004.

O'Neil, Dennis, and Neal Adams. *The Green Lantern / Green Arrow Collection*. Vol. 2. DC Comics, 2004.

O'Rourke, Shane. *The Cossacks*. Manchester University Press, 2007.

Oyola, Osvaldo. "Marked for Failure: Whiteness, Innocence, and Power in Defining Captain America." In *Unstable Masks: Whiteness and American Superhero Comics*, edited by Sean Guynes and Martin Lund, 19–37. Ohio University Press, 2019.

Pak, Greg, and Carmine Di Giandomenico. *X-Men: Magneto Testament*. Marvel, 2009.

Pappe, Ilan. *The Ethnic Cleansing of Palestine*. Oneworld, 2006.

Parker, Robert. "Religion in Public Life." In *Sparta*, edited by Michael Whitby, 161–73. Edinburgh University Press, 2002.

Parkin, Lance. *Magic Worlds: The Extraordinary Life of Alan Moore*. Aurum, 2013.

Passmore, Ben. *Your Black Friend*. Silver Sprocket, 2016.

Paz, Octavio. *The Labyrinth of Solitude*. Trans. Lysander Kemp, Yara Milos, and Rachel Phillips Belash. New York: Grove, 1985.

Pekar, Harvey. *Bob & Harv's Comics*. Four Walls Eight Windows, 1996.

Pekar, Harvey. *Not the Israel My Parents Promised Me*. Hill & Wang, 2012.

Peterson, James Braxton. "Graphic Black Nationalism: Visualizing Political Narratives in the Graphic Novel." In *The Rise and Reason of Comics and Graphic Literature: Critical Essays on the Form*, edited by Joyce Goggin and Dan Hassler-Forest, 202–22. McFarland, 2014.

Plant, Richard. *The Pink Triangle: The Nazi War against Homosexuals*. Henry Holt, 1986.

Powell, Anton. "Dining Groups, Marriage, Homosexuality." In *Sparta*, edited by Michael Whitby, 90–103. Edinburgh University Press, 2002.

Prince, Michael J. "Alan Moore's America: The Liberal Individual and American Identities in *Watchmen*." *Journal of Popular Culture* 44, no. 4 (2011): 815–30.

Proszek, James Michael. *Drawn Apart: Visual Representations of the Persian Wars in Contemporary Graphic Novels and Film*. Carbondale: Southern Illinois University, 2015.

Quart, Alissa. "The Age of Hipster Sexism." The Cut. *New York Magazine*, October 30, 2012. https://www.thecut.com/2012/10/age-of-hipster-sexism.html.

Ratner-Rosenhagen, Jennifer. *American Nietzsche: A History of an Icon and His Ideas*. University of Chicago Press, 2012.

Reibman, James E. "Introduction." In *Seduction of the Innocent*, rev. ed., v–xliv. Main Road, 2004.

Reich, David. "Gray Matter: How Genetics Is Changing Our Understanding of 'Race.'" *New York Times*, March 23, 2018.

Richards, Jeffrey. *China and the Chinese in Popular Film: From Fu Manchu to Charlie Chan.* I. B. Tauris, 2017.

Richardson, Alan, and Omaar Hena. "Primitivism." In *The Princeton Encyclopedia of Poetry and Poetics*, edited by Roland Greene et al., 4th ed., 1108–9. Princeton University Press, 2012.

Rifas, Leonard. "Racial Imagery, Racism, Individualism, and Underground Comix." *ImageTexT: Interdisciplinary Comics Studies* 1, no. 1 (2004), http://www.english.ufl.edu/imagetext/archives/v1_1/rifas/index.shtml.

Robbins, Trina. "Babes and Women." In *The Complete Women's Comix*, vol. 1, vii–xiii. Fantagraphics, 2016.

Roediger, David R. *The Wages of Whiteness: Race and the Making of the American Working Class.* Verso, 1991.

Roediger, David. *Working toward Whiteness: How America's Immigrants Became White: The Strange Journey from Ellis Island to the Suburbs.* Basic, 2005.

Rosenkranz, Patrick. *Rebel Visions: The Underground Comix Revolution, 1963–1975.* Fantagraphics, 2002.

Royal, Derek Parker. "Introduction: Coloring America: Multi-ethnic Engagements with Graphic Narrative." *Melus* 32, no. 3 (Fall 2007): 7–22.

Sacks, Karen Brodkin. "How Did Jews Become White Folks?" In *Critical White Studies: Looking Behind the Mirror*, edited by Richard Delgado and Jean Stefancic, 395–406. Temple University Press, 1997.

Said, Edward. *Orientalism.* Pantheon, 1978.

Sammond, Nicholas. *Birth of an Industry: Blackface Minstrelsy and the Rise of American Animation.* Duke University Press, 2015.

Schumacher, Michael. *Will Eisner: A Dreamer's Life in Comics.* Bloomsbury, 2010.

Sedgwick, Eve Kosofsky. "Epistemology of the Closet." In *Literary Theory: An Anthology*, edited by Julie Rivkin and Michael Ryan, 912–21. Blackwell, 2004.

Shane, Scott, et al. "Trump Pushes Dark View of Islam to Center of U.S. Policy-Making." *New York Times*, February 1, 2017.

Sharrett, Christopher. "Batman and the Twilight of the Idols: An Interview with Frank Miller." In *The Many Lives of the Batman: Critical Approaches to a Superhero and His Media*, edited by Roberta E. Pearson and William Uricchio, 33–46. Routledge, 1991.

Shelton, Gilbert. "Smiling Sergeant Death and His Merciless Mayhem Patrol." *Radical America Komiks* 3, no. 1 (1969).

Shyminsky, Neil. "Mutation, Racialization, Decimation: The X-Men as White Men." In *Unstable Masks: Whiteness and American Superhero Comics*, edited by Sean Guynes and Martin Lund. Ohio State University Press, 2019.

Sides, Hampton. *Blood and Thunder: The Epic Story of Kit Carson and the Conquest of the American West.* Anchor Books, 2006.

Siegel, Jerry, and Joe Shuster. *The Superman Chronicles.* Vol. 1. DC Comics, 2006.

Simon, Joe, and Jack Kirby. *The Kid Cowboys of Boys' Ranch.* Marvel Comics, 1991.

Simon, Joe, et al. *Golden Age Captain America.* Marvel Worldwide, 2014.

Slotkin, Richard. *Gunfighter Nation: The Myth of the Frontier in Twentieth-Century America.* HarperCollins, 1992.

Spiegelman, Art. *Maus: A Survivor's Tale.* Pantheon, 1997.

Spiegelman, Art. *MetaMaus: A Look inside a Modern Classic, Maus*. Pantheon, 2011.
Spooner, James. "Foreword." In *White Riot: Punk Rock and the Politics of Race*, edited by Stephen Duncombe and Maxwell Tremblay, xiii–xvii. Verso, 2011.
Stegner, Wallace. "Walter Clark's Frontier." In *Walter Van Tilburg Clark: Critiques*, edited by Charlton Laird, 60–75. University of Nevada Press, 1983.
Steinberg, Stephen. *The Ethnic Myth: Race, Ethnicity, and Class in America*. Atheneum, 1981.
Stevens, J. Richard. *Captain America, Masculinity, and Violence: The Evolution of a National Icon*. Syracuse University Press, 2015.
Surman, Steven. "Alan Moore's *Watchmen* and Rorschach: Does the Character Set a Bad Example?" *Steven Surman Writes*, January 20, 2015. https://www.stevensurman.com/rorschach-from-alan-moores-watchmen-does-he-set-a-bad-example/.
Tano, Duy. "Addressing Ebony White—Was Will Eisner Racist?" *Comics Cube*, May 2010. http://www.comicscube.com/2010/05/addressing-ebony-white-was-will-eisner_26.html.
Thrush, Glenn, and Julie Hirschfeld Davis. "Trump, in Poland, Asks If West Has the 'Will to Survive.'" *New York Times*, July 6, 2017.
Tochluk, Shelly. *Witnessing Whiteness: The Need to Talk about Race and How to Do It*. Rowman & Littlefield Education, 2010.
Trump, Donald. "Bring Back the Death Penalty. Bring Back Our Police!" *New York Times*, May 1, 1989.
Turner, Patricia A. *Ceramic Uncles and Celluloid Mammies: Black Images and Their Influence on Culture*. University of Virginia Press, 2002.
Van Ness, Sara J. *Watchmen as Literature*. McFarland, 2010.
Waid, Mark, and Mike Wieringo. *Fantastic Four: Imaginauts*. Vol. 1. Marvel, 2003.
Ware, Chris. *Jimmy Corrigan: The Smartest Kid on Earth*. New York: Pantheon, 2003.
Webb, Bob, et al. *The Best of the Golden Age Sheena*. Edited by Stephen Christy. Devil's Due, 2008.
Wertham, Fredric. *Seduction of the Innocent*. Rev. ed. Main Road, 2004.
Whitby, Michael. "Two Shadows: Images of Spartans and Helots." In *The Shadow of Sparta*, edited by Anton Powell and Stephen Hodkinson, 87–126. Routledge, 1994.
"White-wash." In *Oxford English Dictionary Online*. https://www.oed.com.
Whitted, Qiana. *EC Comics: Race, Shock, and Social Protest*. Rutgers University Press, 2019.
Wilson, G. Willow. *Ms. Marvel: No Normal*. Marvel, 2014.
Wood, Amy Louise. *Lynching and Spectacle: Witnessing Racial Violence in America, 1890–1940*. Chapel Hill: University of North Carolina Press, 2009.
Wright, Bradford W. *Comic Book Nation: The Transformation of Youth Culture in America*. Johns Hopkins University Press, 2001.
Zimmerman, Nadya. *Counterculture Kaleidoscope: Musical and Cultural Perspectives on Late Sixties San Francisco*. University of Michigan Press, 2013.
Zimmerman, Ron, and John Severin. *The Rawhide Kid: Slap Leather*. Marvel Comics, 2010.
Zwigoff, Terry. *Crumb*. Superior Pictures, 1994.

INDEX

Abel, Jessica, 175–76, 186–92
Achebe, Chinua, 72
alternative comics, 174–75
Andrae, Thomas, 23, 24–25
Anzaldúa, Gloria, 174–75, 177, 186–87, 198, 204

Baldwin, James, 161
Bandy, Mary Lea, 47
Barbour, Chad A., 48, 55
Batchelor, Bob, 107
Batman, 4, 21–22, 76–77, 104–5
Batman: The Dark Knight Returns, 222–23, 225–29
Black Panther, 80–86
Brodkin, Karen, 154, 159, 164, 168–69
Burroughs, Edgar Rice, 22, 23

Captain America, 4, 18, 28–29, 77, 79, 93, 126; in *Captain America: Winter in America*, 267–69; in *Civil War*, 214–16; identity crisis, 88–89, 120–23; as Jew, 38–40; as legionnaire, 20–21; in *Truth: Red, White & Black*, 258–62
Carter, John, 22
Civil War, 216–19
Coates, Ta-Nehisi, 266–69
Comics Code, 51–52, 91, 128
Comics Magazine Association of America (CMAA), 91, 95, 98
Costello, Brannon, 123
Creekmur, Corey, 127–28, 130–31, 147–48
Crumb, Robert, 5, 7, 127, 129–51

Dery, Mark, 82
DiAngelo, Robin, 3, 246
Dubey, Madhu, 112
Du Bois, W. E. B., 42, 198, 203

EC Comics, 91, 95, 99–100. *See also* Gaines, William
Eisner, Will, 5, 7, 11–12, 34–36, 41–42, 152–63
eugenics, 16–17, 19–20, 23

Falcon, The, 93, 120–23, 126
Fantastic Four, The, 113–17
Fawaz, Ramzi, 90
Feagin, Joe, 3, 10
Frankenberg, Ruth, 100
Fu Manchu, 27

Gaines, William, 5, 91, 95, 98, 100–101
Garvey, John, 8
Gavaler, Chris, 21
Glazer, Nathan, 135, 152, 154–55
Green Arrow, 123–24
Green Lantern, 30–31, 123–25, 251–56
Gruenwald, Mark, 216

Haney López, Ian, 26, 155, 225, 234, 242
Hassler-Forest, Dan, 238
Hernandez, Gilberto, 175–86
Hernandez, Jaime, 175–86
Hex, Jonah, 44–45, 55–59
Holy Terror, 240–43
Hulk, The, 4, 115–17
Horn, Maurice, 52, 56

Ignatiev, Noel, 8, 59, 203
Iron Man, 4, 79–80, 86–88, 248–51

Jackson, Jack, 5. See also *Lost Cause*
Jeffries, Judson, 122
Jimmy Corrigan, 192–96
Johnson, Charles, 140, 147–48
Jones, Charles, 122
Judaism, 4–5, 19, 36–40
jungle comics, 68–76, 80–86

Kaufman, Jonathan, 161
Khan, Kamala, 262–65. See also *Ms. Marvel: No Normal*
Kid Cowboys of Boys' Ranch, The, 44, 49–50
Kimmel, Michael, 46, 61–62, 103, 105, 200
Kirby, Jack, 18, 106
Kominsky-Crumb, Aline, 164, 167–71
Ku Klux Klan, 16, 21–22

Lane, Lois, 17
La Perdida, 186–92. See also Abel, Jessica
Lee, Stan, 5, 92, 106, 110–18. See also Marvel Comics
Legman, Gershon, 41
Lepore, Jill, 34
Lieberson, Stanley, 154
Lipset, Seymour Martin, 154–55
Lipsitz, George, 247
Lost Cause, 45, 59–62. See also Jackson, Jack
Love and Rockets, 176–86

Martinot, Steve, 106
Marvel Comics, 91–92, 106, 113, 117–18. See also Lee, Stan
Maus, 165–67. See also Spiegelman, Art
Medhurst, Andy, 208
Miller, Frank, 5, 221–45
Morrison, Toni, 4, 6
Moynihan, Daniel Patrick, 135, 152, 154–55
Ms. Marvel: No Normal, 262–65

Nelson, Brandon, 132
Nietzsche, Friedrich, 16, 18
Nyberg, Amy Kiste, 92, 95, 107

Olson, Joel, 247

Pekar, Harvey, 7, 171–73
Peterson, James Braxton, 233
Prince, Michael J., 200
Proszek, James, 235

Quart, Alissa, 149

Raab, Earl, 154–55
Rawhide Kid, 44, 52–55, 62–63
Robbins, Trina, 169
Roediger, David, 4, 17–18

Said, Edward, 30
Scalped, 45, 64–65
Schumacher, Michael, 11
Sgt. Fury and His Howling Commandos, 117–18
Sheena, 70–71, 73–76
Shock SuspenStories, 91, 95–101, 103–5
Shuster, Joe, 5, 18, 24–25, 28
Sides, Hampton, 49
Siegel, Jerry, 5, 18, 24–25, 28
Simon, Joe, 18
Sin City, 223–24
Slotkin, Richard, 43–48
Spider-Man, 4
Spiegelman, Art, 7, 165–66. See also *Maus*
Spirit, The, 34–36. See also Eisner, Will
Steinberg, Stephen, 154
Stevens, J. Richard, 18, 28
superheroes, 16–25, 76–77
Superman, 4, 18, 24–28, 37–38, 56–58

Tano, Duy, 11
Tarzan, 22, 23
300, 234–40

underground comix, 126–31

Van Ness, Sara J., 207

Ware, Chris, 7, 176, 192–96
Watchmen, 197–214

Wertham, Fredric, 13, 16, 41, 91–106
western comics, 43–45
white fragility, 3
white Indian, 44, 48–49
whiteness, 3–4, 8–9, 17
white racial frame, 3, 5, 10–11
white supremacy, 5
Wonder Woman, 17, 32–34, 102
Wright, Bradford, 88

X-Men, The, 4, 92, 106–13

Yellow Peril, 16, 26–33, 79, 80
Your Black Friend, 269–71

Zimmerman, Nadya, 127

ABOUT THE AUTHORS

Credit: Alyssa Nepper, University of Wisconsin–Parkside

Josef Benson is associate professor of literatures and languages at the University of Wisconsin–Parkside. He is the author of *Star Wars: Triumph of Nerd Culture* (Rowman & Littlefield, 2020), *J. D. Salinger's "The Catcher in the Rye": A Cultural History* (Rowman & Littlefield, 2018), and *Hypermasculinities in the Contemporary Novel: Cormac McCarthy, Toni Morrison, and James Baldwin* (Rowman & Littlefield, 2014). He is working on his fifth book, *The Sniper: A Cultural Reading of Jeffrey Dahmer* (University Press of Kentucky, 2021).

Credit: Alyssa Nepper, University of Wisconsin–Parkside

Doug Singsen is associate professor of art history at the University of Wisconsin–Parkside. His work has been published in *Modernism/Modernity*, the *Journal of Graphic Novels and Comics*, *Key Terms in Comics Studies* (Palgrave Macmillan, 2020), *The Grove Encyclopedia of American Art* (Oxford University Press, 2011), and *Art History Teaching Resources*. He is working on a textbook titled *Art: A Global History* for Oxford University Press.

www.ingramcontent.com/pod-product-compliance
Lightning Source LLC
Chambersburg PA
CBHW030610230426
43661CB00053B/1918